Encore Adulthood

Encore Adulthood

Boomers on the Edge of Risk, Renewal, and Purpose

PHYLLIS MOEN

OXFORD
UNIVERSITY PRESS

Oxford University Press is a department of the University of Oxford.
It furthers the University's objective of excellence in research, scholarship,
and education by publishing worldwide. Oxford is a registered trade mark of
Oxford University Press in the UK and in certain other countries

Published in the United States of America by Oxford University Press
198 Madison Avenue, New York, NY 10016, United States of America

Library of Congress Cataloging-in-Publication Data
Moen, Phyllis, author.
Encore adulthood : boomers on the edge of risk, renewal, and purpose / Phyllis Moen.
pages cm
Includes bibliographical references and index.
ISBN 978-0-19-935727-7 (hardcover : alk. paper)—
ISBN 978-0-19-935728-4 (pbk. : alk. paper)
1. Older people—United States—Social conditions.
2. Baby boom generation—United States. 3. Retirement—United States.
4. Lifestyles—United States. 5. Aging—Psychological aspects.
6. Adulthood. I. Title.
HQ1064.U5M64 2016
305.260973—dc23 2015032486

For the grandchildren: William, Matt,
James, Kiri, and Tara
and, of course,
for Dick

Contents

Appendix B is an online supplement at www.oup.com/us/encoreadulthood.

List of Figures

Encore Adulthood

1

An Encore to Conventional Adulthood

AFTER 25 YEARS at Cornell University, I made the move to the University of Minnesota, in part because two young grandsons lived within a short drive. That first summer, I was invited to the Wright County Fair to watch James, age 13, show his chickens. His two-and-a-half-year-old brother William got pretty bored watching the 4Hers display their poultry to the judges, so we walked around, looking at pigs, goats, and sheep. I asked if there was anything else he wanted to see—cows or horses, perhaps? William replied, "camel."

Being a good professor, as we continued to trek through the muddy fairgrounds and buildings, I lectured him on the distinctions between farm animals and zoo animals, citing many examples. Camels, I explained, were zoo animals. Though you could find them in the Middle East, you would not find them on Minnesota farms or at county fairs. William said not a word. I went on about how some zoos do in fact have a few farm animals as a sort of petting zoo, but the division between farm and zoo animals is key. William walked on with his head down, stomping in every puddle, saying nothing.

We turned the corner. And, lo and behold, there was—a camel. I laughed and laughed—who's smart now? It turned out William had seen the camel with his father the night before. Chagrined, I even agreed to ride the camel with William.

People and groups create categories like farm animals, zoo animals, career paths, retirement, and life-course stages so that we can organize, talk about, and make sense of the world. But these mental maps take on a life of their own.[1] In other words, they become set beliefs and social arrangements providing order and meaning to our lives.[2] The problem is, as with my assumptions about camels and county fairs, we are living in a time when taken-for-granted categories and rules about schooling, work, careers, and retirement are out of date.

As with the second industrial revolution at the turn of the last century,[3] we are once again living in times of profound change. Economic, technological, demographic, and policy forces are disrupting the conventional linear life course (first schooling, then work, then retirement and with it old age). These forces include population aging with extended healthy life expectancy, a global economy dismantling job and economic security, rapidly advancing digital technologies automating jobs, improving medical care and blurring temporal and spatial boundaries, and declining social protections, such as reductions in or the elimination of social welfare supports and pensions. These changes are at odds with existing temporal categories—the established clocks and calendars defining work time, careers, education, family care, and retirement. And yet, even though career paths and retirement exits are in flux, most individuals and organizations continue to operate under a very outdated linear lockstep template of first learning, then working for advancement or at least security, then retiring once, all at once. This template leaves out things like family care or layoffs, returning to school or living healthier longer. Accelerated technologies combined with the shortened time horizons of organizations and their shareholders are transforming economies and labor markets as we move in fits and starts from linear to nonlinear ways of working and living.[4]

Conventional adulthood is unraveling to be sure. It is most evident around the edges as boundaries increasingly blur. On one edge, scholars find early adulthood is lengthening as Millennials (born 1981–1996) move through it,[5] with many getting more education but finding no clear career paths or job security once they graduate from high school or college. (Figure 1.1 shows the composition of the US workforce by cohort.) There are no longer crisp markers of entry into adulthood that used to be characterized by the end of schooling, a full-time job, marriage, and parenting in quick succession. Some call this new life stage through the twenties *emerging adulthood*, a time between

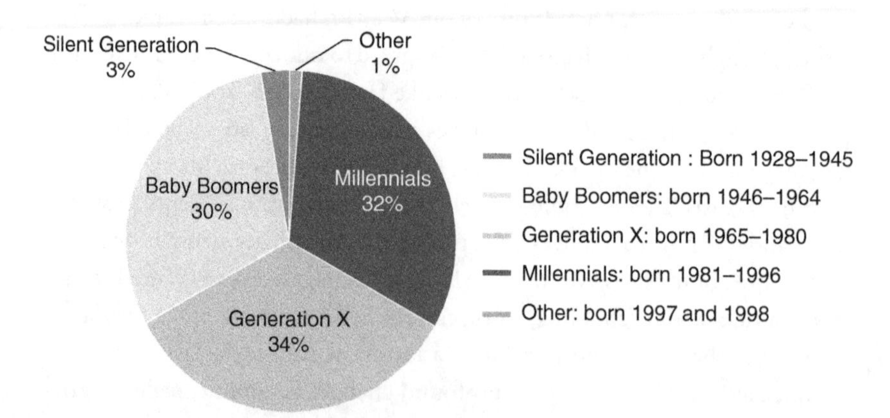

FIGURE 1.1. 2014 US Labor Force Composition by Cohort: Ages 16+

adolescence and conventional adult responsibilities. Millennials themselves are helping to define its characteristics and parameters. Much has been written about this new stage, with its very name—emerging adulthood—contested.[6]

This book is about another new stage, what I call *encore adulthood*, sandwiched between traditional careers and childrearing and old age. This is a time of varied paths, including for some ongoing engagement in meaningful activities made possible by medical advances and lifestyle changes improving population health and longevity. It turns out that the bonus years of life expectancy are coming not at the end of life but sometime around 55 through 75, as the infirmities associated with being elderly are postponed. As a result, Boomers (born 1946–1964) are like Millennials in that they both confront ill-fitting blueprints for the future. Both generations are moving beyond conventional life stages to—they are not quite sure what. It is hard to plan for the future when expected verities like education leading to stable employment, seniority leading to employment and economic security, and retirement leading to a carefree golden age no longer apply.

The linear, predictable life course has become nonlinear and unpredictable. Neither turning 65 nor retirement now signal the end of work or the beginning of old age, much less economic security. Boomers are retiring both earlier or later, and sometimes several times. Most are seeking new sources of purpose and usefulness: a second act of work, civic engagement, or family care. Just as founder and CEO of encore.org Marc Freedman speaks of encore careers, I see this new stage as an encore to adulthood.[7] The large cohort of Boomers now moving through these years are helping fashion this new life stage, even as categories like careers, retirement, and the life course are disassembling.

Thus we see major alterations at both ends of adulthood—emerging adulthood and encore adulthood. The rhythms and seasons of life are changing.

Unfortunately, the conventional clockworks, categories, and logics underlying workdays and workweeks, career paths, family care, education, and retirement have not kept pace with these changes. The lockstep model of first education, then continuous full-time work, culminating in full-time retirement leisure may have been an historical blip, unique to life in the middle of the twentieth century. But contemporary women and men of all ages and families at all stages remain constrained by the policies, practices, and mindsets it spawned.

This book examines this new encore stage between conventional adulthood and conventional old age as a tangible indicator of how careers and the life course are shifting before our eyes. How can we foster these bonus years as a time of potential and purpose? New life stages—much less a recalibrated life course—don't come about evenly or easily. But adolescence was created in the

1920s, and retirement was institutionalized in the United States with Social Security in the 1930s and 1940s. The conventional life course is changing in part because of the new longevity, but also because we are living through unsettled historical times, experiencing a whole range of uncertainties and disconnects. This reflects what sociologist Richard Sennett calls a new institutional architecture involving the delayering of organizations, the casualization of the labor market through short-term contracts, and the nonlinear task-oriented sequencing of work, all shortening organizations' and workers' time frames.[8] Mid-twentieth-century mindsets and institutional logics feel out of date, especially the clocks and calendars defining whether and when to go (or return) to college, where and what hours, days, and weeks to work, the shape of family care and career trajectories, and when to retire. And yet these rigid clockworks designed for life and work in the last century continue to limit the options shaping contemporary lives.

A New Life Course for the Twenty-First Century?

The linear lockstep life course—first education, then work, then retirement—was based on the orderly career tracks of white middle-class and unionized blue-collar men in the middle of the last century. It no longer fits the reality of most lives and never fit women's experiences, leaving out as it did the family-care obligations that fell mostly to them.[9] Neither has it fit the experiences of minority, immigrant, or poorly educated men and women, those on the outside of stable career paths for a single employer or in a single occupation. Moreover, the lockstep is no longer lockstep. Career pathways feel uncertain; some are disappearing all together. Seniority no longer means job security. And retirement is becoming less straightforward and more ambiguous, a process rather than a single event.

I argue in this book that it is time to think about and design more customized and sustainable life-course templates that better fit and recognize the risks of the demographic, technological, and economic realities—and time horizons—of the twenty-first century. New life stages at both ends of adulthood are reflective of the fact that deeply held beliefs about and outdated policies dictating linear careers and linear lives simply don't capture the contemporary human experience.

The Way Things Are

This book is very much about categories and conventions—how they are structured and named, and how they continue to structure our lives even when they no longer fit. "Old" or "elderly," for example, seem to be well past their usage dates for so many Boomers now entering their sixties and seventies, but the idea of age 65 as constituting old age continues to underpin public and organizational policies, employment options, cultural expectations, and imagined possibilities. So too do categories like "career," "workweek," "full time." Categories are in our heads as much as in policies and practices. In other words, they become institutionalized.

Many books have been written about institutions, and I will discuss this concept in depth in chapter 2.[10] Here I'll just say institutions represent existing beliefs and arrangements—the rigidities of the way things are, such as separating zoos from county fairs, for example, work from retirement, careers from casual jobs. These beliefs often morph into norms about the way things *should* be. I was convinced that camels should not be at the county fair, and most people are convinced that schooling, careers, and retirement should come in precisely this sequence and at pretty set times. Most continue to accept the increasingly false career mystique that long-hour, total dedication to work is *the* path to fulfillment,[11] although we have all known extremely committed workers who were unceremoniously laid off. These mindsets may be obsolete, but our biographies, organizations, and social policies continue to be ordered by assumptions and practices established sixty or seventy years ago. We are experiencing the deinstitutionalization of time as we know it while living with education, work-time, career, care, and retirement roles and rules designed for a different labor market, different types of work, different technologies, and different family configurations in a very different and much more unsettled world.

Boomers, members of the large post-World War II spike in births that occurred between 1946 and 1964, have always challenged prevailing clocks and calendars. The first Boomers, the leading edge born 1946–1954, embraced new music, created new lifestyles, and reacted to the draft and the Vietnam War in the 1960s. The trailing edge (born 1955–1964) came of age in a very different world than their older brothers and sisters. But most Boomers—leading edge and trailing edge—challenged ideas about family-related calendars standardized when their parents were adults. Many Boomers made the idea of cohabitation seem normal, even as many more ignored time and age clocks around whether or when to leave home, marry, have children, buy a house, divorce, remarry.[12] Still, the mid-twentieth-century calendars of public life known as the linear life course—of schooling coming early, continuous work throughout adulthood, followed by the leisure of retirement and with it old age—remain set, even though only educated white-collar and unionized blue-collar white men a generation ago were best able to actually follow its lockstep. This path was bolstered by public, labor, and business policies and practices undergirding the prevailing structures, logics, timetables, and mental markers of adult life.

Just as the division between types of animals is embedded in the institutions of county fairs and zoos, the ways governments, schools, unions, and businesses divide up time—distinguishing workdays from weekends, for example, or fashioning careers and the lockstep life course—also seem natural. But such classifications are socially constructed, designed in past times under different circumstances.

Categories of all kinds may be useful, even essential, as guideposts to living. But they are decidedly *not* immutable. Time and life-course categories, in particular, are so basic that those of us in the United States and Europe can hardly imagine a world without workweeks and weekends, 9 a.m. and 5 p.m. rush hours, holidays off from work. In the same way, we rarely stop to question the stages constituting the mid-twentieth-century life course: first childhood, adolescence, and years of education; then many years of employment in adulthood; followed by years in retirement, leisure, dependency, and old age.[13] From happy hour to teenager to golden years, our clocks and calendars are taken-for-granted rules, routines, and rigidities setting the rhythms and textures of our lives.[14]

I argue in this book that such life-course, career, and work-time classifications are both outdated *and* in flux, a combination stalling *and* inviting improvisations and innovations in the ways members of all generations work and live.[15] Twenty-first-century life in North America and Europe is changing in remarkable ways—lives last longer, life stages are less tied to specific ages, and people find themselves on more diverse and often risky pathways at all stages of the life course.

Consider, for example, the risks confronting Boomers. One in four (24 percent) Americans ages 50 to 59 lost a job between 2008 and 2013, as did one in five (20 percent) ages 60 to sixty-four. And one in eight is currently unemployed.[16] Some are trying to make themselves irreplaceable to stave off job loss. Some are hoping to work—for income, for meaning, or for routine—as long as they can. Some are quitting dead-end jobs to seek new possibilities. Some are testing the waters through phased retirement, "not-so-big" jobs,[17] or volunteer work. Some are seeking second careers or self-employment, retooling and reinventing themselves. Some are leaving the workforce entirely to help ailing parents, grandchildren, or community service organizations, or else to focus on improving their own health and well-being. Many want a sense of purpose, what entrepreneur Aaron Hurst defines as a sense of community and the opportunity for self-expression and personal growth.[18] But, like Millennials in emerging adulthood and GenXers in what used to be conventional adulthood, all are moving through this next phase of their lives with outdated blueprints. What comes next for the advantaged and especially for the disadvantaged is ambiguous at best.

Why Encore Adulthood Matters

Understanding the possibilities and perils of this new encore adult phase promises pragmatic and policy, as well as scientific, value. The large number of Boomers moving through this age period is not just an American phenomenon. Europe, Australia, New Zealand, and Canada also experienced a rise in postwar fertility (a little later than the United States), and an even greater rise in life expectancy. Recognizing the potentials of encore adulthood could help manage the rising costs of social security, pensions, and health care as this Boomer cohort moves through their fifties, sixties, and seventies. Given the aging populations in North America, Europe, and Asia, how Boomers spend their time in the encore years matters for their own and their families' life quality, to be sure. But their collective and often constrained choices also affect the sustainability of social welfare programs as well as health care systems worldwide. For example, Boomers engaging in health-promoting lifestyles will slow the rising costs of medical care. If they continue to work for pay, even part time, Boomers contribute to—rather than draw down—government coffers and social security systems. Some follow something of a hybrid path, such as the working retired, drawing on social security benefits and continuing to pay taxes to support such programs. Over half (54 percent) of employed Americans 65 to 74 say they are "retired but currently working," as do 17 percent of those 57 to 64 in the labor force.[19]

There is a third payoff as well. Boomers' leaning in to new forms of paid or unpaid work mean that organizations and communities can continue to draw on the experience and expertise of the vast numbers wanting to make a difference, mentor the next generation, transfer knowledge, and contribute in meaningful and useful ways. Tapping the time, talents, and skills of Boomers leaning out from demanding, often unrewarding, and increasingly risky career jobs but who feel they are not yet done makes sense on a variety of levels.

Decision-makers would do well to figure out how to promote and sustain Boomers' continued voluntary public engagement, and indeed, that of adults of all ages. I have concluded that to do so requires designing appealing, purposive, and flexible forms of work, as well as easy, affordable options to return to school or get the training necessary in today's job market. The difficulties facing encore adults only underscore what is happening at all ages and life stages. Linear careers and long time frames enabling people to feel secure and to plan for the future are disappearing.[20]

A key challenge is to break open standardized work times, education and career paths, and retirement exits, inventing a range of viable pathways through work and through life, including new narratives around what constitutes good jobs, sustainable (though nonlinear) careers, satisfying retirements, and new models of career and life success. Another challenge is to ameliorate patterned disparities in the social inclusion of people differing by education, gender, race/ethnicity, health conditions, and skills, as well as age. Recall the wide age spread within this cohort—some 19 years from the birth of the first US Boomers in 1946 to the last, in 1964.[21] There is equally wide variety in their goals, values, obligations, relationships, resources, and lifestyles. Some are seeking to remain in or establish full—and fulfilling—careers. Others less advantaged are less able to follow paths to new opportunities given health considerations, care obligations, or the age, gender, and other discriminations built into how gatekeepers think about careers, college students, workers, retirees, and productivity.[22] Policy developments that enable time shifts like delaying retirement but reducing hours, working in flexible part-time, part-year jobs, or inventing new ways of helping others and promoting the greater good could lift some of the risk of job and economic insecurity and open up new and satisfying life pathways. Nine in 10 older workers in the United States describe their ideal job as one making use of their skills and talents—the chance to do something worthwhile in a friendly work environment.[23] Many Boomers don't want to lean into their current jobs *or* step into total retirement.[24] Rather, they want to explore new ways of engaging with the world.

Key Themes

Along with others who may call them various names,[25] I see great possibilities in the windfall years of encore adulthood. A key theme of this book is that there are similarities in the changes at both ends of the adult life course. Because emerging adulthood has already been studied intensely, I draw on the concepts and findings about the transition to adulthood to see if they similarly apply to the transition from traditional careers and childrearing into what are becoming varied paths replacing conventional retirement.[26] Generations today are more similar than different from each other in their beliefs and values.

A second theme is that times of rapid social change such as these enable people to experiment, opening up opportunities for some to fashion new ways of working and living. In the chapters that follow I chart improvisations by Boomer women and men who, like Millennials in emerging adulthood, are literally making up this new life stage as they go along. In doing so, many are challenging outdated norms around both the full-time career lockstep and the full-time retirement lockstep, as well as norms relegating higher education to early adulthood.

Also like many Millennials, many Boomers teeter on a moving platform of mounting job and economic insecurity, as well as health and retirement insecurity. While some are actively fashioning what's next, others find themselves unwillingly in the workforce or unwillingly retired. An AARP survey found one in four (24 percent) employed Boomers (45–74) thought it was "somewhat" or "very" likely they could lose their job or that it would be eliminated within the next year.[27] In the middle of the last century the seniority associated with long tenure in a company meant job security. This is no longer the case.

A third key theme, then, is that as is true for emerging adulthood, opportunities for reinvention and renewal as well as heightened risks of economic hardship, distress, and disability are not equally distributed across those moving through the encore adult years. Education, social class, gender, race, health, and age expand or narrow life chances and life quality. For example, the AARP survey shows workers in minority groups feel more vulnerable than white workers; fully two in five (39 percent) of employed African Americans ages 45 to 74 saw job loss as a possibility, as did one in three employed Hispanics.[28]

A fourth theme is the distinctly gendered pathways that women and men follow through life, what I call the gendered life course.[29] Women and men chart or are allocated to different work and family paths, with enormous consequences for their financial, physical, and emotional well-being. This perpetuates and accentuates gender disparities already evident for those youngsters in the emerging adult years as well as for GenXers still deep into building their families and trying to hang on to their careers.

These last three themes—opportunity, uncertainty and risk, and the gendered nature of lives—capture possibilities and disparities characterizing the twenty-first-century life course from emerging to encore adulthood and beyond. I focus on the new encore to adulthood, defined as yet by a disconnect between today's uncertainties and dislocations and traditional expectations of a set retirement exit involving, at its best, a steady stream of income and a little travel. But what is going on in this encore adult stage is rife with larger insights about an evolving life course characterized by both hazards and prospects for personal growth and purpose, with some better positioned than others to bend the arc of their lives.

A Triple Agenda

How can individuals, families, governments, and organizations reduce the risks, enhance purpose, and benefit from the promise of the bonus encore years? This book is about two sets of choices. First, how are contemporary Boomers choosing to respond to twenty-first-century uncertainties and opportunities in the face of outdated timetables around work, careers, and retirement? Boomers (and soon GenXers) seek to customize their own pathways. But they can't do it on their own.

This leads to the second set of choices. Will organizations, communities, and governments redesign and update work, career, schooling, service, care, and retirement in the face of population aging, digital technologies, global economies, and insufficient safety nets? We need to legitimate new language, customs, and policies, discarding twentieth-century scripts locked into rules and routines around schooling, work, careers, and retirement. I argue for an overhaul of research, policy, and action agendas, aligning them to twenty-first-century exigencies and opportunities. In the pages that follow I describe three major challenges for individuals and families, for scholars, and for leaders in the private, public, and social (nonprofit) sectors. Though my focus is on life in the encore years, these challenges pretty much apply to emerging as well as encore adulthood and, indeed, to what I see as a more customized life course for those of all ages.

Agenda #1: Recognizing Inertia

First is to simply recognize institutional inertia, the outdatedness of existing, taken-for-granted rules, regulations, mindsets and logics fashioned around a mid-twentieth-century vision of a very gendered, very lockstep, and very unequal life course. Yesterday's clocks and calendars of work time and school/career/retirement paths simply don't fit today's shortened time frames, uncertain futures, and rapidly developing technologies. The first step in transformation is *recognizing the need for change*.

Recall from your high school science classes that inertia refers to things that remain still or remain in motion. Things persist in their current form.

Inertia also exists in institutional logics around work, careers, higher education, and the life course. Governments, corporations, unions, universities, and community organizations find it easier to keep prevailing standardized educational, work-time, career, and life-course templates rather than reimagine and reinvent new ones, even though both work and the workforce have changed in so many other ways. For example, four out of every 10 (40.2 percent) Americans ages 55 and older were in the workforce in 2010, an increase from less than a third (32.8 percent) in 2000. By contrast, fully eight in 10 (82.2 percent) of those ages 25 to 54 were in the labor force in 2010,[30] suggesting that many Boomers are voting with their feet—or are being pushed out of paid work.

Ideas, identities, and institutions about schooling, career paths, family care, age, gender, retirement, and the life course came about and persisted through a series of choices made by nineteenth- and twentieth-century leaders. They are all examples of institutional inertia. These firmly established—inert—policies created for a different time, different economy, and different workforce are now limiting the paths open to Boomers for whom retirement may not come at a particular age, if at all, or too early because of layoffs, health problems, or unsatisfactory working conditions. Others sandwiched between caring for elderly parents and children or grandchildren may leave the workforce to do so, or keep working for the needed money or the respite from family concerns jobs can provide. Others with the skills and the will to contribute to their communities do so through unpaid civic engagement, second careers, or part-time or self-employment. Still others may want second acts, but can't figure out how to get there.

Another way of thinking about institutional inertia is what Matilda White Riley terms structural lag.[31] In times of rapid social change, cultural expectations, laws, rules, and regulations can't keep pace, changing at a glacial pace.[32]

Agenda #2: Time-Shifting Improvisations

Second is to investigate, track, and support Boomers' own informal improvisations, expectations, and claims as to what they want and need as they move through this new phase of adult life. The challenge for Boomers as well as for Millennials and GenXers as individuals, couples, and collectivities is to improvise the lives they want, despite twenty-first-century risks and uncertainties and the weight of institutional inertia bound to the outdated linear life course.

One by one, or as couples and friends, Boomers are strategically improvising creative personal solutions for making paid work, family care, civic engagement, and leisure fit their needs and goals. In doing so, they are collectively transforming the landscape of the conventional linear and lockstep life course. As with Millennials moving through emerging adulthood and any large-scale social change, this shift is happening in fits and starts, as people watch their friends flourish and flounder, and choose or are forced by layoffs, sporadic or chronic unemployment, or health problems to follow established or alternative paths. From these myriad individual transitions and trajectories, we can begin to see the flow of change. Some pathways in this new encore stage are obscured from public view, as individuals and families struggle to make ends meet or care for grandchildren or aging parents, aunts, and spouses. Others seem dominant, as advertisers and the media glorify this stage as a sort of extended vacation made possible by buying certain types of insurance, financial services, or pharmaceuticals.

Boomers blessed with good health and economic security can often carve their own paths, and these may be suggestive of ways to develop realistic and sustainable options for those less advantaged. As with Millennials constructing emerging adulthood, we must learn from, acknowledge, and facilitate Boomers' improvisations as both adaptive strategies and increasingly normal ways of living. Boomers are seeking to live the lives they want and need. The absence of guideposts is especially evident as they begin thinking about and try to plan for—or else are unexpectedly thrust into—second runs. Taking their preferences seriously and tracking their transitions and trajectories and the outcomes of different paths can inform cogent, flexible policy.

Obsolete timetables, automation, and unsettled economic times foster apprehension, but they also open up opportunities for improvisation and reinvention. Consider how new technologies are dismantling established clockworks, bringing transformations to leisure as new platforms permit people to enjoy movies and television programs, listen to music, play games, and connect with one another on their own timetables. In fact, in every life arena, normative clocks and calendars are morphing—what I call *time shifting*. This is the ability to rearrange the once-standard clocks and calendars of life, hopefully in ways that better fit with people's goals, abilities, and preferences. Voluntary time shifting promotes a sense of control and purpose. For example, young people have always taken easily to the speed and wide-ranging temporal rhythms offered by changing communication and information technologies. For Millennials (those born 1981–1996), smart phones, entertainment on demand, wearables, and social media are firmly entrenched institutions—taken for granted as both the way things are and the way things should be. GenXers and Boomers have increasingly adopted these same technologies, fashioning lifestyles of their own by changing the speed, sequencing, and allocation of their leisure time. Together with their younger and middle-aged colleagues, some Boomers are also time-shifting paid work.

Time shifting in all its forms is coming to be a hallmark of contemporary life. GenXers (born 1965–1980), Millennials (born 1981–1996), and what some call "the 2020s" (born since 1996) may have led change in the time shifting of everyday life through social media. But Boomers (born 1946–1964) have been the movers and shakers behind *life-course* time shifting. They dismantled outdated age scripts dictating the time and timing of when to complete schooling, move into or remain in jobs, relocate to a new city or country, live together, marry or stay married, become a parent, buy a house. And their improvisations are driving the customization of the twenty-first-century life course—expanding, rebranding, and blurring the boundaries around the once lockstep timetables of family, careers, conventional adulthood, conventional retirement, and now encore adulthood.[33]

Boomers are more similar to members of younger cohorts than to those of their parents; their wide-ranging improvisations have paved the way for acceptance of the diverse paths of those currently moving through their twenties, thirties, and forties.[34] Both Millennials and Boomers are in what sociologists Phillipa Clarke from the University of Michigan and Blair Wheaton from the University of Toronto call a "sorting period."[35]

Agenda #3: Innovations

The third challenge is to investigate, design, and implement innovations in the public, private, and social (nonprofit) sectors that offer a wide range of interesting, flexible, financially sustainable, and purposive options for paid work, learning, and civic engagement in this encore stage that mesh with Boomers' family-care work, financial needs, and the effective management of their health conditions. So, too, must scholars and policymakers consider Boomers' own goals for what is next, their very valid concerns about sufficient future income, and their desire to leave stressful career jobs for more fulfilling if less well-paid or even unpaid work. There are so many problems that could benefit from the expertise, experience, and energy of those in encore adulthood.

Tapping this resource in ways that work for Boomers, organizations, and communities makes practical sense. We *can* create, investigate, and scale innovations in logics, policies, and practices that open up educational, work, and service opportunities across the life course. And we can do so in ways that maximize both individual and societal renewal, creating magnets that retain, attract, and support those moving through these bonus years. Schools, public agencies, labor unions, businesses, and community associations must build on the early rough sketches of Boomers' own improvisations to design a range of innovative options for those in this new life stage. Encore adults aren't forever young, but they're not old either. And many have much to contribute as well as the motivation, skills, and energy to do so. But this requires institutional work, "the practices of individuals and collective actors aimed at creating, maintaining and disrupting institutions."[36]

We need new institutional logics, practices, and policies—innovative laws, rules, regulations, norms, mindsets, and strategies widening the pool of options for purposive and willing but also flexible engagement in work and civic activities across the life course, including for those seeking new possibilities the second time around.[37]

Innovations are also needed that recognize and remedy the fact that both risks and opportunities for individual reinvention and renewal in encore adulthood are shaped by what the famous developmentalist Urie Bronfenbrenner called people's social address—their age, health, gender, race/ethnicity, nativity, sexuality, education, and occupation.[38] As with emerging adulthood, risks and prospects in this new encore stage are also shaped by the people in their lives—partners, children, grandchildren, parents, siblings, bosses, coworkers, friends, and neighbors. Boomers with fewer resources, skills, and social ties are less equipped to time shift their lives in ways they might prefer. Existing institutional logics and labor market regimes reinforce age segmentation, stereotypes, and discrimination even as they codify unequal career and retirement pathways for Boomer women and men with different educational levels, races and ethnicities, and biographies.

Moreover, even as more privileged Boomers are improvising new ways of living, they bump up against existing rules, regulations, and expectations of work and retirement juxtaposed with the new insecurities around work, income, and future prospects. Their options are limited. Outdated time clocks package jobs as full-time, full-year, often fully inflexible, and retirement as a one-way, one-time, irreversible exit. This sustains age discrimination and makes time-shifting Boomers feel like they're all doing it on their own. No map, no net.

My argument for policy innovations to actualize encore as well as emerging adulthood and indeed to customize the life course is not about getting rid of all structural categories and arrangements. Structures organize and give meaning to our lives. Institutionalized rules, routines, logics, and activities provide a sense of coherence and stability, offering predictability to social behavior. But existing structures can be redesigned, institutional logics updated, and new social inventions created to include a range of alternative paid work, care work, education, retirement, and lifestyle options. The evidence suggests that many in this life stage who can afford to are willing to trade off some income for satisfaction, purpose, flexibility, and time. Addressing ways encore adults' talents can be repurposed and put to work to promote the common good; ways public and organizational policies must shift to accommodate an older workforce and longer, healthier life spans; and how we support those who take on caregiving roles within community and family structures would touch on solutions to key twenty-first-century challenges.

A Road Map

This chapter has provided an introduction to encore adulthood and several intertwining threads serving to define, open up, or shut down its possibilities. How can we appreciate, support, and capitalize on this new life stage? I maintain that to institutionalize encore adulthood as a new and welcomed life stage, reducing its risks and opening up purposive opportunities to a broader pool of Boomers, requires the triple agenda previewed above.

First, we must recognize the institutional inertia and obsolescence of existing clockworks that create structural lag between outdated twentieth-century labor market and retirement policies and twenty-first-century work, families, and workforces. Throughout the book, but especially in chapters 2 and 3, I describe ways this mismatch between obsolete norms and the explosion in the numbers of older workers and younger retirees is constraining the opportunities for an encore to adulthood. Chapter 2 delves further into careers and the life course as institutions—created and outdated—as well as related concepts. Chapter 3 describes the institutional inertia of standardized work practices that persist even with globalization, automation, and concomitant changes in the social contract among employers, their workers, and retirees. And then there is precarity—the very real shakiness of employment and economic security across the life course, made unsteady by mergers, layoffs, automation, forced early retirements, and the existential difficulty of obtaining new jobs for people age 50 and beyond.

We next look at the improvisations Boomers in this life stage are making, time-shifting the way they work and live by leaning out from conventional work roles and expectations. Given the absence of guideposts, Boomers who feel reasonably healthy and have sufficient income are reimagining themselves and regenerating their lives. Many are seeking or creating second chances, challenging the existing choices of full-time demanding jobs or full-time undemanding retirement. Others find the employers they were loyal to are not loyal to them, as they are suddenly on the outside looking in. Many are time-shifting to remain vital, achieve long-held dreams, or give back or subsist instead of stepping quietly into the margins of mainstream society. In chapters 2, 4, and 5, I introduce the idea of voluntary time shifting as a new way of improvising working and living. Boomers are customizing as they are able their careers, work hours, retirement timing, and second acts to better fit the lives they want as opposed to the lives of their parents or grandparents encrusted in existing regulations. They are also providing new visions and new narratives of life on the edge, many of which are interspersed throughout the volume.

Third, crucial to realizing the promise of a more customized twenty-first-century life course is institutional work—efforts at disrupting existing logics and pioneering policies and practices in the private, social, and public sectors that tap into the talents, energy, and purposive engagement of encore adults while also promoting their well-being. Social and corporate entrepreneurs of all ages are becoming undeniable movers and shakers, leading change by exploring and fashioning new pathways. Chapter 7 highlights institutional work in the form of pockets of change—small-scale social inventions challenging taken-for-granted assumptions and reflexive beliefs about jobs, work time, careers, retirement, and the life course. Such initiatives, often local, offer prototypes for larger policies that might accommodate and even capitalize on the time shifting of paid and volunteer work in ways that better fit the realities of Boomers' values, needs, and goals.

Taking these pockets of change to scale will help legitimate encore adulthood as a recognizable stage of the twenty-first-century life course. Doing so requires changing language and customs, but also laws and regulations. Chapter 8 describes ways to move away from outmoded templates of work, schooling, career paths, and retirement; ways to move away from age as a marker of ability and disability; and ways to recognize the personal and societal possibilities of institutionalizing encore adulthood as a distinct life stage.

I end this chapter with a second camel story. Another grandson—Matt—was about eight years old when we went to the zoo in Washington, DC. We could see three camels in the distance, on top of a hill. Matt asked if they were real or statues. "Of course they're real," I told him. "They move!" But, wisely, Matt rattled off examples of statues that move. Together we pondered the existential question of what it is that makes something real. And then we went to see the pandas.

In the chapters that follow, I recount the perils and promise of encore adulthood, a time fabricated from the bonus years of extended healthy life expectancy; the heightened risks associated with new technologies, automation, and globalization; the enduring inequalities stitched into women's and men's life paths that are also confined by different social addresses; concerns about the aging of the population; and the large numbers of Boomers now moving through their fifties, sixties, and seventies. Like the camels, the question becomes, how do we know if this new life-course stage is real? Perhaps the better question is whether it's a useful addition to the ways people—from Boomers themselves to scholars and corporate, social, and public decision-makers—think about, divide up, and regulate the contemporary life course. As with past time clocks and calendars, both emerging adulthood and encore adulthood will become real only after being improvised, lived, and legitimated by individuals, families, organizations, communities, and governments. The challenge is to make the promise of these new twenty-first-century stages and indeed a more customized life-course actualities, reducing their risks by opening up, normalizing, individualizing, and standardizing new possibilities.

This is why I wrote this book.[39] Like Millennials, Boomers are on the edge—improvising a new life stage in the face of a disappearing social contract between employers and employees; a more varied, longer, and possibly healthier and purposive life course; and the inertia and upheavals of outdated or disappearing educational, labor market, and retirement policies, practices, and customs in the face of digital technologies, global economies, and the aging of the population. All of which makes their life chances and life quality both uncertain and unique.

AGENDA #1

Recognizing Inertia

2

Outdated Career and Life-Course Templates

INDIVIDUALS WHO SEEM similar may follow very different life paths. For example, my friend Donna and I are about the same age, but I had my first child at 19, while she had hers at forty. So while Donna was raising a preschooler, my two daughters were in college. Although we are in the same birth cohort, we are at very different family stages.

Still, Donna and I are more similar to each other than to our mothers, having benefited from the women's movement opening up opportunities in education and employment, doors that were closed for most in our mothers' generation. We both returned to school and earned PhDs, something not possible for our mothers, their friends, or many other women our age.

Our biographies are also more similar to each other's than to men's. Like many Boomer women, we have followed convoluted career paths. Donna and I are the same age, the same cohort; we have lived through the same historical times and experienced the same outdated gendered regimes around work, schooling, careers, family care, and the life course. But I was also Donna's graduate advisor, and my daughters babysat hers. This underscores the individualization but also the social organization of the life course, the patterned yet distinctive pathways we take through life.

What is striking is that the life course is both outdated *and* changing before our eyes. Let's step back from the introduction in chapter 1 to define in this chapter concepts key to my argument. What exactly do we mean by the life course? What precisely are institutions and institutional inertia? And how do both relate to the concept of careers? I illustrate these concepts by drawing on the experiences of the people I have interviewed,[1] concluding by describing other related concepts: age (along with gender), cohort, and historical period.

Careers and the Life Course as Institutions

The famous life-course scholar Glen Elder, the University of North Carolina sociologist who captured the lives of children in the Great Depression, describes the life course as "age-graded life patterns embedded in social institutions and subject to historical change."[2] Even in its definition, the life course is related to age, institutions, historical time periods, and life patterns. The concept of career has traditionally been defined as the large middle portion of the life course, an orderly, continuous, and hierarchical progression up occupational or seniority ladders, most commonly in professional and unionized blue-collar occupations. But both careers and the linear lockstep life course are twentieth-century inventions, institutionalized in now outdated laws, logics, and language.[3] And yet, like Donna, myself, and many women as well as men of all ages, actual career and life-course pathways often diverge considerably from the expected sequence of first education, then a lifetime of continuous full-time work, then total retirement. Still, both life-course and career concepts operate as metaphors, mindsets, and organizing principles, providing a way of describing experiences, expectations, and self-conceptions. We identify with our life stages—I am a student, new father, retired, for example—and our paid work—I am a doctor, janitor, teacher.

Studies of occupational careers and the life course are necessarily about time, with careers investigated as processes of job development, mobility, plateauing, transitions, exits, and entrances. But the notion of careers is a function of historical time as well—a modern invention, emerging as a social fact only with the development of corporations, bureaucracies, and white-collar as well as skilled blue-collar employment. As Columbia University sociologist C. Wright Mills pointed out,[4] prior to the Industrial Revolution most people worked in either agriculture or a family business. Though individual farmers, craftspeople, and family entrepreneurs may have had life plans, they did not have careers. The whole idea of career is thus really a product of industrialization and the development and bureaucratization of occupational lines. As paid work for others, particularly in corporations and governments, became central to twentieth-century society, the work career and the salary it provides came to shape life chances, life quality, and life choices in virtually every arena.

When in the middle of the last century C. Wright Mills wrote *White Collar*, editor of *Fortune* magazine and distinguished professor at Hunter College William Whyte wrote *The Organization Man*, and Harvard University historian Charles Walker together with Dartmouth industrial psychologist Robert Guest wrote *The Man on the Assembly Line*,[5] they were describing bureaucratic managerial practices that produced what I call the career mystique: that is, seeing long-hour continuous commitment to one's job throughout adulthood as the only path to upward mobility and success. In the United States this was the path to the American Dream.[6] But these and other classic publications on careers were based on the assumption that men in white-collar or unionized blue-collar occupations could focus completely on their jobs because they were free of family-care obligations.[7] Someone else—a wife—was presumed available to take care of their families, their households, and the men themselves. Careers of upward mobility were what everyone aspired to, even though many minorities, women, and the poorly educated found no rungs to climb. By equating career, success, and the life course with paid work and occupational paths, a vast amount of social activity coming under the rubric of unpaid work—whether for a family business, doing one's own household and family-care work, being a community volunteer, or informally helping out neighbors and friends—was rendered marginal to the "business" of society, and, consequently, the business of those making public policy or conducting mainstream social research.[8]

In 1930, sociologist Karl Mannheim described career as a series of steps: "At each step in it one receives a neat package of prestige and power whose size is known in advance. Its keynote is security; the unforeseen is reduced to the vanishing point."[9] This framing can be seen in the early career literature focusing on vocational choices by Columbia University psychologist Donald Super,[10] University of Michigan psychologist John Holland,[11] and others. There were lots of opportunities out there. Young people simply had to choose the best fit.

The notion of career is also closely associated with the scholarship in the 1960s of an organizational sociologist from the University of California, Berkeley, Harold Wilensky. He emphasized the dimensions of an orderly career path—continuity in terms of stability of labor force participation; mobility that could be upward, flat, or even downward; and coherence in that there were no unrelated job shifts. What is clear is that occupational career paths became an indispensable means for individuals and families to achieve life quality or at least make ends meet and for businesses to create an effective, productive workforce. But a global economy, new digital and computational technologies, and the individualization of risk are resulting in more contingent jobs and less orderly career paths, calling for new ways of framing work, careers, and the life course, as well as the social protections undergirding them.

German sociologists Karl Mayer and Walter Mueller describe institutional careers as the orderly flow of persons through segmented institutions (such as schools for training, a series of related jobs, and retirement).[12] Despite the fact that career paths today—men's and women's—are more contingent than orderly, the career concept still constitutes a bridge between organizations, individuals and families, a window for viewing the life course.[13]

Assumptions about careers remain based on the mystique of continuous hard work and commitment as the path to both security and success, but that is an out-of-date model given the uncertainties and risks associated with today's global economy, automation, outsourcing, offshoring, and restructuring. We are living in what MIT professors Brynjolfsson and McAfee call the second machine age, a time when digitalization is transforming work, career paths, and essential skills. It is also challenging existing models of the life course and promoting, I argue, the creation of both emerging and encore adult stages at the two ends of conventional adulthood. The first machine age—the Industrial Revolution—institutionalized time, including temporal rules and expectations around careers and the lockstep life course. The second machine age is upending them, creating what MIT and London School of Economics sociologist Richard Sennett describes as foreshortened timeframes in organizations and in individual lives.[14] Consider, for example, the idea of portfolio or "boundaryless" careers, recognizing the permeability and shifting nature of contemporary work paths.[15] The contemporary challenge is to investigate, understand, and manage both continuity and change in time as manifested in work, careers, labor markets and the life course in a climate characterized by uncertainty and continuous, rapid-paced technological change.[16]

Institutionalized time is changing at the macro level. This plays out at family and individual levels in the form of job transitions and trajectories, by definition life-course processes that play out over time, but are often studied at one point in a person's life. There is, however, a growing body of scholarship examining the dynamics of men's and women's career paths.[17] Boomer women have typically followed "disorderly" trajectories and their narratives may anticipate the increasingly tenuous connection to jobs and organizations of the early twenty-first century. Consider the case of Jessie, for example, who at age 62 reflects on her "messy" pathway:

> I quit college early, worked as a nursing assistant. And then took off across the country, eventually ended up on a Christian commune, just working in the kitchen and with children. And then got married, and took a part-time job in a fabric store. Ended up going back to school. I thought I was going to get a degree in programming, but absolutely hated programming

> and switched to nutrition. Thought, "Oh I really don't want to tell people what to eat." So I ended up doing a degree in elementary education and never worked in education. Got a divorce as I was finishing up that program, and moved back from Oregon to Connecticut. Worked as a sub, trying to, you know, work myself into a job. And that summer just took a temp job when the subbing was over for the school year. And they offered me a full-time position with benefits. I had two young children and I jumped on it, doing customer service work in the manufacturing sector and just kind of stayed there. Went through a few lay-offs and then ended up taking the position that I have currently in an alternative healthcare office managing the office and taking care of patients.

Today, both men's and women's occupational paths are increasingly uncertain and contingent, reflecting technological innovations together with the disappearing social contract we'll discuss in chapter 3.[18] Years spent in the labor market are declining, not always voluntarily.

Consider Jeff in Los Angeles, who at age 57 has watched cameras on cell phones destroy his career:

> With commercial photography, there is a point of diminishing return basically. The pie has always been small for the available work, but it is even smaller now and there are more people vying for that pie. When I started my work I was competing against established giants in the field. Now I am competing against people with an iPhone.

Jeff is currently doing contract work while looking for another job:

> I still have to work. I still have to make an income. The economy isn't such that anybody can sit around and do nothing, otherwise you continue to burn your candle down to nothing and you lose your home.

Boomers like Jeff find themselves at odds with the conventional clocks and calendars of work and the life course, even as taken-for-granted verities like the security that used to accompany seniority disappear before their eyes.

Career and Life Stages

Career and life-course stages have to do with where people are in terms of their occupational or family circumstances, how they identify and evaluate themselves, and how others identify and evaluate them. For example, people raising young children are in very different situations compared to those who remain childfree or whose children are grown. And someone in a new job is very different from a 20-year veteran. Usually, but not always, occupational and family stages are aligned with age.

Consider the case of Marc and Robin, two Boomers who lived together in the 1970s while attending Stanford University, postponing marriage till their midthirties, and divorcing in their late fifties, after their last child entered college. Or Angela, who married and had two children early in her twenties, returned to school then became an elementary school principal in her late forties. These time shifters have not followed the mid-twentieth-century ordered patterns of completing school, finding a job, marrying shortly after, and soon having a child—patterns that characterized the life courses of many middle-class individuals in their parents' generation.

Boomers are increasingly empty-nesters, as was Marc before he divorced Robin. Now he finds himself unable to plan for retirement given that his encore includes a new marriage to a younger wife and a second round of parenting. Remarried and raising a new family, Marc is essentially perpetuating childrearing into his eighties. Robin, too, is reimagining her life, planning to move back to where she grew up, aiming to use the expertise gleaned from her career in a federal agency to help her struggling hometown. Marc feels a bit stuck: "I can never retire—have to put two small kids through college." Robin, on the other hand, says:

> I am not planning on scaling back, but scaling *up*. If I can devise programs to help communities in Africa [in her career job], surely I can do something for the small town in Texas where my relatives still live.

Life stages as we know them have emerged historically through a process of differentiation, with first childhood, then old age, then adolescence being demarcated from the rest of life.[19] Social observers propose new stages when existing formulations seem out of date, usually because of a mismatch between new demographic and social realities and current policies and practices. We have seen childhood, for example, be unpacked into preschool, adolescence, even toddlers and tweens. Right now life-course researchers like me are focused on two change-points in the contemporary social organization of the life course: emerging adulthood throughout the twenties, where young people with sufficient resources are able to experiment with various adult roles,[20] and a third age or encore adulthood, coming after the career- and family-building years.[21] Boomers are experimenting with alternative ways of living and working, hoping to postpone the "fourth age" of infirmities associated with the last years of life.

Just as adolescence was first ill-defined,[22] but became part of the institutionalized life course in the early part of the twentieth century and further honed by middle-class teenage Boomers as consumers and activists in the 1960s and 1970s,[23] "emerging adulthood" and "encore adulthood" remain ambiguous terms while still capturing recognizable periods on both edges of conventional adulthood. Both of these stages are increasingly fraught with risks, uncertainty, and ambivalence, as well as interesting possibilities. Both render existing logics and structures organizing the life course out of date—those mindsets, norms, and assumptions based on strict divisions between schooling, work, and retirement; between productivity and dependency; between men and women; between youth, adulthood, and old age.[24] Both reflect time shifting—either delaying or moving out of conventional adult roles—in the context of an uncertain and unsettled economic, labor market, and digital climate.

I make the case in this book that many of the experiences of Millennials in emerging adulthood also apply to Boomers in encore adulthood, even though they differ in important ways. Twenty-somethings experiment with various adult roles though they "aren't quite there yet in part because traditional career paths are eroding."[25] Many are experiencing considerable difficulty establishing economic independence, carrying heavy student loans and floundering in uneven job markets. Emerging adulthood has to date been frequently marked by financial and residential dependence on parents, adolescent-like irresponsibility, and indecision.[26] It is portrayed through various expressions such as "failure to launch."[27] But this is indicative of the dislocations in the social organization of careers and the life course. Fortunately, many have parents (Boomers) who provide the scaffolds and safety nets that assist them in forging their paths toward adulthood.[28] By contrast, Boomers themselves have no such scaffolds or safety nets.

Still, the similarities are remarkable. Consider the taken-for-granted divide between adolescence and adulthood once associated with graduating high school or college and moving, lockstep, into career jobs, marriage, and parenthood. This has evaporated. Similarly, the taken-for-granted divide between paid work and retirement signaling the arrival of the golden years is also evaporating. I like Purdue University sociologist Kenneth Ferraro's concept of "soft" life stages.[29] There are no hard edges on either side of emerging or encore adulthood. Still, the argument for a period of life after raising children and career-building but before the infirmities of old age has merit. For example, most fifty-somethings are reasonably healthy, and seven in ten (73.6 percent) Americans ages 65 to 74 have no disability—no severe vision or hearing problems, no cognitive difficulties, no trouble walking or caring for themselves, fully able to live independently. This does change over time, but over half (55 percent) of those 75 to 84 are still disability free, compared to only 27.5 percent of those 85 and older.[30]

Emerging adulthood reflects the dismantling of expectations about the "right" ages to marry, buy a house, or have a child—the ambivalence of young people about taking on conventional adult roles especially in the face of their mounting debt, insufficient earnings, and the inability to plan for the future.[31]

Encore adulthood also reflects the dismantling of deeply ingrained mindsets. It was first characterized as a third age by historian Peter Laslett,[32] an interlude produced by medical advances and lifestyle changes improving population health and longevity.[33] He saw this as an active period of ongoing engagement in meaningful activities; others define this as the third chapter or the encore years.[34]

Finally, both emerging and encore adulthood incorporate a wide range of divergent and unequal paths.[35] These are new phases of adulthood with new and different risks, responsibilities, and opportunities, all informed by the insights, resources, and deficits the people living them have accumulated from life thus far.

Time Shifting

Except for a few like Marc, Boomers in their sixties and early seventies are time shifting away from the conventional adult roles of raising children and building careers. Or simply time shifting the way they work. New digital technologies may have upended the life course as we know it, but they also make it possible for many to work—or appear to work—at unconventional times and places. Jackie is a well-established Boston lawyer who delayed becoming a (single) mother until her early forties. She composes a series of emails in the evenings, setting them to be sent automatically at 5:30 the next morning. This subtle subterfuge sustains her reputation for putting in long hours, even as it frees Jackie to enjoy breakfasts with her daughter before going into the office. Brad is a buyer in his early fifties who regularly skips traffic jams by working out at the gym most mornings, delaying his commutes to and from work until after the morning and evening rush hours. Natalie has worked her way up the ladder: at 58, her job means long, intense Skype sessions with an international team. She regularly works from home, taking early calls to connect with team members in India. And Patrick has worked in health care for 20 years and has to be at work for certain prescribed times. Unlike many other shift workers, he feels lucky to have his schedule for the next three months and the ability to switch shifts with coworkers online without supervisor approval. He and his coworkers appreciate the ways this advance self-scheduling is a sort of "perk" of working at their particular organization.

Time shifting in all its forms is coming to be a hallmark of contemporary life. People move the time and timing of television programs, movies, communications, and work hours. They also time-shift key life-course experiences by going back to school, switching career paths or romantic partnerships, postponing parenting. From adolescence on, Boomers have led the transformation of the temporal rhythms of roles and relationships, refashioning the conventional life course. GenXers (born 1965–1980) and especially Millennials (born 1981–1996), and what some call "the 2020s" (born after 1996) may be leading change in the time shifting of everyday life through new communication and computational technologies. But Boomers (born 1946–1964) have been the movers and shakers behind life-course time shifting. They dismantled age scripts dictating the time and timing of when to complete schooling, move into or remain in jobs, relocate to a new city or country, live together, marry or stay married, become a parent, buy a house. As University of Oklahoma historian Steve Gillon observes: "Boomers grew up in a unique moment in the nation's history—a time of unprecedented economic growth and unparalleled expectations about the future."[36] Even as these expectations have morphed into uncertainty and the inability to plan for the future, Boomers,' GenXers,' and Millennials' contemporary improvisations are driving the individualization of the twenty-first-century life course—expanding, rebranding, jump-starting, delaying, or blurring the boundaries around once-lockstep timetables of families, careers, conventional adulthood, and now emerging and encore adulthood.[37]

Those in all stages of adulthood—emerging, conventional, and encore—value personal, social, and societal purpose, defined by entrepreneur Aaron Hurst as seeking a sense of community and the opportunity for self-expression and personal growth.[38] Some in the new encore stage have the education, skills, savings, networks, and health to make the most of their bonus years by working to renew themselves and society. Others are at risk of employment and economic insecurity, with Boomers finding neither scaffolds nor safety nets—in the United States at least—for themselves.[39]

In line with the Millennials in emerging adulthood, there is also considerable ambivalence around this later adult stage. Consider Bill, who at 64 is thinking about leaving his job as a financial advisor in an international firm:

> I always said that one more serious health problem would push me out the door, but now I have decided not to wait for that bell to ring. This job is addictive... it would be impossible to scale back and still do it right. I can't go part time. Which is why I want to leave next year, at sixty-five. I might go to 66, but no more. I want to spend more time cooking, reading, traveling, fixing up the house. It will take a minimum of two years to fix up the house. I have had to let it go. And I want to cook more, things I left behind... studying, reading. And I expect to volunteer... I do some volunteer work but I could do a lot more.

Note that Bill doesn't use the word retirement. He talks about "leaving" or "going," but he feels in control of when this happens. Bill wants to pick up on things he "left behind," taking the time in encore adulthood for what he has had to overlook for his career job. He views retirement as risky, pointing out, "I am getting increasingly risk averse. What will it mean to no longer work?" Like Marc, Bill has a range of new possibilities and new limitations to consider—one can start a new family and the other a new lifestyle, but neither feels like a full, old-fashioned retirement is a safe or available choice.

Like Bill, Jenn also followed the career mystique linear lockstep at an international medical product company where she rose through the ranks, becoming the director of public relations reporting to the Human Resources vice president. Describing her job, she says, "I really loved it, and it was an insane job. I was working like 60, 70 hours a week, 24/7 sometimes." When she got laid off, it was totally unexpected:

> My manager called me in at 8 and asked if this particular communication project with England was done. I said "No, not yet, because we have to wait 'til 10 for it to be six hours ahead of our time." So he said, "Ok, great, come back at 10."... At 10... I gave him the wrap-up and he said okay, "I am glad that is done, and, oh, by the way your job is gone and you have to leave tomorrow." I thought he was kidding! No—he was dead serious... Horrific. I'd been with that company for 18 years. If it didn't happen to me, I would have said things like that don't happen.

Jenn was blindsided and felt too young to retire. Luckily, she was able to eventually find another job, working part time for a nonprofit. She recalls:

> I was very fortunate that both my children were out of the house at the time. They're grown up, they're older. Had they been home or in college, we would not have been able to afford their tuition. Without a doubt. So it was a very crushing blow, but it could have been worse... that's why I really like what I'm doing now, because I feel so sympathetic to those poor souls that are just scrounging from check to check.

Like Bill and Jenn and like Millennials, tens of thousands of Boomers are strategizing for or being thrust into whatever comes next in their lives. They are coming to a wide range of conclusions, improvising a second run at adulthood and in all likelihood shaping this new life-course stage for coming generations.

Keep in mind that Boomers in their fifties, sixties, and early seventies don't feel at the end, but midcourse.[40] As with my friend Donna and myself, there is unprecedented divergence in the sheer range of ages at which Boomers' family and employment pathways play out. Donna and I are moving to a more similar life stage in that neither of us have children at home, both of us have cared for elderly parents, and we are both working in encore jobs. Yet I am now a grandmother, while her daughter is in graduate school.

It is true that Boomers' earlier experiences—such as getting a college education or dropping out of the workforce to raise children—have enormous consequences throughout their lives. But many who can afford or are inclined to are reshaping their futures and redefining themselves by deliberately time shifting roles and relationships. What looked like inevitable trajectories and transitions are no longer certain. But individuals seek to take control, resetting their options by going back to school; switching from the private sector to nonprofit engagement; becoming a social entrepreneur; getting divorced, married, or remarried; taking up a regime of healthy eating and exercise, moving across the country, and so on. These are, indeed, times of uncertainty and risk. But Boomers blessed with health, energy, and education—and even those less advantaged—may have time to try on several second acts, wiser this time around, with a 20- or 30-year run of what's next before they consider themselves old.

Institutional Inertia

Another key concept is institutional inertia, discussed briefly in chapter 1. Institutions are taken-for-granted schema and logics about appropriate behavior—formal and informal rules and assumptions representing collectively developed patterns of living. Institutionalized beliefs and behavior often reflect the answers of powerful actors—in governments, organizations, and communities—to past problems and uncertainties or simply the borrowing of others' ways of doing things.[41] Institutions constitute the cultural logics and structural edifices organizing both outdated mid-twentieth-century educational, career, and retirement timetables and the gendered life course dividing family and work obligations, resources, and expectations by whether one is a man or a woman.

Structure refers to the configuration of resources, roles, and behavior, while culture consists of the mental maps, mindsets and logics defining how people perceive, evaluate, and anticipate their situations. University of Wisconsin historian William Sewell Jr. makes the point that "structure," the noun, always implies "structuring," the verb.[42] That is, even though they may be outmoded, twentieth-century structural arrangements continue to shape what people believe, value, and do.

Consider a simple idea: driving on one side of the road. This rule prevented chaos as drivers happily took to their automobiles in Europe and the United States in the early twentieth century. Brits chose to drive on the left, others chose the right. This discrepancy remains in place. Institutional inertia is this very rigidity characteristic of past decisions. It might make economic and practical sense to choose one side to drive on so all cars would be similar, but such structures and cultures become deeply engrained and difficult to change.

Another example of institutional changes around autos that continue to affect Americans: the dismantling in the twentieth century of streetcar rails in US towns and cities to literally pave the way for automobiles. In the 1950s, President Eisenhower championed a national highway system that would institutionalize cars, not public transportation, as the way Americans travel to their jobs, their homes, their vacations. Institutional inertia means Americans continue to move, for the most part, in cars—not trains, trams, or buses, much less by bicycle or feet. The absence of trains, networks of subways or light rail beyond New York, the Eastern corridor, and the Bay area—and in many places even of sidewalks and bike paths—has enormously impacted how Americans live, work, and spend their time.

Similarly, a range of mid-twentieth-century corporate and labor solutions to postwar problems of attracting and retaining employees tied medical insurance and pensions as nonwage benefits to full-time, full-year employment.[43] Public solutions to economic turbulence came in the form of social welfare and unemployment benefits—restricted and low in the United States—and led to the expansion of social security programs in Europe, and public retirement pensions everywhere, at age 65 or earlier. Though some are being scaled back, these are the institutional arrangements we live with today.

A classic sociological dictum (discussed further in chapter 6) is sociologist William I. Thomas's "What is defined as real is real in its consequences." Because standardized work and education/career/retirement timetables have been realities for Boomers throughout most of their lives, those patterns seem inevitable. But as they move through their fifties, sixties, and seventies many Boomers are coming to see that these assumptions and regulations don't work for them. Given the technologies associated with industrialization, it once made sense to have workers on assembly lines and in offices start and end work at the same times, take the same breaks, work consistent hours, and retire at the same ages. But the digital economy and its more efficient communication, computational, production, and medical technologies along with corollary risks and rapid pace are calling these outdated ways of working into question.

Work as an institution serves to structure virtually all aspects of men's, women's, and family members' lives, directly and indirectly, but in different ways, at different times, and with different consequences. Since the 1950s, jobs have historically provided both household incomes and an organizational blueprint for life, at least for white-collar and unionized blue-collar men who followed the lockstep of first education, followed by years of paid work and then retirement.[44] In the United States, most men and growing numbers of women aspired to the American Dream, seeking to follow the career mystique promising the good life in return for hard work, long hours, and continuous employment.[45] For those living long enough, this culminated in a retirement mystique promising golden years of continuous, financially secure leisure.[46] Retirement was the carrot at the end of the stick. But how many of us have watched fathers or grandfathers live to enjoy only two or three of these golden years? That is what is changing, as growing life expectancy contains the seeds of new possibilities.

Many industry leaders and elected officials are slow to recognize the need to provide both greater flexibility and more reliable safety nets around unraveling work and retirement paths. And yet existing inflexible, standardized full-time work arrangements contribute to Boomers' exits. For example, Sally's job in a Title 1 federally funded program (serving elementary school students who were falling behind) became increasingly difficult:

> I got physically exhausted. It was a job where you would go around the school to many, many of the classrooms and work with children directly in the room and it was a lot of walking. It was a heavy schedule of children and dealing with many teachers. And I think physically—physically I got worn out. I have a knee with arthritis and that would really provoke that by then end of the day.

There was no "give" in her job, so she made the decision to leave:

> It turned out there were no ways to accommodate me. And the Human Relations, I thought—I asked if we could change this to a part time, like 30 hours a week instead of thirty-eight. And the Human Resources guideline was no—that it needed to be these hours a week to best serve the students.

More flexible arrangements around the time and timing of work might keep Boomers like Sally working longer, but the outdated institutional structure of work invites little give.

Unfortunately, powerful actors in organizations *are* questioning and often eliminating the pension and health care benefits developed to lure and retain workers in the past. Other historical protections, against layoffs and economic insecurity through seniority provisions, for example, or workers compensation programs in the face of a work-related disability, are eroding as well. So the workforce, the workplace, and even work itself are shifting, but workers and employers as well as colleges, universities, communities, and government agencies still adhere to 1950s timetables. This matters, because these outdated clocks and calendars don't work for adults of all ages and effectively exclude older workers and retirees from many educational, employment, and civic engagement opportunities.

What Makes Something an Institution?

Three things make something an institution: language that develops around it, taken-for-granted customs, and a body of rule and laws.[47] As with Millennials in emerging adulthood, for GenXers trying to hold on to their jobs, and for Boomers on the edge of their occupational careers, all of these are in flux. Together with sociologist Sarah Flood at the Minnesota Population Center and along with Duke University's Angela O'Rand and others, I find that retirement is now less a normative, lockstep exit than a fuzzy transition; it is no longer a one-time, one-way, universal, irreversible, age-graded event.[48] Workforce exits are now occurring both before and after the age of 65; they are also both voluntary and involuntary, such as when a layoff leads to an extended period of unemployment that morphs into calling oneself "retired." Community service is equally fuzzy but less age-graded than employment. What is variously called unpaid work, volunteering, or civic engagement is less institutionalized by language, custom, or law, while home and family care remains institutionalized as women's unpaid work, even though Boomer men are increasingly becoming care providers for their aging parents.

Consider as well the language of work and retirement. We have no language for people who are retired from their career jobs but employed in a different job, working for themselves, or even doing the very same jobs they retired from. We have no language to describe the civically engaged retirees whose jobs, albeit unpaid, offer purpose and fulfillment, but are not always recognized.[49] And we have no language to delineate expectations with regard to voluntary but stipended community service.

Language is also problematic for characterizing people in their late fifties, sixties, and early seventies: they are not "old," but they are not "young" either, and middle age can refer to people ages 35 or fifty-five.[50] In other words, for growing numbers of people of all ages, the standardized linear tripartite—first education, then work, then retirement—no longer works. Boomers are finding themselves midcourse, literally and figuratively, in what is seeming like an encore to adulthood. We don't know how to categorize them, what to call them, or how to support them.

Sources of Institutional Inertia

Like emerging adulthood in the twenties, I see encore adulthood occurring somewhere between 55 and 75 as both an actual age period *and* a state of mind. In these bonus years of longer, healthier lives—including chronic health conditions made far more livable by medical advances, new technologies, and lifestyle changes—some, like Bill, the financial advisor, and Jessie, whose messy career path has led at last to a job in alternative health, are dusting off long-held values and goals, reaching for things once left behind in the rush of job and family demands. Others imagine and work toward personal and social renewal in the form of new dreams, skills, projects, and identities, like Robin, who wants to scale up in retiring from an international development agency to help her old hometown in Texas develop economically.

Significant numbers of Boomers have already moved on—leaning out of their old jobs because of downsizing, health problems, too stressful work conditions, or a simple desire to reset their lives. This is the case for Jenn, the high-flying public relations professional at the top of her game when she was laid off; Jeff, the commercial photographer who now must compete with iPhone pictures; and Sally, who can no longer cope physically with a full-time special ed job. They are all seeking to reshape their biographies in ways that will provide them a living and a new lease on life. Whether by choice, the press of circumstance, or some combination of the two, Boomers' lives are unlike their parents' experiences. And, despite growing numbers of how-to and inspirational books,[51] they seem to find no ready or realistic scripts for this new life stage.

Scholars of institutions underscore the instability of social structures and logics that have become outdated.[52] Today we see old ways and old timetables around working, schooling, and retiring challenged by historical, demographic, economic, technological, and policy developments. In the case of both career paths and the golden years, outdated policies and practices as well as language and customs increasingly seem irrelevant. There are so many Boomers, some 76 million now in their fifties, sixties, and moving into their seventies. Like those in emerging adulthood, a convergence of circumstances has left them in uncharted waters.

Next I examine three fundamental concepts key to understanding Boomers' lives and prospects, as well as the outdatedness of existing career and life-course blueprints: age and gender (two concepts, but better viewed together), cohort, and historical period. I take the time to clarify these terms because what we know about people of a certain age—in their fifties, sixties, or early seventies, for example—is based on studies of past cohorts in past times who faced very different challenges and followed very different career and life-course paths. It is not at all clear we can learn about the experiences of Boomers and their families or about the new encore stage by analyzing survey and interview data collected from people who grew up in very different worlds. Unfortunately, even contemporary scholarship is often looking at a rearview mirror, drawing on surveys fielded decades ago or simulations based on past behavior. This is to be expected, of course, since one cannot study, for example, the retirement timing of a cohort until most have already made that status passage. Thus much of what we know about career paths and the life course is based on the experiences of prior cohorts and is very probably out of date. To appreciate the uncertainties, risks, and possibilities for personal renewal and social purpose of encore adulthood necessitates understanding how Boomers' lives articulate in new ways with age and gender, cohort, and the historical times—all of which shape and are shaped by the structures and scripts that cross-cut Boomers' lives.

Age and Gender

Most people understand age as a concept related to time since birth. What they don't realize is that chronological age is itself an empty category, explaining very little. To be sure, age is related to human development, including physiological and neurological changes that occur over time. But there is wide variation in the physical and cognitive capacities of people at any one age.

Aging has long been fraught with negative meanings associated with poor health, frailty, and general mental and physical decline. This framing has fostered and been reinforced by a social system of age stratification,[53] institutionalized in deeply embedded beliefs, policies, and practices that simultaneously reward people of certain ages—with, for example, pensions, social security, Medicare, and "senior" rates for movies or public transportation—*and* remove them from the mainstream of society. Boomers who lose their jobs (like Jenn) or are seeking new ones (like Jeff) can speak to the reality of age discrimination.[54] Indeed, date of birth has become a dominant method for tracking individuals as citizens, patients, and customers.

Chronological age may or may not reflect a person's biological age, psychological age (including age identity), or social age (including age-related roles).[55] Both chronological and social age intersect with gender to create greater risks of poverty and disability for women. Their longer life expectancies mean longer periods of time during which injury and illness may arise and over which savings and retirement funds must be stretched. And women's often nontraditional career paths, combined with gendered stereotypes and bias allocating men and women to different jobs along with discriminating against them in hiring, earnings, and promotion, mean that women are at greater risk than men of economic and retirement insecurity in encore adulthood.

There is as well a widening disparity in life expectancy between women with a college degree and those without a high school diploma.[56] Boomer women who may have seen their mothers outlive their fathers worry about their own long lives. Some, like Sally, are looking for a not-so-big job that isn't too physically taxing or stressful,[57] but, also like Sally, not getting callbacks on any job prospects that would support them for long.

Still, Boomers are growing older. Populations and workforces in Europe and North America are aging in unprecedented ways given medical advances, healthier lifestyles, and declining fertility.[58] What this means for individuals, families, workplaces, and policy development, for risks as well as personal and social renewal, and especially for a purposeful encore to adulthood, is the topic of this book.

Boomers' constrained choices as to whether and when to shift down from full-time work cannot be understood apart from gender.[59] For the first time in history large numbers of women have careers they will retire from. Women Boomers are less likely than men to be married, explained in part by the fact they are also less likely to remarry following divorce or widowhood, as well as by their longer life expectancy. Many women outlive their husbands and they are more apt to be caring for grandchildren and infirm relatives, both of which frame their constraints and choices in encore adulthood.

Men are living longer as well, such that the gender gap in life expectancy appears to be narrowing. The demographic trends extending the lives of Boomer men and women, combined with the low savings and dismantled private pensions that characterize the United States at least, concern scholars as well as those setting health care, entitlement, and economic policy agendas. Also unique to Boomers and the GenXers following in their wake is the fact that couples must now plan and strategize around two sets of retirement exits, with multiple possible scenarios—one partner exits first, both exit together, both want to delay final workforce exits as late as possible, one wants to do that while the other wants to exit as soon as possible, or both, one, or neither take on an encore job in paid or unpaid work.

Decisions are often tempered by gender, with wives historically timing their retirements to match their husbands, even though they may wish to work longer. Both single and married women tend to exit the workforce earlier than men. Women's exits may also be moved up in order to care for aging relatives who are themselves living longer, or for their partners.[60] Many Boomers, single or not, worry about being able to afford to retire at all or outliving their resources. This is an enormous cohort living far longer, and most organizations and communities are unprepared for the challenges of these demographic realities.

But age and gender are far more than biology or demography. They are also taken-for-granted markers of social and subjective time in the form of the gendered life course:[61] the complex set of beliefs and structures perpetuating gender inequality by opening up and closing down options and risks for women and men at different ages. I examine age and gender from a sociological perspective, as the socially constructed ways that roles and resources are unevenly distributed in contemporary society, such as how family-care work is allocated disproportionately to women and powerful occupational positions are allocated disproportionately to men. As with Bill (the financial advisor), Jeff (the struggling photographer), Sally (the former special ed teacher), and Jenn (the laid off PR exec), there is wide variability in how Boomer women and men are moving through their life courses.[62] Along with race/ethnicity, social class, nativity, sexuality, and citizenship, age and gender intersect with biology and family, on the one hand, and organizations, social policy, social movements, demography, and social change, on the other. Boomers' disparate pathways both promote and perpetuate inequality in the distribution of material and personal resources, such as health, educational degrees, savings, wealth—and risks, such as job insecurity, low wages, few benefits, chronic diseases, disability, unemployment.[63]

And then there is subjective age.[64] Both age and gender are also tied to identity—personal and collective beliefs about age and gender groups (even one's own). Age is distinct in one regard: while few people change their gender or race/ethnicity, everyone, if lucky enough, moves through a wide range of ages.

Because age is a key way of categorizing people, it contributes to age stereotypes (assumptions about abilities and behavior) and age discrimination (ageism), which, like gender and race discrimination, cut people off from opportunities.[65] Take the risk of poverty. The twentieth century witnessed the development of important age-related safety nets (in the United States, Social Security and Medicare) that dramatically reduced the poverty of those in their midsixties and older. Still, in 2014, about one in 10 Boomers in the United States was below the official poverty line. This differs by gender, with 11.8 percent Boomer women officially poor compared to only 9.9 percent Boomer men. Age and gender also intersect with education (see figure 2.1) in shaping the risk of poverty. Trailing-edge Boomer men (those born 1955–1964) with a college degree are the least apt to fall below the poverty line

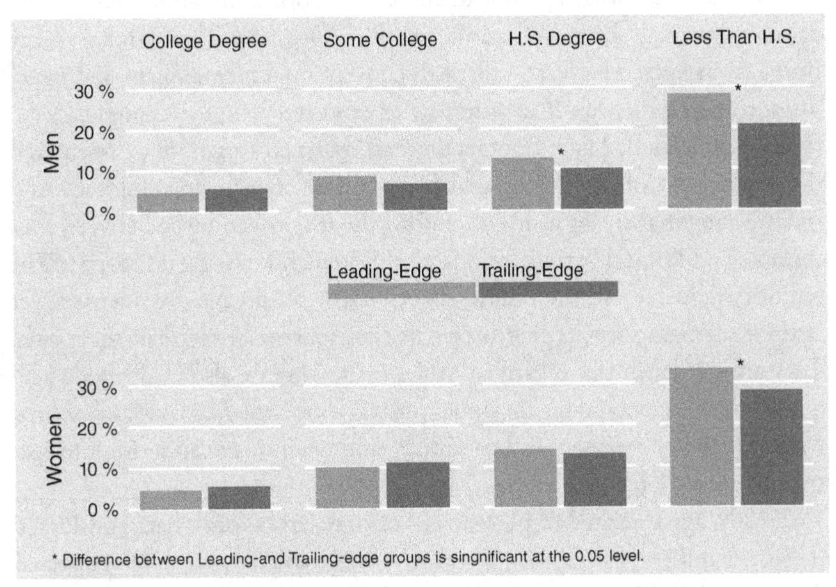

FIGURE 2.1. Percent of Leading- and Trailing-Edge Boomers Below the Poverty Line in 2014 by Gender and Education

(.5 percent), while one in three (33.5 percent) Boomer women without a high school diploma are likely to be poor.[66]

Age and gender are also markers of biographical pacing—that is, the timing, duration, and sequencing of transitions and trajectories such as marriage, parenting, divorce, widowhood, and career entries, pathways, and exits.[67] For example, seven in 10 Boomer men in their fifties are married and living with their spouses, compared to only six in 10 Boomer women in this age range.[68] Along with changes in their resources and relationships over time, these and other markers are linked to the schooling, family, work, and retirement experiences of Boomers.

But classic age divides *are* blurring. For example, age 65 no longer signals the passage to old age or even to retirement, though it continues to color our expectations and our identities. Recall that at age 55, Jenn felt she was too young to retire, a reflection of how she has internalized age norms. When asked if she gave serious thought to retiring following the loss of her job, Jenn replied, "No, I can't retire. I'm not old enough. Ask me in a couple of years." Boomers typically feel that people become "old" in their seventies,[69] but they may change their minds as they edge closer to the seventies themselves.

Boomers have always questioned age—that is, the number of years one has lived—as a way of assigning roles. In the 1960s, in the midst of the Vietnam War, young Boomer men challenged the legitimacy of the draft (mandatory "selective service" with sign-up required at age 18), sometimes even sending back or burning their draft cards. In the 1960s, 1970s, and 1980s many Boomers navigated paths at odds with conventional mental maps and structures, cohabiting rather than marrying at expected ages, for example, or delaying parenthood. Many Boomer women returned to school or re-entered the workforce in their thirties and forties, often after having children. And today Boomers are navigating and crafting the space opening up between conventional adulthood (a time for raising children and moving up corporate or seniority ladders) and the frailties associated with old age. Boomers are yet again challenging scripts that better fit their parents' lives than their own. They are similar in this regard to Millennials, who are also challenging age-graded roles—customizing their own timetables for when to finish schooling, when to take on partners and parenting, and when they can move into reasonably secure jobs.

Finally, age is related to perceptions of time left before what's considered the inevitability of disability or what *is* inevitable: death. The renowned Stanford scholar Laura Carstensen and her colleagues describe her theory of socioemotional selectivity:[70] older people become more selective in the relationships they wish to nurture and sustain, given their limited time horizons, in terms of the time they feel they have left to live.[71] Many also make strategic selections in their social roles and lifestyles, leaning out from the status quo of their lives by seeing this encore phase as an opportunity to make midcourse corrections.[72] Some Boomers are leaning out from career jobs in order to time shift away from demanding, high intensity, and often unbounded work.[73] For instance, Jenn may feel too young to retire, but she is now working no more than 30 hours a week in her job for a nonprofit outplacement company. In her career job, she'd had no choice: "I was working like 60, 70 hours a week, 24/7 sometimes." Jenn deliberately chose her encore job so that she

> can have parameters about what I will do... I am *not* my career. My career in public relations ended. The career is over. It's just mutated into something more quiet, something more mellow.

Jenn reflects what many Boomers want: a simpler, more "in control" life, with opportunities to grow and contribute to their communities as well as savor these encore years of adulthood. Millennials and GenXers want more control also, but often find even fewer options at their ages and life stages.

Cohort

Cohort and generation are other age-related terms.[74] Both are used to categorize people by the dates they were born, capturing the intersections between history and biography, such as the Millennial Generation, the Boomer Generation, or Generation X. Generation is also used to capture family location or stage, such as the grandparent generation, or in discussing intergenerational relationships between parents and their adult children or between grandparents and their grandchildren.[75]

The large Boomer cohort is a result of the high rates of fertility right after World War II; the United States' fertility rate was 3.1 in 1954 and 3.6 in 1962, but had been 2.5 both before and after the Baby Boom.[76] The sheer size of the Boomer cohort—around 78 million babies were born in those years in the United States—has precipitated changes in organizations and communities, from the maternity wards in which they were born (some were born in hospital hallways because there truly wasn't enough room for all of the arriving infants) to the new schools built to educate them. Colleges, communities, and the military had to respond to their outcries against the Vietnam War and for civil rights and women's rights; workplaces had to come to terms with a large cohort moving through their ranks.[77] Note that this isn't just an American phenomenon: the world's population increased by around 400 million people in the Baby Boom years.[78]

The definitions and ages associated with particular cohorts are defined in a variety of ways. I find the divisions assigned by the Pew Corporation most useful (see figure 2.2). We know the Boomers (born 1946–1964) are very different from the cohorts coming before them: the Silent Generation (born 1928–1945) or the Greatest Generation (born before 1928). As figure 2.2 shows, every generation has a unique relationship with history. The years when people reach a certain age or life stage are also points in historical time (see figure 2.2). That period can open up or close down possibilities for education, occupations, career paths, and a worry-free retirement.

Like other cohorts, Boomers share a common social history of events, opportunities, constraints, and culture, with formative experiences in early adulthood especially consequential for shaping their worldviews.[79] As the Boomers grew up, they saw the civil rights movement and the death of the Rev. Dr. Martin Luther King Jr.; the escalation of the Vietnam War; the Great Society programs of President Lyndon Johnson; the women's movement; and the Watergate scandal together with President Richard Nixon's resignation.

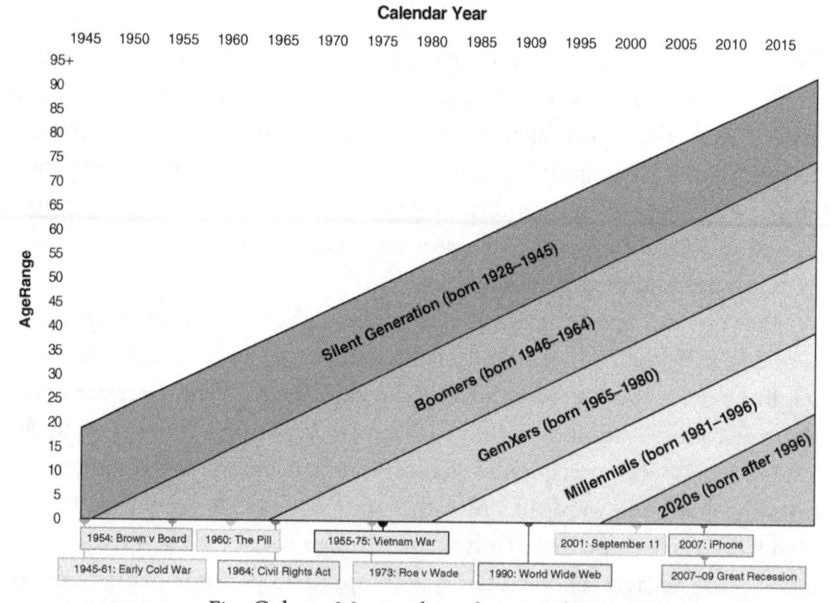

FIGURE 2.2. Five Cohorts Moving through Age and History: 1945–2017

Millennials, by contrast, have come of age with a black president, a fast-paced digital economy, social networks maintained by social media, and a climate of risk and uncertainty in terms of safety, global warming, occupational and economic security, and their own futures. Boomers are an historical event unto themselves; their very numbers have had implications for society and for individual lives.[80] Millennials are another, even larger, demographic force moving through and changing history.

The famous sociologist C. Wright Mills defined the sociological imagination as becoming aware of these relations between history and biography within society.[81] Thinking sociologically means realizing that what we take for granted isn't the way things have to be. Categories are created and discarded, attitudes can change, and the world is different when viewed from another's perspective. Though Boomers are described as a single cohort, they span a 19-year period and may be better conceived as two distinct subcohorts. Accordingly, in this book I sometimes focus on the life chances and life quality of four subgroups divided by age and gender: women and men in the leading edge of the Boomer cohort (those born 1946–1954, right after the end of WWII and during the Korean Conflict) and the trailing edge (born 1955–1964, during a period of economic prosperity before the escalation of the Vietnam War).

These four groups are quite different (see table 2.1 in appendix B). Consider that 30 percent of leading-edge Boomer men are veterans, compared to only 13.7 percent of trailing-edge men (only 1.4 percent and 1.8 percent of leading-edge and trailing-edge Boomer women, respectively, are veterans). And more leading-edge men are white than trailing-edge men (76.7 percent to 70.5 percent), as is the case among Boomer women (73.8 percent of leading-edge women define themselves as white, compared to only 68.8 percent of trailing-edge women). More trailing-edge Boomers are likely to have never married (13.4 percent of trailing-edge compared to only 8.2 percent of leading-edge Boomer men; 10.9 percent of trailing-edge compared to only 7.6 percent of leading-edge Boomer women). But trailing-edge Boomer men lag somewhat in educational achievement in terms of obtaining a college degree (30.4 percent compared to 34.6 percent) and advanced degrees (12.2 percent compared to 14.7 percent). By contrast, leading-edge and trailing-edge women are more similar in educational achievement, with 30 percent having a college degree and 11 percent obtaining an advanced degree.[82]

These Boomers come with different backgrounds for improvising what's next in their lives, and it is easier for some than others. Sally is part of the leading edge of the Boomer cohort. Recall that she left her job in special education because it was too arduous and is looking for but not finding a less demanding, part-time job. Jenn is part of the trailing edge and has the skills that served her well in public relations, as well as the financial and emotional support of a working husband. Clearly, she has better prospects than Sally, in part because of age discrimination, in part because of the experiences and resources each brings with them, with Sally's health limitations a real impediment. Though Jenn didn't necessarily want to lean out from her career job, she says it has let her reorder her priorities. When she was in public relations her priority was:

> Work. Then family. Then all the housework, and if there was any time left over, I'd split it between friends and God, and God usually got a sleep-in on Sunday. Now it's family first. God. Friends. And work is somewhere down at the bottom.

The women's movement and the shift toward a service economy, together with stagnant wages from the 1970s on, transformed women's and men's education and employment experiences,[83] bringing together many aspects of women's and men's life patterns. Boomer couples increasingly face the orchestration of two careers and two encores:[84] his and hers, so to speak. Same-sex couples may see advantage and disadvantage in encore adulthood in terms of the mingling of finances, the red tape of policies built for opposite-sex families, and more closely aligned life experiences and expectancies. Boomer women increasingly think about and must deal with retirement, typically a male transition. Still, there remain enduring gender inequalities across the life course, producing for women what is often an accumulation of disadvantage in incomes, pensions, and health.[85] Thus, leading-edge Boomer women average a personal income of $33,950, compared to $58,671 for leading-edge men.[86]

Many in the Boomer cohort have always been unique. In addition to cohabiting, they have led in more later-adult divorces, along with more second, third, or same-sex marriages; more single-person and blended households; more adult children returning home. Many have been on the forefront of changes in assumptions, with more women in full-time jobs, more single parents, more singles, more couples facing two retirements. With Boomers came demographic shifts—more older workers and minorities, as well as greater healthy life expectancy, more with living-though-aging relatives. And Boomers have led in two educational changes—more college graduates and adult learners. Many of these trends constituted remarkable transformations for Boomers, but are now considered normal by GenXers (born 1965–1980), Millennials (born 1981–1996), and the latest cohort, the 2020s (born after 1996).

Historical Period

Closely related to the concepts of cohort and generation, period captures the importance of historical events and cultural trends. Boomers share a history of the Vietnam War, hair, hippies, Flower Power, the best music (I may be biased), the civil rights and women's movements, the Reagan years, Clinton's economic boom, 9/11, and the wars in Iraq and Afghanistan. Many middle-class Boomers had stay-at-home mothers in early childhood, and they were raised according to the latest parenting manuals written by Dr. Spock and other child development experts. Many lived in suburbs designed for breadwinner–homemaker families with children.[87] The leading edge of the Boomers grew up in a time of unprecedented prosperity, and Boomers have typically enjoyed higher standards of living than their parents and, for that matter, than their children will experience.[88] Boomer women began entering, re-entering, and remaining in the workforce in unprecedented numbers in the 1970s (see figures 2.3A and B). The Vietnam War and draft deferments for college enrollees encouraged leading-edge Boomers to enter, remain in, and graduate from colleges and universities. In time, trailing-edge Boomers also attended or completed college.[89] Enrollments in college more than doubled and the labor force grew by 42 percent between 1965 and 1980. Boomers were well-educated and gainfully employed.[90]

More recently, Boomers have, like everyone else, experienced the enormous social and economic dislocations of the financial crisis, with unemployment peaking in the United States at 9.7 percent in 2010. The financial crisis and its fallout further underscore the ways new technologies and a turbulent global economy are making Boomers' contemporary lives vastly different from the lives of their parents when their parents were the ages they are now. In the 1970s, workers (mostly men) in their fifties and sixties had little doubt as to when they would retire; age 65 was built into legal regulations and corporate policies. There were other timetables as well, such as the 90-year rule for some teachers (the offer of full pensions to those whose age—say, 57—and tenure—33 years of teaching—added up to 90) or similar combinations for pensions in state agencies and large private-sector organizations. Most white-collar and unionized blue-collar workers also had a sense of economic security; in the 1950s and 1960s rising wages accompanied seniority, "good" jobs—those with full-time, continuous employment and medical benefits—included generous

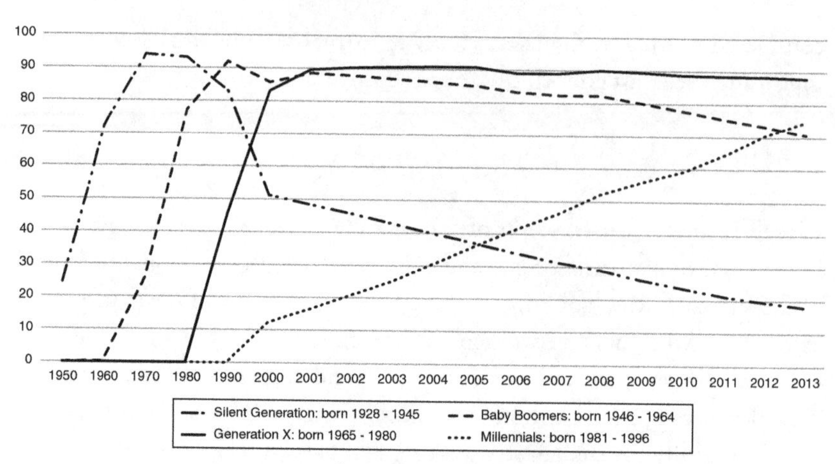

FIGURE 2.3A. Proportion of US Men in Labor Force by Cohort: 1950–2013

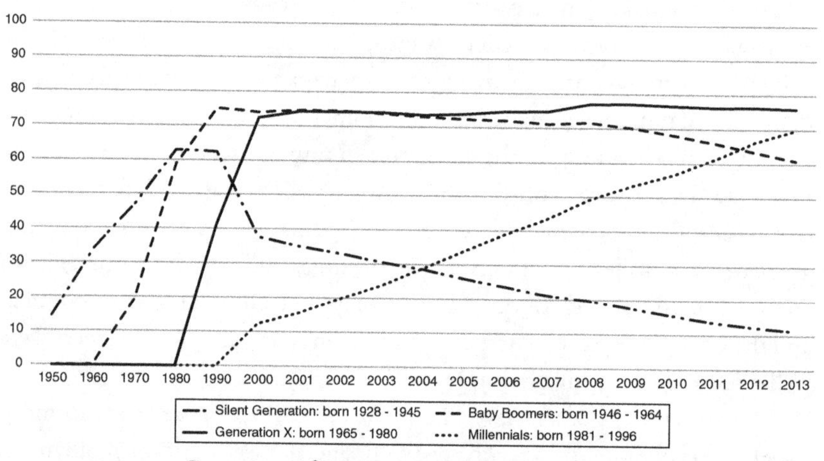

FIGURE 2.3B. Proportion of US Women in Labor Force by Cohort: 1950–2013

private pensions, and all could count on the limited but real protections of social security. But beginning in the late 1970s in the United States, these protections began to unravel.[91]

Today, a competitive international workforce and new digital technologies in this second machine age are literally reconfiguring *time*,[92] with coworkers in different time zones working together, disrupting conventional time clocks as people rise early or stay up late to phone or Skype into team meetings. American IT workers describe the time strains they experience as workloads ratchet up, including the difficulty of meeting these new time demands and 24/7 accessibility while still being expected to be "at work" during regular hours.[93]

That's just one example. All kinds of Boomers are caught up in the multi-layered dislocations and ambiguities of early twenty-first-century life. Our digital global economy means a corresponding restructuring of work and risk. Protective policies and practices are no longer enforced or available. Boomers and their younger colleagues are experiencing more stringent time binds on the job concomitant with temp jobs, greater intensity of work expectations, enforced efficiency, multitasking, and e-work that crowd out their ability to accomplish high-value work or to have reasonable hours on the job when some get too few hours and others way too many.[94] But sometimes, and for some people in innovative organizations, these same technological advances can also facilitate the time shifting many Boomers want, letting them create flexible work scheduling, return to school, change their involvement in paid and unpaid work, fashion bridge jobs, and reconfigure retirement and leisure.

Another marker of this particular historical moment is that conventional family and gender expectations seem outdated. Cohabitation, divorce, and blended families are now normal; there are growing numbers who live alone; same-sex marriage is widely accepted. So, just as research on agrarian life in the 1850s would have little to inform suburban life in the 1950s, twenty-first-century changes challenge the value of past assumptions and past research for understanding Boomers' contemporary lives. Why have different family forms become so widely accepted while old-fashioned work rules remain operative?[95] As they improvise new life pathways in this new encore stage, Boomers are breaking down outdated mindsets and expectations about how older adults "should" live and work.

Conclusions

All of these social dynamisms—the institutional inertia bound up in conventional mid-twentieth-century career, life-course, age, and gender scripts and disparities, the experiences of different cohorts at different historical periods, the growing ambiguities and uncertainties around work and retirement, the various ways Boomers are moving through life—are serving to fashion encore adulthood differently depending on people's social address.[96] By social address I mean Boomers' locations in multiple communities based on their gender, age, education, social class, health, immigrant status, sexuality, race, and ethnicity. Still, despite these wide variations and disparities, Boomers' encore adult years are, for the most part, similar to Millennials' emerging adult years in terms of no longer being a single transition but rather a series of projects taking place over time. The larger projects of fashioning new phases of adult life remain embedded in outdated institutional contexts characterized by both inertia and upheavals, a world at odds with Millennials' and Boomers' own experiences, values, and preferences.

Individuals, families, workplaces and other institutions are changing over time but at different rates. Clearly there is also a subjective side to both careers and the life course: people generally consider their lives as a whole, punctuated by significant experiences, and compare their situations with their expectations and with others in their social networks.

This is an exciting and sometimes scary time for those in both emerging and encore adulthood. I have shown how life-course and career paths are dynamic links between individuals and families, on the one hand, and public as well as organizational policies and practices, on the other. Both career and life-course concepts are important prisms through which to understand the range and impacts of patterned social arrangements and disruptions channeling Boomers' as well as Millennials' life paths.[97] What a combined institutional and gendered life-course approach provides is a way of linking prior experiences with subsequent life paths and tracking disparities as they play out in distinct ways for women and men.[98]

The life-course concept of accumulating advantages or disadvantages underscores ongoing and widening inequalities.[99] This again relates to Boomers' social addresses and the undercurrents of career paths. As we will see in chapter 5, Boomers with high levels of education and few health limitations tend to remain involved in paid work longer, volunteer more, and are therefore more socially connected than those with fewer such resources. Their advantage builds; those who are healthy and actively engaged throughout conventional adulthood are apt to continue being healthy and active in encore adulthood. This leads to wide gender, educational, and ethnic disparities in Boomers' incomes, occupations, pensions, and health insurance coverage, as well as in disability, exposure to stress, and overall health. Whether encore adulthood is a further accumulation of advantage or disadvantage, or a turning point, depends on both the inertia *and* the visionary innovation of institutions restricting or enhancing the ability of Boomers to time shift as well as make ends meet, crafting their own ways of living and working that fit their abilities, preferences, and needs. As with emerging adulthood, advantages and disadvantages accrued over time help determine whether encore adulthood is mostly a time of constraints or choices, but individuals and couples strategize to achieve their goals, and sometimes things can turn around in unexpected ways.

In the chapters that follow I emphasize the dynamic intersections of lives, rapid social changes, and lagging institutions. I do so by focusing on the institutionalized and gendered nature of the life course—the intertwining relationships, roles, rules, and risks affecting men's and women's options, experiences, and resources across their lives. The linear life course emerged only in the twentieth century. Prior cohorts in previous times may have also faced risks and uncertainties. But the fact is, lives today are confined by outmoded institutional logics, policies, and practices that are changing too slowly even as digital technologies and global economies are ramping up dislocations. This constitutes the backdrop against which both emerging and encore adulthood are evolving.[100] Like Millennials, Boomers—women as well as men—are on the edge of history and time, balancing on a remarkably unstable platform of multilayered social and personal ambiguities.

In the middle of the last century, both career and life course referred to orderly paths. Today there are wide patterns of movement across jobs and other roles throughout adulthood but especially on its edges, as emerging adulthood and encore adulthood are beginning to take shape. The question is, with the insecurity associated with a global digital economy and a dismantled social contract, how are twenty-first-century careers and life courses coming to be shaped? We take this up in the next chapter.

3

Context

INERTIA, UPHEAVALS, INEQUALITY

WORK IS ABOUT time and place, taking up most of the waking hours of many people for most of their adult lives. I learned this in the early 1960s on my first job. I was 17, having just graduated high school and hired by an insurance company in downtown Atlanta, Georgia. I filed correspondence and contracts for those customers whose last names started with MA- to MM-. Sometimes, when someone was sick or if I were especially efficient, I got to file in other parts of the alphabet, an exciting event! We "girls" all punched in and out on a time clock, and we were permitted 10 minutes twice a day for bathroom or smoking breaks and 20 minutes for lunch. Since these breaks came for everyone at the same time, most of the 10-minute breaks were spent smoking while waiting in the bathroom line. I didn't know anyone then who didn't smoke. The few older women supervising us seemed to have a bit more flexibility. The men were in suits and offices with windows; they occasionally walked along the aisles of the big open room filled with desks, observing us girls at work.

This was during the civil rights revolution; changing buses on the way to and from work, I would find myself smack in the middle of sit-ins at lunch counters.[1] In the fall, also by court order, first-graders across the city would become the first integrated class in our city's public schools. Soon all the public swimming pools in Atlanta and its suburbs would be closed rather than follow a court order to allow everyone to swim.

As the world changed outside, I was learning the rules and routines of paid work. My first lesson was that work was about time and place. It was about being at my desk in the middle of a room filled with white girls for eight hours. It had little to do with what I actually accomplished during those hours. No matter how fast I did my filing, my supervisor would bring new stacks to keep me occupied until 5 p.m. rolled around. My second lesson was that staying with an employer may bring some benefits for some white women, but they were never comparable to those allocated to white men. Though there were lots of older girls working around me, I couldn't see myself there for long. In the fall, I opted for college instead.

I hadn't yet figured out whether I would pursue a career; I was thinking about teaching or marriage and a family. What I could see, however, was that I would have to choose one over the other, that it was impossible to have what I wanted, which was both. My mother and her friends were all full-time homemakers. I didn't know any women who had professional careers, except teachers, nurses, and librarians, and assumed they were all single. But recall that this was in the early 1960s. The women's movement, the ongoing transition to a service economy, changes in public and private-sector policies and practices, and increased education would soon open opportunities for women in general, and for me in particular. Gender and racial/ethnic discrimination—what sociologist Chuck Tilly calls "durable inequality"[2]—remains very much with us, but the world in which Americans now live and work is enormously different from the 1960s South.

Recall from chapter 1 the importance of categories. Tilly depicts inequality as durable because "people who control access to value-producing resources solve pressing organizational problems by means of categorical distinctions" such as social class, race, and gender.[3] Though researchers and policy leaders are more aware of unequal opportunities related to class, gender, nativity, and race/ethnicity,[4] *age* is also a common source of what Tilly calls "categorical distinctions" and another sociologist, Cynthia Fuchs Epstein,[5] labels "deceptive distinctions."

Though well behind in wages, advancement, leadership positions, and benefits, women and minorities—at least those with a college education—have seen more opportunities open to them over time. Still, gender, race and ethnicity, and other markers continue to reflect durable inequalities in resources, risks, and opportunities. They intersect with age and life-course stage as well as with fraying safety nets to perpetuate and even accentuate inequalities in encore adulthood.[6]

This chapter describes the confluence of upheavals and inertia producing new risks and uncertainties, but also possibilities for the encore life stage. It describes new and enduring inequalities resulting from an unraveling social contract and an unraveling retirement, asking the question: how did we get here? Social forces are upending the conventional, albeit gendered, linear life-course template—first learning, then working, then retiring—developed in the middle of the last century and continue to guide beliefs and expectations, though not necessarily the reality of adults of all ages.[7]

The chapter concludes with three fundamental mismatches confronting Boomers but also people of all ages and life stages in this early part of the twenty-first century. Identifying and challenging the inertia built into the institutional logics (customs, beliefs, practices) and policies constraining education, work, career trajectories, care work, and retirement are the first steps in responding to these mismatches.

Three Institutional Logics

Recall the institutionalization of time is a result of decisions creating a set of formal rules and laws establishing the timing, duration, and ordering of activities.[8] This includes mandatory schooling for children, minimum ages for employment and for receiving public pensions, and age norms and expectations about career paths and retirement timing.[9] These policies, practices, and logics produced the linear, lockstep life course, cementing floors around the ages at which people can vote, marry, join the military, enroll in social welfare programs (such as Medicare), become eligible for pensions and social security, and take the minimum required payouts of savings plans. This template is characterized by three interrelated mindsets and institutional logics, enduring sets of assumptions and beliefs shaping expectations and behavior.[10]

The Unencumbered Worker Institutional Logic

Work, career path, and family-care norms have always operated differently for women and men, reinforcing the separate spheres idea of work and home. Households that could afford it after World War II prioritized paid work for men and unpaid family work for women. This perpetuated, in the middle of the last century, a lockstep career mystique for men[11]—the belief that fulfillment came from continuous, full-time commitment to and employment by a single employer or a series of related jobs. But the career mystique was based on what Betty Friedan named the feminine mystique, that women's fulfillment came from caring for their families and supporting their husbands' careers.[12]

Combined, these two myths encouraged male breadwinners to focus totally on their jobs. When married women were employed, their work was expected to be intermittent, in jobs that permitted movement in and out of the workforce and in and out of part-time work so they could prioritize their family-care responsibilities and their husbands' careers. Good jobs were typically white-collar or unionized blue-collar ones occupied primarily by white men. Bad jobs were those held by most women and men with little education and few skills—often immigrants and minorities, but also the rows and rows of white women working like I did in my first job—in filing or typing pools. This secondary workforce had neither the security nor the prospects associated with the career mystique.[13]

Recall that the term "institutional logic" refers to an enduring set of assumptions and beliefs shaping expectations and behavior.[14] The clocks embedded in the social organization of workdays, workweeks, and for some 24/7 availability remain characterized by the institutional logic of the *unencumbered worker*. For married men who could afford it in the 1950s, having homemaking wives freed them to focus like a laser on their jobs. However, women now constitute half the workforce, most workers (men and women) have no backup on the home front and most are or will be caring for infirm relatives, children, or grandchildren. Despite this altered empirical reality, the logic of the unencumbered worker still governs where and when employees are expected to work.

The Lockstep Institutional Logic

Second, institutional inertia is reflected in public-, social-, and private-sector regulations and expectations that enforce the rights and responsibilities of those moving through age-graded structures such as schools and workplaces. This institutional logic captures mindsets and assumptions about the lockstep life course—that education occurs early, adulthood is about full-time continuous work, and retirement is the passage to old age. This predictable routine is gone forever, but institutions still hold to its assumptions.

Universities still think about their clientele as between the ages of 18 and 22, while companies (and nonprofits) look for entry-level workers in their twenties or early thirties. Social Security policies in the United States originally defined retirement as occurring at age 62 or sixty-five. Some of these regulations had built-in gender and racial restrictions, such as jobs advertised to or assumed to be open only to men or women, but not both. Even social security protections were devised with the breadwinner-homemaker family and the career mystique model in mind: those following low-wage, intermittent employment trajectories—typically women, high-school dropouts, immigrants, and minorities—qualify for lower benefits than those with long-term steady employment.

The lockstep logic is also embedded in the ways a series of positions became organized in certain sequences of progression. For example, students move through different grades in elementary school, high school, and college in set ways. And law school and MBA students pursue rigid, typically three-year pathways through professional programs. Careers in academia and law, like many occupations and organizations with set procedures for moving up organizational ladders, follow established sequences over a set period of time.

I argue that this lockstep logic is outdated. Linear sequences of predictability are gone, even though they remain embedded in the thinking behind labor market, organizational, educational, and social welfare policies and practices that have yet to be updated.

Despite the popular belief that individuals today are free to choose their own life paths, their choices are constrained by the ways education, employment, career paths, retirement, and the life course have been standardized and are currently unraveling. Even though age borders seem invisible, people carry in their heads age-graded expectations and organizations have institutional timetables and routines constituting the lockstep life course. They also confront concrete barriers around when to go to school, seek a job, move up occupational ladders, and retire. For example, it is easier to get off the career train than to get back on. In this way, both processes of individualization and standardization operate to fashion lives, including the encore adult years.

The "Hard Work Pays Off" Institutional Logic

The institutional logic about hard work and commitment to the organization being rewarded in rising salaries and advancements along with job, economic, and retirement security is deeply embedded in the American Dream and European as well as American beliefs about the ideal worker. Public and organizational policies as well as individual and family plans for the future have assumed this was the case. But wages have been stagnant, layoffs and downsizing are now common regardless of age or seniority, and pensions as well as retiree health insurance in the US are being scaled back or dropped altogether.[15]

Institutional inertia is particularly difficult in times of rapid social change like we are experiencing today. Unraveling employer/employee and retirement contracts reflect technological, demographic, economic and policy transformations. These changes juxtaposed against inertia in institutional logics, policies, and practices are creating three mismatches, described further below.

An Unraveling Employer/Employee Contract

Globalization, new communication, computation, and information technologies, increasing longevity together with an aging workforce, and the privatization of risk are overturning the traditional social contract that linked organizational seniority to job, economic, and retirement security in the middle of the last century.[16] Despite the fact that those in the encore years often have considerable capabilities and seniority in their jobs, many find themselves vulnerable to layoffs or buyouts due to mergers, bankruptcies, off-shoring, automation, and downsizing.[17] Though Boomers had lower unemployment rates than their younger colleagues during the last major economic downturn, those laid off remained jobless longer.[18] Age stereotypes, age discrimination, and mismatched skills continue to keep unemployed or discouraged Boomers out of good jobs—that is, those with adequate salaries and benefits—and out of the running for even entry-level positions. This despite the fact that many need jobs to make ends meet and others want the structure and sense of purpose employment provides.

Economic and employment precarity—a teetering instability that keeps people from counting on their jobs and resources being there day to day, including having enough retirement income—and the institutional inertia of established norms and regulations around education, work, careers, and retirement, constitute significant forces shaping workers' lives and prospects, including how they spend or shift time in encore adulthood. For some, like Jessie and Jeff (chapter 2), this encore is about ideally seeking useful or meaningful work to use talents, improve community, and add purpose to this bonus stage of life, but being willing to take any job. Hopefully they can find something that will provide an adequate paycheck, but that's less likely these days, too. For others, encore adulthood has meant early, often unexpected, and sometimes even unwilling full-time retirement.[19] How did we get here?

The Way Things Were

In the years following World War II an implicit contract—or explicit, in the case of union jobs—developed between employees and employers. It went like this: Boomers' white-collar and unionized blue-collar fathers traded their work hours, effort, and commitment for what was frequently a lifetime job, or at least a steady income and job security geared toward seniority.[20] Jobs following standardized, continuous, and rigid full-time clockworks together with identifiable ladders of progression were good jobs, typically rewarded with higher wages, health insurance, vacation time, pensions, and protections such as unemployment insurance and security with seniority.[21] Women were rarely in such good jobs. Most worked like I did at the insurance company, in clerical or repetitive tasks even though, to be sure, some were teachers, librarians, nurses.

The idea of uninterrupted commitment and uninterrupted employment became widely accepted as the path to success and personal fulfillment, a career mystique defining in the United States the route to the American Dream. Though not available to all, those in good jobs could expect an economically secure pension, health insurance, and enough pay to support a house, a wife, and children. They could expect a certain rhythm to their lives, and could plan for the future. Of course women, minorities, immigrants, and the less educated were often outside this career mystique designed in the mid-twentieth century for husbands free of care responsibilities. But recall that the career mystique was predicated on the feminine mystique that Betty Friedan famously named in 1963.[22] Still, after the civil rights and women's movements it came to be the lifestyle most—even those on the margins of the workforce—aspired to.[23]

Policies were based on this career mystique and reinforced it. Labor market, educational, health insurance, pension, welfare, and retirement policies developed in post-World War II North America and Europe were all shaped around the institutional logics of a linear and lockstep life course of education, full-time employment, and then the continuous full-time leisure of retirement.[24] Labor market, pension, and employment policies, in turn, forged regulations and expectations institutionalizing the standardized clock-works of work and retirement: 40 or more hours, five days a week, for most weeks of the year, for most of adulthood, ending abruptly with a gold watch, a firm handshake, and often a lifetime pension. Sixty-five was presumably postprime and equated with old age. And many who were retirement-eligible exited their career jobs as soon as pensions kicked in, in their fifties and early sixties.

With the advent of industrialization and bureaucratic white-collar jobs, work truly became about time and place, just as I discovered at age 17 in Atlanta. This was institutionalized with the 1938 Fair Labor Standards Act and the many union contracts defining how workers' time at the workplace would be traded for income, benefits, and security. The social rules about when, where, and how long to work became widely agreed upon, ordinary routines of everyday life.[25]

Institutionalized work-time clocks and calendars provided a sense of routine, but made it difficult and costly for people to time shift in and out of jobs or career paths. Middle-class Boomer women who left the workforce to care for their families found it easy to step off the career track, though clearly household budgets had to be rethought, as men's wages began to no longer keep pace with the rising costs of living. But women opting out have found it hard—sometimes impossible—to get back to old career paths. Those who scale back from full-time to part-time work or exit the workforce for a period to care for children or ailing parents pay an enormous price for doing so.[26] They lose salaries, opportunities, and credits for future Social Security benefits in the years they were out of the workforce, often returning to jobs with low wages, low job security, no pensions, and little potential for advancement.

I first learned about the status differences between full-time and part-time workers in my second job, at Orkin Exterminating Company. I worked in the afternoons, after finishing my morning classes at Georgia State University. In this job I learned that rules, not individuals, matter. I was doing a wide variety of tasks with and for Janet, executive secretary to the vice president of the company, Mr. William B. Orkin. Janet had her own small office, and I had a tiny desk squeezed in the corner of it. Most of the other "girls" in the company headquarters were simply filing documents, sitting before cabinets in a large open room. (Note to younger readers: before computers, all records were in the form of hard copies that needed to be filed.) Apparently, women were better at filing—I never saw a man doing this job. When Janet was sick, on vacation, or even gone for lunch, I did the bidding of Mr. Orkin.[27]

He was the first millionaire I ever met. I thought my presence in the halls of power, working for a person whose father had started the company, was a big deal, and I loved my job. I even invented a more efficient way to send letters to those who cancelled our exterminating service, and was quite pleased when Mr. William B. approved and adopted this form letter that nevertheless had a personal touch. At the Christmas party, I received my cash bonus, $50 wrapped in a brown envelope. This was a terrific windfall, since I only earned $1.15 an hour. I believed I was being recognized for my work streamlining the mailings. But a mistake had been made. Turns out, the envelopes had gotten switched. The $50 was for a full-time filing employee; my envelope held a $10 bill. I worked half time, but did not even get half of her bonus. I was sure she was less productive than me, but it simply didn't matter. I was marginal: recently hired, less than full-time, minimally trained, easily replaceable. Because of organizational rules, the full-timer was simply more valuable than me.

The men in the Orkin corporate headquarters—managers and department heads—worked at a different rhythm and with different expectations than most of the women, still called "girls" at the time. Men put in more than full-time hours as a matter of course, and their purposive, energetic strides from meeting to meeting suggested full dedication to their careers, if not their current jobs. Listening to their banter with Mr. William B.'s executive secretary, I could hear they expected to move up in the company, shift to one with better prospects, or even start a rival firm of their own. They were, in the early 1960s, following the career mystique. They believed the best life for themselves, their homemaking wives, and their children would result from a lifetime of career-building.[28] But again, their ability to follow that path revealed the feminine mystique in action: men could devote their lives to their jobs because their wives were taking care of them, their children, their homes, pets, and relatives, while secretaries like Janet were taking care of them at work.

The Way Things Are

Today's work-time rules remain based on the carefree unencumbered male worker logic, even though half the labor force in the United States is now female and few workers—women or men—have homemaking partners.[29] The out-of-date clocks and calendars of work together with more intense job demands challenge dual-earner couples, singles, single parents, and others with family care obligations to prioritize both careers and a satisfying, fulfilling family life. Part-time, shift, contract, temporary, and intermittent jobs are increasingly common, but remain marginal positions with few protections. These ways of working are outside the mainstream career mystique ideal of linear lockstep career development with a single employer or in a single occupation, a mystique more in people's heads than in the real world of work. These types of peripheral jobs have tended to be allocated to women, immigrants, the less educated, and minorities, thereby perpetuating and often expanding existing inequalities.[30] But now even educated professionals find themselves with a portfolio of often unrelated short-term jobs.

Even though most workers live in households in which all adults work for pay, some semblance of the gender divide allocating breadwinning to men and caregiving to women remains. Even when women make more money or work more hours than their husbands, most come home to a second shift of family-care and domestic work.[31] As several scholars have pointed out, the gender revolution is unfinished in many ways.[32] Inflexible work times and inflexible career paths remain geared to a workforce without family-care responsibilities.

What is key is that women's intermittent work paths and secondary career status have increased their risks of both economic and employment insecurity in encore adulthood.[33] Those who moved in and out of the labor force and in and out of full-time employment in light of family responsibilities—caring for children, parents, and spouses or moving to new cities, states, and even countries for their husbands' jobs—are finding these accommodations have long-term implications: not only lower wages and little advancement, but also resulting in no or low private pensions, lower Social Security benefits, few financial assets, and sometimes even economic privation, especially for widows and divorcees.[34] As a case in point, Shin-Kap Han and I found that when large corporations in upstate New York downsized in the 1980s, women were typically ineligible for the generous buyout packages because they had not been employed in these organizations enough years; accordingly they were laid off or encouraged to retire without such benefits.[35]

Many Boomer women purposefully sought jobs that would permit them to time shift when necessary in order to care for their families. They have paid a heavy price for doing so. Cultural norms assuming such informal caregiving as women's work have fostered both sudden crises and ongoing strains for workers trying to successfully combine work and family goals and obligations. Job and family overloads and disconnects mean that conflicts between work and home are increasingly common for everyone, men as well as women.[36] Moreover, the fact that women bear more responsibility for family care has produced and reproduced distinctly gendered pathways. Though it needn't be so—remember that institutions can and do change—middle-class Boomer men have, insofar as it's possible, worked continuously and full time, with Boomer women often shifting to part-time jobs or taking time outs from paid work. This gendered life course has led to economic, power, and status disparities between women and men throughout their lives.[37]

Beginning in the 1980s the implicit contract I observed at Orkin, where men's full-time, continuous work was fully rewarded, began to disappear. Globalization—in the form of internationalization of markets, the intersection of competition due to deregulation, wide communication networks and automation of tasks based on new digital technologies, and the rising importance and vulnerabilities of markets—have produced an international labor market characterized by risk and uncertainty.[38]

The enormity of these transformations cannot be overemphasized; decades of outsourcing, offshoring, and automation have led to decades of stagnant wages and corporations shedding workers, hiring contractors and temps. As economist David Weil observes:

> The large corporation of days of yore came with distinctive borders around its perimeter, with most employment located inside firm walls. The large business of today looks more like a solar system, with a lead firm at its center and smaller workplaces orbiting around it.[39]

The full force of connectivity and computational technological advancements have ushered in what MIT professors and digital experts Erik Brynjolfsson and Andrew McAfee term "the Second Machine Age."[40] They believe we are now at an intersection point, with "digital technologies to be as important and transformational to society and technology as the steam engine."[41] The steam engine ushered in the Industrial Revolution, what these authors call "humanity's first machine age." Their point is that just as machines greatly expended people's physical power, so too are digital technologies expanding our mental power. The sheer pace of digital technological development is astounding.

People are quite adept at fashioning and adapting to technological inventions—from steam engines to digital devices helping us to remember, calculate, and communicate as well as live healthier longer. We are less adept at fashioning and adapting to *social* inventions, such as new ways of organizing work, career paths, retirement, and the life course. For example, as factories developed during the Industrial Revolution, for a while the traditional agricultural model persevered: everyone from children to old folks worked from sun to sun. It took time for new ways of working to emerge. It was not until the Fair Labor Standards Act of 1938 that the 40-hour work was legitimated by requiring time and a half pay for any hours over forty. My point is that just as the first machine age called for new ways of organizing work and life, so too is the second machine age necessitating the invention of new logics and innovative policies and practices.

Today, both women and men are trying to stay on track by leaning in to increasingly demanding careers and full-time, full-force jobs as ways of making a living and remaining on evermore shaky job ladders. But a combination of new technologies fostering the second machine age, global competition, an increased emphasis on the bottom line, diminishing union membership, and a decline in the enforcement of labor protections has undermined the reciprocal employer–employee relationship.[42] While job insecurity has always been a fact of life for workers in the secondary workforce, the speedy restructuring of good jobs in the primary workforce jobs to reduce company costs has resulted in downsizing and risk for older as well as younger workers—even college-educated ones—in North America and Europe.[43]

This is not just a US phenomenon. For example, when unemployment peaked in the Netherlands in 1983, permanent employment contracts were replaced with fixed-term contracts that could be more easily dissolved.[44] There was also a decline in the labor force participation rates of older workers; in 1971, 80 percent of Dutch men ages 50 to 64 were in the labor market, declining to 55 percent by the early 1980s.[45]

Precarity was exacerbated with the historic economic downturn becoming widespread in the United States in 2008 and lingering in the form of chronic job insecurity for workers of all ages and retirement uncertainty for a large portion of the Boomer population.[46] The unemployment rate has since declined, but the inertia of outdated rules and rigidities continue to matter, constraining innovation and perpetuating outdated work times and lockstep career paths. This limits Boomers' opportunities to time shift work, such as by reducing their positions to 80 percent or 50 percent time, voluntarily moving to contract or project work, or in other ways tailoring their own jobs or their own late career paths as many would prefer. Inertia tied to age bias and discrimination also limits Boomers' chances to learn new skills, train for new occupations, or to scale back or move into flexible new jobs that give them a sense of usefulness, purpose, and meaning while also opening up time to pursue other passions, be it caring for a grandchild, taking up yoga or other health-promoting activities, or relearning to play the piano.[47]

An Unraveling Retirement

Retirement has meant permanent later life withdrawal from the workforce, typically in conjunction with eligibility for public or employer-provided pension benefits. It has also been traditionally defined as a passage from prime adulthood to old age. This cultural formulation of desk chair to rocking chair is clearly out of date for those in the encore years who want to remain purposefully engaged, as well as for those wanting or needing a secure stream of earned income. All are approaching or moving through the conventional retirement years in a time of extended life expectancy, declining pensions, and rising economic insecurity.

The Way Things Were

Retirement was first institutionalized in Germany in 1893, when Otto von Bismarck decreed age 70 as the age of entitlement for public pensions (later reduced to age 65 in 1916).[48] With the enactment of Social Security in 1934, the United States also adopted age 65 as the age of full eligibility.[49] The British civil service pension plan was launched even earlier, in 1859, as a way to retain workers.[50] Public and private retirement pensions developed to transition older workers out of the labor force as their skills and health declined, thus opening up jobs for younger cohorts.[51] In the 1950s and 1960s, US corporations also offered private retirement pensions even as government agencies offered civil service pensions as defined benefits, meaning a certain income every year for life, aimed at attracting and keeping desirable workers. Employer-provided pensions were seen and used as useful perks for recruiting and retaining valuable talent. Stay longer, and you get a better pension, and the company or agency can save money by not having to continuously hire and train new workers. Then leave at 65 or earlier to make room for a youngster. This works fairly well when there are relatively even numbers of people entering and exiting the workforce each year. But you can see how it might go wrong if there happens to be a sudden population shift—say, 76 million in the United States now moving into conventional retirement ages at a time of extended life expectancy. But we'll get back to that.

Both social welfare and organizational policies—in the United States, Social Security, SSI, Medicare, Medicaid, pensions, and retirement packages—legitimated in the second half of the twentieth century were predicated on the leisure model of retirement. Institutionalized sources of public financial support along with employer-provided pensions and retirement communities for those 50 or 55 and older have been fundamental in shaping the later adult life course and leading to the golden years model of retirement.[52] Those with generous pensions as well as those having health conditions began retiring at progressively earlier ages. And substantial buyouts encouraged high-wage workers to leave the workforce earlier than they planned.[53] European policies throughout the latter half of the last century encouraged early retirement with large public pensions as a way of responding to changes in the labor market, containing unemployment rates, and opening up jobs for younger people.[54]

Retirement may be a relatively recent social invention, but it has come to be a key individual, family, organizational, political, and cultural phenomenon. It has become an important dimension of the conventional life course and for most workers, an almost universal status passage.[55]

The Way Things Are

Today the whole edifice around a one-way, one-time, irreversible, and reasonably secure retirement is crumbling. Existing policies, practices, and logics are increasingly problematic. Some traditional social protections such as private pensions, social security, and in the United States retiree health insurance are being delayed, scaled back, or dismantled; others are out of step with the needs and desires of a significant segment of Boomers to work beyond conventional retirement ages but in unconventional ways.[56]

Early retirement policies began to be reversed in the 1990s, as, in the face of growing numbers of older workers and retirees, governments sought to increase the costs of early withdrawal and delay the "normal" retirement age. For example, Germany increased its legal mandatory retirement age to 67 and limited the possibilities of early retirement for older employees experiencing long bouts of unemployment.[57] The United States set age 66 as the full retirement age (FRA), the age when workers would receive full Social Security benefits, phasing to age 67 as the eventual age for full benefits. Thus US Boomers need to work longer than 65 to receive full benefits, with the trailing edge of the Boomer cohort not eligible until sixty-seven. Congress also established the Delayed Retirement Credit (DRC) for those who wait to claim their Social Security credits beyond the FRA, maxing out at age 70.[58] Remain in the workforce another three, four, five, or six years, and you will get higher benefits.

In the corporate sector most defined benefit (DB) guaranteed pensions for the rest of one's life were replaced by defined contribution (DC) plans based on returns to investments made by employees with funds contributed by both themselves and their employers. The shift from DB to DC plans is important—it's the difference between a guaranteed income for life and worries about outliving one's savings along with betting on the vagaries of the stock market. US Boomers with only DC plans have highly individualized risk and no guaranteed retirement income other than Social Security.[59] Investigative reporter for the *Wall Street Journal* Ellen E. Schultz describes the results as a failure: "Employees save too little, too late, spend the money before retiring, and can see their savings erased when the market nosedives."[60]

However, these changes appear to have fulfilled their promise of pushing Americans to work longer. Men ages 62 to 69 saw an average annual drop in their full-time employment rate of 2.23 percent from 1955 to 1986, but from 1988 to 2010, their employment increased 1.21 percent annually. Women ages 52 to 59 increased their rate of employment from .4 percent each year from 1965 to 1988 to a fairly steady 1.8 percent per year from 1988 to 2010.[61]

While social security and pension reforms in Europe and North America have aimed to postpone the age of full retirement, University of California, Irvine economists David Neumark and Joanne Song show that there are two confounding factors.[62] First, age discrimination makes older people harder to re-employ if they lose their jobs. A job loss for an older worker is more likely to become a not-entirely-voluntary retirement. Second, with age, the physical demands of work become more challenging. Some Boomers are like Joe, a fifty-something construction worker I interviewed who is wondering how long he can keep up with his coworkers and the demands of his job.

To be sure, laws against age discrimination have served to increase the employment of older workers covered by them,[63] but require fighting through the courts and arbitration and lots of legalese for jobs and chances many may feel aren't really worth fighting for. This is not a cheery, retirement party exit from the workforce. Recall how Jenn (chapter 2) was told in her early fifties that her high-level public relations job at a Fortune 500 company would simply be *gone* the next day. The announcement was so sudden she thought the VP firing her was joking. He was not. After being laid off, Jenn described herself at age 55 as "temporarily retired," or "involuntarily retired." She finally found another job working for a nonprofit placement agency assisting low-wage workers, but feels she has only a 50/50 chance of keeping this one. As her husband Claude says, "it looks like that company's in transition too, as they all seem to be."

After unexpected dislocations the meaning of work often changes. Sarah, a marketer for a large firm, was also unexpectedly laid off. She even went back to talk to her boss a week later to see if there was any way to salvage her job. There wasn't. She was out of work for a year and a half, finally finding a temporary, lower-level job. She now works as a retail distributor, preparing and sending packages to online customers even though she has an MBA in marketing. She would prefer another marketing job but has gotten no response from her repeated applications. About her current job, Sarah reflects, "It's certainly not a job I would have chosen, but I have to put some food on the table." She feels strongly that she needs to continue bringing in income. Even though she is married to a pharmacist earning a good salary, they can't make all their monthly payments on his income alone.

We are experiencing two conflicting trends regarding retirement planning and possibilities. On the one hand, the retirement transition is embedded in established social and organizational policies, practices, and institutionalized logics based on men's continuous work paths in the mid-twentieth century. It has come to be normatively defined in terms of timing and legitimacy, a well-deserved exit from decades of employment. On the other hand, this institutionalized transition is, in reality, very much in flux. Mergers, downsizing, restructuring, automation, changes in the employer–employee contract, and the high salaries those in their fifties and sixties typically command, all mean employers may well view them as both costly and expendable. Jenn's husband Claude, a former school superintendent now doing consulting, observes about his wife's former workplace:

> Companies, as we all know, are pretty much heartless I guess. So they don't know who you are. They just do things and get caught up into it. I think she took it very personally, and that's hard for me to see.

Claude retired because of the introduction of an incentive in the state retirement system designed to move expensive older employees off the payrolls. His was an easy decision. He describes his former job as one where

> the pressures and the concerns and the problem solving is nonstop, 24 hours a day... As far as what I want to do in my older years in my life, that's not what it is. So I needed to get out from under, so that I could do things that were just more personally, not relevant, say, but rewarding.

Many Boomers want, like Claude, to get "out from under," but without his generous pension, they can't figure out how to do so.

Many employees continue to believe that if they put in long hours and accomplish mounting work demands, their jobs will be secure; "the hard work pays off" institutional logic. But Boomers like Sarah, Claude, and Joe in this chapter and Jenn (director of public relations), Jessie (following a messy career path), and Jeff (the photographer whose job is challenged by cell phones) in chapter 2 know that it isn't so.

Americans in particular equate productivity exclusively with paid work and seem to prioritize income and advancement over life quality. But meanings of work are also changing as Millennials, GenXers, and Boomers survey their options. Many workers feel they are at a point in life where they want to prioritize quality of life over quality of output, earnings, possessions, or status. Significant numbers of Boomers know that life quality has to do with a sense of purpose and personal growth, and accordingly want to lean out but not *check out*. But recall that social innovations like reinventing retirement, offering alternative pathways, or institutionalizing a new life stage are harder than technological innovations.

Times of Transition: Three Mismatches

The story thus far is that periods of rapid social change produce structural lag between the inertia permeating outdated work, career, and retirement rules of the game and new demographic, technological, economic, and policy realities.[64] The confluence of these forces during what MIT professors Brynjolfsson and McAfee call the second machine age mean that Boomers are moving through the encore adult years at a time when established regimes around education, work, and retirement are both out of date and in flux.[65] Figure 3.1 shows the shifting composition of the US workforce, as different

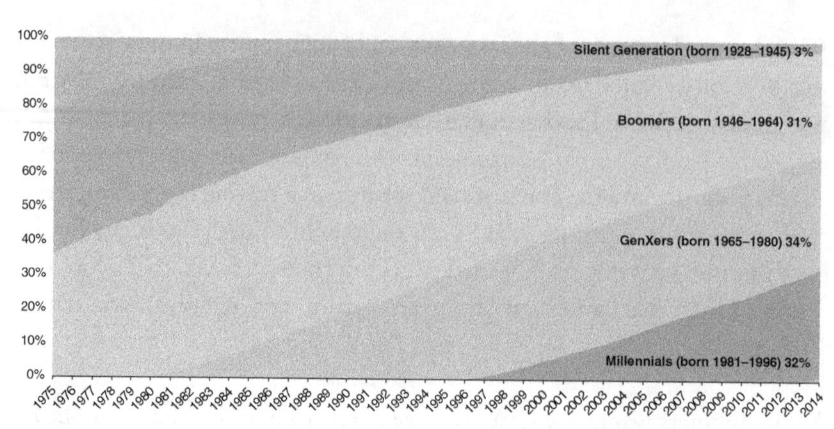

FIGURE 3.1. Forty Years of Labor Force Composition by Cohort: 1975–2014

cohorts move through different ages and historical time. It shows Boomers at a point where the unraveling of conventional work and of conventional retirement is challenging what they might have expected, even as many are seeking ways to repair and even reset their lives.

Structural lag in flexible opportunities for purposive engagement as an encore act is mirrored by its counterpart in the lagging development of practical arrangements that acknowledge the blurring of boundaries around paid work, unemployment, and retirement. This is exemplified by the experiences of Sarah, Jenn, and Claude—all of whom are in their fifties and working, but not in the jobs they trained for or have years of experience in. Only Claude, with his state pension and buyout package, calls himself "retired"—even though he also works, consulting 10 to 12 hours each week. He chose to exit his career job; Sarah and Jenn did not.

I see three fundamental mismatches characterizing this structural lag between Boomers' lives and obsolete governmental and business policies, practices, and logics guiding expectations: the work-time mismatch, the life-course mismatch, and the risk-safety net mismatch. All necessitate social inventions opening up the ways we work and live at all life stages—from those just entering the workforce to those already retired. I focus here on the case of Boomers on the edge of encores to their previous lives.

The Work-Time Mismatch

Conventional work-time institutional logics are mismatched with Boomers' as well as Millennials' and GenXers' needs and preferences. Global competitiveness together with the technological advances characterizing this second machine age have resulted in both work intensification—the time pressures associated with doing more with less—and extensification (being available 24/7), even as many contemporary workers, men and women of all ages, hope to lean out of or at least contain long-hour work to better focus on family, civic, and personal goals and obligations.[66] Despite lip service to offering workers greater control over their time, the fact is that few public or corporate policies deal with the time strains, work–life conflicts, or overloads experienced by workers of all ages. Instead, they remain geared toward the career mystique, assuming employees can—and will—focus like a laser on their jobs. The reality for many Boomers as well as their younger coworkers is a sense of too much to do, too little time.[67] Rigidities around work hours as well as when and where work is accomplished are at odds with the responsibilities of all workers, including Boomers who may be caring for children, grandchildren, ailing spouses or partners, parents or other infirm relatives, and who may be looking for personal, social, or societal purpose, not total investment or burnout in their jobs.[68] Boston College professor of social work Marcie Pitt-Catsouphes and colleagues find that unions are more likely to work for benefits like health insurance for part-time workers than for flexible work options.[69]

What, then, is the new ideal vision of integrating and sustaining work, family, and personal life for the twenty-first century that will get us to gender equality at work and at home? The fact is, there is none. The preponderance of the contemporary workforce in the United States is saddled with improvising its own work-life "balance" in a world based on a workforce and work arrangements that no longer exist. The career and feminine mystiques seen as ideal in the middle of the twentieth century, replaced during the women's movement with the norm of both men and women following the career mystique, with two-career couples as models of the pathway to equality, hasn't worked out as expected.

Today's workforce necessitates new, more flexible work-time logics and practices more in keeping with life in the twenty-first century. Most children are now raised in households in which all adults work for pay. Many grandparents are employed,[70] reconfiguring the shape and culture of childhood in ways dictated by the time and psychosocial demands of parents' and grandparents' jobs. Family time is often both scheduled and frantic, leaving less free time for everyone. And, given new communication technologies and social media, the lines between paid work and home are increasingly blurred.[71] Employees are expected to use technology to make themselves available to coworkers, customers, and managers even during purportedly nonwork evenings, early mornings, and weekends.[72] Recall what Claude said about his work expectations as a school superintendent: "The pressures and the concerns and the problem solving is nonstop." This is the case for many workers of all ages.

Such demands are also at odds with Boomers' goals and needs to reduce stress at this time in their lives. Claude confides:

> I'm not sure if we ever talked about it before. I'm a polio victim, and at this age, you begin to get the post-polio syndrome, which causes a lot of pain and a lot of muscle fatigue and a lot of balance problems. A lot of that is predicated upon the amount of stress that you have in your life. By reducing that level of stress, I have improved hugely. So that's a major plus from retirement.

Claude was fortunate in that he could afford to retire and continue to use his skills as much or as little as he wants as a consultant. But most jobs remain demanding in terms of time, intensity, and availability expectations, even as Boomers discover new health conditions, reset the amount of stress they are willing to live with, or devise plans for projects offering them a sense of purpose and renewal. In contrast to standardized work times, there is in fact unprecedented divergence in the sheer range of actual family, personal, and employment clockworks. Most often, they simply don't match up. As employers gain flexibility to reset their workforces, workers seem to lose it. It is hard to find the flexible, reduced work hours in purposive work Boomers and others increasingly want or need.[73]

The Life-Course Mismatch

The life-course mismatch captures the gap between the existing social organization of the lockstep career mystique and contemporary real-life career paths, personal experiences, and preferences of the people living them.[74]

The mid-twentieth-century labor market constituted an environment in which professionals, managers, and skilled blue-collar male workers with seniority and the willingness to work hard could expect security and, hopefully, advancement. But this is no longer the case. The linear and lockstep life course is possible for an increasingly smaller portion of the professional and managerial workforce, much less for those in less-advantaged occupations.[75] This model was also based on the unencumbered worker logic that employees—husbands—were carefree and totally devoted to their jobs. This out-of-date logic makes it difficult for dual-earner families to prioritize and pursue two careers even as stalled wages and the press for gender equality make it difficult or undesirable to support households on a single income.

In their younger days, many Boomers bought into the traditional employment contract. With the women's movement, many women joined men in investing in building careers and seniority. Now men and women find themselves on the edge, having lost much of their sense of security as employers maximize *their* flexibility. Corporations in the United States and Europe now have the flexibility to hire, reduce or increase hours, and fire employees essentially at will. Call it the privatization of risk. Some, like Jenn, accept their unemployment as only "temporary retirement." Others, like Sarah, accept stopgap jobs while still seeking out prospects for rebooting their careers. Either way, to be out of work or worried about losing their jobs and yet feeling too young to retire leaves many Boomers up in the air. Their experiences do not match the traditional life course, and they're unprepared for this predicament.[76]

In Europe especially, the word "flexibility" often refers to a set of contemporary practices permitting employ*ers* to downsize or shift their workforces in tandem with changing demands, including offshoring jobs to developing countries with lower wage rates.[77] Employer flexibility was brought about by the rising competitiveness of globalization, new digital technologies automating work and blurring the spatial and temporal boundaries around where and when work is accomplished, and the absence or lack of enforcement of policy protections for employees. A tighter labor market may help Boomers keep or find jobs, but possibilities remain characterized by uncertainty.

In tandem with greater employer flexibility and the rising pace of technological innovation, older workers are often seen as outdated.[78] Once regarded as valued employees who would be difficult to replace, older workers are now seen as less skilled, more difficult to train, and more expensive than younger workers.

Consider the case of Germany. Though such employer flexibility appears to be less prevalent in Germany, older German workers have often found themselves in declining industries, at risk of obsolescence. Strict boundaries around occupations and occupational tracks have standardized and stratified the German labor market, obliterating re-employment options for many older workers. Moreover, the German pension scheme is generous, providing about 70 percent of preretirement net earnings. So, as new industries sprang up and older workers became less valuable, unemployment insurance policies let firms dismiss employees at age 57—the workers could then count on legal retirement pensions as early as age 60.[79] Workers in their fifties and early sixties in Europe and North America are, like Jenn, Claude, and Sarah, thus encouraged to leave the workforce through layoffs and early retirement incentives. Pension policies, especially in Europe, have even made it lucrative for some to retire.[80] Until recently in the United States, Social Security and other regulations penalized those past 65 who continued to work or who chose to return to work after retirement.[81]

Older workers with little seniority or in low-paying jobs—recall these are typically women, the less educated, immigrants, and minorities—have always been vulnerable to a changing economy. But today's competitive global and digital economy in this second machine age means that even the most advantaged—educated, white, male Boomers with considerable seniority at the peak of their careers—are no longer immune to layoffs. Moreover, the absence of ongoing educational and training options for older workers is a real impediment to Boomers who need skill upgrades or new certification to maintain or seek new employment. Greater employer flexibility has led to an increase in temporary contract employment, including the hiring of employees through temporary work agencies. In the Netherlands, for example, both younger and older workers are more apt to have temp jobs.[82]

This life-course mismatch is grounded in age-graded institutional logics and actions. It is evident in hiring policies and practices assuming that new hires are young, not older adults, both in the United States and abroad.[83] It is also evident in how older workers are treated. Studies have found two-thirds of those ages 45 to 71 report experiencing age discrimination at work.[84] Research shows that younger job candidates are more likely to be offered an interview and actually hired.[85]

What MIT professors Brynjolfsson and McAfee call the skill–work mismatch I see as part of the life-course mismatch.[86] Workers of all ages need more and continuous opportunities to develop and upgrade the skills necessary in this second machine age. Higher education needs to reimagine and reinvent portals to learning that offer new skills, certifications, and personal growth across the life course, a real effort at what is truly lifelong learning. The need is for flexible careers—a redesign of educational, career, and time-out options for people of all ages and life stages.

The Risk-Safety Net Mismatch

Boomers also confront a mismatch between risks and available safety nets. The privatization of risk to individuals and families and away from employers or government reflects a shift in the burden of economic downturns and uncertainty. In the United States and parts of Europe, this has involved retrenchment, the lowering or elimination of welfare regimes.[87] For example, Italy has two pension schemes: one kicks in after 35 years of contribution regardless of age, and one after 15 years of contributions combined with age 60 for men and 55 for women. But 1992 reforms reduced the generosity of Italy's pensions, and in 1995 Italy moved from a defined benefit to a defined contribution program and started to delay the age of statutory retirement—that is, the age at which full eligibility for social security benefits occurs. Still, employers and governments continue to use early retirement as an adaptive strategy in the face of high unemployment rates to get high-cost older employees off payrolls. Spain has economic problems and early retirement programs similar to Italy's; though the standard old age pension is not available until age 65, as of 2008 only 36 percent of Spaniards ages 55 to 64 were in the labor market.[88]

These risk shifts in Europe and North America are occurring as employer and public protections erode. The flexibility of employers to fire at will has spawned various policy responses. Denmark is an interesting case, with the Danish labor market characterized by a mix of flexibility and security. The emphasis is on *employment* security, not *job* security. Known as "the golden triangle of flexicurity," the Danish scheme consists of low employment protection in terms of remaining in particular jobs, generous welfare programs, and an active labor market policy in the form of help with job searches, skill upgrading, and retraining.[89] In Denmark, there are active policies to keep those who want jobs in jobs—it just may not be doing the work they'd prefer.

Global financial crises and chronic uncertainties associated with the rapid pace of digital change have accentuated the mismatch between heightened risks related to the economy and unsettled futures on the one hand, and social protections or safety nets, on the other. Like younger cohorts, Boomers live on the edge of a competitive global economy in which automation, downsizing, cutbacks, mergers, and layoffs have become facts of life.[90] Unfortunately, so too is age discrimination, along with scaled-back social welfare policies around job, economic, and retirement security. Risks are increasing, and safety nets are wearing thin. Social innovation in protections against the vulnerabilities and risks endemic to contemporary society and in ways to retrain, retool, or start something new are key for sustainable families and lives at all ages and stages.

Conclusions

Career and retirement have become contested—and ambiguous—concepts. Full-time, full-year, paid work provided the organizational blueprint for much of mid-twentieth-century life, at least for white, middle-class, and unionized blue-collar men in North America and Europe. This linear lockstep career mystique presuming (family) care free working husbands with caretaking wives went hand-in-hand with a retirement mystique—the promise of golden years of full-time leisure as a well-deserved and subsidized ending to a lifetime of full-time employment. These mystiques have never fit the experiences of women, minorities, immigrants, or low-wage workers, and nowadays many in privileged professional occupations are also living with employment and retirement insecurity. Still, this institutionalization of time provided people with a narrative of their lives, enabling them to make long-term choices like buying a home and to plan for the future.[91]

Planning is a lot harder today. All kinds of families and all kinds of family members are caught up in the multilayered dislocations and ambiguities of the global digital economy described by Brynjolfsson and McAfee as the second machine age, given its corresponding restructuring of work and risk.[92] Legal and organizational frameworks endorsing gender equality and decrying age discrimination are stymied by institutional logics that reinforce gender and age stereotypes and bias. Social welfare protections are being scaled back and, in most countries and companies, few policies consider the time scarcity and overloads characterizing the lives of Boomers and their younger colleagues, or the fact that many Boomers as well as Millennials and GenXers want to lean out of inflexible, demanding, long-hour jobs to something that feels more sustainable, purposeful, and sane. Now that seniority no longer means job security, chronic uncertainty and anxiety is becoming the norm. Boomers, GenXers, and Millennials are having to become pathfinders in the search for new-fashioned careers, training, and life paths for a more customized—but also more risky—twenty-first-century life course.

Clearly, the meanings and institutional arrangements behind the metaphors of the career and retirement mystiques are out of step with reality. The result? Work-hour, life-course, and risk-safety-net mismatches. The inertia and social dislocations contributing to these mismatches constitute the context constraining the options and accentuating the risks of Boomers as well as members of later cohorts, especially those with few material, social, or personal resources. We are experiencing what Richard Sennett calls a "shortened framework of institutional time," as adults spend less of their lives in paid work. Both Millennials and Boomers find themselves on the cusp of the workforce, looking for but not always finding ways to contribute their talents and passion, or simply make a living.[93] These mismatches constitute impediments for the advantaged as well as disadvantaged of all ages, as they seek to triangulate their thinking about and ability to fashion sustainable life paths—hopefully infused with personal, social, and societal purpose in an uncertain, nonlinear, and disorienting climate of change.

AGENDA #2

Time-Shifting Improvisations

4

Improvising Plans for the Future

IN 2002 AND partly in response to the experience of 9/11, my husband Dick Shore and I sat down for a serious conversation about our future. We ultimately decided we would remain in Ithaca, New York for the rest of our lives. It seemed like a rational choice; our friends were there, and we valued the farmers' market, restaurants, concerts, gorges, and other charms of this lovely college town. Dick had retired and was volunteering five mornings a week at a local grade school, helping young folks learn to read—his best job ever, he said. I enjoyed my job at Cornell University and had an especially smart coterie of graduate students and a large research grant. Accordingly, we not only painted and fixed up our condo; we also, with some other neighbors and at considerable expense, bought up the land behind the condos to protect the lovely view of woods and a pond.[1] But then I was recruited by three different universities, including my alma mater, the University of Minnesota, and suddenly we found ourselves selling our condo and loading a moving van. Somehow having three schools courting at once changed our calculus as to the gains and losses of a move—especially at a moment when we were thinking about the arc of our lives and were still shaken, like most people, by the terrorist attacks of that previous September. As it turns out, decision-making is not as rational or permanent as most of us suppose.

This chapter is about Boomers' decisions in what is a yet to be defined, unsettled period I call encore adulthood. Most research on the planning and decisions of older workers is about their expected or actual retirement timing, drawing on data from Boomers' parents' generation or the cohort born during World War II. But as the preceding chapters have shown, just as tens of thousands of Boomers are turning 60, 65, or 70 every day, increases in healthy life expectancy and education together with a range of technological advances and insecurities tied to a global economy and the second machine age are unraveling conventional careers and the conventional life course.[2] The confluence of these forces are opening a window of risk but also of potential prime time, a new life stage coming after career- and family-building but prior to the infirmities associated with old age. Recall that Millennials are finding themselves in a new life stage of emergent adulthood, planning differently, if at all, and often postponing traditional work and family transitions, such as buying a home or having children. Boomers too need to plan for new and uncertain exigencies in the face of a combination of institutional inertia coupled with multilayered demographic, economic, and technological transformations. Because encore adulthood is yet to become a taken-for-granted life stage, Boomers are having to make their own contingent plans, develop their own contingent expectations. In other words, they are improvising encore adulthood, whatever they may call it. This chapter considers the variability of plans for new ways of leaning out from conventional career paths and leaning in to new lifestyles. It also describes decision-making under uncertainty, and the elusiveness of choice for some, as well as offering an institutional framing of the ways plans and structures reproduce the gendered life course. Concluding sections address whether couples plan together, along with singles' plans and possibilities.

The New Leaning Out

Author and COO at Facebook Sheryl Sandberg has famously encouraged women (and men) to lean in to their jobs, to confront the institutional inertia around work-life issues and gender discrimination by being ambitious, assertive, and taking initiative to advance their careers.[3] But many Boomers have reached a stage in which they would like to lean out. Unlike their parents, however, many don't want to lean out of their careers in order to pursue full-time passive leisure. As economists Kevin Cahill, Michael Giandrea, and Joseph Quinn observe:

> Substantial changes have occurred to all three legs of the traditional retirement income stool—social security, private pensions, and savings—altering the relative attractiveness of work and leisure later in life, nearly always in favor of additional work.[4]

In addition to the financial incentives to working longer, many see added years to explore other options and other facets of their lives, to repair their physical and emotional health, to seek renewed purpose and reset the second half of their adult life course, reimagining who they are and how they want to spend their time. However, outdated institutional logics and retirement rigidities reinforce either continuous, full-time work or continuous, full-time retirement, providing few seemingly possible alternatives. Sandberg's focus is on career-building; she doesn't address what to do when you no longer want to lean in to a given career, how to scale back or use your get-up-and-go to, well, get up and go. Opportunities for leaning in to career jobs are important earlier in the life course, to be sure, and remain so for a segment of Boomers; but so are opportunities for leaning out of career work in order to lean into purposeful activities like volunteering, family care, or not-so-big jobs,[5] that is, those that are part time, part year, or at least have built-in flexibility.

How is the leaning out process in the twenty-first century different from that experienced by prior generations retiring from their career jobs? First, leaning out or committing to leaning in to a social sector or volunteer job can last longer. Prior generations could not count on the unprecedented life expectancy characterizing the contemporary life course. Second, this is the first generation in which older women are both in the workforce and retiring in large numbers. Women and dual-earner couples are confronting this new encore to adulthood from new vantage points, often making it up as they go along. Third, all generations have unique relationships with the social changes of their times, but the sheer pace of contemporary economic, technological, and demographic transformations along with the demise of the social protections developed in the last century make leaning out to retirement or new beginnings more problematic.

As individuals and couples, Boomers are finding they must improvise new ways of living and working on their own. A MetLife survey of the oldest Boomers, those turning 65 in 2011, found that on average, they won't consider themselves to be "old" until they are almost 79.[6] A 2009 Pew Survey shows differences by age cohorts in the age they think people become old. Twenty-something Millennials think it is at age 60; those 65 and older think it is at age seventy-four. Four out of 10 (44 percent) think a person is old when they retire from work. Only one in 10 (10 percent) still sees 65-plus-retirement as a marker of old age.[7]

The social forces extending health and longevity along with the increasing proportion of the population in their sixties and seventies are postponing "old." The space opening up between career- and family-building and the infirmities of old age—the encore to adulthood—is uncharted territory. There are no blueprints, guidelines, or time-tested strategies to guide those suddenly laid off in their fifties or sixties, or those with the health and privilege to consider whether or when to leave career jobs; whether or when to seek out another career; whether or when to negotiate or look for part-time work, bridge jobs, or opportunities for civic engagement; and whether or when to move or stay in current homes and communities.

My Cornell colleague and friend, the developmentalist Urie Bronfenbrenner,[8] always pointed out that we are the people in our lives—that our individualized biographies are deeply intertwined with those of others—linked across relationships and across generations. Families have always functioned as economic units, operating as "role budget centers" by making strategic allocations of family members' time, money, skills, and energy in ways that sustain everyone.[9] For example, some Boomer parents have welcomed their Millennial children home again when they can't make it on their own. These strategic processes of allocation, coordination, and distribution are called the *family economy*. Family members also strategize about ways to achieve noneconomic goals—their children's (or grandchildren's) optimal development, the quality of their relationships, adequate care for failing parents, a sense of personal renewal and purpose, and a healthier lifestyle to reduce stress, manage health conditions, and promote quality of life more generally.

Words like "strategy" and "coordination" imply a sense of agency, the ability of individuals and families to make and implement choices. But existing realities constrain most Boomers' choices, as do family members' health, education, networks, and material and psychological resources. For example, increasing life expectancy means that Boomers' parents are more likely to live longer, which means they are also more likely to require assistance and care from their Boomer children who themselves are in their fifties, sixties, and seventies. And then there are chance events—a health scare, a layoff, a death or divorce, a child's or parent's or grandchild's car accident—that push Boomers and their families off course. Even expected transitions—moving across the country or a long-planned retirement from a career job—can create unexpected strains.

Like Millennials in emerging adulthood, Boomers' choices and the degrees to which they plan for the future in encore adulthood are related to their sense of personal mastery and control, the opportunities or constraints they face, the people in their lives, and the new risks and ambiguities of life in the twenty-first century. And the decisions they make go to the core of their identities, spirituality, and values just as surely as they affect savings accounts, social security benefits, and simple questions of how to spend one's time. They are, in short, part of a major life-course *project* or series of small projects in encore adulthood, even as decisions about education, occupation, and family define early adulthood and decisions about end of life care shape senescence or old age.

Planning and Decisions Under Uncertainty

The early Industrial Revolution followed the agricultural template of lifetime work; most employees worked until they died or were totally disabled. But by the 1960s and 1970s, as a result of safety nets like social security and pensions guaranteeing an income, retirement had become a major, taken-for-granted transition for older workers in North America and Europe. Often it required few decisions: career paths and retirement into total leisure and old age were pretty rote for middle-class and unionized blue-collar workers. Parameters around the timing of career exits were set by laws such as eligibility ages for early and full social security benefits, by corporate policies and union negotiations setting pension eligibility rules, and by social convention. The main decisions were whether to retire early if retirement eligible—that is, pension eligible; whether to move to warmer climates, smaller homes, or retirement communities; and whether to move away from or nearer to their adult children. Most couples experienced just one retirement, replete with a gold watch and big send-off. If wives were employed, it was usually in retail or service jobs with few protections, and no or else very small pensions. Many married women's exits from the workforce were simply exits, not any formal retirement. Being retired generally indicated that both husband and wife were no longer working outside the home. This was true even for women who were homemakers; I recall my mother saying "we're retired" when my father left his military career.

This standardization of retirement as part of men's normal life course made it an expected transition, as established as other transitions like graduating high school or starting first grade. Both careers and retirement came to serve as what sociologist Leonard Pearlin describes as durable arrangements: standard patterns organizing people's experiences as well as how they view and think about the world and act toward it.[10] Even those on the margins of the labor force accepted this career/retirement mystique, often looking to social security at age 62 (the earliest possible age for reduced benefits in the United States) as the first time in their lives they would receive a secure and steady stream of income, however minimal.

Today, as we saw in chapter 3, the realities and risks around both career and retirement paths are in flux. Nothing can be taken for granted. Except for a few occupations, there is no longer any mandatory retirement age in the United States. By law, managers and human resource personnel can't encourage or even inquire about their employees' plans or retirement timing. Rather than marching lockstep to a taken-for-granted exit, retirement is becoming a series of improvised or, for some, forced transitions in activities and lifestyles in the bonus years of encore adulthood. These years that begin for some in their fifties and end for some in their late seventies involve a number of decisions about job shifts, work exits/entrances, lifestyles, relationships, and resources, including worries about having enough money for the long run of living longer, desires for a sense of purpose, and vagueness about how to spend the looming resource of time.[11]

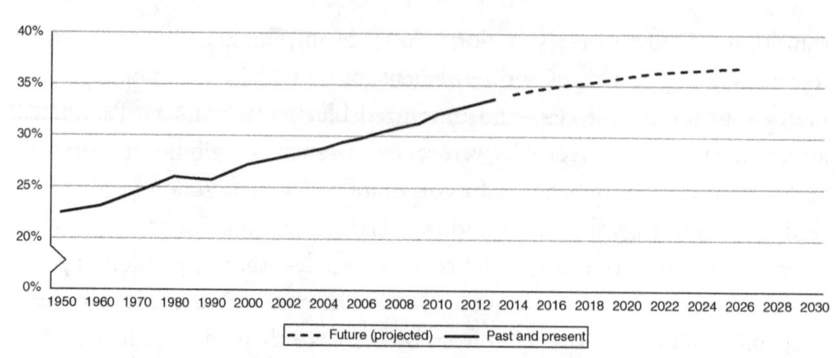

FIGURE 4.1. Percent of US Population Age 50 and Older: 1950–2030 (Projected)

A lot of people are or will soon be at this stage. Over one in three (35 percent) of Americans are 50 or older (see figure 4.1). Converging demographic, technological, economic, labor market, and cultural transformations—in tandem with institutional inertia—are reshaping the second half of the adult life course and complicating decision-making.[12] This is highlighted by the importance two prominent career coaches, Lois Frankel and Susan Picascia, place on the *final five*: the last three to five years a Boomer spends working before moving into postretirement activities.[13] Sounds ominous, precarious, and very little like the golden years Boomers' parents took for granted.

Risky Choices

We tend to think we make decisions rationally as economists suggest,[14] weighing our options in light of perceived costs and benefits as well as preferences. Dick and I did just that, even making a list of pluses and minuses in deciding to stay in Ithaca. But sociologists and psychologists emphasize that decisions are typically made pragmatically within the shifting contexts of risks, opportunities, meanings, and constrictions.[15] As sociologist Barbara Hobson at Stockholm University says, "What one would choose is bound up with the real opportunities to choose."[16] That is, you choose from the options you see as available to you. While much research assumes that individuals are active, purposive agents in planning careers and retirements, their decisions are constrained or opened up by the historical, cultural, and organizational environments they find themselves in. It makes sense, then, that the research evidence shows that the age at which workers choose to retire from career jobs often shifts in response to changes in incentives and disincentives.[17]

The difficulty is that seemingly rational choices aren't always that rational—think of how quickly Dick and I went from planning how to protect our view in our Ithaca home to packing boxes for Minnesota. And when laid off, insecure, burnt-out, well-heeled, or enterprising Boomers seek what's next in the face of ageism and essentially two institutionalized choices, full-time work or full-time retirement, the encore adult years become an improvisational work in progress.

Psychologist and Nobel Prize winner in economics Daniel Kahneman, together with cognitive and mathematical psychologist Amos Tversky,[18] leaders in advancing scientific understanding about decision-making, observe that "making decisions is like speaking prose—people do it all the time, knowingly and unknowingly." In response to the difficulties of a rational choice approach assuming that individuals and families make cogent choices, Kahneman and Tversky developed prospect theory to explain decision-making under risky conditions.[19] This is what Boomers moving through their fifties, sixties, and seventies face—what Kahneman and Tversky call "decision problems." Retiring from the workforce in the 1960s or 1970s was for older workers a rote decision. Such a decision was not even possible for older workers in cohorts living before social security and other protections. Today, retiring from a career job and exiting the workforce have become decoupled. And both have become ambiguous and tricky, "risky choices" made "without advance knowledge of their consequences."[20] Boomers now confront decisions about shifting jobs, starting a business, joining a nonprofit, enrolling for social security benefits—often without fully comprehending the consequences. Some fortunate Boomers constitute the last large group receiving lifetime pensions, giving them a sense of financial security. One couple I talked to had four such pensions between them, given prior career moves. But even for the advantaged the future is uncertain, and so the pros and cons of each choice, whether to retire in their fifties or not for example, let alone a multitude of them, are uncertain, too.

What Kahneman and Tversky have shown is that rationality is bounded.[21] In making decisions, we tend to be 1) risk-averse, avoiding bad or risky outcomes; 2) present- rather than future-focused, preferring a smaller payout now than a larger one some years down the line; and 3) reliant on our own past experiences, considering our life experiences unique and informative, even when facing new and unfamiliar situations. Economic geographers Gordon L. Clark, Kendra Strauss, and Janelle Knox-Hayes agree,[22] writing that decisions such as saving for retirement typically involve intuition, habit, and imitation, with the social environment setting the parameters for behavior.[23] They note that for most Americans, "life is calibrated against the temporal rhythms of the economy."[24] In a good, stable economy people are more likely to invest because they see less risk. Indeed, economists Marco Angrisani and

Michael Hurd from the RAND Corporation, along with Erik Meijer from the University of California, show that low expectations about possible returns limit Americans' decisions to invest their savings in the stock market.[25] How expectations shift when conditions, economic or otherwise, shift is a key research and policy issue.

Social Contexts

Boomers' decisions depend on their social identities, goals, values, ages, health, and future income streams, as well as their relationships with others. Given the prevailing economic and policy climate, Boomers' plans to time shift to more flexible work, new careers, volunteering, full-time family-care work, or full-time recreation often feel like risky choices. By risky, I mean they are made without advance knowledge of other contingencies, such as future health, job security, or the sufficiency of whatever savings they may have.

Kahneman and Tversky conceptualize outcomes in terms of gains or losses relative to a given reference point, rather than as final assets, with losses looming larger than gains. Exiting the workforce or defining oneself as retired after a layoff can represent potential gains and potential losses, depending on the context, and especially the reference point. For Boomers in their early or mid-fifties the reference point may still be full-time paid work, and so leaving involuntarily or losing a career could be seen as a major loss. Recall Sally (chapter 2), who reluctantly left her job as a special education teacher because she couldn't handle the physical demands and HR personnel could not or would not change the job configuration to part time. She is still looking for work, and doesn't want to consider herself retired at her age. By contrast, Boomers in their early or late sixties may mark other retirees as their reference point, focusing on either the potential gain of early Social Security benefits at age 62 in the United States or the potential loss of higher benefits they would receive by postponing these benefits to 66 or even seventy. Depending on reference points, then, volunteering or informal family-care work might be framed as a gain in meaning and purpose, while continuing in an unfulfilling, stressful career job could be framed as a loss of energy and time.

Consider Colleen, who has been divorced for over 30 years and defines herself as single more than divorced at this point. She hadn't planned much for retirement, thinking just a bit about finances for the last 10 years or so, with no plans at all as to how to live in retirement. In fact, she fully expected to keep her job in hospital administration in Northern Virginia until she was at least 67 or sixty-eight. Colleen found her work demanding but interesting, typically putting in 10-hour days. She described her job as pretty flexible, but there was little time off. She had a lot of autonomy and authority. But when a new CEO came in, Colleen told me he was "forcing me back in a box." Very quickly, they were at odds.

Since Colleen knew she wanted to move into risk management, she attended a class in managing risks in health care settings in the spring of 2013. While there, "I heard myself so angry at what I was putting up with. I realized I really did have choices." So, at age 64, Colleen "came back and decided to sell my house, leave my job and move to Arkansas" to start anew. She said her other two daughters in Northern Virginia didn't need her, but her oldest daughter

> has a demanding job as a manager in the Arkansas Health Department, a two-year-old, a husband in law school, and another baby on the way. My house [in Virginia] was too big with a yard that was more I wanted to take care of. It sold in three days above the asking price.

She loves her two young Arkansas granddaughters, but isn't interested in babysitting full-time.

Colleen describes her decision-making style: "I can be plodding along and then suddenly do something unexpected." That is an understatement. By July, she had purchased a home in Arkansas and started looking for what comes next. Colleen saw this as leaving a stressful, unhealthy workplace and starting a new chapter. She thought it would be easy to pick up at least a part-time job given her wealth of experience. Unfortunately, that was not the case. She wanted something in risk management, but could only find unpaid volunteer positions.

Boomers like Colleen and Sally are making decisions with imperfect information. Others fall in between. Colleen and Sally are both looking for work, with little luck. Neither wants nor can afford to be fully retired. Colleen is trying hard not to take her Social Security until she is eligible for full benefits, but is financially strapped in ways she could never have imagined.

Boomers as individuals, couples, family members, and a generation are trying to improvise the career paths, second acts, and retirement exits they want, but bumping up against the realities of age bias, the risks of a digital economy, and rigid institutional logics around the clockworks of schooling, work, career paths, and retirement. Though millions are making decisions about what is next in their lives, they are essentially crafting them alone or as couples, not yet having enough examples of successes and failures among their peers to have a good sense of the best decisions to make or the possible outcomes of a variety of constrained choices. Too, many as individuals and couples live in a chronic state of risk and uncertainty. But like Colleen, many are willing—and often even eager—to take the leap into what's next. Leaving a bad boss and selling the house she raised her children in felt like burdens off Colleen's shoulders. But buying a new place in Arkansas before landing a job now feels a bit unwise.

Those working in emotionally unhealthy situations like Colleen or in physically demanding jobs like Sally worry how long they can keep it up. Recall Joe, a fifty-something construction worker (chapter 3), who confides that he is not sure how long he can keep up with his coworkers who are 20 or 30 years younger. He has given years to this job and the company he works for. But what matters is how he is doing today, and whether he is holding others up. Joe knows he does not have the skills to get work that is less physically demanding, and his age is a barrier to finding another construction job. Like Joe, Boomers without a college education and even some of those with a college degree see no option other than keeping their current jobs—if they can avoid layoffs—until eligible for social security. Others exit through a disability path.[26]

Further, with fewer defined benefit (DB) pensions—that is, a steady income that will be paid out indefinitely after retirement—many Boomers in the United States are uncertain as to whether their defined contribution (DC) plans such as 401Ks, limited savings, or Social Security income will be enough when stretched over a lengthening life span. By contrast, European public pensions are comparatively generous and alleviate some of this anxiety; however, by 2040, over a fourth of the EU population will be over 65, prompting concerns about pension reforms.[27] Regulations in the United States have reduced the penalties of working while receiving Social Security payments, as well as extending the age of full benefits to age sixty-seven. These initiatives are aimed at encouraging ongoing employment.[28]

As a result of these changes along with an uncertain economic climate and extended life expectancy, a subset of Boomers are planning on delaying complete retirement from the workforce indefinitely. Sometimes this is because of financial need or the possibility of higher social security benefits at a later age, sometimes because they love their jobs, sometimes because early retirement options are limited, and sometimes because they want to do something else—a different job that will make a difference or at least be different from what they currently do. Those who value the income, status, and purposeful activity their career jobs provide may envision exiting these jobs as a loss. Indeed, research confirms that well-educated men in professional jobs are likelier than most to work longer and be more financially stable.[29] Recall Bill (chapter 2), the financial advisor who thinks about leaving but pushes it back a year at a time.

Others change jobs but not employers. Mary, age 62, explains why she is moving from being a VP of human resources into an encore career in the same health care organization:

> I am tired of human resources. I have been doing it for too many years. I negotiated with my current boss [in a public health organization] to move into something else, something that will directly help people, make a difference.

Mary plans to work in this encore job for five or six years, long enough that her organization "will receive its return on giving me this opportunity." This decision gives her time for meaningful work but also for planning what comes next.

While Mary will continue working full time, her husband Don has just retired from a high-level position in a state agency, and she's hoping Don doesn't become a "couch potato, in front of the television." They plan to travel. Mary says, "I always take my full vacations." And Mary has been careful to maintain a healthy lifestyle, "exercising regularly."

Good jobs with high wages and generous benefits like Mary's and Don's open up choices in encore adulthood. While poor health or highly stressful work environments can motivate early moves to less strenuous jobs or precipitate unexpectedly early exits,[30] good health and economic stability can bolster planning for new careers, bridge jobs, or early retirement to start new projects, including fulfilling lifelong ambitions.[31] One former VP in manufacturing told me he'd left his high-paying, high-status job to sell hot dogs in a baseball park. Mary's husband Don (age 66), retired for only a few weeks when we talked, has been cycling every day. He began planning on retiring at this point in his life five years earlier, even though Mary knew she wouldn't be ready to retire with him. Don set a specific date and, even though he loved his work, he was ready when that time came to leave his stressful leadership position.

Sometimes Boomers forgo the life they planned as new opportunities or constraints appear on the horizon. Colleen had planned on continuing in hospital administration for years; however, a new boss precipitated her sudden exit. As an example of the vagaries of decision-making, I learned that Don, who had long planned on retiring completely at age 66, was back at work seven weeks into his retirement. His old agency asked him to step in as an interim director of a major program, and he agreed. Don had planned to retire completely, but is suddenly back in full-time work.

Relational Contexts

This is a good place to remember that while decision-making is typically discussed and studied as actions of individuals, it often takes place within couples or other groupings, such as coworkers or friends. Mary and Don planned together to pursue different pathways, even as Don's certain plans are now up in the air. Another example is Denny, who has lived in the same small southern town in Alabama all his life and worked at the same job for most of it. Denny was an electrician working on a nearby army base, as did many of his neighbors and friends. The job involved an hour-long commute—each way—every day, so a group of workers bought a beat-up car to park in a grocery store lot, using it only for the Monday through Friday ride to and from the army base. On this daily trek they would talk about the future, eventually deciding they would all retire together. And they actually did so, when all were in their middle fifties. Their jobs for the military afforded them generous lifetime pensions, making these early exits possible. Denny's wife Becky retired from teaching first grade several years before he did, according to Denny, "to get everything ready," presumably for his retirement.

After their daughter's unexpected divorce, though, Denny and Becky's plans changed. They are now helping raise two grandsons who live close by while helping out with yet another grandson living further away, in South Carolina. Grandparenting has become their full-time job—one they share and enjoy tremendously. Though they haven't ended up with the retirement they expected, Denny and Becky recognize that they are making an enormous difference in the lives of their grandsons. The new routine is also giving them a second chance at active parenting,[32] with time out on Tuesdays for Denny to golf with the guys.

Their experience is far from unusual. US Census data shows that one in five preschoolers whose mothers are employed are cared for primarily by their grandparents.[33] Research shows Boomer grandparents and parents typically provide more assistance to their adult children and grandchildren than they receive.[34]

Ambivalent Planning in an Unsettled Climate

Psychologists, sociologists, demographers, and economists have all found that decision-making in the form of plans and expectations does, in fact, predict actual behavior. Boomers' subjective expectations such as about spending habits, health, or when they will retire matter because they are powerful predictors of future experiences.[35] For example, older workers expect to spend less after retirement and it turns out that they do, especially those who retire on time (at 62, 65, or when retirement eligible) or when they expected.[36] Though some like Denny and his friends pick a date to retire and stick to it, other Boomers are more ambivalent and ambiguous about when they will move on from their career jobs to something else. Recall Bill, the financial consultant in chapter 2, who had said he would "go" at 65, but as that date creeps closer, says he "may stay on another year." Mary, who told us about her encore job, isn't quite sure when she will stop working altogether. A 2013 MetLife study of the oldest Boomers (those born in 1946, turning 66 in 2012) found that of those who had not yet retired, three in 10 changed their plans over the course of a single year, expecting to retire later than they had a year earlier.[37] Note also that 54 percent of the fully retired had retired earlier than they expected, while 8 percent retired later than expected.

Consider Gray, born in 1946 and rising to the position of vice president in a large corporation:

> I never thought about retirement. It's like death. It just never occurred to me! Probably, intellectually, I knew retirement was somewhere down the road, but it just seemed so far off in the future, I just didn't embrace it. I don't think it's pretending it's not there, it's just not something I looked forward to.

But when the company was sold, he suddenly found himself retired.

Recall from chapter 2 that the renowned Stanford University psychologist Laura Carstensen and colleagues developed an important model of socioemotional selectivity, theorizing that in later adulthood individuals recognize the finiteness of life and make choices as to which relationships to continue to pursue.[38] I find a similar model of strategic selection of social roles, lifestyles, and time spent in them, as individuals and couples seek better fit between their needs and goals and their experiences.[39] This is also congruent with the selection, optimization, and compensation model of adult development proposing that people choose to engage in activities they can accomplish, compensating for loss of abilities in some spheres by optimizing other abilities or activities.[40] But, as with Kahneman and Tversky, I find the choices Boomers as individuals and couples make are often more strategic than goal-centered, sometimes made in the absence of desired options.[41]

Beth is a software developer at the firm I and my colleagues in the Work, Family, and Health Network studied.[42] When first interviewed, she reported both high job satisfaction and no desire to leave. Five years later, at age 66, Beth reports low job satisfaction and is now putting in 65 hours a week compared to 49 hours five years earlier. Layoffs have meant that she is expected to do more with less, making for an "impossible" job. Beth is looking elsewhere simply because she can't scale back in her current job:

> It would be nice to have an option to transition into retirement by having "part-time" job options at [this company] that would allow you to maintain your health insurance.

Plans and expectations surrounding work—its continuation, duration, and cessation—are changing across cohorts, with Boomers increasingly expecting to work beyond age sixty-five. It's also clear that many, many other factors, including changes in health and in job conditions, converge to modify plans. Studies show that expectations about retirement timing are more likely to change with health changes than with shifts in income or wealth.[43]

A 2013 government survey of Americans ages 50 and older found almost half (47 percent) of those working and not yet retired say it is very likely that they will do some work for pay during their retirement, with another third (35 percent) saying it is somewhat likely.[44] Another 2013 study by AARP finds 72 percent of older workers ages 46 to 74 plan to work in retirement, with 52 percent wanting to work part time and 13 percent wanting to start their own business.[45] And yet institutional inertia, in terms of typically rigidly full-time or longer hours along with the age-graded ways human resource personnel recruit and hire job applicants, means many are unlikely to actually do so. The 2013 AARP study found only 5 percent of workers in this age group want another full-time job and only 1 percent say they want to retire completely. Melissa Wooten, a sociology professor at Amherst, together with Andrew Hoffman, professor of sustainable development at the University of Michigan, note that institutional theory "asks questions about how social choices are shaped, mediated, and channeled by the institutional environment."[46] This dovetails with Kahneman and Tversky's emphasis on contexts and perceptions of gains or losses.[47]

An Institutional, Comparative Framing

Boomers' plans and decisions reflect distinctions, risks, and inequalities built into existing occupational paths as well as across different subgroups and nation-states. Boomers confront constrained choices, hemmed in by existing rules and possibilities. They are the pathfinders in shaping the new encore to adulthood, but are traveling this uncertain terrain with different resources and protections.

Consider the similarities and differences in Boomer experiences across countries. Germany, which is currently debating whether to raise the retirement age to 67, nevertheless has generous pensions. Marg, a 60-year-old teacher working for 30 years in a public elementary school in Bonn, can count on her plan, which is good, because her stamina is waning even as demands are increasing:

> My workload is probably higher these days than in the past, as work demands for teachers have generally increased substantially... I will reduce my work hours at age 62 and retire completely at sixty-four. I believe that I will no longer have enough strength at that time to do my work as well as I want to.

Still, she recognizes the importance of what she does for her sense of self:

> I know I will very much miss my work and the confirmation it provides me with. I hope I will be able to live a satisfactory and full life also without my occupational work.

Marg has no financial worries given her generous pension. Note that Germany also provides paid "time outs" when needed. Marg recalls:

> Seven years ago I took time off (four months) after back surgery, herniated disk, returning stepwise with initially six hours/week to my original workload. This so-called Hamburg model is often used in Germany after long and serious illnesses.

By contrast, despite the Family and Medical Leave Act providing *unpaid* leave in the United States, caregiving for others or one's own health difficulties push some older workers out of the workforce. Marjorie, a 61-year-old professor at a small university in Connecticut, tells a different story than Marg in Bonn:

> If you are ill, the University is not very forgiving. They'll say "Don't come to work if you're sick," but if you're out for two days with pink

> eye, they're after you. "Where are you?" You don't even have to tell them why, and we're not required to bring a doctor's note, but they act like you should. It's a real strange thing, it makes you feel like they don't trust you. But that's just part of the sweeping administrative, watch-dog crap.

Both these women—in Germany and the United States—can be characterized as Boomers planning what is coming next. Marg sees her timetable as first scaling back and then fully exiting by age sixty-four. But for Marjorie, not retiring is also a plan. She has no intention of retiring in the immediate future because she "can't afford to," doesn't want her "brain to dry up," and because she "likes her job." Note that the institutional arrangements and especially the social protections provided are strikingly different for these two women.

Life-course researchers like me recognize how "planful" individuals—those with more resources and more advantages—can and do shape their futures.[48] For the less advantaged, the encore adult years can be a roller-coaster ride, with improvised responses to layoffs, health problems, disappearing pensions, unexpected family-care needs, and the siren call of early Social Security benefits. One factor shaping choices is the enormous disparity in income among retirees, a source of inequality that has not been adequately addressed.[49] Minorities in the US are particularly at risk, with Hispanic Boomers having less education, less income, and poorer health—though, surprisingly, greater life expectancy, the so-called Hispanic paradox—all of which adds uncertainty to planning and choices.[50] But there is no simple race/ethnicity story. For example, almost one in four (24 percent) older African American workers in the 2012 AARP survey plans to start their own business, as do 18 percent of older Hispanic American workers and only 11 percent of white workers.[51]

Institutional rigidities further constrain options. As described in the previous chapters, the fact that work and career/retirement mindsets and policies remain geared to married men's lives in the middle of the twentieth century, not the realities of the twenty-first, is producing structural lag,[52] mismatches between the existing social organization of days, weeks, and life courses and today's realities. Most organizational and governmental policies are designed for either full-time employment or full-time retirement,[53] with few options in between. And yet Boomers' situations and preferences become ever less likely to match that binary set-up. Many are able to improvise in spite of the rules and regulations conspiring against them. For example, AARP found that almost half (48 percent) of US workers ages 65 to 74 works 30 or fewer hours a week, as do 28 percent of those 57 to sixty-four. But finding or crafting flexible, not-so-big jobs requires persistence, luck, social networks, and creativity.[54]

Denny and Becky could plan their early retirements because both teachers and civil service employees have identifiable retirement exits and pensions, even though public pensions are no longer as secure as they once were. Lyle, a contract worker in retail, and his wife Dawn, who works at a pharmaceutical headquarters, are in their midfifties and already planning for Lyle's encore job as a history teacher, a long-held ambition. They are saving money so that he can go back to school to get certified. This plan will push Lyle out of his current job early, but delay his retirement from the workforce. Dawn would like a phased exit from work, spending some time volunteering, with lots of time for travel and relaxation. But there are no guidelines as to how to make their ideal happen: there are no clear or financially viable paths for Lyle to return to school and Dawn's employer does not offer any form of gradual exit. And yet it seems clear both the couple and society would benefit enormously from Lyle entering the teaching profession and from Dawn gradually transitioning to community service.

Many Boomers are like Lyle and Dawn. Research shows most in this cohort don't want to retire completely, but hope to leave demanding and long-hour jobs. Some of those I interviewed use the word "trapped": wanting to cut back on the hours they work, they can't find a path to do so. In a study following employees over time, I discovered that workers in their fifties and sixties who had preferred to but were unable to scale back on their hours were more likely to retire completely over the ensuing two years.[55] Like Beth at 66 (the software developer) and Dawn at 55 (working in HR at a pharmaceutical company), they believe they have to retire cold turkey given the inflexibility of their jobs and the limited possibilities on the horizon.[56]

What Boomers want is a wide variety of options. The 2012 AARP survey of workers ages 46 to 74 shows that equal proportions—three in ten—say they will work in retirement because they enjoy working (31 percent) and for extra money (30 percent). Another one in five say it is "to have something interesting to do" (21 percent). Other reasons given are to stay physically active (14 percent), stay mentally active (11 percent), and support yourself (10 percent). But note this is a survey of older workers; those who wanted to retire or were forced out are not in the sample.

One institutional change in the United States—the Affordable Care Act—may well transform many Boomers' plans and expectations. Health care insurance has been traditionally tied to full-time employment. This made the years before turning 65, the age of eligibility for Medicare, particularly problematic. Many US Boomers, including those with health conditions, have continued in stressful jobs rather than retire, simply because they needed the health insurance.[57] Others would move to another full-time job offering health insurance rather than scale back or exit the workforce. But with affordable health care insurance now available, the choice set in encore adulthood is suddenly broader. For example, more Americans in their fifties and early sixties may now consider becoming entrepreneurs or consultants rather than remaining tethered to jobs that are too demanding, boring, or both until Medicare eligibility at age 65, just for the health insurance they provide.

Planning (or Falling Into) the Gendered Life Course

Decisions as to whether and when to shift down from full-time work cannot be understood apart from gender and the ways that gender has historically been embedded in mindsets and policies related to work, careers, families, and retirement.[58] The career mystique defining continuous work as the path to fulfillment became a full-blown part of the culture following World War II, hand-in-hand with the feminine mystique promoting homemaking as the path to women's fulfillment. Middle-class and unionized blue-collar life meant the pursuit of the lockstep career path for men, backed up by their wives' full-time homemaking. With the women's movement in the 1960s, 1970s, and 1980s came the push for opportunities available to men to be available to women. As women sought to escape the feminine mystique, they traded it for the seeming equality of the career mystique. Still, most men and women retained the conventional values of what it means to be the good wife, the good mother, and the good breadwinner/husband/father. Men's images as family breadwinners in the United States have persisted, but with several important changes. Few men and even fewer women have the backup of a full-time homemaker or wages to sustain a middle-class or even working-class lifestyle on just their salaries, which have failed to increase over time. Men's and women's jobs are now more intense, with digital technologies blurring the boundaries between work and the rest of life. Many feel, with good reason, more insecure in their jobs. Growing numbers of men have wives who earn more than they do. And, as is the case for Millennials and GenXers, many want to spend more time with their children, aging parents, friends, or, more broadly, to have a *life* as well as a job.

Women's lives have also become a lot more complicated. Women who lean into careers typically follow a career mystique plus—the plus being multiple family-care decisions and distractions. We have no ready model of the twenty-first-century ideal worker successfully combining career, care, and a personal life.

What has emerged instead is a new metaphor of balance as the hybrid solution, purportedly enabling women especially to have it all, balancing their work and family obligations by working less, aiming lower, and occasionally leaving work altogether. In other words, many women manage by *not* leaning in to their jobs. But the very language of balance reinforces the artificial division between paid work and unpaid family work, as well as the gender divide between the two. Women typically do the family balancing, while their husbands invest time, energy, and commitment in their jobs. The fact is, the mid-twentieth-century career mystique based on married men with no family care obligations is incompatible with contemporary family care. As a number of researchers have pointed out,[59] many Boomer women who followed the lock-step clockwork based on men's careers did not marry or else got divorced, or else had fewer children later in life, remained childfree, or else, in effect, as Arlie Hochschild documents, outsourced their lives, hiring other women to be the homemakers and caregivers for their families.[60] These adaptive strategies only underscore the fundamental structural disjuncture between family-care work and the ratcheting expectations of greedy careers perpetuating the gendered life course.[61]

The distinctive life courses of women and men in the conventional adult years lead to gender distinctions and disparities in encore adulthood. Research shows that the vast majority of men and women in their fifties and sixties engage in at least some preretirement planning, but men tend to be significantly more likely to plan.[62] What planning is done is more about finances than future lifestyles. The whole process of retirement planning and expectations is different for women than men, in part because of the historical differences in their attachment to the labor force. In the last century when men left their jobs they were exiting a role that had typically dominated their identities and their adult years.[63] That remains the case for most Boomer men today. By contrast, Boomer women typically come to retirement through different, more winding, paths.[64]

Now large numbers of women have careers to retire from, with the intersection of age and gender producing distinctive life-course patterns. Women age 50 and beyond are less likely than men to be married, more apt to be caring for infirm relatives, and more apt to have health problems, all of which frame their constraints and choices in the encore adult years. Women who moved in and out of the workforce or in and out of part-time work are disadvantaged in retirement and pension schemes.[65] Accordingly, I find that women are typically vague when asked about particular ages and dates for transitioning away from their current jobs; they are less sure about their future financial resources and more likely to link their exits to particular contingencies. Mary, for example, did not, as implied above, go straight from her HR job to her encore position with the same organization. She left the HR job she'd had for many years when her stepmother required hands-on care, and remained out of the workforce to care for her father. After both passed away, Mary was lucky to avoid the typical age discrimination faced by fifty-somethings in the job market, using personal connections to secure another HR job. Only after a number of years in that job could Mary begin planning and negotiating her encore career, moving to something she felt would provide a sense of purpose, of making a contribution to the broader community as well as the organization.

Women tend to consider their retirement decisions as not always controllable, partially because of the lower valuation of women's careers within heterosexual couples, because they have greater caregiving obligations, because of health conditions, and because there's less of an historical pattern established around women's retirement.[66] Once an emergency such as a health crisis or the needs of an elderly relative has passed, early exiters are often unable to find the types of full-time, flexible, or part-time jobs they want, with some never even hearing back from any job application. Some decide or default to volunteering or informally helping out neighbors and friends, traveling, or taking up new hobby. This even though some would like to take up—and many need—at least some paid work.

Do Couples Plan Together?

Also unique to today's and tomorrow's older workers and retirees is the fact that couples must now plan and strategize around two retirements, his and hers,[67] often within the context of caring for aging relatives or one another. Most Boomers are part of dual-earner couples, navigating two not always linear career paths and deciding about both their lives in this new life stage. Research as well as organizational and public policies and practices, however, still see these passages as individual, not paired, experiences. Planning programs when they are offered typically focus on individuals, not couples, and exclusively on retirement timing and retirement income, not on dynamic life planning, much less assisting Boomers in considering how they will spend the bonus years of life expectancy driving this encore to adulthood.

Europeans who have resources along with the generous safety net of public pensions and other supports find planning a bit easier. Marg, the elementary school teacher in Bonn, is married to Klaus, a physician. At age 59 and "with the entry of a partner into my medical practice," he developed a plan for gradually scaling back on his work obligations. His current workload is about three-fifths of what it was at the peak of his career. Now he takes "an annual reduction of my workload by four percent." His strategy involves:

> Initially cutting out one workday per month, typically a Wednesday. That week then consisted of only two sets of two workdays, which proved beneficial and increased my joy in work. In the second year I then cut out two days, which lead to two four day weeks each month. At age 64 I only had four-day workweeks...I found that it is better and a positive experience to reduce work with increasing age and declining health—in part because my load was very heavy, some 60 hours per week.

Klaus plans to take his "final step into retirement...in about three years. I'll be 69 years old then and my wife [Marg, the elementary school teacher] will also retire at that time." Note that Klaus and Marg are planning together, but with slightly different timetables: Marg, as we've seen, plans to "reduce my work hours at age 62 and retire completely at 64."

For some couples there might be a division of labor in planning the next stage, in the same way there is a division of labor in bill paying, housework, and laundry. That is, planning the next chapter of their lives may be like mowing the lawn—a "chore" typically assigned to one spouse. In fact, in past cohorts planning has been exactly like mowing the lawn, with men being the family planners, possibly due to men's more frequent roles as breadwinners and organization men,[68] and, as mentioned above, their careers typically having priority in dual-earner households.[69] Studies also show that women tend to have a lower sense of control or personal mastery and less free time,[70] meaning that like Scarlet O'Hara in *Gone with the Wind*, they take an "I'll think about that tomorrow" approach to the future. Since dual-earner wives may feel less equipped and more pressed for time in thinking about and planning their next steps, husbands' plans might well shape wives' plans and expectations, but not vice versa.

Importantly, research has also found that wives in dual-earner, middle-class couples tend to coordinate whatever retirement plans they have made to better mesh with their husbands' plans. A study of people in European countries by Kim Denaeghel, Dimitri Mortelmans, and Annelies Borghgraef at the University of Antwerp in Belgium finds that men's circumstances shape their wives' retirement timing.[71] A 2010 MetLife Survey found that only one in three US women (34 percent) ages 50 to 70 said they are most responsible for financial and retirement planning in their households, compared to six in 10 men (61 percent).[72] Many therefore expect to retire earlier or later than they'd like if the choice were solely up to them.[73] Other things come into play. For example, a 2013 survey of the oldest US Boomers—those born in 1946—found a third (33 percent) had inherited from their parents, an average of $110,000, something that can change retirement planning.[74]

Katie (age 58) and Jerry (age 60) have planned together for the timing of their career exits, but not for encore adulthood. Jerry is a computer control specialist, while Katie is a hospital nutritionist. They expect Jerry to retire first, with Katie supporting the household for six months and then retiring also. They plan lots of travel right away. Katie defines their goal as "to be able to retire young enough, when we still have our heath and to be able to do the things we want to do." This follows Kahneman and Tverksy's theory about making decisions based on loss-avoidance—here, the potential loss of their health and ability to enjoy travel is shaping their plans. Katie talks about people she has met working in the hospital, seriously ill patients who would say things like "I was going to do so and so, but then I got this disease and now I can't do that," or "I waited until I retired and within two months, three months, can't do that anymore." Still, apart from planning their treks around the world over first six months, Katie and Jerry have not thought much about how to spend the many years they will likely be retired together.

This was common among prior cohorts: few men and even fewer women planned for life after retirement, focusing exclusively on financial planning, with the possible exception of golfers setting lots of tee times. But things are changing. Many contemporary wives seem more likely to plan for future lifestyles, while their husbands continue to be more likely to plan financially. Research finds three factors related to both husbands' and wives' degree of planfulness: a heavy workload in their current jobs, a sense of control or mastery, and an adequate income. Women with greater schedule control and flexibility as well as women with health problems are more apt to plan for what comes next. Men working in the private sector are less apt to plan than those in governmental or nonprofit sectors.[75]

Looking specifically at the leading edge (born 1946–1954) of the large Boomer cohort when they were in their fifties,[76] the evidence suggests that unlike previous cohorts, wives' planfulness now has a positive influence on husbands' planfulness, but husbands' planfulness does not predict their wives' planfulness. This may reflect the engagement of Boomer wives in their own careers, and, consequently, in thinking about and planning for their own encore years. Two factors positively predict leading-edge Boomer wives' planfulness: their age and their sense of mastery. For this Boomer group, husbands still tend to plan for and worry about their financial futures, while their wives are starting to engage in both financial and lifestyle planning.

When interviewed in their forties, younger, trailing-edge Boomers (in this study, those born 1955–1964) appeared to plan on their own, not as couples. Traditional factors—education, income, mastery, health—did not predict whether these Boomer husbands planned in their forties, but trailing-edge wives with a sense of mastery and income adequacy tended to plan more, as did wives in poor health. As time goes on, given the uncertainties and risks one or both partners now face in our global digital economy, Boomer husbands and wives' plans and expectations about the future may be developing as possible contingencies independently of one another.[77]

Todd and Karen represent just such a case of independent planning for the future. Karen (now 68) is older than Todd, who is her second husband, albeit of over 30 years. She left the workforce 10 years ago. She now has some health problems, but spends time with their two granddaughters. Todd, also married for the second time, is now 62 and finds it difficult to anticipate when he will actually retire from what is already an encore job: the nonprofit consultancy for K-12 education he started after two decades in higher education. Todd plans to begin drawing on Social Security at age 67, scaling back on his work hours at that time. Asked about when he will retire completely, Todd says he "doesn't see that happen[ing]." He says he's in peak health, running several miles every day, and, when asked about his ideal lifestyle he says, "it is pretty much here." This couple's independent planning points to the importance of age differences between partners. Karen was ready to retire long before Todd had even thought about his own future retirement, which even now seems far away.

My research shows that couples where one is employed and one is retired report the greatest marital conflict, and Karen and Todd are finding less and less in common.[78] On the whole, though, men tend to be happy when their wives are not working, since it gives them a full-time homemaker. Their wives feel very differently, though, for precisely the same reason. Women also tend to be unhappy when they are working and their husbands are fully retired, feeling that their husbands do too little around the house. Their husbands by contrast, enumerate all the household tasks they are performing.

Many wives worry about having their husbands around so much when both retire completely from the workforce. Dual-earner couples are used to being together for just portions of the day and week. A dual-retirement may mean adjusting to less alone time, planning around two encore schedules that may be packed with caregiving, friends, and volunteer work, or even feeling supervised by one's spouse. One woman described *her* ideal retirement as "having my *husband* work part time." She went on to explain that having him at home all the time means less free time for her, as she will be busy fetching him coffee, watching his favorite television programs, and staying around the house when she'd rather be out with friends.

Having one or both spouses move out of the labor force completely is clearly a major transition affecting couples' relationships. Happily, once both are retired from the workforce for a couple of years, couples seem to develop a new rhythm to their lives and their relationship.

Singles' Plans and Possibilities

A growing number of Boomers—one third—are divorced, widowed, separated, or never married singles.[79] Their situations and experiences vary depending on their gender (see table 2.1 in appendix B). For example, more Boomer women (38.7 percent) than men (32.1 percent) were in this nonmarried category in 2014. And more women are likely to be widowed (7.3 to 2.6 percent in 2014), even as more men are likely to never have married (11.2 percent to 8.9 percent). Looking just at the leading-edge Boomers (those born 1946–1954), only six in 10 (60.9 percent) women were married and living with their spouses in 2014. Two in 10 were either divorced (18.4 percent) or separated (2.7 percent), and one in 10 was widowed (10.2 percent). Even fewer (6.7 percent) had never married. One in five (20.3 percent) lived alone.

By contrast, seven in 10 (71.3 percent) men in the leading-edge group were married with their spouses present; only one in six were either divorced (13.9 percent) or separated (1.4 percent), and only 3.9 percent were widowed. Fewer (7.1 percent) of the leading-edge men never married, and slightly fewer (17 percent) of the leading-edge men live alone compared to women (20.3 percent). The biggest contrasts between leading-edge and the trailing-edge Boomers are that a greater proportion of trailing-edge men (14.4 percent) and women (11 percent) have never married and fewer (1.4 percent men, 4.7 percent women) are widowed.[80]

Nonmarried Boomer women and men differ in expected and unexpected ways from each other and from those who are partnered (see table 4.1 in appendix B.) For example, consider the interplay between gender and marital status in terms of personal income. Married women had an average personal income of $33,936 in 2013, compared to married men's personal income of $66,788. There is a disparity, but a smaller one, between nonmarried men and women in personal income ($41,035 compared to $34,279).

Additional difficulties faced by nonmarried Boomers are a consequence, in part, of marriage being a normative role, part of the expected twentieth-century lockstep life course. Moreover, marriage typically provides a built-in source of social and financial support. Marrieds are advantaged in mental and physical health including low disability, in income and other resources, and in prospects for future income streams.[81] Jenn, the PR strategist, was devastated when she was laid off, but had the financial and emotional back-up of her husband, Claude (chapter 3). Contrast her experience with that of Colleen, single longer than she was married, who confidently left her job because of a bad boss but then found herself in a new city and state without financial or emotional support. Still, Colleen has plenty of resources, compared to most divorced, singles, and widowed in her cohort. Nonmarried Boomers in the United States are more apt to be below the official poverty line (22.7 percent nonmarried women, 20 percent nonmarried men, compared to 4.8 percent wives, 5.2 percent husbands). And more apt to be receiving SSI (Supplemental Security Income)[82]—7.6 percent nonmarrieds, compared to only 1.3 percent marrieds (see tables 2.1 and 2.2 in appendix B). Single, widowed, and divorced women ages 65 and older tend to rely on Social Security for fully half of their income. For some, it's all they can count on.[83]

Bill, the financial advisor discussed in chapter 2, and Joe, the construction worker discussed earlier in this chapter, are both divorced and coming up with encore plans on their own. But the difference in their financial resources is striking: Bill can think about leaving, while Joe is trying hard to hang on to his job.

Conclusions

Boomers can expect to live long lives and want to enjoy them along the way.[84] Their parents had little to plan for—retirement was an expected transition to full-time leisure, to be taken as soon as possible. Today, as with Millennials in the emerging adult years, nothing is as expected, or else expectations shift with changes at work, at home, or in workers' health or that of their parents or their partners.

Decision-making reflects a combination of choice, mindsets, resources, risks, and others' circumstances. This underscores the importance of dynamic planning for various possible scenarios. Women and men ages 50 to 70 interviewed in 2010 anticipated living to ages 85.3 and 83.3 respectively. Moreover, two in five women (39 percent) anticipated living into their nineties, as did one in five men.[85]

They also don't feel "old." A 2012 MetLife survey of those born in 1946—the oldest Boomers—found one in five feel they won't be old until they are in their eighties or older, with an overall average of 12.5 years before this oldest group feels old. Boomers of all ages recognize they have the time for a second run, an encore to adulthood. But they plan on time shifting in myriad ways: leaving some jobs, entering or re-entering others, scaling up to more meaningful work, or scaling back to fewer job demands; retiring to start a business, moving into volunteering, or working in the social sector; providing care for their grandchildren, parents, or husbands; traveling; or simply adopting a healthier lifestyle. Whether and when they improvise a new life path depends on their own proclivities and the options and constraints they face. Unlike the transition to retirement for most in the 1970s, there is no one way.

Given the growing uncertainties around both job security and retirement income, along with their extended life expectancy and care-providing expectations, Boomers in encore adulthood need to move from retirement planning to dynamic life planning, anticipating various contingencies. They would do well to begin planning early, both financially and for the lives they want. Some are not planning at all, given their uncertainty and ambivalence about what's next. Of course, plans may shift. Don, for example, left the life of total retirement he planned after only a few weeks, taking on something short-term, interesting and meaningful: another stint at his state agency. But he swore he planned for five years to stop work cold turkey. Colleen planned to retire at 67 or 68, but left her job unexpectedly at age 64 when she got a new boss who didn't appreciate her. Gray (the VP) gave no thought to retirement, but found himself suddenly retired when the company was sold. What is clear is that most can count on a longer life course, but that is about all. And yet couples may well live together in these encore adult years longer than they were together in conventional adulthood. And singles may spend more time in encore adulthood than they did in previous marriages or previous jobs.

Planning for various possibilities takes on heightened importance in times of rapid social dislocations, when taken-for-granted scripts no longer fit. How can adults of all ages prepare for the decisions they will confront throughout the evolving twenty-first-century life course? This is a challenge for Millennials in emerging adulthood as well as for Boomers in encore adulthood and GenXers in the middle. Life-course sociologists like John Clausen point to the value of "planful competence," observing variability in the degree to which individuals and groups—including couples—not only make decisions in the present but also develop expectations, goals, and strategies for the future.[86] Psychologists Kimberly Prenda and Margie Lachman theorize that planning may well be an outgrowth of a sense of being in charge of one's life. In these unsettled times, planning may help people structure and take control of events, both predictable and unpredictable.[87] However, Boomers with little ability to shape what happens next are unlikely to believe they can effectively make decisions about and plan for the future. Joe, for instance, can't imagine a time when he can ever retire, even though he knows he can't keep up with the younger workers on his construction team. He avoids thinking about what's next in his life.

Studies and statistics also show that educational achievement, key to planfulness, is important in shaping lifestyles and life quality in encore adulthood. A college degree promotes a future orientation and has historically been the gateway to occupations with the kinds of pensions and savings arrangements conducive to planning. Todd and Karen's education and income have meant that she could stop working in her late fifties and he could plan and then move to his encore career as a social entrepreneur. Those with less education, including many blacks and Hispanics, miss out on the income and rewards, such as better health and higher employability, but also on that feeling of control over their futures. Recall that a significant portion of African American and Hispanic American older workers hope to start their own businesses after retirement, but whether this will come about is not at all clear. They are more apt to time shift because of health difficulties or layoffs, which, together with few resources, limit planning and the ability to execute their ideal encores. A college education is no guarantee of security, either. Jenn's education and high-status job didn't help when she was laid off out of the blue. She eventually found an encore job, but one that uses neither her skills nor her education.

Women have a generally lower sense of mastery or control over their lives than do men. Often without their having planned on these exigencies, they tend to take up the informal family-care work for their parents, in-laws, adult children and grandchildren, spouses, and siblings, all of which shapes their encore adult years. Luckily, age itself can actually bolster a sense of mastery for both men and women, especially as older Boomers—those on the leading edge—feel they are in fact taking control of their lives. In the Work, Family, and Health Network study of a group of high-tech Boomers whose firm was being merged with another corporation,[88] we found that those who subsequently retired reported feeling better. An example is Kumar, who left earlier than he had expected, something that is quite common:

> My last year at [the company] was the worst in my 38 years with that company. Since leaving I feel wonderful and my life is wonderful. Best move I ever made was leaving that company. I planned on staying another two years, but the manager I reported to and the person he put in place to run our team were the worst. How some people are selected to be managers is beyond me. Taking my concerns to HR was a total waste of time. They gave me no support. I am grateful every day that I was retirement eligible and I could leave. Life is wonderful for me now.

Katarina, who also retired after the takeover feels an increased sense of control:

> I think that my approach to retirement has made my personal life wonderful and kept me healthy. When people asked me what I was going to *do* after retirement, I always said that I didn't know. That wasn't what was important to me. I wanted to focus on how I wanted to *be*, not what I wanted to *do*. I wanted to be relaxed, stress free, healthy, present in the moment, creative, and peaceful, and to feel like I was making a difference in the lives of others—that is, my family members, friends, and people in the larger community. I decided that those things would constitute my decision process for anything I *did* after retirement. I only do those things that contribute to how I want to *be* and *feel*. I say "no" to anything else, with no regrets.

Having resources shaped Katarina's and Kumar's ability to improvise and customize the encore years. But they also responded to push factors. Like Kumar and Katarina, men and women in jobs with heavy workloads are apt to plan more, and difficult managers or bosses like Colleen's make retirement begin to look like a welcome respite, with exit dates moved up. Similarly, Boomers with health difficulties typically exit their current jobs earlier than expected, as did Sally, the special ed teacher, in order to regain or maintain their health. Almost half (47 percent) of the oldest Boomers (born in 1964) reported in 2013 having a major health challenge in the past year, even though most (82 percent) are positive about their health.[89]

The life-course concept of cycles of control,[90] combined with the stress process model,[91] points to how particular life events, including retirement, may be both a stressor and a respite from stress. As figure 4.2 shows, a sense of control ratchets up when resources exceed demands or needs, going down when needs exceed available resources. These cycles of claims, resources, and

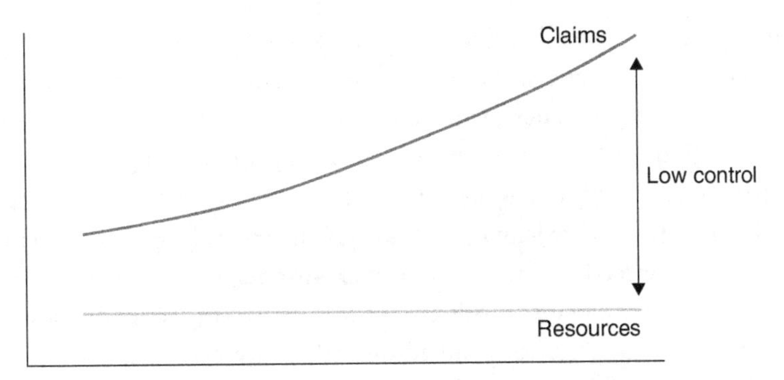

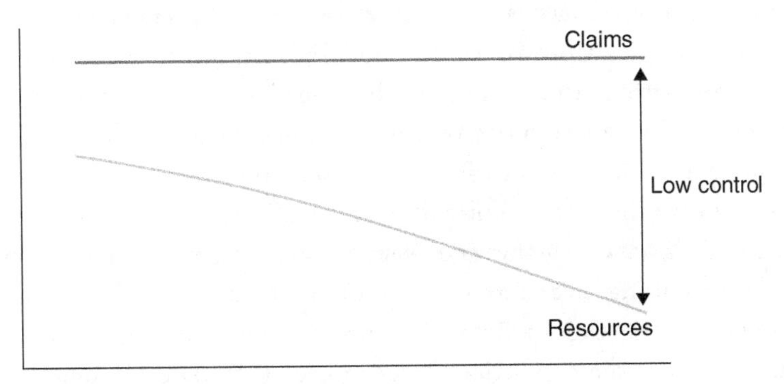

FIGURE 4.2. Cycles of Control

control occur throughout the life course, with some groups more consistently feeling in control than others. Cycles of control as well as a sense of well-being or distress are related to whether exiting, remaining, or re-entering work or retirement are voluntary or involuntary time shifts. Voluntary or involuntary transitions predict how in control people feel over their lives and choices. Changes at work or in home life may create cycles of more of less control over time.

Boomers—as individuals, couples, singles, coworkers, and friends—are improvising encore adulthood, often by contingency planning for alternative scenarios that fit their very variable situations. Most of these plans involve some sort of time shifting away from the conventional lockstep life course. Todd plans to never retire from the nonprofit business he started, his full-time encore job. Joe hopes to never retire, but only because he can't afford it, even though his body would surely be grateful for the opportunity to stop the physical labor of construction work. Dawn wants to move into some form of civic engagement, but can't figure out how to make a gradual transition out of an inflexible workplace. Lyle wants to go back to school in order to teach high school history, but can't afford to do so. Beth wants a gradual retirement but can't make it happen in her current company, so she is looking elsewhere for a not-so-big job. Colleen took control by quitting and moving, but can't find the part-time or full-time job she needs to make ends meet, suspecting age discrimination. Neither Jenn nor Claude planned on exiting their career jobs, but Jenn was forced out and Claude took advantage of a generous buyout package. He feels good; she feels bitter, though is trying to let the bitterness go. Denny and Becky both planned on early retirements—just not for the part about caring for their grandsons.

Encore time shifting projects are often the result of personal plans and expectations, but can happen out of the blue. The institutions of both work and retirement continue to fluctuate, much of our health is unpredictable, and new bosses, new opportunities, or new family needs may push or pull people into and out of the workforce. These and other improvisational plans are just that—improvisations that shift with events and exigencies. What seem like personal decisions of whether and when to leave, stay, or do some unconventional time shifting have enormous implications for social welfare costs, labor markets, and communities, along with the health and well-being of this significant segment of the population. Three in five of the oldest Boomers (born 1946) were already retired in 2013; with over half of these retirees (54 percent) saying they retired earlier than expected.[92] Boomers' plans and life in encore adulthood matter for individual and family life quality, but also for society.

5

Improvising Work, Civic Engagement, Retirement

MY HUSBAND DICK spent a quarter of a century at the Department of Labor in Washington, DC. An encore job at Cornell University's School of Industrial and Labor Relations lasted for five years or so before he declared he was ready to time shift again, this time out of paid work all together. Given that I, 13 years younger, was still in the prime of my career, I worried about him sitting around the house. We talked about what he would do. He didn't play golf or bridge, wasn't interested in a new hobby, and didn't want another job. He coveted time to read and the flexibility to travel with me on business trips and vacations. But he also recognized he needed something to structure and occupy his time, a way to feel useful and to "give back."

After considering various options, Dick reinvented himself as a volunteer, focusing on helping the next generation by teaching first-graders to read five mornings a week at a grade school down the street. Everyone was happy. One young girl called him "the most perfect person in the world," and other children (whose parents surely wondered how they had become friends) would shout "Hi, Dick!" as we walked in downtown Ithaca. Dick felt a real sense of purpose, saying this was "his best job ever." When I accepted a position at the University of Minnesota, he quickly found a similar spot in Minneapolis' Inter-district Downtown School, this time helping third-graders with math.

Dick's portfolio of time shifting—first to a new, different, and challenging part-time job at Cornell and then as a volunteer—are emblematic of the ways encore adulthood can be a time of personal and social renewal, distinct from both full-time career employment and full-time retirement. His experience also shows how customized the time shifts in this new life stage can be, encompassing several reinventions over time.

This chapter documents how individuals and couples are improvising, responding to the challenges, risks, and opportunities of life today, and in so doing helping to define the contours of an evolving twenty-first-century life course. The bonus years of extended life expectancy are not coming at the end of life, adding to years of disability and decline. Neither are they extending the middle adulthood period of raising families and building careers. Despite the uncertainties and ambiguities of this new encore adult stage, many Boomers—the largest, most educated cohort in history until their children, the Millennials, came along—feel on the edge of their career- and family-building years but not yet done.

This chapter also charts the unevenness of this evolving paradigm of a more voluntarily customized life course. What many want, but can't always find, are chances to reset the time clocks of their lives, often in the form of different combinations of flexible, frequently less-than-full-time work, volunteering, learning, caring, and leisure, including more healthy lifestyles. Despite the absence of institutionalized options for such configurations, growing numbers of Boomers are indeed resetting their lives and their identities, making them up as they go.

Millennials are participating in the same paradigm shift but at the beginning of adulthood, making choices about schooling, partners, parenting, and jobs in the face of unraveling established transition-to-adulthood norms and career paths. Along with GenXers, both Millennials and Boomers find themselves navigating life choices at a point in history when the standardized social contract has disappeared, promulgating uncertainty, in the United States at least, regarding employment and economic security, along with retirement timing and retirement security.[1] We define ourselves by what we do. And yet neither Boomers in encore adulthood nor Millennials in emerging adulthood want identities exclusively tied to career work.[2]

Chapter 4 focused on Boomers' plans and expectations, as well as the dislocations of unexpected events. In this chapter I describe their actual time shifting of work, retirement, civic engagement, and leisure—the improvisational pathways Boomers are taking through encore adulthood. Sometimes they are time shifting in response to past experiences, such as watching fathers who worked too long or retired too early go downhill, or divorced or widowed mothers worry about money. Sometimes they are responding to the lay of the land, such as watching their own or coworkers' jobs disappear, a husband's health deteriorate, or the windfall of an unexpected inheritance. Like Millennials at the beginning of adulthood, Boomers are finding past scripts or guidelines simply don't fit the uncertainties, risks, and promise of this new phase of the life course.

Four Pathways through Encore Adulthood

Prior generations of men and a few women also made decisions about how to live out their later lives. But the sheer pace of change in what MIT professors

Brynjolfsson and McAfee call the second machine age, combined with extended longevity and delays and declines in social protections,[3] make the experiences of Boomers feel unique. Widening disparities in income, savings, and health translate into widening disparities in possible paths.

As we saw in chapter 4, Boomers don't plan much financially, but are much more likely to plan for their financial needs than to anticipate how they will spend their time during these bonus years.[4] And, as Boomers, GenXers, and Millennials can all testify, plans are often upended. With no cultural traditions or role models to guide them, many are improvising, time shifting their own pathways.

The point I make throughout this book: many Boomers are thinking about or have already moved away from the roles that occupied most of their adult lives—active parenting and full-time, career-related jobs—but do not consider themselves anywhere near old age. Medical advances and healthy lifestyles help them both prevent and manage most chronic health difficulties, and middle-class Boomers typically feel in relatively good health. They are looking forward, not back, aiming to recalibrate this stage of their lives and reinvent themselves in exciting new ways. While this typically includes retiring from jobs they have spent years in, some are also seeking or imagining ways to configure work, family, community connections, and leisure that will provide them with a new lease on life. This new encore adult stage is being fashioned out of the micro-level time shifts of individuals and families, as people with skills and enthusiasm like Dick pursue meaningful engagement by helping others, taking on new types of work, and enjoying a bit more free time.[5] This is the promise of encore adulthood for those with the resources to make it happen. For others—also enacting micro-level time shifts—the future is a big question mark, replete with anxiety about keeping needed jobs, having sufficient income, and worries about poor health.

One Boomer segment aims to prolong their working years purely for economic reasons. They simply can't afford not to work. Others may expect one scenario, but find they are not immune to layoffs, market fluctuations, and economic uncertainty. Still, paralleling Frank Furstenberg's and Jeffrey Arnett's conception of emerging adulthood as a new period of exploration and opportunity for those in their twenties,[6] other Boomers with the ability to do so are time shifting by postponing exits from challenging, purpose-driven jobs or looking for flexible and less demanding work that challenges them in new ways. Others seek purpose by taking up unpaid volunteering or engaging in what are often low-paying jobs in the social and public sectors, using their skills and talents so they can continue to grow, give back to their communities, and promote the common good. This can also be a time to downsize homes and possessions, relocate, reignite old interests or take up new ones—sometimes in a spirit of personal renewal, other times as pragmatic decision-making. From civic engagement to involvement in the lives of their grandchildren, Boomers in the encore adult years are doing just about anything but taking up residence in a rocking chair.

Cost, constrained opportunity, and family or personal care demands restrict the choices available to Boomers who are poor or in serious debt, have major health conditions, have limited and outdated skill sets, or are deep in care work—for aging parents, infirm spouses, adult children in need, and grandchildren, among others. Further, people over 50 are discriminated against and many lack the experience and networks that would gain them entry into new workplaces, much less onto civic boards. Despite the absence of institutionalized options for flexible and shifting combinations of working, learning, caring, volunteering, and pursuing healthy lifestyles, growing numbers of Boomers are indeed resetting their lives and their identities, making them up as they go.

As I have underscored throughout, rigid mid-twentieth-century time infrastructures—40 or more hour, five-day workweeks, set career assumptions, the built-in age segmentation undergirding the tripartite education/work/retirement linear lockstep—narrow the options of Boomers. But so do their preferences. Some want to exit the workforce as soon as possible, while others cannot afford anything less than full-time work. Still others want to time shift in order to combine some elements of work, family care, education, civic engagement, and leisure. As is the case with Millennials, Boomers may lack blueprints or institutional supports, but are engaging in wide varieties of improvisational time shifting when it is possible or necessary to do so.

Based on surveys and in-depth interviews over the last fifteen years,[7] I have identified four broad, patterned pathways through encore adulthood. Even as Millennials are improvising the new early adulthood, Boomers are improvising the new encore adult years, sometimes beginning on one path and then shifting to another as they adapt to unexpected exigencies or opportunities, or else sense that they might be on the wrong track. Others may seek change, but find the train has already left the station.

Pathway #1. Neotraditional Time Shifting

First is a neotraditional retirement exit, often earlier than conventional retirement age. Significant numbers of Boomers want this early version of total retirement, especially those in stressful jobs, those with heavy family-care responsibilities, a retired spouse, or their own health difficulties, and those who want a more relaxed lifestyle.

The fact is, despite governmental efforts to encourage delayed retirement, most older workers are still exiting the workforce early, in their fifties or early sixties. Over half the oldest US Boomers, those born in 1946, are retired, and 43 percent are already opting for early reduced Social Security benefits.[8] In fact, a third of college-educated, leading-edge Boomers were taking Social Security in 2014, as were a fourth of those with just a high school education. Three in 10 of those without a high school degree received Social Security (and 11 percent qualified for SSI benefits;[9] see tables 5.1–5.4 in appendix B).

Boomers following this neotraditional path often retire from their jobs before they are eligible for full social security benefits because of health conditions that make their jobs difficult or impossible. Others are voluntary time shifters with government or private-sector pensions, and those less interested in leaning into their careers by pursuing more income or climbing occupational ladders than in leaning out to less stressful and healthier lifestyles. Many following this pathway seek to travel and have time for other leisure pursuits, including making lifestyle moves such as downsizing from large homes (and lawns) in suburbs to city apartments and condos, or moving to warmer climates. These are neotraditional improvisations in that they retain the conventional one-way exit from the career job and into full-time retirement, but time shift exactly when this departure occurs. The risk here for such voluntary early exit time shifters is that those who change their minds later on may find it difficult to re-enter the labor market.

Martha made just such a neotraditional exit this year, at age 57, a couple of years after her husband passed away. A package handler for a large delivery service, she has been planning this exit for five years:

> Into my 50s, I started paying attention to the contract language and realized that after age 57 with over 30 years of service, I could leave with health insurance at a reduced rate from the company.

Martha is but one of many in the United States who told me that health insurance has been key in their decision-making around retirement. How this will change with the Affordable Care Act is yet to be seen. Her exit also shows how important continuous full-time employment is in making Boomers eligible for pensions. Though this is changing for more recent cohorts, few women Boomers are like Martha, in that she has 30 years of seniority, having worked steadily for one organization. Many are more like Jessie (chapter 2), with decidedly unstandardized career paths, in and out of the labor market, in and out of a range of occupations.

Multiple circumstances can precipitate the decision to retire early. In addition to her pension eligibility and health insurance, Martha felt the introduction of new automotive technologies had changed her job and her worth to the firm. Early on, she felt challenged by having to memorize addresses and where to put the packages.

> So you would take a look and say, "This goes into middle yellow, this goes into top brown." It was within the last, maybe around 2000, that the whole knowledge-based value that I had changed because they came up with a little sticker that tells a sorter that it goes to top yellow. It would say that on the sticker. So it had gone through a scanner somewhere that knew how to put that information on the sticker. My value as someone who had knowledge went away. Anyone could do my job after that sticker showed up. That was a game changer.

And her job, which was always inflexible, became much more demanding. Newly hired and much younger supervisors made sure of that:

> They would be like drill sergeants. "Hurry up, you are not doing this fast enough." That was constant. That was getting progressively worse... There was no job satisfaction, nothing like that. It just became an endurance. That's all it was at the end.

Neotraditional retirement, of course, does not preclude social engagement. Martha is currently improvising by taking a class at a local community college and considering volunteering.

> That's really feasible just because the social connection is totally needed. I think that is a really integral part of a healthy retirement—that is, staying socially connected. That is one reason I took the class. And it proved to be really awesome that way. I live in a remote, rural setting... so the social, being involved with people, I think is important.

Martha is well aware that the social contract discussed in chapter 2 worked for her, but is disappearing:

> I know I did my part working those years as required, and then my promise was a retirement and a pension. I did what I needed to do to get

> to the end goal. But when I see things like what is happening in Detroit, where the same people did their part and all of a sudden the structure is saying "Detroit is in bankruptcy. We are going to have to go after the workers' pensions." If they get away with it—and I don't see how they will not—that will be setting a precedent that other places will look at.... And if they did that along with Social Security, if they get to go after that, then I mean what happens? The middle class is at such a dangerous point.

A surprising number of Boomers in the United States are following this neotraditional time-shifting strategy. Consider the leading edge of Boomers—those born 1946 to 1954, who were ages 59 to 68 in 2014 (see figure 5.1 and in appendix B tables 5.1–5.4 by educational level).[10] Three in 10 (31.9 percent) of the college-educated women who didn't work last year call themselves retired,[11] as do a fourth (25 percent) of college-educated men. A few more leading-edge Boomer women (35.2 percent) and men (28.5 percent) with only a high school diploma check the "retired" box. Similar proportions of leading-edge Boomers with less than a high school degree are retired (33.6 percent of the women and 27.3 percent of the men). But note that others are not in the labor force whether they define themselves as retired or not. For example, in 2014, 28 percent of all Boomers with less

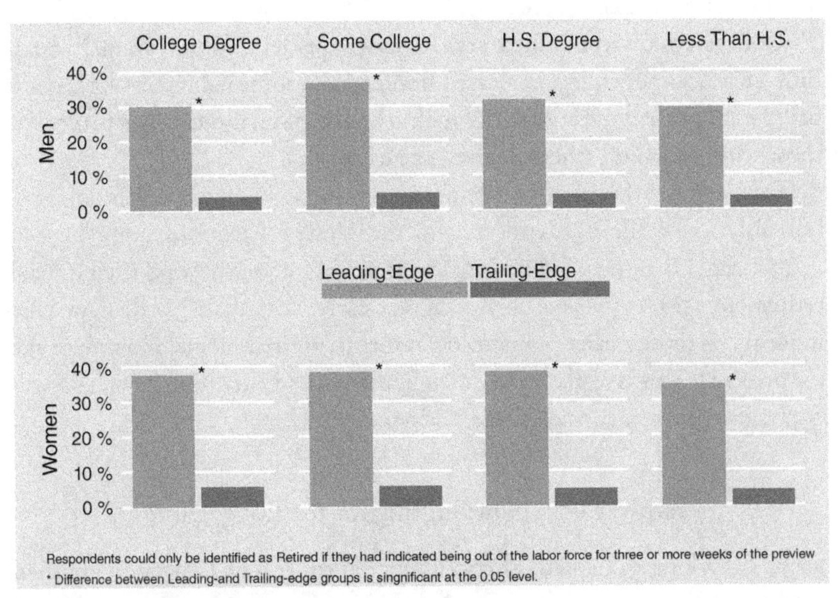

FIGURE 5.1. Percent of Leading- and Trailing-Edge Boomers Who Reported Being Retired in 2014 by Gender and Education

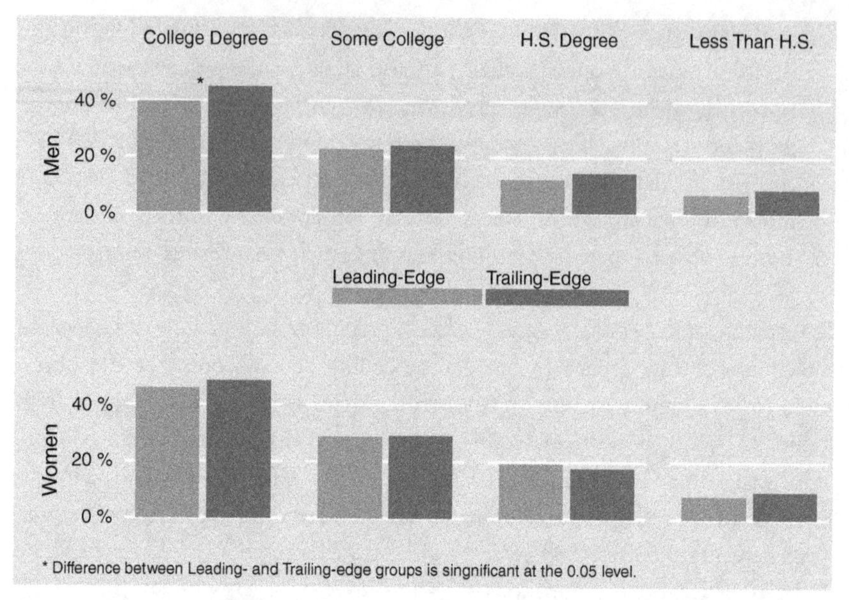

FIGURE 5.2. Percent of Leading- and Trailing-Edge Boomers Who Reported Volunteering in 2013 by Gender and Education

than a high school diploma report never working last year because they were ill or disabled, compared to 14 percent of high school grads and only 3 percent of those with a college degree.

College-educated Boomers are also more apt to be volunteering. In 2013, fully 46 percent of college-educated Boomers did some volunteer work, compared to 18 percent of those with a high school diploma, and only 8 percent of those without a high school degree (s.ee figure 5.2).

Early exit neotraditional retirement is not just an American phenomenon. For instance, while it is true that in the United Kingdom more women (40 percent) than men (19 percent) work at least a year beyond their official retirement ages, 25 percent of women take early retirement.[12] British men are more apt to retire earlier (42 percent) rather than their official retirement age (33 percent). This is explained by men in the United Kingdom having greater coverage by private pensions than women.

Pathway #2. Time Shifting for the Long Game

Second is a long game path of continuing on the job or moving to another, working well past conventional retirement age, often without a specific goal set for retiring or a final exit from the workforce. This can involve various improvisations: remaining in the career job, becoming an entrepreneur, or moving from building careers and bonuses to using one's skills, service, and expertise in the social sector.

Despite all the public discussions about the need for working longer and social security incentives designed for encouraging older workers to do so, the long game path in career jobs remains a road less traveled. Still, for an important, if small, subset of Boomers, working past traditional retirement ages in one's career job represents business as usual.

Michelle, at age 64, is a case in point. She is divorced and living with a new partner. She works as a case manager and would like to retire in two years, but doesn't feel it is financially possible. Events like her divorce and decisions along the way—especially buying a new house—have limited her degrees of freedom:

> I wish I wouldn't have bought a house when housing was so high. So I am one of those near retirement that is stuck with a big mortgage. And so, if I can't retire at the age of 66 or 68, it is because of that home I bought when houses skyrocketed.... Every month, because my Social Security is not going to be as much as my house payment is, I am going to have to pull out of my retirement account to pay for my house payment, or, if I sold it, pay for my rent or whatever.

Michelle feels resilient, but is unwillingly playing the long game because she lacks the resources to do anything else.

By contrast, an important segment of Boomers—often in professional jobs—love their jobs and would like to continue working as long as possible.[13] Some in this long game path might hope to scale back a bit on their workloads and to have more flexibility, but do not see retirement on their horizons for many years, if ever. Others continue to lean in to their career jobs. Postponing their exits is a way of retaining their identities, and they are truly in it for the long game. Many feel they *are* what they *do*, and can't imagine life without work. Recall Mary, age 62, who switched from her human resource job in public health to another high-status encore job for the same nonprofit (chapter 4). She has no plans to retire:

> My identity is wrapped up in work. Many of my friends are retired, but they seem self-absorbed, disorganized. People having too much free time are all about "me." I need to be more stimulated.

Even though their same-age friends and coworkers may be scaling back or leaving jobs, some Boomers following the long game strategy are putting in even more hours and doubling down on their work. For some this is because of the nature of their jobs. For others, working more intensively is a strategy to increase their value, a way of hopefully reducing the risks of being laid off. Rob is a merchandise planner for a large retail organization who feels he can't retire until he is eligible for full Social Security benefits:

> I am in the first group of Baby Boomers based on Social Security that can't retire until I am 66, instead of sixty-five. I really do not expect to be able to retire until I am sixty-six. If you want to ask the question when would I *like* to retire? Well, it would be May 1 of next year. I would be 59 and a half and could start drawing my 401(k). Unfortunately with the cost of medical coverage now, that would be impossible.

Rob is working hard, hoping he can keep his job until he is 66:

> Hopefully I will stay employed for that entire seven years.... I have made [it through] all the cuts up to now, and I hope that is because I do a good enough job and I am doing what they are looking for me to do. As time goes on I just—to be completely honest, I just hope to stay employed for the next seven years and 13 days.

Rob is in the long game in a risk environment replete with periodic cuts in his organization's workforce; his resilience hinges on keeping his job for another "seven years and 13 days" so he can qualify for full Social Security benefits. Whether the Affordable Care Act will change his calculus is unknown. He was interviewed after it launched in 2014, but doesn't seem to see it as a consideration. Unlike others who derive a sense of purpose and renewal from their work, Rob represents a group of Boomers who are postponing any personal development or renewal until they get through a requisite number of working years.

Getting an encore job is another way of pursuing the long game that can both postpone resetting identities, provide purpose, and improve finances. Debra is in just such a situation. She left her career job as a consultant because of a round of health problems and related surgeries. Simultaneously, she was undergoing separation and divorce. We interviewed her as part of our study of people involved in SHIFT,[14] a small Minnesota nonprofit for people in midlife transition. She began looking for work once she finally regained her health, and she feels fortunate to have found a full-time encore job as an office administrator. During the job search Debra was regularly getting together with a group of women (ages 50 plus) all looking for work. But unlike the others, she took a very pragmatic approach to finding any job:

> Many of those women held up for their kind of dream job career path and, to my knowledge, only one of them is employed except for me. A couple of them went back to school. And I just looked at it practically and said, "I need a job with benefits. So I am going to do what I have to do and try and find something that is pleasant." And I was successful in doing that. But I think I was viewed... with a little bit of disdain perhaps. I was going to be an office administrator. But, hey, I am working and bringing home a paycheck and like going to work every day, so that is all right.

She plans to keep working:

> Oh, I am going to work until at least 66, and, if I am healthy and still enjoying [it], I will probably work beyond that. My current position, I would have the option of maybe going part time or being an on-call if I just wanted to work for a little extra spending cash in retirement.

Even though she is working full time, Debra does not have to put in long hours, and so is free to pursue other interests:

> One of the things I like about my job right now is that my hours are capped. I can't work more than 42 1/2 hours, so it does leave me time to have a life.... So, many of the things I would rather have pursued as a career when I was younger or at a different place in my life, I can now do on a volunteer basis. So I am doing a lay care ministry training class, where you do hospital visitations or grief support, that kind of thing.

Debra exemplifies the resilience and renewal of Boomers in the face of the risks of this life stage, especially for women. She spent her life prioritizing her husband's career and raising children, with her own consulting business taking back stage. Now single, she is improvising a new way to work and live. She needs to work for the money and is making the long game work for her. But her success hinged on someone willing to take the risk of hiring an older worker. That person has become a great boss:

> We just clicked as people, and she treats me with a lot of respect... she treats me like she values me and what I do is valuable, and that doesn't happen everywhere. We just have a lot of fun, we laugh a lot. So to me that is worth a lot.

Labor markets governed by frequent restructuring, uncertainty about the future, and an older workforce with extended life expectancy mean that significant numbers of Boomers, in the United States at least, are delaying a total exit from the labor market because of financial concerns like Debra's. Even though they may wish to retire or are less able to function well in physically demanding jobs like construction (recall Joe in chapter 3), many Boomers and their families are squeezed with increased debt and the financial needs of their younger, college-age or older children, needing to prolong working lives to make ends meet as publicly provided safety nets shrink and private-sector pensions disappear.[15]

Others pursue the long game by becoming self-employed entrepreneurs, freelancers, and consultants, generating their own start-ups and clienteles while also setting the parameters of their own careers. For example, one retired administrator started her own yoga practice for fifty-somethings. Another couple translated a hobby into an online jewelry business. A Canadian Boomer I discuss later on started a housing swap business. And a physician has begun taking on urgent care slots rather than working regular clinic hours. If their years in career jobs have afforded them the chance to save money and create strong networks, these long-game years may be a time of unprecedented success and enrichment.

That is the case for Hugh, a 58-year-old independent industrial contractor laying floors. He started his own business as an encore six years ago, in order to be in charge of his life. He plans to continue working, in part because it is fundamental to his identity and sense of purpose:

> I play golf, but I am not a golfer. I fish, but I am not a fisherman. I sail, but I am not a sailor. I mean, I couldn't do this as an avocation/vocation. That is not me. I am not going to move to the Caribbean and do that. I could do that for a week. That is not part of my psyche.

Hugh plans to work through his seventies, as long as he is physically able:

> I enjoy working. I enjoy the field that I am in. I think there is some value to what we do. I would love... writing and gardening. But I

couldn't do any of those things full time, and I couldn't do them for long durations. That is why I would rather work. Maybe not 12-hour days... but maybe four to five hours a day, four or five days a week.

Those following the long game, time-shifting full-time retirement to some future date, if at all, are what public decision-makers concerned with the costs of social security and health care consider ideal. But this is a relatively small group, distinctive in terms of education and gender. In March 2014, more college-educated men (58.5 percent) in the leading edge of Boomers (born 1946–1954, ages 59–68 in 2014) were employed full time, compared to same-age men with just a high school diploma (47.2 percent) and those with not even that (35 percent) (see figures 5.3A and B and in appendix B tables 5.1–5.4). Leading-edge women with a college degree were less apt to be working full time (42.5 percent) than similarly educated, similarly aged men (58.5 percent), but more likely to hold full-time jobs than leading-edge women with only a high school diploma (29.3 percent) or less (15.1 percent). Leading-edge college-educated men are also more likely (as is the case with Hugh) to be entrepreneurs (15.5 percent self-employed in their own businesses), than women with a college degree (8 percent), high-school educated men (8.7 percent), high-school educated women (3.8 percent), or those without a high-school diploma, only 5.8 percent of men and 2.7 percent women without a high-school

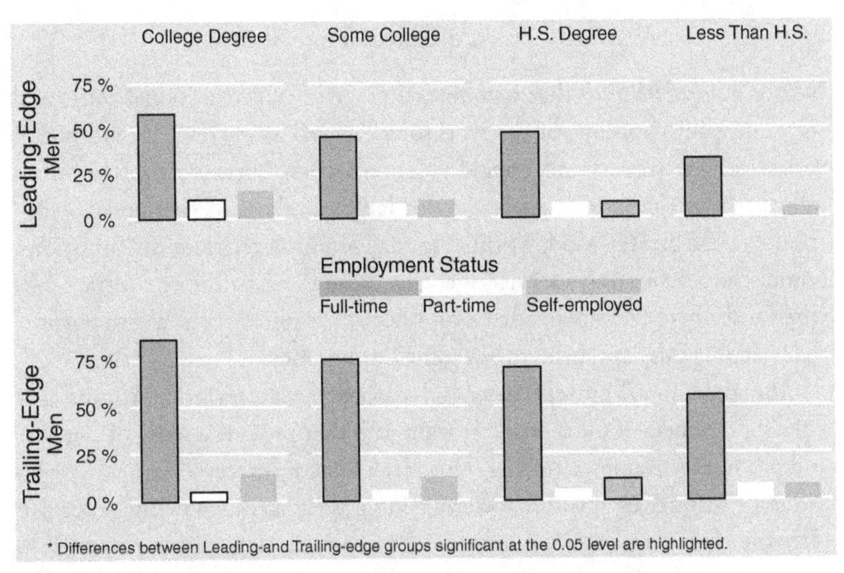

FIGURE 5.3A. Employment Status of Leading- and Trailing-Edge Boomer Men in 2014 by Education

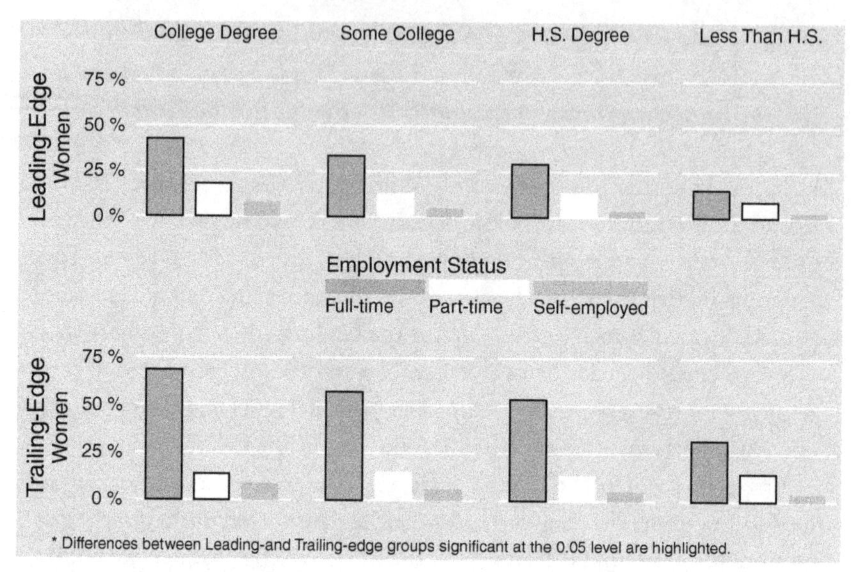

FIGURE 5.3B. Employment Status of Leading- and Trailing-Edge Boomer Women in 2014 by Education

diploma are self-employed.[16] Less-educated Boomers and women may need to play the long game to make ends meet, but the risk is that many lack the skills, networks, and health to make it happen.

Pathway #3. "Portfolio" Time Shifting

Next is a *portfolio path* that combines a range of improvisational starts and stops, dips into and out of the workforce, as well as moves into and out of various service careers and unpaid volunteer work. Portfolio configurations offer perhaps the best opportunity for large numbers of Boomers to contribute to the greater good, working for pay or not in religious organizations, schools, and community service agencies, often in part-time or contract jobs when and where they are needed. For others, portfolios are less about purpose than keeping busy and bringing in some extra money.

The great social entrepreneur and visionary Marc Freedman finds that growing numbers of older workers want jobs that provide a sense of purpose and promote societal well-being—his idea of encore careers.[17] For those who can afford riskier or possibly lower-paying positions, this new life stage can offer the chance to both lean out and lean back in, time shifting away from career jobs to follow a dream or make a drastic change from working for the money (or status or benefits) to working to make the world a better place.

This subset of Boomers often shifts from the private to the social (nonprofit) sector, and some need and manage to find both money and meaning.

Gray, the VP of a large corporation who found himself retired when the company was sold, took on a couple of encore jobs, including working another fourteen and a half years full time as the director of a homeless shelter. This was a joint decision. His wife Marjorie recalls:

> He came home and said "I would really like to do this. I realize its altruistic work and will drastically change our finances," but it just felt right for both of us. I was in a position where I was working as a fixed-term adjunct, making better money in those days than I do now in a tenured position, and we were financially secure before the crash, and there was no question. It was like, "Absolutely. If this is something you want to do, do it." He loved it. He was successful, completely overhauled the program and made it a working program. It made him happy—he's happy, I'm happy! You want your partner to be fulfilled in their work. It turned out to be the right thing to do.

After what amounted to a whole new career (nearly fifteen years) in this encore, Gray eventually retired from that as well, but continues to be actively engaged as a leader in his community:

> When I retired, it wasn't just that I wanted desperately to retire, I just didn't want to do what I was doing anymore or at the *pace* I was doing it. If I ever updated my CV, I've served as chair over six or seven boards by now.

Many Boomers are seeking greater control and flexibility, or, like Gray and my husband Dick, want opportunities for meaningful paid or unpaid activities that offer a rhythm and routine to the day and week as well as a sense of purpose. Gray may yet take on another encore job:

> It's funny, I still look at the want ads every weekend. I just figure, maybe some NGO would be looking at needing some part-time person.

What characterizes portfolio time shifting is the wide assortment of pathways these Boomers are following in improvising this stage of their lives. For many, jobs are looking more like how musicians view gigs: temporary respites from chronic unemployment, nonemployment, or retirement that provide extra income, might be fun, and might make a difference. Recall Jessie (chapter 2), who pursued what she calls a "messy" career path. She has had several encore jobs, and expects she may have more. But can't figure out how she can retire:

> I don't think it is really going to be an option for me. I just haven't, I haven't figured out how that is going to work and, you know, luckily I like what I do. But who knows, anything can happen. And I may find myself looking for another job. And so I am always kind of strategizing financially how to make that happen. And in my other corporate jobs I was able to—I had a 401K and I was able to save, even though I wasn't earning a lot of money, I knew I needed to. Now with this job I haven't, I have not, just because there are no benefits, there is no matching. So that is always the puzzle, you know. It always feels like a juggling act of where does—how is this going to work?

Other Boomers who don't need the money from a paying job turn to a portfolio of civic engagement. The notion of service—giving back to community, helping those less fortunate, and working toward a greater good—by volunteering for local or national organizations runs deep in American culture.[18] It provides the glue connecting citizens to their communities. Hannah, married to Hugh, the self-employed contractor (this chapter) who plans to never retire, lost her job, but is enjoying volunteering:

> I don't understand people who are afraid of not working. I think it is because I have so many interests and so many things that I don't have time to do them all, even now when I am not working.... I would like to be more in things that interest me like the Nature Center. Right now I volunteer with things that I have a personal interest in and enjoy. Given more time, I will probably volunteer in areas that maybe are a lot more difficult. Now, personally, I would like to help people more.

Don, married to Mary, who at 62 is in an encore job, is another excellent example of portfolio time shifting. He was making major strides in social renewal in his career job as executive director of a state agency, but felt he had accomplished what he wanted there. Now he wants to spend more time as board chair of a small, international nonprofit. Don had planned his retirement carefully, but was recruited back by his boss to another temporary job after less than two months of being a retiree. After that stint he plans to ramp up his nonprofit work, but is also talking with another Boomer about a small start-up. Portfolio time shifting often occurs just like this, as opportunities open up or close. Note that routes to paid or unpaid service work are not clear-cut, and may not even exist for Boomers without rich social networks.

We don't know the extent of portfolio time shifting in the United States or Europe, or whether, like the long game, it also follows an education/gender gradient. The only data about voluntary paid work captured by the US Census' Current Population Survey is about wanting to work part time. As we see in figure 5.2, volunteering is more common among Boomers with college degrees. Similarly (see figures 5.3A and B), among those with college degrees in the leading edge of the Boomer cohort in March 2014, 12.2 percent of women and 6.6 percent of men report working part time because they want to. Among those with high school diplomas, 7.5 percent women and 4.7 percent men are voluntarily working part time, as are 4.7 percent women and 2.8 percent men without a high school diploma.[19] Part-timers may well be pursing portfolio paths, with the college educated most apt to be willingly working less.

Another insight about portfolio career paths may be found in job shifts. Census data tells us that trailing-edge Boomers are most apt to have switched jobs in the past year (6.2 percent of men and 3.8 percent of women ages 50–58 in 2014 had changed jobs in the past year), but we don't know whether such job shifts are voluntary or involuntary (see table 2.1 in appendix B). However, the fact that Boomers in this age group with a college degree are most apt to job shift (7.7 percent men, 6.6 percent women) suggests that for some, this may well reflect portfolio shifting.[20]

Neither is it clear whether portfolio time shifting occurs principally in the United States and not elsewhere. Data on Germans born during the Second World War (1940–1945), however, show that only 6 percent of men and women were re-employed after they transitioned to retirement.[21]

Pathway #4. Unanticipated Time Shifting

Portfolio transitions certainly take some juggling and a willingness to tolerate uncertainty. But some Boomers are finding themselves retired unexpectedly and unwillingly.[22] These constitute the fourth, unanticipated exit path—those less-than-voluntary withdrawals that refashion unemployment or a sudden health problem, one's own or a family member's—into unexpected retirement. This path is bleaker, given the limited choices for future improvisations available for those on it.

Labor market risks together with age discrimination, age-based stereotypes, and institutional logics supporting an age-stratified labor market presuming entry level jobs go to young people, for example, make it difficult for laid-off older workers to become re-employed or for retirees to find postretirement employment.[23] Accordingly, older adults suffer from long-term unemployment more often than younger counterparts.[24] As repeated, unsuccessful job searches turn them into what the census calls discouraged workers, many become unwilling retirees or nonworkers, dropping out of the labor force altogether. Consider the case of Paul, forced into retirement at sixty-four. At first he wasn't devastated by the downsizing. He was sure he could get a part-time bridge job,

> thinking that there might be something I could do without full-time employment because work there [former employer] could be a bit demanding. And I thought, "Maybe I can get out of this grind, but still do something within the field, but not full time."

It didn't work. As the months passed Paul couldn't find any job, full-time or part-time, in his field of industrial design or otherwise. He missed the sense of purpose he'd gotten from his career job:

> A lot of times it was rewarding. There is a lot of junk you have to do, but when you came to a point when you knew you were producing something not only of value but of intrinsic—you said "Wow." With all your cohort, as Obama said, you didn't do this yourself. It was a team effort. Just knowing that there was an object there that could be admired and helpful, all those kinds of things. So the rewards, the psychic rewards were quite critical.

Paul would like to continue to contribute:

> If I could be in some position where I could be of assistance and help people design or build things and I didn't have to work 50 hours, do the all-nighters, I would like that. I'd like to get back. I still enjoy building things. It is a high when you can do it.

Paul, who never married, led a middle-class life filled with purpose until he was laid off. He would like another job, but is currently volunteering and enjoying that.

Others have always lived on the margins. Unfortunately, as is the case for many Millennials navigating early adulthood, the opportunities and advantages associated with—possibly even the entire experience of an encore to adulthood—are limited for those who live with the accumulated disadvantages of personal and institutional discrimination in tandem with the enduring inequalities built into our stratified society.

Whereas unemployed or discouraged workers in the second half of their sixties in the United States may at least qualify for Medicare and Social Security benefits, unemployed men and women in their fifties and early sixties have wholly inadequate safety nets. Unlike those in European countries, tight limits on welfare income and short-term unemployment benefits will not help them sufficiently or for long enough so that they might reach an age to receive federal benefits, and they're often still too far from an anticipated retirement to have planned or saved much in advance. Their children, if they have them, are likely to be in college or looking to establish secure jobs of their own, making Boomers' economic difficulties problematic for both generations.

Some know if they lose or leave their career jobs they must get over the hurdles of age bias. Even if they find work, they will never command the salaries they had come to expect.[25] Concerns over the loss of health care benefits in the United States is now less of a problem given the Affordable Care Act implemented in 2014, but the costs may still be prohibitive for those with a sudden drop in income. Other Boomers are taking the early retirement provision of Social Security at age 62, accepting the penalty of a lower payout because they have been laid off (or are fairly certain they will be), can't find employment, have health problems, want to try something else, or need the money.

Health issues often produce unexpected exits, not always labeled as retirement. Over one in 10 (10.5 percent) of leading-edge Boomer men and slightly fewer leading-edge Boomer women (9 percent) report quitting or retiring in 2014 for health reasons (see table 2.1 in appendix B). But this varies from only 4 percent and 5 percent for men and women with a college degree to 18.2 percent (men) and 12.9 percent (women) for those without a high school diploma (see appendix B, table 5.3). Clearly, Boomers with little education are often out of the workforce for reasons other than voluntary retirement. Over three in 10 of leading-edge Boomers without a high school diploma (32.4 percent women and 30.8 percent men) are not working because they are ill or disabled (as are 14 percent of women and 15.8 percent of men with a high-school diploma, compared to only 4.5 percent of women and 3.9 percent of men with a college degree). Others are not in the workforce because of family care (5.1 percent of leading-edge women and 1 percent of leading-edge men who are college graduates are homemakers, as are 7.6 percent and 1.4 percent of women and men with just a high school diploma, and 9.9 percent and 1.3 percent of women and men with less than a high school education). In all, 45.9 percent, 59 percent, and 76.9 percent of leading-edge Boomer women with college degrees, high school diplomas, and less than high school education, respectively, were not in the workforce in March 2014, as were 34.7 percent, 48.9 percent, and 62 percent of trailing-edge Boomer men.[26] These data point to an educational as well as gender gradient; those with more education are more likely to be engaged in paid work, with men with a college degree the most apt to be working for pay.

In chapter 3 we saw that continuing occupational changes, rapid information, communications, and computational technological shifts, and a multitude of trends associated with globalization and the second machine age of digitalization are increasing competition, cost-cutting, outsourcing, offshoring, automation, bankruptcies, and mergers.[27] These produce diminished job opportunities and employer commitment to older employees, despite the lowering of the unemployment rate. Much has been made of the risks confronting Millennials navigating job and credit markets and often needing assistance from family and friends as they seek to get on their feet. Many of their Boomer parents are in precarious positions of their own, also lacking social protections and at risk of both age bias and health difficulties.

Varieties and Inequalities in the Encore Adult Experience

Boomers are moving through the encore adult years with unique biographies, which, in turn, shape their risks and possibilities for reinvention. And yet their talents and experience are a resource for both personal and social renewal. We have seen that educational levels and gender combine to shape gradients in both paid work and civic engagement at this life stage, with college-educated men typically the most advantaged and women without high school diplomas typically the least advantaged in terms of remaining engaged. These inequalities reinforce existing racial disparities, too: college-educated Boomer men and women are typically white. By contrast, the majority of poorly educated women and men are nonwhite (see tables 5.1–5.4 in appendix B). Consider Boomers without a high school diploma: 37.6 percent of women and 35.5 percent of men without high school degree are Hispanic, almost 15 percent are African American, and another 9.3 percent of women and 3.7 percent of Boomer men characterize themselves as "other."[28] Behind these statistics is the fact that race- and ethnicity-based disadvantages beginning early in life contribute to ongoing stratification in education and health that in turn shape opportunities and resources in the encore adult years.

Boomers long ago bought into the linear lockstep life course replete with the career mystique promise of ladders leading to success, happiness, and security, only to find in their fifties and sixties that the ladders they counted on are extremely unstable, if they exist at all. Like the workers at Boeing and public-sector employees in Detroit, many Boomers are witnessing the demise of economic security.[29] They counted on generous pensions, but insufficient funds combined with payouts to shareholders, bankruptcies, offshoring, automation, and other deals made in headquarter offices or city halls are quietly destroying those promised—and earned—benefits for many.

Prior decisions about marital and parental timing along with sometimes unexpected divorce also continue to have implications. Boomer women who delayed childbearing until 39 or 40 and men who started second families with younger second wives are a long way from an empty nest, especially in light of the extended transitions to adulthood of their Millennial children. Boomer parents still caught up in childrearing may have to delay plans to reinvent themselves in encore adulthood. One man I interviewed had become a new father again in his fifties, some twenty years after his first son was born. He started counting up how long it would be before his youngest finished college, before he could even think about retiring. Like Marc, who also started a second family (chapter 2), he was aghast at the number he came up with.

The old adage about the rich getting richer and the poor getting poorer seems to apply in the encore adult years as well, given that successes and adversities tend to accumulate over time.[30] Large educational, gender, and race/ethnic disparities in income, health, and other resources become magnified in encore adulthood, as Boomers' families, health, economic circumstances, and goals and expectations tend to branch out. Boomers also vary widely in their degree of uncertainty and ambivalence about what comes next and in their sense of control over this next phase of their lives.[31]

Still, despite considerable diversity, most experience continuity in their sense of self, attitudes, and behaviors, even as they may be moving into new situations. In his study of Americans born in the 1920s, sociologist John Clausen (1993) found that adolescents who exhibited planful competence made better life choices and, as a result, had smoother and more satisfying lives, including more stable careers and marriages. But whether the Boomer generation's early planning produces stability later on is doubtful, given the pace of social change they are experiencing. Even the best-laid plans feel tentative, even precarious, today. Advantages and disadvantages in encore adulthood—such as economic security—come from educational credentials, occupational attainment, continuous or unstable career paths, and unexpected events such as layoffs or a health scare. Pensions, social security payments, and personal savings and investments are contingent on stable career paths and earnings. As we saw in chapter 3, individual retirement accounts are quickly replacing defined pension-like retirement benefits, part of a larger trend called the individualization of risk.[32] Turbulence in career paths increases Boomers' sense of unpredictability. All shrink the improvisational options for encore adults.[33] In the meantime, there are events that can shift trajectories in positive ways, such as when Pam, another woman placed at financial risk by divorce once the children were launched, inherited both land and money when her parents passed away. This offered the economic security that enabled her to reassess her spiritual life. She now regularly attends religious retreats and volunteers for her church, living a life filled with purpose.

Linked Pathways

The focus in census data and most research on individuals can obscure the *linked lives* aspects of the life course[34]—that is, the ways we all lead intertwined lives, making decisions with or responding to experiences of the people in our lives. For example, their Millennial children's stressful divorces, layoffs, and money problems create tensions for Boomers,[35] as do their aging parents' increasing frailty, confusion, and possible isolation. Another example of linked lives is that retirement or employment can create pressure for both spouses. Don (chapter 4), who planned his retirement carefully but was recruited back to the agency he helped put on the map, expects to leave Minnesota's cold winters for sunnier climates for several months at least. His increasingly heavy engagement in unpaid leadership work for a nonprofit in Africa provides the flexibility for him to do just that. He is proud of his past career accomplishments—literally rewriting the scripts and redesigning his state agency's mission. This career work remains an important component of his identity, providing a sense of both personal and social purpose. (Others are more ambivalent about identifying with their past jobs, especially when restructuring at work serves to push them out of door.) Now Don's growing civic investment provides that satisfaction, and, at age 66, one key project is self-exploration. But his wife Mary is full time and full steam into her challenging and paid encore job. Don says he is hoping that his going south next winter will make Mary want to begin scaling back on her work obligations.

Conclusions

The twenty-first-century life course is being recast as demography, the economy, technology, and the temporal rhythms of life open up space for—and indeed sometimes necessitate—time shifting work, family care, schooling, retirement, leisure, and civic engagement. Like Millennials encountering an uncertain early adulthood, most Boomers are in considerable flux; improvising by time shifting away from set timetables and the last century's linear and lock-step life course. What we saw in chapter 4 was that Boomers expect to engage in some form of work. What we see in this chapter is that real life rarely conforms to their expectations. A few, the long-game time shifters, plan to continue to lean in to paid work—sometimes their career jobs, sometimes social sector or unpaid volunteer jobs—indefinitely. Neotraditional and portfolio time shifters want to lean out, even as those in the fourth pathway, the unanticipated time shifters, are forced to do so. Many laid off or with health-precipitated exits discover they can't get back into the workforce, finding disability or family-care responsibilities become paths to retirement.

This chapter underscores the unevenness of the encore life stage, the multiplicity and disparities in paths taken or not taken. Boomers may improvise by moving in and out of the labor force, from full- to part-time jobs and back again, or from career-like to noncareer employment. They may do so voluntarily or involuntarily. Large segments are opting to retire from their primary career jobs early, regardless of incentives in federal policies to keep working,[36] often in order to improvise new lifestyles and portfolio time shifting.

This chapter also points to the utility of Matilda Riley's concept of structural lag in addressing the disconnects between the growing numbers of capable older individuals and the opportunities available to them in paid and volunteer work.[37] Significant numbers of Boomers are on the margins, retired from their career jobs but not yet feeling old. And, as we will see in the next chapter, many are improvising around chronic but not debilitating health problems. Significant numbers—even those with chronic health conditions—want to continue some form of social engagement, but are finding that most jobs come prepackaged as full year and full time, that age discrimination is alive and well, that volunteering can be hit or miss, and that most retirements are still regarded as all-or-nothing, irreversible exits.

6

Improvising Health, Well-Being, Purpose

ONE MORNING SEVERAL years ago I got a call from my husband, who had just learned that our oldest grandson James (age 19 and in college) was in a Texas jail. It seems James and a friend had driven from Minnesota to Texas to watch a football game, had a car accident while drinking, and could not be released until they paid a fine ($5,000). James said he did not want his parents to know, so he was calling us. As I waited for Dick to pick me up from my office, my heart was racing. We decided to get the money from savings and then wire it to his lawyer. As we drove, I tried—unsuccessfully—to reach James's cell phone. Before we sent the funds electronically, Dick sought, also unsuccessfully, to reach James's lawyer. It turned out that there was no such person listed in the Texas Bar Association. Only then did we realize we were the victims of a scam. I finally reached James—he was walking to class at the University of Minnesota, Morris, dumbfounded by my story about Texas, his alleged broken nose, and the very idea that we thought he would drink and drive.

This is an example of the importance of the meaning of events. Nothing had happened except a trick phone call, where someone who sounded like James might if he had a broken nose, convinced Dick and through him, me about the reality of this situation. Our emotional reactivity skyrocketed, and it was days before we recovered our equilibrium. Moreover, we remained sort of angry at James for several days, even though he has no car, doesn't drink, and would never go to Texas for a game. It's just one example of the observation by the famous sociologist W. I. Thomas: what people believe to be true has enormous consequences. We came uncomfortably close to losing thousands of dollars. We were panicked. We felt cross toward our own grandchild, who had actually done nothing wrong.

Similarly, when it comes to paid work, family-care work, retirement from a long-held job, or final exits from the workforce, how individuals "see" their situations matters. It is not that certain jobs or activities are inherently fulfilling, it is how we define them that imbues meaning.

This chapter describes improvisations to reduce stress and promote physical health, well-being, and purpose, as well as the forces—from institutional inertia and economic dislocations as part of the big picture to an aging mother's fall and broken hip or a new and terrible boss as part of real life—that can change meanings and move the wheels increasing or decreasing Boomers' sense of control, producing the cycles of control described in chapter 4. Moreover, far more than previous cohorts, many educated Boomers are improvising healthy lifestyles—deliberately making decisions to get healthy. This chapter also underscores that the stress, health, and happiness of Boomers are a result of both external conditions and their improvised plans and paths through encore adulthood described in chapters 4 and 5, along with those paths' meanings and especially Boomers' sense of control along the way.

For example, those with little education are more apt than the college educated to experience the onset of functional limitations and chronic conditions, even as those with low incomes are apt to experience the further progression of these limitations and conditions.[1] As discussed in chapter 4, having little education and insufficient income also translates into feeling less control over one's life. The reality of actual control over life circumstances and a subjective sense of control are, in effect, different but intertwined pieces of how Boomers approach and experience encore adulthood.

Many Boomers, especially those with a college degree, take on an encore project around health. They strategize to become or remain fit, seeking to eat right, sleep enough, and exercise sufficiently to stave off the next stage—infirmity associated with old age. Many see the encore years as a time to aim for good health, seeking to manage any chronic conditions they may have.

The questions become: What is good health? And how are Boomers doing? In 1948, the World Health Organization defined health broadly as "a state of complete physical, mental, and social well-being and not merely the absence of disease." This extends well beyond the traditional medical model that has focused almost exclusively on curing specific maladies, not preventing them, and not on promoting life quality. A good way to begin to move outside "merely the absence of disease" is to examine variations in happiness, health, and well-being across nation-states and subgroups. This provides a window into patterned social disparities in life chances and life quality.

Consider, for example, a simple measure of how happy people feel. Cross-national surveys report that more than 10 percent of Americans say they are "not too happy" while one-third say they are "very happy." For comparison, fully 60 percent of Danes report being "very happy."[2] But do these statistics on large populations hold specifically for those in encore adulthood? I next describe the social contexts and determinants of stress, happiness, and health, including both age and cohort effects, then look specifically at work and retirement. The chapter concludes by pointing to three important protective factors promoting the health, well-being, and purposefulness of Boomers: education, engagement, and a sense of control. These personal resources help people of all ages strategize ways of responding to adversity as well as to opportunity, and are especially important in the encore years.

Health in Context

The experience with our grandson James described above is an example of W. I. Thomas's dictum: "What is defined as real is real in its consequences."[3] Recognizing the validity of this Thomas theorem is key to understanding Boomers as they move through encore adulthood. Specifically, those who feel in control and see this time of life as a chance to reframe and reset their lives are more apt to actually do so. They feel happier and healthier. "What is defined as real" also matters in terms of how encore adults perceive their own situations—that is, the meanings they ascribe to circumstances or events.[4] For example, research evidence suggests that it is not paid work or family-care work or civic engagement or retirement that matters for health and well-being. Rather, it is whether these activities are seen as *voluntary* or *involuntary*, a matter of personal or forced choice, providing a source of purpose and recognition or just mindless and mind-numbing activity.[5]

Chapter 2 described the differences and overlaps between age, historical period, and cohort. All of them shape the contemporary expectations, health, and well-being of Boomers, but they are often confounded with one another. Consider Mary, a Boomer born in 1951 (first described in chapter 4) who was 63 in 2015. It is hard to say whether it is being in the encore years, her awareness of extended life expectancy, her experiences as part of the large Boomer cohort, living in the technologically advanced years of the early twenty-first century, or none of these factors that motivates her commitment to helping others in her new encore job for a health care organization. Certainly she believes she has many good years ahead of her and wants to use those years in purposeful ways.

While biological aging increases the incidence of both chronic diseases such as arthritis and acute diseases such as a stroke, age differences also reflect other processes. For instance, more leading-edge than trailing-edge Boomers have a college education, and education is a key resource. Age, cohort, and historical period also matter for those engaging in, reading about, or trying to learn from research; we must consider who is in the sample and when the study was done in relation to historical circumstances such as medical and technological advances.

Consider, for example, that as people grow older those who smoke heavily are more apt to die. This leaves a greater proportion of nonsmokers among surviving Boomers and could be interpreted, wrongly, as meaning that large proportions of Boomers never really enjoyed tobacco.[6] This is called a *selective survival effect*, and may result in older adults appearing healthier and happier than those at younger ages simply because those who weren't as happy or healthy have died off, moved to institutional care, or stopped participating in surveys.

Another difficulty in making comparisons across different cohorts is that there are now earlier and more accurate diagnoses than ever before. This means Boomers have a higher likelihood of being diagnosed as having health conditions than did their parents or grandparents, even though their parents or grandparents may have suffered from the same problems. It only looks, on paper, like Boomers are sicker. An important recent study compared Boomers' health with that of their parents' generation when they were the same age and found higher rates of chronic disease, disability, and lower self-rated health. Another study examined different cohorts' health when members of each cohort were ages 51 to 56, finding that leading-edge Boomer men rated their health as only slightly less healthy than those in an earlier (1936–1941) cohort at the same age. Leading-edge Boomer women in the first half of their fifties in 2004 rated their health worse than Boomer men as well as worse than women in the earlier cohort at the same ages. Again, it is not clear whether Boomers have more health problems, have more health care, are being diagnosed with previously undiagnosed conditions, are more attuned to health conditions given the commodification (through advertising) of pharmacological solutions, are more apt to survive than did prior cohorts, or, of course, whether they are in fact in poorer health.

Historical trends, such as the recent massive rise in the proportion of adults of all ages who are overweight, clearly make a difference. Obesity is a key risk factor for many diseases, and contemporary men and women in their forties, fifties, and sixties report the highest weight levels in the United States. Among all Americans, they are the most likely to be overweight. In fact, almost three in 10 leading-edge Boomer men and over a third of Boomer women were obese in 2004; in the previous cohort at the same ages, just one in five men and one in four women was obese.[7]

The Social Determinants of Health

To understand how Boomers in encore adulthood are strategizing in response to ongoing or unexpected stressors and the conditions that seem to promote health and well-being requires stepping back to more general theories. Scholars have long theorized social structures and contexts as central to physical and emotional health. This "social determinants of health" framing has generated a lively field of research on the social causes of illness, health, and subjective well-being.[8] It emphasizes the embeddedness of individuals in particular social structures, with corresponding risks, rules, claims, and resources that shape their health and subjective well-being.[9]

Four theoretical threads have guided much of the research on the social determinants of health. Sociologists have drawn on stress process theory developed by Leonard Pearlin and colleagues focusing on structural conditions producing stress that affects subjective well-being,[10] as well as on fundamental cause theory developed by Jo Phelan and Bruce Link explaining the ongoing relationship between socioeconomic status and health/well-being outcomes in light of the unequal distributions of resources such as health knowledge and access to quality care within society.[11] A third thread is the considerable interdisciplinary scholarship by Robert Karasek and Töres Theorell,[12] who developed the job strain theoretical model defining strain as the result of high demands combined with low control and low support, circumstances leading to poor physical and mental health. The fourth thread can be found in the studies by Michael Marmot and colleagues on the social gradient, that ones' occupational status in conventional adulthood predicts health, well-being, and mortality.[13]

Stress has been defined as the mismatch between claims and resources, or the mismatch between a person and his or her environment.[14] Theory and research depict stress in the form of both crises and chronic strains as occurring when a gap between resources and claims (or needs) reduces people's sense of control.[15] Chronic stress, such as role strain, or "the felt difficulty in fulfilling role obligations,"[16] is often associated with conflicting role obligations, such as when Boomers are expected to devote themselves full-time to their jobs while also caring for a parent or husband with dementia.

The stress process approach also theorizes change over time, as stresses increase or abate, shaping the dynamics of "fit" between resources and claims/needs and enhancing or reducing people's sense of control over their lives.[17] Thus becoming unemployed or taking on caregiving of an aging parent increases stress and reduces feelings of well-being.[18]

Stress process as well as life-course scholars underscore shifts in both resources and claims (i.e., the demands, needs, and expectations that individuals face) alter the social environment over the life course, creating what University of North Carolina sociologist Glen Elder describes as cycles of control (see figure 4.2 in chapter 4) where a sense of control goes up or down depending on the match or mismatch between demands and resources.[19] Social psychologist Leonard Pearlin points out the importance of observing "how deeply well-being is affected by the structured arrangements of people's lives and by the repeated experiences that stem from these arrangements."[20]

Note that the stress process approach also underscores the inequality in stress and well-being based on mostly invariant status locations like gender, race, and social class. This conforms with the literature on social stratification that depicts what Tilly calls enduring disparities.[21] This again underlines the pervasive theme of disparities throughout this book. Both time-shifting pathways and how people see and define them are shaped by inequalities that cumulate over the life course, leading to wide differences in stress, health, happiness, cognitive ability, and even life expectancy in encore adulthood. British epidemiologists Michael Marmot and Richard Wilkerson and colleagues, as well as Johannes Siegrist, a medical sociologist at the University of Dusseldorf, and Harvard's Lisa Berkman, point to the social gradient of health, with those in higher status jobs the most healthy mentally and physically.[22]

The structural arrangements of work are fundamental to health and well-being, given that work remains pivotal to identity, meaning, routine, and status as well as income. It is also an activity that occupies most of the waking hours of many adults. Job conditions are theorized as triggers of the stress process impacting health. This suggests that the structural arrangements (or absence of them) and conditions around conventional retirement also matters, although the prevailing research focus has been on the timing of the retirement exit and financial assets, not other retirement conditions.

Achieving an occupational (sometimes called work, job, or career) identity is a challenging aspect of emerging adulthood in the twenty-first century given the uncertainties and insecurities young people face. My University of Minnesota colleague Jeylan Mortimer and coauthors conclude that "increasing insecurity, turbulence, and technological change make the transition from school to work more difficult and prolonged as youth are increasingly faced with transient employment and nonstandard contracts, recurrent job losses and spells of unemployment, and shifts in career lines as they attempt to adapt to the changing labor market." Similarly, University of Hawaii psychologists Vladimir Skorikov and Fred Vondracek emphasize that "adjustment to the nature of careers in modern economies progressively depends on establishing and maintaining a strong sense of proactive, dynamic, and highly individualized occupational identity."[23] These are stressful times for emerging adults, but also for Boomers who are similarly seeking new identities and purpose around a more varied and prolonged path through the encore adult years.

Physical Health

I recall one interviewee in Elmira, New York who was wheelchair-bound as a result of diabetes. Even though she was unable to walk, when asked about the quality of her health on a scale of 0 to 10, she said she was a ten. The interviewer noted that she was in a wheelchair with a bum leg and foot related to diabetes, and said that he would have ranked her as a 2 or a 3 at most on any health scale. Had we not interviewed her in person we would have had a very different impression of her health, recording only the "perfectly healthy" way she saw herself. So even one's sense of health follows Thomas's dictum: this woman sees herself and acts "healthy," even if the interviewer would tell a different story. Defining one's self or situation can also be an improvisational strategy.

Boomers in general seem to be in the odd position of having or being aware of more chronic conditions than their parents or older siblings did at the same ages, but nevertheless defining themselves as healthy. Even though encore adulthood reflects the bonus years of extended healthy life expectancy, studies show that as they age Boomers report more physical limitations. A qualitative study by Toni Calasanti and colleagues found that when asked about their health, people would say their health is fine, though they "have arthritis;" or that they "have allergies," but are "healthy."[24] In other words, the meaning of health seems to be related to serious conditions, not the chronic ailments typical of encore adulthood.

Having several health limitations, however, takes a toll on how at least some Boomers' perceive their health. The 2014 Current Population Survey shows about one in 10 men (10.3 percent) and women (11.2 percent) in the leading edge of American Boomers describe themselves as having only "fair" or "poor" health, while almost one in five say they have a work-limiting difficulty (18.4 percent and 18.1 percent of leading-edge Boomer men and women, respectively).[25] This also differs by labor market status: only 1.2 percent of Boomer men and 1.6 percent of Boomer women working full time say they have a work-limiting health difficulty, compared to 69.3 percent and 49.8 percent of Boomer men and women who are neither in the labor force nor retired. Less than one in five nonworking retirees (18.9 percent Boomer men and 14.9 percent Boomer women) report a work-limiting difficulty (see appendix B, tables 6.1–6.4).

Estimating the odds of their surviving to age 75, men in a 2004 study of the leading-edge Boomers gave themselves only a 60.7 percent chance on average, with women estimating a 66.2 percent chance.[26] These are lower than the odds given by previous cohorts at these ages. This matters because how people subjectively appraise the quality of their health has been shown to have a strong relationship with their subsequent happiness and longevity.[27] Such self-observations are not only strategic assessments, they also matter for the long run.[28]

Health risks leading to heart disease and other maladies also vary by cohort. The rising obesity mentioned above is associated with multiple adverse health outcomes, including type-2 diabetes, cardiovascular disease, high blood pressure, and some cancers.[29] In one study, diabetes was reported at a slightly lower rate for Boomer men than earlier cohorts, while 11 percent of Boomer women are diabetic, compared to 8.5 percent of those born 1936 to 1941. A higher proportion of Boomers also report being in frequent pain—at about a 9 percent increase over the earlier group, regardless of gender.[30]

Many Boomers are reassessing their health risks and strategizing about how to avoid or minimize health problems that may curtail the quality and length of their lives. For example, Boomer women interviewed in 2004 were less apt to smoke (19.4 percent, compared to 26.8 percent of women in the 1936 to 1941 cohort when they were the same age).[31] Note that even though Boomer men smoke less than previous cohorts, they are more apt to smoke than Boomer women (26.2 percent compared to 19.4 percent). Also, compared to the earlier cohort, fewer Boomer men or women report having ever smoked (62.2 percent of Boomer men, 47.3 percent Boomer women, compared to 73.8 percent men, 54.7 percent women in the 1936 to 1941 cohort). Keep in mind, of course, the timing of the study—it is certainly possible that some Boomers who smoked heavily were not around to answer such questions by 2004.

Boomers are also confronting ambivalence about their identities and their self-definitions around age. Later adulthood in the West, at least, is devalued, associated with disability and disease. Boomers who are no longer employed or raising children thus want to avoid the stigma of labels and connotations many see as negative such as "old," "senior citizen," or "elderly."

Older adults also tend to think of themselves as younger than their chronological age. We do know that Boomers feel younger than they are—on average, at least 10 years younger. A third of Americans ages 65 to 74 say they feel 10 to 19 years younger than their actual age. And one in six feels at least 20 years younger.[32] Over time, that gap between subjective and real age widens.[33] As the large Boomer cohort moves through their fifties, sixties, and seventies, then, new age and activity categories such as encore adulthood, retirement jobs, partial retirement, and encore careers are helpful in providing positive alternative identities.

This can even be seen in pop culture, as advertising and media outlets, seeing a ready market, are substituting new images, identities, and definitions of what it means to be in one's fifties, sixties, and seventies. However, the picture painted seems to be about getting more insurance, a new financial planner, and buying vacations, Cialis, Testosterone, and other pharmaceuticals, cars and other possessions. In turn, these idealized cultural tropes are helping legitimate, inform, and shape what people expect of and plan for their physical and emotional health, as well as their aspirational next steps, making it sometimes seem easier to jump into a new life than it really is.

Boomers increasingly face chronic health conditions, but are these conditions likely to produce a decline in their actual life expectancy? The answer appears to be no. Analyses show that leading-edge Boomers who were 59 in 2005 (born 1946) had a 31 percent lower mortality rate compared to an earlier (born 1923) cohort of Americans who were 59 in 1982.[34] Advances in biomedical preventions and treatments for chronic diseases like diabetes and hypertension suggest that most Boomers are likely to be able to live well and even work despite chronic health problems. They are also likely to live longer, with corresponding implications for the costs of and policy development around Social Security, Medicare, health care, and family-care work.

While healthy people die and those with poor health may live long lives, researchers recognize that the most objective measure of poor health—and the easiest to compare across different populations—is mortality. A study published in 2013 by the National Research Council and the Institute of Medicine concludes that even though the United States is among the wealthiest of nations, it is definitely not the healthiest. Life expectancy has been extended worldwide, yet "Americans live shorter lives and experience more injuries and illnesses than people in other high-income countries."[35] A growing body of research is calling attention to the life expectancy gaps across different countries. For instance, from 1980 to 2006 life expectancy for US women was extended by over two years, compared to a four- to five-year extension for women in Australia. A prime reason for this distinction is smoking. US women's smoking increased over the 1950s and 1960s; Boomers who were heavy smokers earlier in their lives are likely to reap the consequences as they grow older.

Recall the social determinants of health thesis: one's cohort as well the historical period and the country in which one lives are tied up with health and health behaviors, as are gender, race/ethnicity, and social class. For example, women are more apt to report poorer health and more health problems but tend to have greater life expectancy, even though the gender gap in life expectancy is narrowing.[36] African Americans and the poorly educated are disadvantaged in terms of risk factors, chronic conditions, and actual mortality. And Hispanics have greater life expectancy but poorer health.

Bottom line: are Boomers in better or worse physical health than previous generations? As we have seen, the evidence is complicated, pointing to the wide discrepancies in Boomers' physical capabilities. "Average" trends mask a multiplicity of experiences—some are feeling healthier than ever, others are in poor health, still others may have one or more health conditions but are managing them well. And many are strategizing to improve their health by adopting healthier lifestyles.[37] University of Texas, Austin sociologist Catherine Ross and colleagues note there is an educational gradient in both self-rated health and mortality. They find gendered changes in educational attainment reduce the gender gap in health and mortality.[38]

This is evident in the differential responses by Boomers to the Current Population Survey depending on their educational level. As seen in figures 6.1 and 6.2,

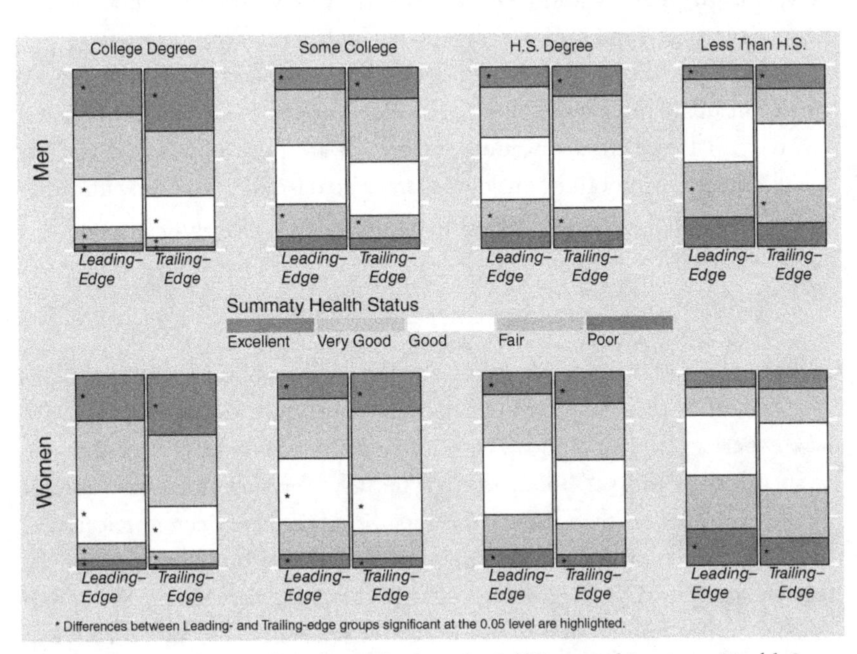

FIGURE 6.1. Leading- and Trailing-Edge Boomer Self-Reported Summary Health Status in 2014 by Gender and Education

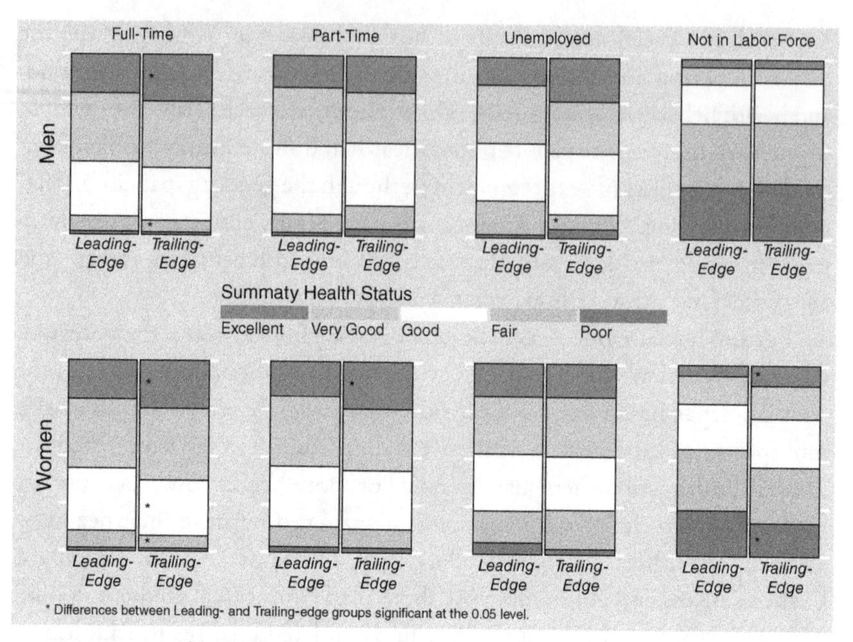

FIGURE 6.2. Leading- and Trailing-Edge Boomer Self-Reported Summary Health Status in 2014 by Gender and Employment Status

most Boomers report being healthy, with the younger trailing edge having better health than the leading edge. Most apt to say they are in poor or fair health are women and men with less than a high-school education.

Advantages like having a college degree promote other advantages conducive to health. For example, Dr. Sarah Flood at the Minnesota Population Center and I find that education and health are positively linked to time spent in health-promoting behaviors such as exercise and negatively linked to health-detracting behaviors such as watching a lot of television.[39]

Cognitive Functioning

A key concern of many Boomers is potential declines in their cognitive abilities. According to a 2009 Pew survey, one in four adults 65 and older say they have experienced memory loss, with low-income respondents at greater risk of such loss.[40] And yet Boomers are typically operating at a higher rate of intellectual prowess than their forbearers. Boomers have been implicated in the "Flynn effect," the thesis that the post-World War II cohort experienced massive gains in IQ.[41] Penn State cognitive psychologists Sherry Willis and Warner Schaie find an increase in inductive reasoning and verbal (but not numeric) ability among Boomers as compared to those born in 1931, with an upward trend for inductive reasoning and a negative trend for verbal ability for the cohorts following the Boomers.[42] Based on years of careful research, Willis and Schaie conclude there is general stability in mental abilities from age 39 through age sixty. But they note that these are averages. Again, averages confound cohort and age, and often obscure a wide variety of patterned changes in mental functioning. Different subgroups have different trajectories of change for different types of cognition: some gaining, some declining, and others stable in their cognitive abilities.

The conclusion? Cognitive abilities are widely variable in encore adulthood, in part depending on whether they are nurtured or permitted to lie fallow. A lot of Boomers get that they are, in part, responsible for their cognitive abilities. Remember Colleen (chapter 4), who left her job in nursing and moved to Arkansas, but still wants to remain engaged and is actively looking for work? Despite the stress of an unsuccessful job search, Colleen has taken up painting as a hobby, telling me that she believes learning new skills will contribute to her intellectual acumen. Health, including cognitive functioning, is seen by many Boomers as something they can help to prolong.

Happiness and Well-Being

The World Health Organization makes the point that health is about more than acute or chronic conditions and poor life expectancy; it also is about a sense of well-being. Subjective well-being is defined as how people experience and evaluate their lives overall, as well as particular aspects of living.[43]

Research on trends in subjective well-being finds that Boomers as a group tend to report less happiness and greater distress than did members of cohorts born before them, but have better mental health and less substance abuse problems than the younger GenXers. In Europe and North America, those born after the Second World War seem to have higher rates of depression than did their parents' generation at that same age, with the age of incidence coming earlier among Boomers and those born after them. The same trend—higher for Boomers than for prior cohorts—appears to characterize reports of anxiety, though there is mixed evidence on younger cohorts. Boomers also have higher rates of alcohol abuse and illicit drug use than did their parents. However, there are differences across communities, cultures, and ethnicities. For example, studies find that Puerto Ricans and Koreans born before 1960 have higher rates of mental disorder than those born since 1960.[44] Why this is the case has yet to be determined.

Sarah Flood and I have looked at life satisfaction in the American Time Use Survey by age, finding that those with poor health report poorer lower average life satisfaction whether respondents are working full time, part time, or not employed.[45] Employment itself seems to result in no discernable patterning of life satisfaction across age groups.

Sociologist Yang Yang from the University of North Carolina examined inequalities in feelings of happiness across age, period, cohort, and other factors.[46] He finds that happiness seems to rise with age, peaking in the encore adult years (ages 50–75), then declining somewhat. Those with a college education have consistently higher odds of reporting themselves as very happy, compared with those with less education, regardless of age. White women used to report being happier than white men, black men, or black women, but this has declined in recent years. Former president of Harvard University Derek Bok suggests that the stress associated with white women's movement into full-time careers might account for their reduced levels of happiness.[47] More women in the labor market, he reasons, makes child care and ailing parent care, conventionally assigned to women, more difficult and increases the strains of daily living. In partial support of his argument, it is the case that work-family conflict is growing. But it is increasing for men as well as for women, as men take on more of the care of their children.[48] And, I would argue, it is not women's movement into the workforce that is the problem, but structural lag in resetting and opening up the clockworks and calendars of workdays, workweeks, and career paths in ways that recognize the nonwork interests and obligations of all workers at all ages and life stages, men as well as women.

Blacks have typically reported being less happy than whites in the United States, but the black-white gap appears to be narrowing, and also seems to narrow with age. Still, white men in their fifties, sixties, and early seventies have the greatest odds of being very happy, followed by white women, then black men, and finally black women. These are clear disparities in well-being in encore adulthood.

Other factors predict happiness, net of people's ages, the time period they are surveyed, and the cohort they are born into. Marital status is important, with the widowed being 70 percent less happy, the divorced 60 percent less happy, and never-married singles about 50 percent less happy than those who are currently married. Those in poor physical health are 70 percent less likely to be happy. The poor—measured by Yang as those in the lowest income quadrant—have the lowest odds of happiness. But the well-off—those in the highest quadrant—are only somewhat happier than those in the middle quadrants. Having enough income is key to happiness, but more money does not appear to buy happiness. Having no children at home is associated with greater happiness, as is attending religious services.

Yang goes on to report that both employment and retirement are positively related to happiness, with the unemployed half as likely to be happy as those who are working.[49] Yang finds those working part time 10 percent less likely to be happy even as retirees are 13 percent more likely to be happy compared to full-time workers. Note that this is across the whole sample, not just Boomers, and includes those who want full-time jobs but can only get part-time hours. By contrast, a study of Australians ages 60 to 69 found that part-time workers were consistently likely to report a higher quality of life and less psychological distress than either full-timers or retirees, as were married men and women, those in good physical health, and those who had a sense of financial adequacy.[50]

Taken together, these findings point to structural inequalities and protective factors—such as working part time, being married, and having an adequate income and good physical health, along with race, gender, and age in various combinations—that lead to disparities in subjective well-being. But what this research shows are average tendencies. Boomers constitute a large and diverse group; one-size-fits-all descriptions can't capture the complexity and variety of ways they view the quality of their lives. A gendered life-course perspective reminds us that even though various protective factors such as marriage, financial adequacy, and physical health may affect women and men similarly, women score lower on measures of well-being across the board, even as they are less apt to be married, have sufficient incomes, or good physical health.

Subjective well-being also changes as circumstances change. In the Work, Family, and Health Network study following people for five years working in an IT division of a Fortune 500 company we call TOMO, we find highly skilled, educated people can sometimes improvise to take control of their lives in ways that promote their health and well-being. For example, consider a woman who worked in IT before it was even called that; she'd been with the company for almost four decades. Shuffling managers and teams as a result of a merger made work "impossible." Recall Kumar (chapter 4), whose last year at TOMO "was the worst in my 38 years with that company." Low job satisfaction led this, another of his TOMO colleagues to retire earlier than she expected—at age 62, and she's much happier in her new life. Those who retire from stressful jobs report higher health and well-being in retirement. This is not the case for those who love and are highly satisfied with their jobs.[51]

Studies show the match or mismatch between planned expectations and realities matter for well-being. For example, men with high prior expectations of working full time at age 62 report considerably greater life satisfaction if they are actually doing so when they reach sixty-two. Conversely, failed expectations of full-time work at age 62—in other words, expecting but not working at that point in time—reduces men's life satisfaction.[52]

Finally, Stanford University psychologist Laura Carstensen and colleagues have also found emotional well-being improves with age.[53] This is a good point to introduce the concept of *role captivity*.[54] Stress, well-being, and purpose are not inherent in employment, family-care work, or retirement, for example. Rather, they come from the fit or, conversely, the misfit between our roles and what we want or choose, as well as how we define our situations. Being a captive worker, retiree, or family-care provider—that is, unwillingly in these situations—is decidedly not good for one's mental health.

The Stress of Transitions and Daily Life

Encore adulthood is a time of many transitions, as Boomers' children leave home and sometimes return; their aging parents, aunts or uncles, and older siblings become more frail or pass away; grandchildren begin to occupy a prominent place in Boomers' lives; intimate or casual relationships dissolve or are formed or reset; and retirement from a long-held job, as well as a final workforce exit, become a reality or else suddenly appear nearer than expected on the horizon. Spouses die, couples divorce, singles move in together, marry, or settle into singlehood; health problems become more nagging; adult children and grandchildren need help or become too busy to get together. Many who can afford it travel extensively. Many Boomers working, traveling, or staying home worry if they will have enough money to support an unknown number of years. How long will they live? How much money is enough? These are big, scary, and generally unanswerable questions.

But, as we've seen throughout this book, Boomers also deliberately time shift, improvising new lives by doing something unusual, at odds with twentieth-century norms "for their age." In my interviews I find fifty-somethings returning to piano lessons after 30 or more years and sixty-somethings training for marathons or lifting weights for the first time in their lives. Boomers also experience a range of labor market transitions: losing or changing jobs or returning to school; retiring partially, completely, or improvising new ways to engage in paid work; taking up family-care work or community work; starting their own businesses or nonprofits or engaging in micro-entrepreneurship by offering services on the Internet.

Transitions, even positive ones, are invariably stressful. Remember marrying? Becoming a parent? Starting a new job? And their longer-term implications are not clear-cut. Even the same transition—such as retiring or caring for ailing parents or partners—can reduce, promote, or exacerbate the experience of stress or well-being for different Boomers with different assessments of the change—whether they feel ready for it, for instance. As a time of multilayered transitions encore adulthood can be stressful, especially in the face of uncertainty and ambivalence.

Beyond such big-picture worries, Boomers, like the rest of us, confront daily stressors, defined by the Pennsylvania State University psychologist David Almeida and his colleagues as

> minor events arising out of day-to-day living, such as the everyday concerns of work, caring for others, and commuting between work and home. They may also refer to small, more unexpected events that disrupt daily life, little life events such as arguments . . . with children, unexpected work deadlines, and malfunctioning computers.[55]

Daily stressors may be less severe than major transitions, but they affect people's lives and may lead to anxiety and depression.[56] They are somewhat related to, but distinct from, chronic stressors, those ongoing stressful circumstances like insufficient income, a too demanding job, feeling isolated, or caring for an aging relative that take their toll on Boomers' mental as well as physical health.

Marjorie, age 61, who finally got tenure two years ago after having returned to school at 40 and working for years as an adjunct professor, recalls the stress—and the necessity—of caring for her mother:

> It was exhausting. I had to put, we had to put our life together—my husband's and mine—on hold for three years. I had to go to her house between classes to check on her, spend the night there, and basically take care of everything. My brother would spot me occasionally, but you know how it is. It goes to the "girls." On the other hand, it's not something I wouldn't have done. She cared for me, so I cared for her. We knew it would be exhausting, so my husband took care of the home and the pets, and I did that. And we went out on a date every Saturday night. I didn't live at home. It was really difficult, but it's just something that you do. Who would not care for their mother?

Transitions, daily hassles, and chronic stressors—all tend to be negatively related to both health and happiness. Boomers are differentially exposed to these stressful circumstances, with some experiencing poor health, income insecurity, job loss, and divorce all at once; others find they are doled out over time, and still others continue in their marriages or single lifestyles and jobs, confident in their abilities to manage. Past experiences and current situations render some people more vulnerable to stress, and some people adapt to stress better than others. Colleen quit her job in Virginia because of a bad boss, certain she could pick up some other work after moving to be near her daughter. But she is feeling vulnerable at the moment, barely making ends meet as she strives to wait to take Social Security until she is fully eligible and confronts age discrimination around every job possibility. Her education, skills, and experiences should make her confident and competent; instead, she is getting worn down.

These key concepts—exposure and vulnerability—help explain the wide variations in the mental and physical health of Boomers. For example, drawing on data from the National Study of Daily Experiences, David Almeida and colleagues found that the leading-edge Boomers, in their forties at the time of their investigation, reported more tensions than trailing-edge Boomers, especially around concerns about other people, such as aging parents and adult children. They also found trailing-edge Boomers, in their thirties at the time, reported more risks around their finances.[57]

This brings up the importance of perceived as well as actual financial well-being. For example, in the IT study of the corporation we call TOMO, we found that perceived income adequacy predicted Boomers' expected age of retirement better than actual income levels.[58] Saving for retirement and taking on bridge or encore jobs are both related to a sense of economic well-being, with both more common among men than women.[59]

Boomers improvise in response to stressful circumstances in a wide variety of ways. Colleen surprised herself when she sold her house and left her job. Though she is not sorry about her decisions, she wishes she had planned and investigated more. Rob (the merchandise planner in chapter 5) finds his job too demanding and is counting the days (and weeks and years) until he can retire with sufficient income. Jenn, the one-time PR executive, has turned to a part-time job for a nonprofit, no longer willing to let her job dictate her identity or her life. Mary quit her HR job to care for her aging parents and in-laws and feels good about that decision, especially since she was able to land another job, and even an encore one later on. Gray (the retired VP discussed in chapter 4) left his stressful full-time encore heading a homeless shelter to get healthy, but remains civically engaged, even hunting the want ads for another, but now part-time, nonprofit stint.

The point is that both transitions and daily experiences can be health-promoting or detracting, depending in part on how they are seen by the individual experiencing them. What also matters are the strategic improvisations people are able to make in response to the stress in their lives. We know, for example, that persistent job insecurity and unemployment have deleterious health effects.[60] Others respond to layoffs by seeking additional training or getting an education in an entirely different field. Some activate broad networks of contacts they have cultivated to locate new possibilities. Still others take to drinking more or taking up (or restarting) smoking to alleviate the tensions of unsuccessful job searches or difficult relationships on the home front resulting from insufficient income. Clearly, some adaptive strategies are more effective and conducive to health and well-being than others. And some options simply aren't possible. Paul was laid off from his job as an industrial designer and can't find another job even though he wants one. However, he has had success in several volunteer positions, working for a museum and then helping to mentor and train high school students. He has skills to offer, but can't seem to get paid to use them.

As insecurity, work intensity, and corollary stresses mount, many workers of all ages are devaluing paid work and careers as sources of identity and meaning. Vanderbilt University sociologist Peggy Thoits theorizes that one self-protective response to chronic difficulties is what she calls "compensatory coping," devaluing the stressful domain while investing oneself in other roles or activities.[61] An important body of scholarship by Washington State University's Monica Johnson, my University of Minnesota colleague Jeylan Mortimer, and other coauthors finds that young adults are shifting their values in relation to jobs and career paths in the face of difficulties they are experiencing, coming to value less what seems unattainable, such as high wages, job security, and high status attainment. Instead, they are moving to value what seems feasible, such as meaningful and creative work, the opportunity to learn new things, and more altruistic jobs that help other people. The centrality of work itself in their lives is also lessening.[62] As a case in point, the circumstances of working-class Millennials are captured in a recent qualitative study by another sociologist, Jennifer Silva at Bucknell University, who finds they are looking inward at their personal development, not at traditional work or career milestones, for their sense of identity and achievement.[63] I am observing similar value shifts by Boomers in the encore adult years who are looking to "turn the page," leaning out from conventional careers to seek purpose and fulfillment. Many are pursuing more control over the clocks and calendars of work through hybrid improvisations, time shifting to encore jobs offering some retirement leisure combined with less than full-time work. Sometimes these involve scaling back career jobs or else moving to public service or volunteer positions that provide personal, social, and societal purpose. Other times jobs are sought for the needed income. Others take up new jobs (one tour bus driver calls it his "retirement job") for something to do, to have some routine in their lives without the stress of inflexible, long-hour work. And as we will discuss in the next section, compensatory coping may explain why those who are fully retired report high levels of well-being, investing themselves in the situation they find themselves in.

Work, Retirement, and Health

Are workers healthier because healthy people tend to remain in the workforce—the "healthy worker effect"—or because working promotes health—the "healthy work effect"? Both processes are likely, of course, with the weight of evidence suggesting that job conditions can promote or detract from health and well-being.[64] The direction of that effect depends on working conditions, the fit between job demands and workers' skills and time availability,[65] the supportiveness of supervisors, schedule flexibility, job security, degree of latitude, and other resources.[66] For instance, a recent Canadian study by Selahadin Ibrahim and colleagues at the University of Toronto's Institute for Work and Health finds that work influences health more than health influences work, with low support at work and job insecurity related to depressive symptoms.[67]

Job and Time Control

A key body of scholarship draws on Robert Karasek's job strain model, implicating both job demands and job control as basic conditions affecting physical and mental health (see figure 6.3). Karasek defines job control as an employee's "potential control over his tasks and his conduct during the working day."[68] As implied by the observations of IT workers at TOMO, there is ample evidence linking job demands and job control to self-reported health, exhaustion, cardiovascular disease, depressive symptoms, happiness, positive self-concepts, distress, blood pressure and mood, and organizational wellness.[69] Job strain imparted by high job demands and little autonomy has long been linked to poor health and even mortality.[70]

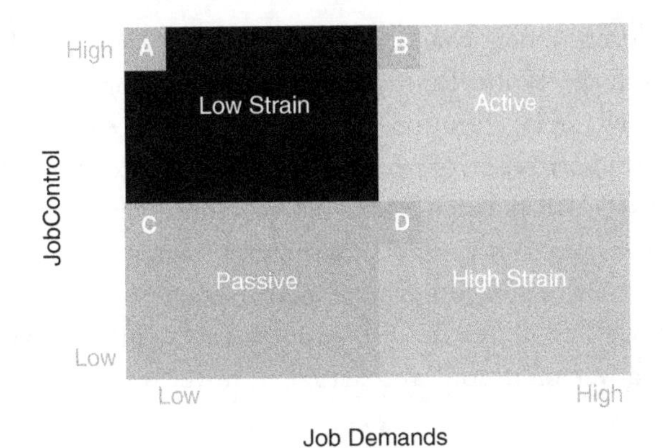

FIGURE 6.3. Demands and Control: The Job Strain Model

But twenty-first-century jobs are often prepackaged with considerable time strain as well as job strain. Heavy job demands and a lack of control over the time and timing of their work also take a toll on employees' health and life quality in the form of 1) higher levels of stress; 2) poor health behaviors such as insufficient sleep or exercise, as well as working when sick, and not going to a doctor when necessary;[71] and 3) the onset of chronic health difficulties such as diabetes, obesity, and high blood pressure.[72] Boomer professionals and managers often report impossible time strains that spill over into the rest of their lives.[73] And Boomers in physically demanding or low-wage jobs are often one injury or one paycheck away from financial disaster. Working under such high levels of job or income insecurity are important risk factors affecting the physical and emotional well-being of Boomers, GenXers, and Millennials at all occupational levels.[74]

Schedule control, the ability to decide when and where to do one's job, has been linked to workers' well-being, given the increasing time pressures, time speed-ups, and work–home time conflicts most are experiencing.[75] MIT professor Erin Kelly and I, together with graduate students, studied the effects of ROWE (Results Only Work Environment) at Best Buy, a major electronics corporation and retailer. The ROWE program permits teams to reimagine and redesign the way they work in order to maximize effectiveness and employees' control over the time and timing of work.[76] We found that ROWE reduced work-family conflicts and promoted health behaviors, including increasing employees' sleep time on nights before workdays by almost an hour. ROWE increased employees' sense of schedule control and time adequacy, both of which promoted a variety of measures of subjective well-being.[77]

In a randomized field trial conducted at TOMO, Kelly and I, together with others in the Work, Family, and Health Network, investigated the effects of STAR, an intervention designed to promote employees' schedule control and supportiveness of managers for their private lives. Like ROWE, we found that STAR reduced both work-to-family conflict and family-to-work conflict, even as it promoted a sense of having adequate time with family. STAR also reduced burnout, perceived stress, and psychological distress, as well as increasing job satisfaction a full year later. It also reduced turnover intentions and actual turnover over the ensuing three years.[78]

Other studies have investigated the health effects of long work hours, linking long hours to poor mental health, self-reported hypertension, poor physical functioning, and smoking.[79] There is also an emerging focus on home demands and home control,[80] with unexpected adult caregiving demands particularly salient—and stressful—for those in encore adulthood.[81] What I see as key is the idea of life-course fit—that the match or mismatch between job circumstances, other obligations, and abilities or motivation change over the life course, with different types of family-care demands and different working conditions exacerbating, preventing, or lessening stress.[82]

Consider the changing nature of career jobs, many of which are becoming more intense and competitive in today's culture of uncertainty and change.[83] Boomers in their fifties and sixties who are still in their main (career or longest) jobs are, like their younger colleagues, caught up in demanding and often unpredictable working environments. As a case in point, during the Work, Family, and Health Network study at the large IT firm we call TOMO, the company unexpectedly announced that they were merging with another. The move precipitated a number of layoffs. Once the announcement was made, some Boomers expressed a desire to leave these high stress jobs, even hoping to be laid off:

> Over the years I have come to the conclusion that I do not fit into a huge bureaucracy... I just can't stand it anymore. I hope to be laid off, but if not, I'll retire at sixty-two.

The culture these IT Boomers describe is taxing, to say the least.

> I work in an "always on" atmosphere from the moment you're in 'til you leave. There is no time at work [to] take a moment, breathe, follow-up on something. The pressure received all day mounts up, and

> once at home I crash very hard. I'm finding myself with less energy and motivation to do anything outside of work because I'm drained by the time I leave.

It is not only North American Boomers who report health problems related to the high demands of their jobs. Franz, at age 58 an art historian working for a large museum in Leipzig, Germany describes his:

> A couple of weeks ago I escaped a heart attack by receiving a stent. I have to move on even if it will be hard. It will be hard as many tasks will be imposed on me, often with tight deadlines. My only option is to convince my boss to move away from a rather hierarchical system and to provide me with more autonomy. I know that many professionals in Germany are in similar situations, but I do not know what they do to make things manageable.

Franz sees the problem, but doesn't know how to fix it. One solution is to retire "once I reach my retirement age at 66," but he is only 58 and already has a stent in his heart. He also has a frail father who is dying, reminding him of the brevity of even long lives.

Many Boomers are like Franz in that they love their jobs, but find the pace near impossible. Others like their jobs, but hate their bosses. And many may find themselves unexpectedly laid off or working under chronic job insecurity. These high pressures together with (in the United States) low or nonexistent social protections have tremendous consequences for their mental health.[84] The US Census asks part-timers whether they want to work part time, presuming that many want, but can't find, full-time work. But few studies ask full-time workers if they would like to work less (or not at all).

Working because you want to, with high job satisfaction, high job and schedule control, manageable demands, and in jobs you feel are meaningful—all these promote health and well-being.[85] These are also the conditions likely to delay total retirement from the workforce. Thus it is not surprising to see Boomers working full time report the highest health scores, while those out of the labor force reporting the worst, and retirees somewhere in the middle. Over a third (34.1 percent) of Boomer men who are not retired and not in the labor force and more than one in five (23.7 percent) women in this circumstance report quitting their jobs for health-related reasons (see appendix B, tables 6.1–6.4).

Retirement

I find that US Boomers frequently move into retirement—whether from career jobs or from the workforce entirely—because they can. This cohort is probably the last in which many have lifetime pensions in addition to Social Security. But most are moving away from stressful jobs, inflexible hours, or bad bosses, rather than toward a new and planned stage of life. At TOMO we found Boomer exits serve mostly as a relief from the stress of their jobs. One 65-year-old woman recounts:

> Since being laid off and deciding to retire, I am much happier and healthier. I can always fit in exercise and am enjoying being able to be active (gardening, yard work, housework) instead of being glued to a desk and on meetings all day. I sleep better and have a more positive attitude. . . . My husband even noticed that I look younger compared to pictures taken soon after I left the company.

Note that this woman feels in control of her decisions. She may have been laid off, but she decided to exit completely, not seeking another job. In part, this was a health strategy. She is into a regimen that keeps her physically active. Another woman at TOMO had to go on disability and retire because of what she saw as a stress-related stroke. Her work was exceedingly demanding, and her supervisor offered neither flexibility nor support.

But retiring from stressful work is not always a panacea. Those in low-wage contract jobs or on the edge of work in some form of partial or even full retirement may experience the stress of income insecurity or worries about future shortfalls. Boomers in their fifties and early sixties are sometimes reluctantly pushed into full retirement by the onset of one of several acute or chronic health conditions.[86] The result is what Hanna van Solinge of the Netherlands Demographic Institute finds, that younger retirees are in poorer mental health. Still, Boomers are generally physically healthy, having low disability rates despite being stressed in their jobs. Most are moving through the encore adult years—their fifties, sixties, and early seventies—in good health as well as good spirits. Moreover, Virginia Tech psychologist Jungmeen Kim and myself also find that the distress of becoming retired dissipates with years in retirement.[87]

Is retirement from the workforce good or bad for Boomers' health? The answer is "yes and yes," depending on how retirement (or employment) is defined and assessed. What matters most is role fit or role captivity—whether retiring, working full time, or finding some more flexible form of time shifting is voluntary or involuntary—and the conditions associated with both work and full-time retirement. University of Vienna's Bettina Kubicek and colleagues draw on data from an older, pre-Boomer cohort to find that men with higher job satisfaction prior to retirement have lower positive psychological functioning after retiring,[88] suggesting that those who enjoy their jobs may reap fewer benefits from a total exit. Similarly for women, viewing one's work as important is associated with greater depressive symptoms upon retiring.[89] Preretirement resources are key, as individuals may gain or lose resources such as social support or self-esteem upon leaving the workforce, with such gains and losses linked to mental health outcomes. But this is viewing retirement as full-time leisure; those willingly engaged in meaningful retirement jobs or volunteering are a different and more positive story.

An important study by Hugo Westerlund and colleagues working at the Stress Research Institute at Stockholm University followed older workers as they transitioned into and through retirement, finding:

> In this large, French, occupational cohort, retirement was associated with a substantial decrease in prevalence of suboptimum health, corresponding to an 8–10 year gain in perceived health. This pattern was remarkably consistent across occupational grades and sex, and, although the effect was stronger for people who had had a poor work environment or health problems before retirement, we also recorded a significant improvement in other groups, apart from those with ideal working conditions.[90]

However, those satisfied with their jobs received no such health dividend with retirement.

Researchers also find that recently retired men who have a wife who is still working report higher depressive symptoms.[91] This suggests that this nontraditional situation, when the wife is working and the husband is not, is difficult for men, possibly reflecting changes in the power dynamics within couples. Employment/retirement transitions may require a renegotiation of housework and lifestyles, underscoring the salience of couples agreeing on their retirement timing decisions as well as the role of planning to help each partner realize their preferred expectations in the bonus encore years.[92]

Research shows that having been in higher status career jobs is related to better mental functioning after retirement.[93] But having worked in poor work environments is also associated with improved postretirement self-rated health.[94] Note that these two studies draw on data from two different employment settings in two different countries (France and the United Kingdom) and include men and women from both Boomer and pre-Boomer cohorts. And they demonstrate the vagueness of what nowadays is considered retirement. Mein and colleagues define retirement as whether or not respondents (all civil servants) were still actually working after the mandatory retirement age of 60 in one of 20 London civil service departments.[95] In contrast, Westerlund and colleagues define retirement as the occurrence of one of three events: receipt of an official retirement pension known as statutory retirement, having a longstanding illness or disability, or else having more than 650 days of sickness absence in two consecutive years.[96] In both studies, however, mental health was impacted—albeit in varying ways—by retirement.

Of the things scholars can say we confidently know, the retired tend to report higher levels of happiness and overall well-being, net of their ages and their health. This can be a *selection* effect—those who are depressed may die earlier or stop taking surveys and those who are happy and healthy may retire to do something else, a *framing* effect—retirees may expect less as they are older and wiser, reevaluating their situations as a form of compensatory coping in terms of no longer valuing paid work, or a *stress reduction* effect—with workers in demanding jobs happy to lean out rather than continuing to lean into or just tread water in their career jobs. The framing effect may be similar to what Jeylan Mortimer and Monica Johnson find is going on in early adulthood. As Johnson concludes: "Valuing what one is able to attain may allow one to perceive one's self in a possible light—capable of achieving desired outcomes and/or living consistently with one's values. Valuing what one does not or cannot have, in contrast, could diminish self-esteem."[97]

How and why people retire also shapes their valuing of work or retirement as well as their health and well-being. A British study following people over time found that both statutory retirement at age 60 and early voluntary retirement predict higher mental health and physical functioning.[98] By contrast, retiring because of poor health was associated with poorer mental health and functioning. But note this group's health may have forced them to retire earlier than expected.[99] It appears that both retiring because you reached the expected age to do so or retiring early because you want to both have positive mental and physical health effects. When poor mental and physical health precipitate retiring for medical reasons, retirees can experience either relief (happy to be out of a stressful situation) or role captivity (wishing they had remained on the job longer), depending on how they define their situations.

Another study in the Netherlands following older adults over a ten-year period by Ellen Dingemans and Kène Henkens of the Netherlands Interdisciplinary Demographic Institute, finds that involuntary retirement followed by full-time retirement reduces life satisfaction, even as an involuntary exit retirement promotes life satisfaction. Note that the involuntary retirees who subsequently take up bridge employment do not experience a loss in life satisfaction, suggesting that postretirement employment can help older adults regain a sense of control.[100]

Back to involuntary retirement.[101] It's actually quite common. A 2011 MetLife Survey of the first Boomers turning 65 in the United States (the very edge of the leading edge, born in 1946) found almost four in 10 (37 percent) who retired earlier than planned gave health-related reasons, while another 16 percent said it was because they lost their jobs. Those who retired later than planned did so because of the need for a salary (27 percent) or else because they wanted to stay active (13 percent). Though there has been an increase in the average retirement age in the United States, the majority (63 percent) of those first Boomers turning 65 were already receiving Social Security benefits; half started collecting Social Security before they had originally planned. The MetLife Survey found most of these first members of the Boomer cohort were not worrying about the continued viability of Social Security; six in 10 Boomers are at least somewhat confident in the ability of Social Security to provide adequate benefits for their lifetime. Seven in 10 of these first Boomer retirees report liking retirement "a lot" while another two in 10 say they "like it somewhat."[102]

What about not-so-big, part-time, phased retirement, self-employment, or contract jobs? Less is known about the health effects of what is variously called partial retirement, bridge jobs, independent contract work, or encore jobs. But there could be selection effects, with men and the more educated more apt to scale back rather exit all paid work.[103] Those in these job arrangements may find their work meaningful and rewarding.[104] If not, and if financially possible to do so, they would seek other encores or exit the workforce altogether.

Still others who are retired seek out volunteering opportunities in order to stay engaged, with corollary benefits to their health.[105] Volunteering is by definition *voluntary*, which may be why it promotes well-being. Those who don't feel a sense of purpose or satisfaction in their volunteer activities for religious or civic organizations or schools are likely to stop doing so—and the power to make decisions is, of course, a bolster for that feeling of mastery and control that seems to affect subjective well-being so distinctly.

Retirement is often depicted as a process,[106] with individuals and couples gradually becoming adjusted to full-time leisure or some sort of encore of paid work or volunteering. Because there are so many diverse paths to and through this status passage, it is not surprising that different studies find different health and well-being outcomes. Experiences in retirement, including work/volunteer/education pathways and sources of social and material support and their impacts on health and well-being, are fertile avenues for future research.

Family-Care Work and Health

Providing care to family members, especially ailing parents and spouses, is often defined negatively, such as in the term "caregiving burden," but care work, too, can have positive or negative health and well-being effects depending on resources, demands, and again whether it is seen as voluntary or involuntary.

Many Boomers are providing care to grandchildren, spouses, or parents while also holding down a job. Women are typically the family-care providers, meaning that women lead contingent lives shaped around the experiences and needs of others: their husbands, children, grandchildren, siblings, and parents. While this is obvious in the early childrearing years, many Boomer women continue to feel their choices involving work or retirement, for instance, are constrained by the choices of their husbands or by the care they provide to partners, parents, in-laws, adult children, grandchildren, or other relatives.

Consider a trailing-edge Boomer care-provider (age 56) who was laid off from TOMO but fortunate to find another job that meshed well with the circumstances of her life:

> My husband has Alzheimer's, so that is a relationship difficulty. I wish I had more time to help my elderly parents; they live independently but could use some "company." This new career is close to home, meaningful, very flexible, and understanding of my personal situation—thank goodness.

Another TOMO worker left because she felt ready to retire at 63, but also to help out her daughter and granddaughter:

> I have been retired for two years. My daughter and granddaughter (just turning two years old) are currently living with us. I help take care of

> my granddaughter and have enjoyed the opportunity to spend so much time with her. Beyond that, I do not feel I have been able to accomplish all I wanted to the first two years of retirement. I feel more tied to the house then I want to be. We plan to utilize more day care for her in the next few months. I plan to find a part-time job in order to offset a bit, the 100% family/home focus of the past couple years.

On the survey she describes herself as working part time, which is what she would like to be doing but isn't, in fact, yet. This kind of family-care work—caring for her two-year-old granddaughter—is generally hidden, not really seen as "working," and it sometimes feels like there is no end in sight. This respondent loves her granddaughter, obviously, but is trying to take control of her life by getting a part-time job.

The same is true for family-care work for parents, partners, or friends; the conditions and the meaning ascribed to that responsibility are key. It remains the case that women do most of the informal care that sustains families as well as health care systems, though Boomer men are increasingly also care providers. For some it is a mission, filled with meaning and purpose. For others, it comes as an unexpected and unwelcome obligation. Some can afford to take time off or retire to do the care work that is necessary; others must improvise as best they can on this new frontier of work–family conflict.[107]

Three Protective Factors

A key concept in understanding Boomers' strategies to reduce stress, promote health and well-being, and achieve or deepen a sense of purpose in life is the idea of protective factors. These are resources that reduce exposure and vulnerability to stressful circumstances while also fostering strategic improvisations in the face of unexpected crises or ongoing daily hassles, such as chronic health conditions. Protective factors reduce the likelihood, severity, and duration of disease, emotional distress, and cognitive decline.

Most scholars agree that three sets of resources long-associated with health, subjective well-being, and longevity serve as protective factors: education, social engagement, and that sense of personal mastery or control described in chapters 2 and 4.[108] All three of these resources are interrelated. All three are socially patterned by Boomers' gender, age, social class, family and career stage, nativity, race and ethnicity. This means that some subgroups are particularly advantaged and others particularly disadvantaged in experiencing and responding to the stresses of their lives. I begin with education, then move to social engagement, focusing especially on the central form of public engagement in contemporary times: working for pay. I then summarize how these two tie in with the third protective factor: a sense of personal control over one's life, concluding with implications for those moving to or through the encore adult years.

Protective Effects of Education

In the 1960s, 1970s, and 1980s, Boomers led the trend in increasing enrollment in higher education, in part because of college deferments for those drafted or about to be drafted for the Vietnam War, in part because the women's movement encouraged so many Boomer women to start, complete, restart or continue their academic lives, in part because of rising demands for an educated workforce. Boomers with higher levels of education have been—and continue to be—advantaged across the life course compared to those with less education. They have better health, material resources, employment security, and economic security. Education is positively linked to exposure to some stressors such as the stress of higher status jobs,[109] but negatively linked to psychological distress.

Why is this the case? Having a college education is a path to gaining other protective resources such as a good income and higher socioeconomic status. Marjorie, the Boomer who got academic tenure as an older adult, describes some of these resources: "You know, I have insurance. I have living wills. I have a pension." Education is also linked to wider-ranging social networks, which could mean more friends, more sources of information and advice, and even a safety net in the face of a sudden layoff.

A college degree is also a path to better health behaviors such as exercising, preparing healthier meals, not smoking, and getting enough sleep.[110] Gray (the retired VP married to Marjorie) saw his second retirement, this time from his encore career heading a homeless shelter, as a way to become healthy. As Marjorie puts it:

> He was well on his way to becoming a couch potato, and he just decided that he didn't want to be that fat old man. He made a lot of decisions with his doctor and he's gotten so much healthier. He's very active and that keeps him, I think, young at heart, young in spirit, and intellectually vigorous, too. It's made a *huge* difference. I used to think, "Okay is he just going to be watching golf on TV for all of retirement?" His personal decisions have made a huge difference. He's much more

> able to do things than he was 10 or 15 years ago. He doesn't get tired. He doesn't get bored. He's a lot of fun to be with!

A college education signals ability and credentials, opening doors for employment, civic engagement, and other prospects. As with Gray, who took charge of his health behaviors, it is also an indicator of planning and problem-solving skills.[III] All of these promote physical, emotional, and cognitive health by opening opportunities as well as financial well-being. An educated, skilled, and well-connected Boomer is more resilient because she has more capabilities and resources to draw upon.

Protective Effects of Social Engagement

Social engagement comes in two forms: the connectedness of relationships and networks, and participation in social roles, what I call public engagement.

Relationships

Engagement with others through close relationships, especially marriage, also serves as a protective factor. People who are married tend to have fewer health problems, become less depressed, and are less likely to commit suicide compared to those who are divorced or separated. In turn, widowhood or divorce can produce declines in happiness. Marjorie, the recently tenured 61-year-old who took care of her mother, describes the value of marriage at this stage in her life, which she says "emotionally supports" her health:

> My job provides the benefits, but having a long-term caring partner obviously supports my health. Having someone who is available, cares about me. It works both ways. I'd do the same for him. His care for me last summer, when I had my knee replaced, enabled me to get back to work in the fall. Without that, I would have had to take the semester off.

Marjorie's husband Gray is seven years older, and she says,

> How do I feel about supporting his health? It's what you do with your loved ones! I don't see it as a duty: it's just, he cares for me and I care for him. It's just what you do. I don't mean that to sound like a martyr, it's just what I'll do.

Right now, this is not a concern; Gray is in increasingly good health. His efforts at not becoming "that fat old man" have paid off. Marjorie notes:

> He doesn't, at this point, have any health issues.... I feel like we have a future. I really, really do. I don't feel like we're in our declining years. I don't have any sense of that.

Social networks also serve to promote health and well-being for both marrieds and singles. Marjorie describes her network of strong and weak ties as "a tremendous help:"

> I'm in a professional world where I have access to friends that are doctors, nurses, teach pharmacy. I have a really strong network for asking a lot of questions. My close women friends, in particular, we trade information all the time. Where to get a good haircut all the way to where to find a good female physician. I've passed my doctor on to about six people! We have each other's back. Work is so busy that our networks provide shortcuts. I can call my friends with questions about how to deal with workplace problems, where it'd be best to have my knee replaced... And it's not necessarily a gender thing, either. I have a lot of great backup from male friends. If I have medical questions, I can talk to Brian [a doctor friend] or other friends about where to get the best care, even things like who's a good dentist. I think the social network has a lot to do with getting good health care.

Marriage may be a protective factor when the partner is supportive, but singles develop their own support systems. Sociologist Eric Klinenberg points to the rising popularity of "going solo," and that "older singles find all the experience need not be either miserable or isolating."[112] Boomers leaning out of their career jobs also have more time to spend with their children, grandchildren, parents, and siblings. A 2009 Pew survey found most (70 percent) Americans 65 and older report that spending more time with their family is what they see as an upside to growing older.[113] But the vast majority don't want to actually live with their relatives.[114]

Public Engagement

How Americans spend their time in encore adulthood also matters for their health and well-being. There is considerable research showing the health effects of engagement in paid work as well as the obvious economic payoffs.[115]

But stressful job conditions can contribute to health difficulties, even for older adults who have since retired.[116] As an example of the negative effects of role captivity in the form of involuntary role loss, those who are laid off experience a major decline in happiness.

Like my husband Dick, those who volunteer or are members of community organizations report greater happiness, as do those who are satisfied with their jobs. There is evidence from studies following people over time showing positive effects of such civic engagement on well-being,[117] mental health,[118] and longevity.[119] More recent longitudinal research reaffirms earlier findings about the positive effects of volunteering: it raises older Americans' cognitive and physical health and lowers their risks of mortality.[120] Rutgers' School of Social Work professor Emily Greenfield and University of Wisconsin-Madison's Institute of Aging professor Nadine Marks show that volunteering has a protective effect on psychological well-being, providing a sense of purpose in life for older adults who may have lost other role identities such as partner, parent, or employee, a finding also supported in a recent German study.[121] The people I communicated with in Germany reinforce the importance of giving back to their communities. For example, Franz, the art historian, serves on a wide variety of boards and provides leadership to other organizations, despite his health concerns and the strains of his job.

Successful Aging or Purpose in Encore Adulthood?

Health and well-being are often linked with the concepts of successful or productive aging. Physician John W. Rowe teamed up with University of Michigan professor of psychology Robert L. Kahn to lead the MacArthur Foundation's Study of Aging in America, bringing together a network of scholars. The results are summarized in their classic 1998 book *Successful Aging*.[122] They define successful aging as a combination of low risk of disease and disability, high mental and physical functioning, and "active engagement with life."[123] Active engagement is further characterized as "relationships with other people and behavior that is productive" in activities that are meaningful and purposeful.[124] This includes paid and unpaid activities. It is contrasted with "usual aging," those who may be functioning well but at high risk of disease and disability.[125] While successful aging is a laudable goal, the emphasis on productivity as well as on individual behavior and responsibility and practices tends to blame those less successfully aging for their own situations. By contrast, this book focuses on the institutional inertia and the need for innovative organizational and state policies critical to promising a sense of purpose in the encore adult years.

Successful aging has been critiqued as part of the North American neoliberal agenda emphasizing the primacy of market forces and paid work.[126] A similar focus on productive aging by Washington University's professor of social work Nancy Morrow-Howell and colleagues broadens productivity to include nonmarket activities.[127] Scott Bass, American University's provost and professor of public administration and policy, and Francis Caro, professor of Gerontology at the University of Massachusetts, Boston, define productive aging as "any activity by an older individual that produces social valued goods or services."[128]

Europeans are emphasizing "active" aging more than successful or productive aging, as a way to move beyond an emphasis on paid work. This conforms to my vision of encore adulthood as a time with hopefully manageable health conditions and active, voluntary (not imposed) engagement in paid or unpaid work or in other activities offering a sense of personal, social, or societal purpose.[129] Note the concept of an encore adult stage avoids the "aging" word altogether. This is important, given its negative connotations.

I believe that subjective well-being is a more useful concept than successful aging. Sarah Flood and I have analyzed the American Time Use Survey data asking people questions about how they felt on a variety of dimensions (meaning, happiness, stress, sad, tired) at different points during the day, when they were doing different activities. The results are quite illuminating. We find, for example, that Boomers' paid work and formal volunteering predict a sense of meaning or purpose. But so does spending time in child or grandchild care, helping out neighbors and friends, and, for women, providing care to an infirm adult. Moreover, working for pay is negatively related to Boomer women's and men's happiness and positively related to their stress. Informal helping out of neighbors and friends is rated as stressful and related to sadness for women, while caring for an infirm adult is rated as stressful for men and linked to sadness for men and women.[130] More studies like this are needed to understand the activities—voluntary or otherwise—that on balance promote rather than detract from a sense of well-being and purpose.

It is clear that the concept of well-being is complex. Activities seen as stressful are also seen as providing a sense of purpose, and different activities during the day shape different facets of well-being, differently as well for women and men. For example, Boomers are on the edge of much more adult care work, which we find is linked to both purpose and sadness. Neither are surprising, as we care for the people who have cared for us, watching as they go downhill. I find no simple prescriptions for or definitions of success in encore adulthood, though clearly purpose matters in addition to happiness. But sadness can feel like the right emotion in some situations.

Protective Effects of a Sense of Control

An important component of life and the ability to handle stress and maintain subjective well-being is a sense of personal control over one's life. Education and engagement each contribute to this sense of mastery, which is related to choice and the ability to make and reach goals. Sociologists Steven Hitlin and Glen Elder define agency (or control) as "an individual capacity for meaningful and sustained action, both within situations and across the life course."[131] Psychologist Albert Bandura points out that having little ability to influence the circumstances of one's life can produce feelings of anxiety, futility, and despondency.[132] And social psychologists Shelley Taylor, Rena Repetti, and Teresa Seeman define a healthy environment as one that "provides safety, opportunities for social integration, and the ability to predict and/or control aspects of that environment."[133] Clearly, a sense of control is a widely agreed-upon factor promoting quality of life. Consider, for example, the case of Colleen, who quit her job because of a bad boss and moved from Virginia to Arkansas. She couldn't find a job, but the fact that she was just able to quit her job and move made her feel strong and competent. As I write this, I just learned that Colleen has at last landed the kind of job she wanted and is flying high.

Sociologists Catherine Ross and John Mirowsky at the University of Texas, Austin underscore that a "sense of powerlessness arises from the inability to achieve one's ends, from inadequate resources and opportunities, from restricted alternatives, and from jobs in which one does not choose what to do and how to do it."[134] A stress process theoretical approach suggests that control in the form of some choice of job tasks, flexibility, and the ability to voluntarily scale back, retire, or continue working may be especially important for health and well-being in encore adulthood.[135] This is why it is difficult to say whether work, caregiving, retirement, or other activities are "good" for Boomers' health and well-being. It is not the role or relationship that matters so much as whether it is voluntarily chosen or a case of role captivity—being in a role involuntarily. This makes intuitive sense: when we have no say in how we live our lives and feel that we can't change bad situations, we are surely, if not depressed, not in a happy-go-lucky mood. Perhaps that is why civic engagement promotes health. Those not wishing to volunteer for nonprofit organizations either don't do so or else drop out, leaving the "ready and willing" in the trenches—those deliberately choosing to make a contribution to the public good.

There are at least two types of control. First is the ability to change one's social as well as physical environment—such as switching jobs, becoming civically engaged, caring for ailing parents, retiring, or unretiring.[136] This is what University of Pittsburgh professor Richard Schulz and University of California, Irvine professor Jutta Heckhausen describe as primary control, in which people are able to change their environments, for instance scaling back to more desirable work hours, or leaving the workforce altogether.[137] Second is the ability to redefine situations that can't be changed, such as when laid-off Boomers redefine their circumstances as voluntary retirement or moments for new opportunities, seeing the glass as half full rather than half empty. Schulz and Heckhausen define this as *secondary* control, responses to challenges one cannot change. People are differentially advantaged or disadvantaged in their control over events and control over their response to events. And their social location matters. By now, my dear readers, you must be noticing a trend—not only for encore adulthood, but for all people's quality of life. As University of California, San Francisco professor in the Department of Family and Medicine Marilyn Skaff points out, "a contextualized view of subjective beliefs about control acknowledges that factors such as income, education, occupation, gender, and race/ethnicity are likely to be more powerful predictors of sense of control than are age, cohort or life stage."[138]

Recall Klaus, the physician in Bonn who has considerable control over his practice, gradually scaling back his workload? By contrast, his brother-in-law Johannes, working in the private sector in Berlin, has no such sense of latitude. He is putting in 10-hour days, five days a week and says:

> It will be impossible to reduce my workload during my professional career. Doing so might be desirable, but unrealistic. I have little control over my workload, which is rather determined from the outside.

A lawyer and head of top management personnel of a large conglomerate that includes a number of companies in the chemistry, coal, and real estate industries, Johannes is taking control by devising an exit strategy:

> I am planning, however, to retire early, at age 62/63, as I hope to have a life after the work phase. Also, my financial situation is such that I will not have to work beyond that age . . . I feel that I will have worked enough for my life by then. Also, my partner, a physician with her own medical practice, is planning to end our working lives together to then begin the new stage of our lives jointly.

Note that a sense of financial security gives a tremendous boost to a sense of control over staying in the career job, scaling back, or having "a life after the work phase."

Security and predictability are key aspects of a sense of control. Though institutional theory is rarely explicitly invoked, sociological, demographic, and social epidemiological understandings of age, health, and the life course are typically about institutional forces. Scholars increasingly emphasize the embeddedness of individuals in particular social-structural contexts replete with different sets of resources, opportunities, logics, and expectations at different stages of the life course. These rules, claims, logics, risks, and resources open up or constrain choices, thereby shaping beliefs, behaviors, health, and life—from emerging through encore adulthood and beyond. But security and predictability are in short supply in light of the disappearing employment contract and reduced social protections in the United States described in chapter 3. As a senior systems engineer at TOMO noted, it is hard to plan in a state of ambiguity and uncertainty:

> I am concerned Obamacare will adversely impact my retirement, my benefits, and how much longer I need to work and save. I just continue to work and save without an exit plan for retirement or my next job.

Like most citizens, this man has little understanding of the ACA legislation's actual intent, costs, and effects, but he is worried at just the thought of it. Not knowing how national health care changes will affect his finances makes him feel he has little control over his retirement.

Today, Boomers confront the offshoring and automating of jobs along with heightened job insecurity, having come through the most precarious economy in almost a century. This often goes hand in hand with feelings of—as well as real—job intensification and extensification; some IT workers at TOMO say they are "on call" 24/7, 365 days per year. All that uncertainty and stress affects the quality of their lives.

Conclusions

There is no one theoretical approach that best explains the mental and physical health effects of paid work, family-care work, civic engagement, or retirement. They all matter, and for a lot of reasons. So in this chapter I combined strands of institutional, life-course, and stress process theories to underscore the dynamics and contexts associated with what are sometimes constrained choices as to whether and when to exit the workforce, seek an encore job, care for grandchildren, partners, or parents, or volunteer for a community service organization.[139] Taken together, these theories provide a framework for understanding the varied transitions and trajectories Boomers are following in this encore to adulthood. Choices by individuals, couples, and multigenerational families are embedded in institutional, technological, and economic environments shaping their options, as well as their current experiences and resource streams. Degrees of choice and control depend on both mindsets and power distributions in roles and relationships.

Implications for those in Encore Adulthood

What are the implications of what we know about protective factors promoting health and life quality for those in the encore years? I glean the following suggestions:

Investigate

Keep learning, and even go back to school to gain new capabilities and credentials. And learn to use the Internet and social media to better assess both useful and so-called useless knowledge. The capabilities and insights garnered by a college degree can be gained or burnished in encore adulthood through both formal and informal routes. There is a wealth of knowledge and insights out there. Use it.

Communicate

Connections are important. Keep or build both casual and family or family-like relationships. You don't need a big social network, but foster relationships that are important to you. Social networks provide support, advice, access, and a platform on which to reimagine and share new goals and identities.

Activate

Take control of your life... either by changing a stressful situation or redefining it. Plan for the future, envisioning several scenarios since the unexpected happens. Consider the possibilities of doing what you always wanted or doing things you never imagined. Try it out first on a small scale. And engage in lifestyles that will keep or make you healthy.

Appreciate

Find purpose in the things you do every day, in the people in your life, and in the promise of these bonus years of life.

Implications for Public Health

Yes, Boomers' health has benefited tremendously from the development of penicillin, the polio vaccine, and a host of immunizations and treatments that are now pretty much taken for granted, but this is a narrow view of health. Equally important are the social determinants of health, purpose, and happiness, including the ways societies organize paid work, care work, retirement, social welfare, and the life course. Boomers improvise ways of promoting health and purpose, but they do so given the hands they are dealt. The three key protective factors that shape exposure, vulnerability, and strategic adaptations to stressful circumstances—education, engagement, and a sense of control—are not available to large segments of the population moving through encore adulthood. These are public health issues—outdated rules, regulations, and logics around the gendered distribution and temporal organization of work, health insurance, retirement, pensions; the absence of support for family-care providers; and the lack of stipends and supports for volunteers in the social sector—having direct and indirect effects on physical health, subjective well-being, purpose, and even mortality.

Involuntary work, family-care work, or retirement are detrimental to health and well-being, as are worries about having a secure and sufficient stream of income. Both family-care responsibilities and couples' joint and singles' individual plans are increasingly salient to the timing of retirement, as well as the health and quality of life of older workers, volunteers, and retirees. Relatives are living longer and needing care, couples face two retirements, and singles feel flush—or, more commonly—financially strapped. The variability in age of retirement and the age of final workforce exits suggests that contemporary older workers have some degree of choice over the nature and timing of these status passages. But the potential opportunities for customizing this phase of the life course are not equally distributed. Some find themselves retired through forced buyouts and layoffs, along with age discrimination preventing their re-employment.[140] Others find they can't afford to leave their often demanding, stressful full-time career jobs. Both are examples of role captivity.

Health and well-being in the encore adult years should be high on any research and policy agenda. We are talking about the quality of life of millions of people, with all its attendant effects on health care systems and costs, economic and retirement security, and the public good. If we are to control health care costs and increase public health, politicians in Europe and North America would do well to fashion social and policy environments and lifestyles that reduce stress and sustain or even improve health, happiness, and life quality in encore adulthood.[141]

Research is needed to advance understanding of people moving through the encore years. These is insufficient evidence of patterned exposures to and experiences of the psychosocial risk factors tied to outmoded organizational and governmental rules, regulations, and logics around paid work, family-care work, civic engagement, and retirement. Such scholarship can illuminate the improvisations, pathways, policies, and practices promoting health and fulfillment through the second half of the adult life course.

We know the protective effects of education, relational and public engagement, and a sense of control. But research is needed on how to promote these protective factors. Will going back to school or getting an encore job increase Boomer's sense of control? What about offering older workers and retirees a range of flexible, part-time, or part-year opportunities to find purpose through paid or unpaid work? What social protections are needed, especially in the United States, for those not yet eligible for Medicare but suddenly laid off or needing to work yet unable to find a job? Scholarship on such innovations may also inspire and provoke the shattering of rigid, out-of-date policies and practices that chip away at the health and happiness of Boomers.

AGENDA #3

Innovations

7

Institutional Work, Pockets of Change

JUST AFTER GRADUATING high school, I was scanning the *Atlanta Journal-Constitution*'s help wanted section, surprised to find four listings: "Help Wanted Males," "Help Wanted Males, Colored," "Help Wanted Females," and "Help Wanted Females, Colored."[1] Remembering that job search now reminds me of how much institutions—and the ideas they embody around gender and race—have changed. To be sure, there is still considerable inequality in opportunity, risks, and resources by race, gender, and the two as they intersect, but at least such blatant discrimination is a thing of the past.

Still, despite policy and social changes that seem to allow or even invite greater access for all, I remembered those terrible ads when thinking about institutional inertia around inflexible age and time conventions tied to higher education, paid work, family care, career paths, and retirement options. Contemporary job ads don't say "Help Wanted, Men and Women under 50," but, given age discrimination, age stereotypes, and age-related expectations, they might as well.

Rather than putting in more hours on their jobs, people who can afford it, including Millennials,[2] may value spending time in leisure or learning pursuits, as well as with their family, religious, and social networks. Nevertheless, the fact remains that the most respected and rewarded activity of contemporary life in modern societies is paid work. This is why retirement became synonymous with old age in the middle of the twentieth century; people 65 and older were relegated to a life stage separate from so-called prime adulthood defined, for men anyway, by full-time, continuous paid work. But as we have seen in chapters 4, 5, and 6, Boomers carving out alternative scenarios in their fifties, sixties, and seventies are directly challenging this arbitrary division involving a one-time exit out of the workforce and into old age. Their portfolio activities constitute a springboard for the new encore stage of adulthood. Boomers' experiences sound awfully similar to what University of Minnesota sociologists Doug Hartmann and Teresa Swartz find about young adults in their late twenties: they see the transition they are making as dynamic and multidimensional, including meeting their own, subjectively defined, goals. And they embrace the "open-ended, diverse, and uneven nature" of this time of their lives.[3]

In chapter 1 I laid out a triple research, policy, and action agenda for redesigning the later adult life course: 1) recognizing the rigidities of institutional inertia; 2) charting and promoting Boomers' own improvisations; and 3) developing innovations opening up options around paid work, volunteering, and other activities. Chapters 4, 5, and 6 describe the improvisations and health implications of Boomers on the edge of their career jobs or retirement, often looking for or trying out second acts or something in between full-time work or full-time retirement. All along, we've examined how, in improvising their own individual pathways, Boomers as collective actors are helping to fashion this new life stage. Like Millennials negotiating lives in emerging adulthood, those moving through these encore years feel in between.[4] Neither group has the language to describe the stages they are in. One by one, or as couples or friends, Boomers are making choices to work and live differently by working less or in different types of occupations, starting a business or a new service, contracting out, going back to school, combining family care with paid jobs or volunteering, retiring earlier, later, or not at all. But their improvisations too often remain individual or family solutions, changing their personal lives but barely denting the institutionalized framing of the lockstep life course.

This chapter addresses the third facet of this triple agenda: investigating and developing policy and practical innovations meant to reflect the reality of encore adulthood and promote, for those who want it, ongoing engagement in paid jobs, self-employment, or unpaid volunteer work. What is needed is institutional work,[5] efforts at upending established, taken-for-granted logics and arrangements. Institutional work often comes in the form of *social inventions*, defined by sociologist William Foote Whyte as

> new elements in organizational structures or interorganizational relations, new sets of procedures for shaping human interactions and activities, new relations to the natural and social environment, new policies in action (not just on the books), or new roles or sets of roles.[6]

To be sure, we are more receptive to technological inventions like the latest iPhone or wearable than to social inventions. But social inventions are essential to solve contemporary social problems. And social inventions also build on technological inventions; mobile devices, for example, permit time shifting as well as geographical mobility.

Innovations customizing and updating the life course can capitalize on a vast pool of talent by harnessing Boomers' continued—and voluntary—public engagement. We have in the past invented novel, imaginative institutions like Social Security, the Peace Corps, and Head Start. Surely we can fashion customized careers and customized retirements, including meaningful opportunities for those moving through this new encore to adulthood. What we see thus far into the twenty-first century are only small pockets of innovation. The challenge is to be even more inventive and to take ideas that work to scale.

Institutional Inertia: A Reminder

My favorite cartoon depicts the Wright brothers in front of their early plane while someone observes, "We can't fly: There are no airports." When people try to tell me why we can't make where, when, and how much employees work more flexible or can't update the twentieth-century schooling/career/retirement lockstep, I visualize them saying, "But there are no airports!"

This is because policymakers, organizations, families, employers, employees, and retirees are all operating under existing arrangements, mindsets, and institutional logics, the taken-for-granted clocks and calendars of work, education, career, and retirement patterns set up in past times. We are all drawing on twentieth-century solutions to address contemporary social problems, solutions that simply don't fit unraveling work and retirement protections, the automation characterizing this second machine age,[7] our global risk economy, and the large wave of retiring Boomers with unprecedented life expectancy straining health care and social security costs. Recall from earlier chapters that this world of social and policy structures and schema was designed for primarily male breadwinners and their homemaking wives in the industrial and white-collar workforce of the 1950s. We continue to live by these obsolete rules and regulations. And yet everything—employees and their families; workforce demographics and diversities; union membership, reward systems, and job security; educational attainments, jobs and technologies; gender and race norms and regulations; economies and public safety nets—has changed.

Structural lag and institutional inertia discussed in detail in chapters 2 and 3 capture the fact that policies, practices, and logics fashioned by governments, corporations, nonprofits, and other organizations typically change at a far slower pace than these demographic, economic, technological, and other social transformations. North America, Europe, Australia, New Zealand, and Japan are all experiencing structural lag in the policies and practices organizing education, work, and retirement over the life course, as well as reduced social protections operating along an age-graded and sometimes gender-graded continuum. Despite the transformations discussed throughout—an aging population, a turbulent global economy, new digital technologies, and the pullback or even dismantling of safety nets—the perpetuation in policy, practice, and public perceptions of the myth of age-divided lives neatly packaged in the form of a systemized lockstep of first learning, then paid labor, and then the leisure of retirement impedes innovations in all three. We have seen how the absence of age-integrative policies and practices effectively closes out opportunities for many to easily time shift back to school, work less, change careers/jobs, or fashion some hybrid of paid work, volunteering, family care, and leisure. Like the Wright brothers, the previous chapters show how those in the encore adult years are having to improvise, landing where and how they are able. For some inventive aviators with no ready airport a field, highway, or even the Hudson River can do the trick. So too for inventive and resourceful Boomers. But too many are left behind.

Most Boomers I have interviewed say they "absolutely" want to work or volunteer after exiting their main jobs. Recall the AARP survey showing that seven in 10 workers ages 50 to 75 expect to do at least some work for pay in retirement.[8] But it is hard for many to even envision possibilities. One high-level administrator in a state agency, just on the verge of retirement, told me as have so many others she would like to work "in something completely different... I don't know what it is yet.... maybe, 'Welcome to Walmart!'" She also plans to volunteer "probably 10 hours/week" for the "church and the homeless." But she quickly became gloomy. "I don't know. I'm sick of seeing the Walmart Greeters... that's what they call them." She went on to describe the meaningful things she has done at church that she would like to expand upon, but that would only be available to her if she had a paid job that provided some income and was flexible enough to allow her the time for her passions. Such aspirations—to work at a flexible, not-so-big job and give back to her community to promote the common good—should not be unattainable. But how does she get there? She was depressed at the limited prospects.

While institutions are typically resistant to change, they do adjust in even settled periods of relative stability and often really revamp in unsettled times when the costs of doing nothing begin to outweigh the costs of change.[9] Consider the enormous effects the civil and women's rights movements in the 1960s and 1970s had on government, business, and community policies and practices. As was the case during the World War II labor shortage, in the latter part of the twentieth century governments and corporations began to at least publicly embrace diversity in terms of including women and minorities in their workforces. In fact, given the changing demography of the labor market and public policies and regulations geared toward promoting equality, a staunch refusal to change would have been calamitous. But in espousing and aiming to achieve diversity goals around race, ethnicity, and gender, what changed most were human resource rhetoric and procedures to be compliant with government regulations.[10] Many wage, hiring, and promotion disparities remain. And, as we have seen throughout this volume, obsolete structures and cultures reifying the rigid clockworks of work and career paths are changing slowly, if at all.

The fact is, the incorporation of women into particular occupations in the 1960s, 1970s, and 1980s did not drive changes in the taken-for-granted clocks, calendars, and cages defining paid work and career paths, despite women's traditional family-care obligations.[11] Employers expected women wanting good jobs—that is, those with benefits and prospects for advancement—to assimilate into existing structural templates based on the career mystique of continuous, full-time work throughout adulthood. All these many decades after the women's movement, there are still no good jobs or career paths designed as if all workers—women and men—have interests, responsibilities, and investments in life beyond paid work. Some European countries have generous paid leave policies, and some states in the United States are leading in providing paid leaves.[12] And there is growing recognition of the need for childcare. But these arrangements in no way challenge the fundamental temporal organization of workdays, workweeks, and work lives or the career mystique, ideal worker framing of putting in long hours throughout "prime" adulthood as the only way of achieving fulfillment and success. We have yet to adopt new mindsets, new visions of careers, retirement, and ideal workers fitting twenty-first century risks and shortened time frames.

When twentieth-century templates of work, careers, and retirement—including set starting and ending times, full-time or more work hours, low vacation and paid sick times in the United States, and the expectation of continuous employment until a one-size-fits-all retirement—don't fit with other obligations and goals, the resulting conflicts and overloads are framed as what C. Wright Mills famously called "private troubles."[13] In other words, the time strains employees experience reflect their own personal failings.

Thus, conventional wisdom blames workers themselves. They need to do a better job of fitting into the existing, yet simultaneously eroding, lockstep or else, if a secondary earner or retirement-eligible, exit the workforce. Few governments or businesses consider the problem as one *they* must address, engaging in the necessary institutional work rewriting institutional logics in light of dismantling time cages.[14] Boomers, like many Millennials, wish to have a life as well as a career. To do so many are retiring completely, when what they want is some ongoing but not-so-big job with a sense of purpose: personal, social, or societal.[15]

What institutional work around existing or novel arrangements can open up options for workers of all ages and life stages, and especially for those moving through this new encore adult stage? We find some clues in promising though small pockets of innovation, possible harbingers of broader shifts to come.

Pockets of Innovation in Public Policy

Government policy innovations are fundamental to redesigning a twenty-first-century life course, since state rules and regulations constitute the constraining and enabling environments in which businesses, community service organizations, families, and individuals operate. State and business policy innovations in Europe and North America toward the end of the last century began to focus on the needs of working parents, and especially working mothers.[16] But the twenty-first-century story will also be about older workers and retirees as well as the bumpy transition to adulthood and the insecurity of job lattices together with the dismantling of job ladders. Will modifications take the form of changes around the edges, in the ways that some policies for US working families (such as city or state paid leave or minimum wage efforts) have emerged? Or can we reimagine and reinvent the social organization of work, education, retirement, and safety nets around a nonlinear, non-lockstep life course?

The challenge is identifying, inventing, and advancing public and private policies opening up outdated rigid clocks and calendars, recognizing new forms of career paths, and the need for social protections. There has been some movement. Key pieces of early legislation in the United States sought to address age exclusion, especially in terms of extending employment. Enactments by the US Congress aimed at recognizing the realities and abilities of older workers and the need for including them in mainstream roles. The Age Discrimination in Employment Act of 1967 (extended in 1978) sought to help job applicants and employees over age 40, and the Older Workers Benefit Protection Act of 1990 prohibited employers from denying health care and other benefits to some employees based on their ages. But these are only baby steps, and did not fundamentally alter age stereotypes, bias, and discrimination.

In light of the graying of both Europe and North America, policies and practices encouraging early and "total" retirement are beginning to be reconsidered.[17] In the United States, a reform delaying full payouts from Social Security progressively (eventually to age 67 for those born 1960 or later) was adopted. And 2012 legislation increased the costs to Canadians retiring earlier than age 65, with a 36 percent reduction in payouts. Those who wait to leave the workforce until they reach age 70 will collect 42 percent more benefits. This is similar to the US system, in which those delaying their social security to age 70 reap maximum payouts. But these policies are only extensions of existing patterns, delaying but not reimagining the lock-step life course.

There are examples of innovations in public policy encouraging delayed retirement rather than penalizing those who do exit. For instance, one part of the Canadian retirement system gives every citizen age 65 and older a monthly payment (Old Age Security or OAS, $540 per month in 2012), regardless of whether they are currently employed. This is untethered from their past employment history. Because it is provided regardless of employment status, this benefit does not push Canadian Boomers out of the workforce. However, payments in Canada's OAS system are projected to quadruple by 2036; the aging of the large Boomer cohort is producing fiscal difficulties.

Another example of innovative action comes from the Netherlands. In 1997, the country transformed its early retirement incentives into prepension arrangements in which workers could both contribute to these plans and engage in work without penalty while receiving payouts from them.[18] Part-time work became a key way to keep older Dutch workers in the labor market, improve women's labor force participation, and reduce unemployment. The policies are also seen as a way of equalizing paid work and family-care work across gender divides.[19]

Canada, the Netherlands, and other countries have created some excellent arrangements, but most public policies in North America and Europe are not very imaginative in trying to increase the options available for engaging in some, but not necessarily long-hour, and more flexible paid work. Rather, the impetus in the United States is on coercing older workers to work longer by pushing back social protections such as delaying the age of eligibility for full Social Security benefits and thereby extending career jobs. This is an unsatisfactory arrangement for many Boomers who aren't physically or emotionally able to continue in demanding, inflexible full-time jobs or who are unemployed and not successful at re-employment. Age discrimination remains a thorny issue. For example, there have been some conversations in the United

Kingdom about job ads giving preference to younger workers.[20] Moreover, an "older worker tsar" has been appointed in the United Kingdom.[21]

Many of those in the encore adult years do want to work longer, but in the United States at least, they find few options, even as their career jobs feel ever more fragile. And yet an AARP survey of older workers found that while over seven in 10 (72 percent) plan to work in retirement, most want not-so-big jobs.[22] Over five in 10 (52 percent) plan to work part time, and over one in 10 (13 percent) plan to start their own businesses, typically working less than full time. Indeed this survey shows that nearly half (48 percent) of older workers ages 65 to 74 are already working 30 hours or less per week, as are almost three in 10 (28 percent) of those ages 57 to sixty-four. Clearly, some are in not-so-big jobs because they can't locate full-time work; others are finding the not-so-big jobs they want, but often in activities they may not enjoy, such as being a Walmart greeter. Note, by the way, that others I have interviewed want this kind of job—something not demanding, but providing them routine and extra money in their pockets. But those who can't find what they want or need simply exit the workforce.

Much institutional work is needed in updating public policies and practices and their underlying logics. The challenge is for elected officials, civil servants, and public agencies to remove restrictive regulations and develop innovations embracing new ways of working more flexibly and more flexible and adequate social protections, while also opening up meaningful opportunities such as stipended volunteering and a wide range of bridge and portfolio jobs in the public, private, and social sectors. The goal should be to encourage and facilitate working longer, rather than forcing people to do so, and providing some income protections for the long-term unemployed or those leaving the workforce for health or family-care obligations.

Pockets of Innovation in Higher Education

Take a look at the brochures from almost any college or university. What you see are terrific photos of 18- to 22-year-olds. Such presentations matter. One economist I know was aghast when his daughter chose to attend Florida State based on hairstyles in that school's promotional material. These brochures mirror the clientele of much of higher education, reflecting its social organization geared to the early or now emerging adult stage of the life course. While these young adults are, in fact, staying in school longer, education remains categorized as an activity for children, adolescents, and twenty-somethings. Older workers or retirees seeking to shift careers or retool by going back to school find it cumbersome, given that the whole infrastructure of higher education, including the mindsets of what students should look like and want, are geared to emerging, not encore, adults. Nor are there in the United States built-in opportunities for vocational training over the life course, making it hard for older displaced workers to gain the skills that might enhance their employability. But there are some interesting examples of structural leads: a few green shoots of social inventions facilitating the time shifting of schooling across age divides and throughout the twenty-first-century life course.

Lifelong Learning

Lifelong learning is widely endorsed by politicians and educators, but, in the United States, lifelong learning is typically a do-it-yourself project. Yes, there are programs specifically aimed for adults. Keep in mind, adult learners are seen as particularly dedicated and able to pay full tuition—both enticing for most learning institutions. For example, the Osher Reentry Scholarship Program offers support for students returning to school after a significant break to obtain their first baccalaureate degree. While 88 universities and colleges in 49 states participate in this program, it has limited funding. There are also Osher Lifelong Learning Institutes (OLLI), a national network operating in 115 institutions of higher education from Maine to Hawaii and Alaska. These innovative institutes were conceived of and supported by the Bernard Osher Foundation for "mature" or "seasoned" adults interested in learning for the joy of it. Another structural lead aimed at deliberately engaging older Americans is Road Scholar, the not-for-profit leader in educational travel since 1975 (formerly known as Elder Hostel), offering 5,500 educational tours in all 50 states and 150 countries.[23]

These are valuable opportunities, but they do not serve those in encore adulthood (Boomers and soon GenXers) interested in more than the joy of learning. Rather than assist those who hope to obtain degrees or additional training for a second career, a different line of work, a part-time job, or civic engagement, these programs are aimed at those wanting and generally able to afford a conventional retirement. They provide important services for people who have left the world of work, but they are about learning as enrichment, not certification or retooling.

By contrast, Denmark, for example, endorses the idea of ongoing educational opportunities throughout the life course, with publicly sponsored opportunities for employed and unemployed Danes. This approach helps older workers and the unemployed update their skills and remain employable in competitive job markets.

Some encore adults do manage to go back to college. A recent survey of colleges and universities by the American Council of Education found that while older adults typically enroll in fine arts and humanities programs, many also seek out programs in business management and entrepreneurship, human services and counseling, teacher education, and health services programs.[24] This points to the desire by some Boomers in the United States for education that facilitates paid or community work.

IT and Encore Education

Taking courses on the web may open up opportunities for Boomers. In fact, these new ways of learning are often geared to adult learners. Those going back to school online are often employed or looking for a job, and such platforms remove age assumptions and expectations. But online classes cannot provide the social interactions and support of a classroom open to intergenerational discussions, and social connection is key for some Boomers at risk of isolation. Consider Martha, who lost her husband and retired at age 57 from a major package delivery corporation, who took a class last year and loved it:

> The social connection is totally needed... I live in a remote, rural setting so it would be way too easy for me to be very remote out here. So the social, being involved with people, I think is important.

The challenge is to develop hybrid innovations—in person and on the web arrangements targeting older workers and retirees who want to gain new skills, additional certification, or new insights into themselves and the world, as well as build new future scenarios and new personal and professional networks.

Learning about Next Steps

Earlier in this book, I discussed how many Boomers have had little time to think about, much less plan for, this encore phase of adulthood. A departure from the workforce may be forced (as with a layoff) or unexpected (as with a sudden decline in health or a sick family member requiring full-time care). And having an IRA is not the same as having a plan. A number of innovative short-term programs have been designed to present options beyond typical financial advice, to facilitate a process of understanding what could be next for Boomers wanting to shift gears. For example, Phoenix, Arizona's Experience Matters has developed an Explore Your Future Program, a workshop for Boomers.[25] Similarly, Minnesota's SHIFT hosts a variety of programs and services to help those in midlife transition.[26] The Life Planning Network consists of a diverse group of interdisciplinary professionals who aim to assist in planning for the second half of life, including paid work, civic engagement, and other activities.[27] Encore! Hartford is another innovative program for managers and professionals who are interested in transitioning to jobs in the nonprofit sector.[28]

Harvard Business School has long had an Advanced Leadership Initiative: "A new stage in higher education designed to prepare experienced leaders to take on new challenges in the social sector where they potentially can make an even greater societal impact than they did in their careers."[29] Portland Community College has Discover Design & Engage, a six-week program for "intentional life planning."[30] And Stanford University launched the Stanford Distinguished Careers Institute, a year of advanced education for leaders seeking new directions and possibly new careers.[31]

But, again, these are high-end opportunities. The bigger challenge is to invent new and affordable initiatives in higher education that can enable large numbers of older workers to plan, retool, and transition into what's next and to engage in learning across generational divides.

Pockets of Innovation in Organizations

As it stands, most Boomers confront two institutionalized choices: total full-time (often long hour, often stressful) work in their current (often inflexible) jobs or total full-time retirement (sometimes earlier than expected). There are few widely recognized and institutionally supported options in between.[32] While some employers and sectors—notably higher education, in which phased retirement by faculty is a long-standing tradition—offer their older employees the ability to retire gradually by scaling back hours or moving to less demanding roles, such opportunities are rare. Still, there are pockets of innovation, new arrangements developed by social entrepreneurs engaging in the institutional work necessary to enhance schedule and even career flexibility, including programs assisting Boomers in moving toward a second career, a less demanding job, or community service.

Enhancing Schedule Flexibility

Several innovative organizations are anticipating and embracing the aging of their workforces, and some policies and practice advances geared for employees of all ages and life stages are helpful for those customizing their encore adult years. Greater employee flexibility and schedule control at work are the newest benefits on the labor market horizon,[33] enabling at least some employees to time shift their work to times and often places that accommodate other spheres of their lives. Note too that low-wage and shift workers are seeking greater predictability in where and when they work, so they can better organize the rest of their lives.[34]

Supervalu's WE Solution

Supervalu, Inc.'s Workplace Empowerment (WE) program is a mobile/flexible workforce strategy for all workers, and it helps in retaining members of their aging workforce. As reported by several people we interviewed, WE recognizes the desire for greater flexibility and new ways of working. WE first meant cultivating an organizational/cultural acceptance of mobile (offsite) and flexible work. The company redefined how and where work got done, focusing on outcomes and individual accountability over hours in the office. Now WE is fostering dynamic and collaborative physical space that better supports mobile work and matches workspaces to the tasks being performed. Their flexible, shared-workspaces have considerably reduced the company's real estate footprint and related costs. Another component of the WE program relates to the use of technology that will enable associates to work where they are most productive. Imaginative use of new information technologies facilitates connections and collaboration while removing barriers to mobility.

Supervalu didn't create WE just to get good press. It's a sound business decision. The program allows the company to shed excess, inefficient space; retain experienced employees who might otherwise leave for more flexible work arrangements; and "do more with less," using fewer resources in more creative ways. The WE solution has resulted in significant cost savings, a remodeling and decluttering of the office environment, improved recruiting and retention of talent, and better employee engagement and morale. Most importantly for top executives, WE has resulted in greater productivity as employees collaborate across departments and hierarchies. It has also helped Boomers work more effectively, enabling those concerned about ice on the roads on bad weather days to work at home, for example, thereby postponing exits.

MNDOT's Customizing Work

Another way to retain an older workforce is by offering flexible options for growth and career customization. Minnesota's Department of Transportation, MNDOT, has a reputation for doing just that. As one manager put it,

> some of these people may have worked here 30–40 years, but they've probably been in a million different jobs... so that there's an opportunity to take on different responsibilities.

MNDOT also emphasizes flexibility in the ways people work. For example, they have initiated the "flex day," where a person works seven nine-hour days, one eight-hour day, then has a day off every two weeks. It seems that in practice workers put the needs of the organization first when it comes to flex days, saying things like, "I'll switch my flex day if I need to, if that would help." Flex day is part of the vernacular of this organization, "the way we work here," as is the opportunity for some to telecommute several days a week.

A Flexibility Experiment

Recognizing the need to change work conditions in ways that reduce work–family conflict and promote health, the National Institutes for Health (NIH) and Centers for Disease Control and Prevention (CDC) supported the Work, Family, and Health Network, a collaborative interdisciplinary project involving field experiments to test the value of increasing supervisor supportiveness for employees' personal lives as well as employees' control over the time and timing of their work. Our study of IT workers at TOMO is part of this larger project.[35]

This field experiment shows the value of work redesigns for today's, not yesterday's work and today's, not yesterday's workforce. We have found that enhancing employees' control over when and where they work while simultaneously increasing supervisors' supportiveness of their family and personal lives reduces work–family conflict, burnout, perceived stress, and psychological distress while increasing job satisfaction and employees' sense of having enough time for their families. This workplace redesign is also good for the bottom line, reducing both turnover intentions and voluntary exits from TOMO, the pseudonym for the corporation we studied.[36] Boomer men randomized to the redesign (called STAR) were more likely to report later expected retirement exit dates than those following usual work-time practices.

Not-So-Big Jobs

I have been impressed with the books by Sarah Susanka about "not-so-big" houses.[37] Her photos and prose elegantly make the point that many Americans don't need or want large houses that require lots of furniture and have a big footprint. Similarly, I find that many Boomers want "not-so-big" jobs.[38] Having gained years of perspective as to what matters to them and how they would like to change their lives, few are interested in continuing to work in long-hour and demanding jobs. Time has become as important—for some, more important—than money. Not-so-big jobs can be part time or full time, but don't feel as demanding. The workloads and physical demands may be less, workers may shed supervisory roles, and the work may be the sort you can "leave behind," rather than worry about constantly.

Darren, for example, would like a not-so-big job, but isn't sure how to get it. He is a senior software development manager in his early sixties, and he leads two different teams in the IT division of TOMO, the Fortune 500 corporation the Work, Family, and Health Network studied. He's worked there for more than 11 years. He loves his team members, but hates his job. Darren recounts he is expected to do more with fewer staff members, and he puts in 55 to 60 hours a week, though he doesn't "want to work even the standard 40-hour workweek." He feels little support for the family side of his life:

> My father passed away recently, and the day that it happened I was here and I got called out of the meeting. I went in and told him [my boss] that I needed to leave and why. And...he was very concerned and told me, "Do whatever you need to do." So I took off the time I needed to take off and got most of the things resolved...when I came back it was like nothing happened, and there's all this crap waiting for me that needs to be done, and it's my fault that it's not getting done.

There is no such thing as a not-so-big job at Darren's organization. On nights he'd prefer to be entertaining his extended Italian-American family, he finds he is expected to work. Even weekends are open to TOMO,

> because something's going on. Production problems, production issues....And there are a lot of times when I just have to do things at home 'cause I didn't have time during the week to get 'em done so, you know I can't always leave it at the door as much as I'd like.

He stays simply for the paycheck, and is looking forward to retiring. There is no way he can lean out to a not-so-big job with this inflexible corporation.

By contrast, health organizations seem especially innovative around career flexibility and the creation of not-so-big jobs. Hospitals and health care organizations like the Mayo Clinic in Rochester, Minnesota regularly have employees on staff at 80 percent time—what amounts to working four 8-hour days a week. This flexibility comes, one person told me, from the nature of health care, which involves shifts. Employees can elect to work more or fewer shifts, and sometimes retirees take on shifts, suiting both their needs and the needs of the organization. It seems easier to move back and forth to and from part- or full-time or reduced hours in this field than in many private-sector businesses. It also seems easier to reengage the organizations' own retirees in regular or occasional part-time work. For the Mayo Clinic, the idea of not-so-big jobs (though they are not called that) is as a way of retaining valued and experienced workers.

Some private sector companies also offer not-so-big jobs. At age 62, Debra works full time in her encore career as an office administrator at a financial firm. Recall from chapter 5 that Debra left her previous professional job after a double whammy—a serious illness and an unexpected divorce—and sought a new job with fewer demands. She needed to earn an income, but wanted to lean out from the incessant demands of her professional career work. When asked about her encore, "On scale of 0 to 10, how much meaning or sense of purpose do you get from the job?" she replied:

> Well, if being Mother Teresa is 10 and being a cocaine dealer is a 0, I would say I am a 7, because I do help people, we do help people. If I were 25 and going into a career, there are probably other things I would do, but I am very satisfied [with an administrative job] for this stage of my life.

Debra is a good reminder that "meaningful" or "purposive" work can come in many different forms. She also reminds us that people want different things at different stages of their life course. At 62, Debra is "very satisfied" with this relatively undemanding job.

Hiring Older Workers

Some organizations are recognizing the value of experience, and, if not actively recruiting a certain age group, at least welcoming older workers. Health care and service organizations appear to be the trailblazers here. For example, most of the drivers for Vinland, a small service organization that provides drug and alcohol treatment for adults with disabilities, are retirees looking for a "retirement job." The executive director points out their value:

> Picking up clients, taking them to medical appointments, taking them to court, bringing them home, that type of thing. It has been fabulous because most of [these older workers] come from a working environment where they know how to interact with our clients, which has been a problem in the past. You know we are picking up people to come into chemical dependency treatment and they are nervous and they are scared. Almost all of [the workers] have had enough experience in their previous lives to be able to be non-threatening, to be able to talk to them, tell them it is going to be ok. They are very reliable. It takes a lot to shake them. That has been a great benefit for us.

Service organizations and nonprofits offer opportunities for not-so-big jobs (paid and unpaid) that provide a sense of purpose as well as the ability to shift back and forth from full to part time. For example, the Children's Museum in St. Paul, Minnesota hires and recruits volunteers as part-timers—mostly college-age students, but also retirees. People are attracted to these jobs and volunteer opportunities because of the nature of the work, including the ability to be with children. Another large public hospital purposefully hires back its own retirees:

> People will retire, but then they will want to come back in a casual capacity where there isn't any set kind of schedule, they can come in when they want to and when there is a need and work a few hours every week. Or… maybe they want to drop down to part-time, maybe they only want to work a 0.4 [16 hours a week]. Most definitely they are eligible for re-hire. The flu season was particularly trying because it did hit so hard and our staffing levels and hospital admissions were so high, we were actually calling a lot of our retired nurses to ask if they would be willing to come in and help and get us through the flu season.

Third-Party Pockets of Innovation

Some, like Martha, who just retired from a national package delivery organization, are spurred to leave their jobs because deskilling and automation have made their once meaningful work seem rote. Martha saw a small technological change in her job become a "game changer":

> I was a package sorter and you needed to memorize addresses and where to put them.... The boxes would come through a moving dump system to get to the sorters and then we would look at the address and then put it into a color-coded box that revolved behind us and those boxes would go down a system and go down to the trucks that deliver in the neighborhoods. Early in my years at a national package delivery organization, I needed to have those addresses memorized. So you would take a look and say this goes into middle yellow, this goes into top brown. It was within the last, maybe around 2000, that the whole knowledge-based value that I had changed because they came up with a little sticker that tells a sorter that it goes to top yellow. It would say that on the sticker. So it had gone through a scanner somewhere that knew how to put that information on the sticker. My value as someone who had knowledge went away. Anyone could do my job after that sticker showed up.

Now Martha wants some kind of volunteer work that will keep her "socially connected" and provide purpose to her life. The issue is how to connect with desirable options for civic engagement. Pathways to volunteering are not typically provided by employers to their retiring employees. And it as not as easy to find the right volunteer position as you might think. Valerie, a semiretired consultant, emphasizes the importance of "fit" and purpose in paid and unpaid work. Talking about options, Valerie mentions a webinar on volunteering:

> It was like, you know, paperwork or stamping envelopes. You have the most skilled people retiring and this is what you can come up with them for what to do? I do not think there is a very good match of opportunities for people matching up with what they are capable of. I think, as a society, kind of our whole vision of what people, of what the potential is for retirement, isn't very good. And there aren't really good supports for people.

Valerie is right about the absence of supports. Pockets of innovation cropping up in the form of third-party organizations helping to put people and paid or unpaid jobs together, provide some hope, however. Following are just a few such catalysts.

Encore.Org

Originally named Civic Ventures, Encore.org is the brainchild of Marc Freedman, a leading social entrepreneur. It aims to maximize the potential of older people as a source of individual and social renewal by building a movement for "encore careers—second acts for the greater good." This organization sees Boomers as "a vital workforce for change," moving from a view of retirement as the freedom from work to "a new life stage that offers the freedom to work in new ways and to new ends." Its programs include the Purpose Prize, the Encore Fellowships Network, the Encore College Initiative, and the Encore Opportunity Awards.[39]

Life Reimagined

AARP has launched this program aimed at helping Boomers consider and find "new possibilities," including jobs, self-employment, or second careers. Life Reimagined for Work provides tips and motivation for finding a job, managing your career, starting a business, and exploring your options. AARP's target audience is those 50 and older—mostly Boomers. It has partnered with several leading corporations that pledge not to discriminate against older job applicants. Richard Leider and Alan Webber, in conjunction with this initiative, published a 2013 book called *Life Reimagined: Discovering Your New Life Possibilities*, and there are Life Reimagined workshops held across the country.

Experience Matters

A nonprofit called Experience Matters located in Phoenix, Arizona, is another leader, offering a number of programs to help make connections between Boomers and nonprofits. In partnership with local Maricopa County foundations, Experience Matters has established an Encore Fellowship Program. Encore fellows are successful, highly skilled professionals transitioning from careers in the for-profit sector and looking to make a significant impact in nonprofit organizations. Fellows earn a stipend (paid by the organizations from which they retired) and work half-time for 12 months at a nonprofit host site.

Service by Design is another innovative program under the Experience Matters umbrella. It brings nonprofits together with volunteers who want to apply their talents and expertise to the common good through the completion of short-term skilled projects. The Share Your Talent program, an online portal through which Boomers can register their skills and interests for engaging in opportunities with a broad range of community organizations, is another connective piece of Experience Matters, as is Explore Your Future, which gives those aged 50+ a unique opportunity to consider "what's next" in their lives. The workshop series focuses on helping participants create a vision for making their future satisfying and rewarding. (Similar to Experience Matters is Centerpoint Institute for Life and Career Renewal in Seattle, Washington.)

Experience Corps and Other Service Innovations

Experience Corps was founded by Marc Freedman and others to engage people over 55 as tutors and mentors in some of the country's poorest neighborhoods and lowest-performing elementary schools. In 2011, Experience Corps become a program of AARP. Now known as AARP Experience Corps, it operates in roughly 20 cities.[40]

Nationally, Senior Corps funds volunteer programs (Foster Grandparents, RSVP, and Senior Companions) for those 55 and older.[41] However, these programs tend to be geared toward "older" Americans, not Boomers, and are often underfunded. Opening up Americorps (originally a year of intensive service for young adults, offering a small stipend) to older people has been a real innovation.

Other such third-party organizations around civic engagement include Volunteer Centre of Calgary, National Retiree Volunteer Coalition (corporate programs), Environmental Alliance for Senior Involvement, and Volunteers in Medicine.[42]

Placement Agencies

Temporary placement agencies can also play a catalytic role for Boomers seeking a different kind of or more flexible work. There are a number of innovative specialty organizations, such as Paragon Legal for attorneys and Experienced Resources for health care leaders (both discussed in chapter 8).[43] And there are more generalist placement agencies, like Jeane Thorne, which places people in a range of occupations—finance and accounting, customer service, inside sales, HR, legal and medical office support. Susan Dircks describes how Jeane Thorne tries to open up possibilities for their clients:

> I don't know if we are the only one out there that does this, but I don't think that every worker who is seeking something new has that innate ability to parlay "what I have done" to "what my skills are" to "where that may play out somewhere else." I think people tend to silo themselves in their careers, and when I look at our recruiters, I am proud to say it that we have recruiters that are outstanding at not just hearing what the person has to say, and "Yup you are a financial analyst but you know you were on a board for a non-profit." Taking all those little experiences—especially when people say, "I wasn't even going to put that on my resume," and turning that into "Did you like doing that?" "I loved it." "Okay why don't you go into this small business and be an HR project leader?" You know it is just that they are excellent at seeing beyond what the resume and what the person even thinks. I don't think everyone can advocate for themselves.

Agencies like this can do much to link encore adults with job openings. While they are not focused on older workers per se, they are looking for *experienced* workers, often coming hand-in-hand with an older clientele. Another long-established placement agency, Robert Half,[44] places highly skilled professionals on a temporary, temporary-to-hire, and full-time basis in accounting, finance, technology, office administration, legal, creative, marketing, and design fields. It is committed to inclusion and diversity, linking to online placement services like retirementjobs.com. Other online portals for finding ways to work and see meaning include jobsover50.com and seniorjobbank.com, all aimed at Boomers.

Collaborative Sharing

A plethora of social inventions have come in the form of dot.com startups and social media's promotion of peer-to-peer transactions, a sharing economy that may be founded by or of interest to those in the encore adult years. Thus some Boomers may use their skills, rent out their cars or houses (or a room), sell things, or donate time to help out others with errands and other tasks by linking to organizations such as taskrabbit.com, zipcar.com, car2go.com, krrb.com, mechanicalTurk, AirBnB.com, craigslist.com, and teamup.com.

For example, Sandra and Wanda, a fifty-something couple in Toronto, are planning their retirement (in two and a half years) around pet sitting. This means they can travel more affordably the world over; staying in people's homes and taking care of their dogs means they won't have to pay for hotels and will be able to cook their meals instead of eating out all the time.

Sandra currently works from home as part owner of a small business facilitating local home swaps (localhomeswap.com). She had worked as an insurance company claims adjuster for 12 years, but was "packaged off" when the company amalgamated with three other corporations. She then wrote a book, *Home Exchanging*. Sandra and Wanda have been together 30 years, and started planning financially for their joint retirement in their midthirties, beginning to talk about how they wanted to live in early retirement in their midforties. They have lived frugally—as Sandra says, they "are not spenders"—and feel they can live the life they have planned for soon. Sandra doesn't want to live like her dad, who retired at 65 and then died a year later. She will be retiring at 53, though keeping a hand in her small business.

Wanda told me that her company (where she is an executive assistant and office manager, supervising some 100 employees) has the "rule of 84"—employees whose age plus years worked sum to 84 can retire with a full pension. They can also retire at age 55 with a reduced pension, and that is what she plans to do. She says she and Sandra are in very good health, love animals, and don't have the stresses or obligations of children:

> We want a different lifestyle... we don't want to live in a city, but to live a quieter life. We love to cycle and travel and plan to take cycling vacations. How our parents thought about retirement and how we think about retirement is all different.

Pet sitting will enable them to achieve their encore dream. Social media and the idea of a sharing economy is opening up possibilities that did not exist for their parents' generation.

Conclusions

Structural leads are the opposite of structural lag and institutional inertia. This chapter has provided just a few examples of institutional work in the form of social inventions—new policies, practices, and logics redesigning and opening up the new nonlinear, life course.[45] Some governments and communities as well as educational, nonprofit, and business organizations are slowly beginning to invest in opportunities for and to invent alternative pathways in education, work, and civic engagement. Others, like third parties and dot-coms, are themselves social inventions, recognizing the experience and expertise of those in the encore adult years and aiming to put this talent to work. To do so often requires breaking or at least bending existing rules and fashioning new, more flexible, and rewarding ways of working and living.

To be sure, the policies and programs outlined in this chapter are just illustrative examples—a patchwork of small-scale structural leads. But they show what is possible. With the right incentives—a wide range of flexibilities, supports, and the removal of constraints associated with long-hour, intensive career work—many Boomers are happy to keep using their diverse talents, developing new skills and insights, making a difference, and improving their communities.

By contrast, an example of role captivity—being caught in a job that doesn't fit one's needs—comes from an interview with an IT Boomer at the Fortune 500 Corporation we studied. She is not yet retired, but expects to leave to do something else in the next several years. I hear words like hers over and over again:

> I would greatly appreciate being in a company where working part time or job sharing was offered, accepted, and supported. The company doesn't talk about these options; nor do they present flexible work hours as an option. It would be so refreshing to have the option at times to work 4/10s or odd hours, 6 a.m.–2 p.m., etc. Since this isn't part of the culture, it's difficult to bring it up without being seen as an "exception," even though our work can accommodate it. It's not a progressive company, and that, plus having a manager that is relatively new to managing people and not confident in being proactive, makes anticipating changes like this seem impossible. But having worked for companies that do offer the above, I know it exists and may need to leave to find it again.

The coercive "stick" approach, wherein reduced and delayed social security and pension benefits serve to leave Boomers stuck in demanding, long-hour or meaningless jobs for lack of other options, doesn't seem to help anyone. Far more useful would be 1) organizations (for profit and nonprofit, as well as government agencies) realizing the *competitive advantage* of opening up options for experienced older workers; and 2) social inventions that facilitate *cooperative projects* (paid and unpaid) across generational divides. Enabling time shifting to new and engaging jobs, less stressful demands, more flexible work, phased retirement, or other arrangements that provide a sense of purpose or at least an income not only encourage continued employment (and continued tax contributions), it also taps the talents of Boomers in ways that enhance both productivity and the public good. Future research on the successes and pitfalls of innovative businesses and programs like those described here can help identify the best approaches and practices for policy moving forward, as well as how to take new social inventions to scale. As Boomers know, we can revise outdated notions (it turns out you can trust at least a few people over age 30!), learn from our mistakes, and reset possibilities. Now, higher education, businesses, governments, nonprofits, and communities must do the same.

8

Transforming Institutions and Lives

I RECENTLY HEARD an "open phones" segment on our local public radio station. The question posed to listeners was, "What would make work better for you?" I was amazed at many of the responses: massages, casual Fridays, free food, the ability to take a dog to work along with on-site pet care. To be sure, some callers mentioned greater flexibility, child care, or safe ways to report bad bosses, but most overlooked the kinds of structural changes in the inflexible clockworks of work and education/career/retirement paths we have discussed in this book.

That so many allude to only modest improvements underscores the deep embeddedness of the status quo: the mindsets and institutional logics of work time and the linear lockstep (and gendered) life course. These are the seemingly immutable categories and rules setting rigid workdays and one-size-fits-best education, career, and retirement norms and paths, despite the fact that for most people contemporary careers and lives are feeling decidedly nonlinear. I argue in this book that today's demographic, economic, technological, and policy developments are creating dislocations, to be sure, but also opening up spaces for reinventing the ways we do work, retirement, family care, education, and the life course. In particular, these forces are leading to two new stages, an emerging adulthood and an encore to adulthood, even as the security and social protections of all aspects of adulthood are being scaled back. These stages introduce new ways of living, being, and defining success across the life course. But to get to a more customized life course requires changing minds and behavior. And that requires changing institutions.

Is a true encore to adulthood, with new prospects and potentials, possible? The answer depends on widespread adoption of imaginative and sustainable innovations opening up opportunities for learning, working, caring, growing, and giving back at all stages of adult life, along with providing reliable social protections. To be sure, we have seen how some enterprising and resource-rich Boomers as individuals, couples, and coworkers are improvising, time shifting by bending rigid clockworks to suit their goals and needs.

A college education has equipped many Boomers—as well as Millennials at the other edge of adulthood—with the tools to shape their own biographies using ad hoc improvisational scripts. They are choosing to become free agents as contractors or consultants, take on a portfolio of project work, help others, go back to school, start something new. In doing so, they may be the vanguard of a social movement helping to fashion visions of what is possible. Outdated rules, regulations, and expectations can be bent for the educated and otherwise advantaged, as we saw in the varieties of Boomer strategies discussed in chapters 4, 5, and 6. But we have also seen the risks confronting the less advantaged. And even educated Boomers in professional occupations are finding that careers and investments once taken for granted can disappear in a day.

Real opportunity will require transforming outmoded time tables, age- and gender-graded assumptions, and policies and practices defining, differentially valuing, and regulating employment, family care, and education/career/retirement trajectories. This is the institutional work that needs doing: purposive actions by people and organizations aimed, not at maintaining, but in this case disrupting the ways things are.[1]

Institutional work also requires visions of a new and different future, a process of discovery. It is hard to design new frames and categories offering more flexible and sustainable career and life-course paths for people of all ages when mindsets remain stuck in old-fashioned ideas about ideal workers, ideal retirees, ideal students, much less success and paths to it. What we have is a failure of imagination.

How do we change the deeply engrained, familiar ways the institutionalization of time in paid work and careers has organized the clockworks of life? That is the challenge... what scholars call the paradox of embedded agency.[2] Leaders in governments, communities, education, business, and social sectors are themselves embedded within the very values, beliefs, practices, and organizational arrangements that need changing. And yet as we have seen, entrepreneurial individuals and collectivities are beginning to refashion assumptions and arrangements to enable individuals, families, and work teams to voluntarily time shift working, learning, caregiving, and leisure in nonlinear ways and to respond to the involuntary time shifts resulting from contemporary organizational focus on profits, automation, and short-term time frames.

Chapter 7 described such pockets of innovation, hinting at some of the kinds of public, private, and social sector policy environments that could open up possibilities for more meaningful and flexible work, career paths and public engagement, regardless of age or gender. Innovative ideas are out there, as individuals and organizations respond to the twenty-first-century challenges of both institutional inertia and multilevel demographic, economic, technological, and policy changes. For example, greater work-time flexibility is beginning to be accepted by some corporate leaders,[3] and topics like paid family leave, sick leave, and sustainability in the form of minimum wages—long norms in other countries—are on the public agenda in the United States. Some American states and cities have taken such purposive actions, and there are some signs of possibility at the federal level. But recognizing and responding to the risks and challenges of a nonlinear more customized life course have yet to occur.

How to engage people and organizations in institutional transformation updating twentieth-century rules and assumptions around the clocks and calendars of our lives is a crucial task for our time. I believe we need to change existing institutions in order to create possibilities for personal and social renewal and reduce risk throughout the life course—for the advantaged and disadvantaged. In other words, more customized instead of age-graded education, career, care, and retirement pathways. This requires sturdy safety nets as well as opportunity, flexibility, and purpose. New types of social insurance are needed for those in between jobs, unemployed, underemployed, or finding themselves retired with insufficient income. Portfolio careers—moving in and out of contract and other work—require a portfolio of supports.

Recall from chapter 3 that there are three fundamental mismatches between the current institutions of work, education, and retirement and the new realities of extended life expectancy, global markets, digital technologies, the coming of age of Millennials, and the sheer numbers of retirement-age Boomers. Recall also that over one in three Americans are age 50 or older (see figure 4.1). Lagging policies and practices have fostered a work-time mismatch, a life-course mismatch, and a risk-safety-net mismatch. Can policymakers, business leaders, HR professionals, and scholars recognize and respond to these fundamental disjunctures—structural lag—drawing lessons from Boomers' experiences and improvisations thus far? And key, can they identify, invent, borrow, and investigate innovations—new language, customs, and policies—to institutionalize and support encore adulthood and a more customized nonlinear life course?

I believe those considering or championing opportunities and social protections for less linear career paths can learn much from the last labor market revolution: women's entry, re-entry, and now firm entrenchment in the workforce. As is now the case, the gender revolution was fueled in part by large-scale changes in the economy, technologies, and demography, but also by ideology, and in particular the women's movement. How can this earlier period of transformation inform the three mismatches confronting societies with expanding older populations and workforces?

1. Fixing the Work-Time Mismatch

Economic, population, and technological transformations generate opportunities for social change, setting the stage for deinstitutionalizing conventional arrangements and legitimating new ones, often through a recombination or reconfiguration of existing elements. Despite the fact that few workers have homemakers as helpmates and that women occupy almost half the US workforce, the temporal organization of workdays, workweeks, work years, and time "off" have *not* changed, with the exception that more workers are working more intensely—often expected to be available 24/7—and feel more insecure.[4] In part, this is the unfinished aspect of the gender revolution.[5]

To be sure, there have been modifications around the edges. In the United States, the Family and Medical Leave Act (FMLA) of 1993 permits workers in firms with 50 or more employees to take at least some unpaid time off for their own or their family members' health difficulties or care without losing their jobs or health insurance. Since the time is unpaid, however, many cannot afford to take such a leave. Moreover, FMLA leaves existing clockworks of work and career paths intact. This both reaffirms and echoes the unfinished nature of the women's revolution, in that paid work remains organized as if workers had someone else to take care of their laundry, their children, their ailing parents, themselves. These same demanding and inflexible clockworks constrain all workers' options regardless of whether they have family-care obligations or other, nonwork interests and concerns.

As they move through this new encore to adulthood, Boomers can be influential in transforming the clocks defining workdays, workweeks, and work years, as well as unsetting the set ages of schooling, work, and retirement. Many are themselves in positions to do so, as social entrepreneurs, elected officials, business leaders, employers, and managers. As individuals and parts of families and friendship networks, Boomers and soon GenXers in leadership positions want options for themselves at this life stage. But most have not translated what they want personally into rewriting the policy prescriptions and reshaping the cultures affecting their own organizations, agencies, and employees.

However, as we saw in the last chapter, some leading organizations are providing built-in impetus for transformation,[6] such as the ways health care establishments actively seek flexible ways of working to retain and tap the skills and experience of their workforces. Simultaneously, forward-looking organizations count the numbers of their employees who are retirement eligible and begin to worry about knowledge transfer and skill replacement. This can become the driver for the development of flexible full- and part-time jobs, contract work, transitional jobs in the social sector, volunteer work with stipends, and phased retirement options for their workforces, especially in today's and tomorrow's economic and technological climate. Chapter 7 describes examples of pockets of innovation suggestive of the kinds of public, private, and social sector policy environments that could open up different work-time possibilities. An easy, early fix could be offering all employees greater flexibility and control over their work time.

Schedule Flexibility and Control

A few insightful employers are already moving beyond existing work-time constraints, beginning to offer greater schedule control and flexibility.[7] This lets their employees—regardless of age—work in ways that better fit their desired lifestyles. However, it remains to be seen whether greater schedule control becomes a taken-for-granted way of working, or whether flexible schedules are doled out by managers to some employees but not others. Moreover, innovative practices are often the first to go in crisis situations, when leaders equate doubling down with going back to previous established, inflexible policies. For example, in the face of bad economic news, leadership at both Best Buy and Yahoo! withdrew their options for employees to work off campus. The companies decided their economic crises required all hands on deck, even as they expect their workforce to be available all hours of the day and sometimes the night and weekends. What many contemporary businesses want are both traditional work-at-work rigidities *and* work spilling over to the rest of life, being able to contact workers at home and expecting them to be responsive 24/7. This combination is intensifying rather than loosening the demands and clockworks of work.

Moreover, few organizations offer career flexibility in terms of offering Boomers, Millennials, and GenXers opportunities to dial down to less stressful work or new, less demanding jobs within the organization. Here nonprofits may lead change. Rising need coupled with few financial resources may herald more flexible options or project-type jobs or volunteer work in the social sector. This would permit Boomers and other workers to negotiate the degree of engagement they prefer, especially when they come with strong motivation, considerable skills, and compelling interest in working to improve the human condition.

The sociologist Richard Sennett calls for a different form of job sharing, with traditional full-time (or longer) jobs divided up in ways that better fit what workers want and need.[8] Health care facilities and social service organizations seem to be more accommodating to employees and volunteers than those in the private sector.

New digital technologies are also transforming education in terms of time and place, making for more flexible schedules and time-shifting arrangements across the life course. Seeking out and serving encore learners as well as their traditional younger clientele could have big payoffs for universities and employers alike.

Leading by Example

Federal, state, and local governments not only serve the public, they also employ a large segment of the workforce (15.3 percent in the US workforce, 28 percent in Wales, and 21 percent in London, for example).[9] Changing the clocks and calendars of this public sector workforce could be extremely influential. If government agencies were to model innovative, flexible ways of training, retaining, hiring, and retiring workers, they would open up—rather than close down—options. Governments at the federal, state, and local levels could be model employers in terms of identifying and speaking out against age discrimination as well as developing not-so-big and bridge jobs for Boomers and others who want to scale back.

2. *Addressing the Life-Course Mismatch*

Organizational scholars have found that transformations are most likely to occur when the costs of doing nothing are greater than the costs of change.[10] Today, elected officials in high-income countries are confronting spiraling health care and social security costs. Business, public, and social sector employers are increasingly faced with older workforces wanting greater flexibility and career crafting even as they worry about being laid off. In truth, workers of all ages and especially Millennials are also seeking these new ways of working and living. Employers are confronting a looming loss: the specter of talent and tacit knowledge about the way things really work lost as retiring Boomers walk out the door.[11] The growing body of retirement-eligible older workers and their amassed institutional knowledge—all of which will be lost to companies bent on outsourcing, offshoring, automating, and hiring fresh batches of interns as fast as they can—may be the tipping point for a true embrace of flexible work and flexible career and retirement path redesigns. It is my hope that more employers like those discussed in these last two chapters begin recognizing the retention or hiring of older workers as a competitive advantage, recognizing also that the linear lockstep is gone, with the customizations Boomers want desired by Millennials and GenXers as well.

Similarly, public policymakers are beginning to realize the social costs of *not* refashioning outdated age-graded life-course templates, including but far beyond the loss of human capital and potential and the rise in social security expenditures. Consider the health costs accompanying the debilitating stresses related to too-demanding jobs for those who can no longer sustain difficult physical, emotional, or long-hour work but can't afford to retire. Then there are the health costs of job loss, unemployment, income insecurity, and age discrimination. And the multilayered costs of the absence of purpose or meaning in the lives of those unwillingly pushed out of the mainstream of society but with many years of time and talent to give.

Most Boomers dismiss their parents' lifestyles as old-fashioned, no longer effective blueprints for living. But what constitutes a vision for the future that can motivate and direct organizational and public policy changes aimed at opening up possibilities in this age of uncertainty?

As previewed in chapter 2, three things make something an institution and need to change in order to redesign work, retirement, learning, family care, community service, and, indeed, the whole structure of the adult course in the twenty-first century. Specifically, these are language, customs, and a body of rules and laws, all of which serve to regularize behavior.[12] The challenge—and promise—of emerging and encore adulthood and a customized life course is that all three are in flux.

The Need to Change Language

During the women's movement, women in organizations, groups, and on their own pushed for changes in taken-for-granted language—recall chairman, mailman, and stewardess, for example. They also challenged cultural stereotypes, mindsets, and media representations, such as doctors and politicians as invariably men, ads of women enjoying their washing machines in fancy dresses and high heels and others like "I dreamed I was shopping in my Maidenform Bra." And they exposed customary community practices such as parent-teacher meetings during the day, when homemaking mothers were presumed to be available, while working fathers, of course, were not.

Now consider the language around aging. Words like elders, aged, senior citizens, and being/becoming old are now being challenged. The reality posed by *Age Power* author Ken Dychtwald that America is becoming a gerontocracy may be true, but the language of gerontocracy has not taken hold, as both Boomers and advanced societies continue to focus on youth and vitality.[13] Language around productive aging or successful aging remains suspect, in part because Boomers don't want to think of themselves as aging, and critical scholars are troubled by mindsets equating success with productivity in the market.[14] Moreover, people of all ages but especially Boomers and Millennials are reformulating success and the good life away from high status and high salaries.[15] Many Boomers are choosing and negotiating new identities, no longer accepting those constructed around career work, retirement, and age. Boomers don't see themselves as elderly, a word and idea they associate with decrepitude and irrelevance.

Old age itself has become a nebulous concept. Classic age divides are blurring: age 65 no longer necessarily signals the passage to old age, at least for those approaching or who have passed this milestone. Clinical psychologists Chris Gilleard and Paul Higgs conclude:

> To be done and outside the labour market is no longer to be old. Old age is a status conferred by others... For the majority, what continues is the symbolic connectedness of individualized lives.[16]

Language and identity are closely related. Who Boomers are as individuals and as family and community members has been tied to their occupations or the organizations they work for. Do people leaving their career jobs identify with what they were, not what they are? Retired in the form of checking out of mainstream society is not a status or identity the best-known Boomers such as Barak and Michelle Obama or Hillary and Bill Clinton—or tens of thousands of the less famous seek. Will the encore adult stage be a time of renewal, providing both the famous and everyone else new challenges and new identities? Or will they remain defined by their past lives?

Encore careers, bridge jobs, second chapters, retirement jobs, transition jobs, encore jobs, semiretired, paid volunteers, civic engagement, social entrepreneurs, and encore adulthood are all concepts providing language to capture multiple life-course pathways that are challenging the equating of age with irrelevance. This is especially important for Boomers laid off or taking retirement buyouts, Boomers needing to work to make ends meet, and Boomers who feel too young to retire or want to continue making contributions to organizations, industries, communities, or the next generation.

In stark contrast, the language around aging and growing older is fraught with negative meanings, associated with sickness, disease, frailty, and general mental as well as physical decline. Refashioning language to incorporate a new temporal space in the life course, an encore period of renewal, is a real challenge. But Boomers are changing language as much as by what they do as what they say. A case in point: in my research I find the terms "working retired" and "encore job" increasingly common.

The Need to Change Customs, Rules, and Laws

In terms of customs as well as a body of rules and laws, different institutions constitute a web of outdated age-graded social structures and cultures based on workers and retirees from the middle of the last century.[17] The challenge is to create new categories and revamp institutions to open up and value education across the life course as well as different types—and amounts—of paid and unpaid work, including recognizing the value of family care for the young and infirm along with personal care, the activities like sufficient sleep and exercise that get and keep people healthy.

The linear, lockstep, and gendered life course was concocted in the twentieth century through a range of education, work, family care, social-welfare, and retirement customs, policies and practices intended to maximize the productivity of an industrial and white-collar labor force by freeing them from worries about the future (with pensions and job security with seniority) as well as distracting care obligations. Homemaking women were expected to provide their white-collar and blue-collar husbands with the respite and recuperation necessary for productivity on the job, in part by taking care of the rest of their lives, including their families and homes. The women's movement of the 1960s and 1970s changed all that. Women—and some men—pushed for social change, for equality of opportunity regardless of gender. Middle-class married women, even mothers, began to seek, remain in, or re-enter paid work.

It is hard to remember how much pushback there was. To protest the election of the first woman to the school board in a small town in northern Minnesota, the other members decided to meet in the men's bathroom. The newly elected woman marched right in with them. I recall the awe with which my youngest daughter Melanie greeted the sight of a woman holding a traffic sign at a construction site. She cranked down the car window to shout, "Way to go!"

But the traditional lockstep linear model of career paths didn't change with the women's movement. Even though the career mystique was based on having someone else—a homemaker alongside the breadwinner—so workers might focus full time on their jobs, the model remained the same as women, the traditional care providers, also sought the career mystique ideal. There was an uneasy acceptance of women as part of the workforce, but no resolution to date around the issues of family care or couples' two sets of career obligations. This has resulted in what sociologist Gøsta Esping-Andersen calls an unstable equilibrium, a basic indeterminacy in terms of guiding people's beliefs and choices given a lack of commonly shared standards identifying what is best.[18] This last labor market revolution—women's increased participation—is what another sociologist, Kathleen Gerson,[19] calls an unfinished revolution, with some policy shifts promoting gender equality but no true structural changes acknowledging the fact that all employees—men as well as women—have nonwork concerns, interests, needs, and responsibilities. Where the women's movement came up short is in redesigning work, career paths, and care. Societies seem slow to recognize that there is, in fact, no border between work and home, nor between occupational and family career paths—that both are experienced in concert, with each providing respites from as well as stresses and resources spilling over to the other.

And both are about time, and the mismatches between time for and the rhythms of life—family and personal life—and time for work. New digital technologies are increasing time pressures but also opportunities for time shifting if we reimagine and redesign new configurations of time, the clocks and calendars of paid work, care work, and leisure. As University of Minnesota political scientist Joan Tronto points out in her book *Caring Democracy*, "care is about relationships. And relationships require more than anything else sufficient time and proximity. Among the most important considerations in rethinking society from a caring perspective, then, is creating time and space for care."[20]

The linear lockstep career path has not only marginalized family and personal care, it has both fostered and been reinforced by a system of age as well as gender stratification, with hiring, promotion, and other opportunities based on age and gender. Age-based norms and expectations effectively reify another putative border—that between active adulthood and what comes next, presumably passive adulthood? These deeply embedded, taken-for-granted mindsets, policies, and practices reward people of certain ages—such as through pensions, social security, Medicare (in the United States), senior rates on public transportation and at movies. But they simultaneously remove them from public engagement opportunities, such as the absence of training and limited access to new projects, leading some older workers to be seen as retired on the job. The way we structure work around age, assuming that retirement-eligible workers should be exiting soon and that entry-level job applicants should be in their twenties or early thirties, for example, limits the options of fifty-, sixty-, or seventy-something Boomers who want to postpone total retirement by adding a not-so-big encore job.[21]

The status quo is backward-looking, continuing to define and shape age, aging, and the life course by the way things were. To be sure, some Boomers can break out to fashion new ways of living. Those who have accumulated advantages over the course of their lives, from being male or white to the health and economic benefits of a college degree, are unique in being better able to follow the paths they choose despite outdated policies and practices. Others, less advantaged, move through this period of life confronting more constraints and fewer options. For them, the years that could be an encore can feel like an interminable maze or even a downward spiral.

Like gender, age stereotypes, bias, and discrimination also impede inventive ways of thinking about and customizing the life course. Older people are perceived positively as warm and kind, but also ineffective. They are too often marginalized, ignored by coworkers, overlooked by hiring managers. What is defined as real—that is, how people believe age to be a marker of decline—thus stands in the way of imagination and innovation.

When thinking about new designs for living, it is easier to contemplate transforming the physical (built) environments of residences and neighborhoods than social environments constituting the clocks, calendars, and time cages of our lives. Without doubt, they will be more difficult to modify than the new bike paths and walkways springing up to encourage people of all ages to become and keep physically active.

In refurbishing existing institutions, elected officials and policymakers need to recognize the wide variations in Boomers' experiences. They come to the encore adult years with no common priors, bringing vast differences in material, human, personal, and social resources and needs, along with a multitude of lifestyle preferences and dreams. To be sure, some want a well-deserved time out, but others want or need full-time work. Even more want to work more flexibly in part-time, part-year, or contract jobs. Some seek to start new careers in self-employment or other occupations; some want to work or volunteer for the social sector giving back to their communities and the next generation of children, but may need small stipends to make that feasible. Most find it difficult to identify suitable positions, to be considered for available openings, or, if interviewed, to be hired. Institutional inertia behind the life-course mismatch remains a key barrier to possibility.

Rewriting Life-Course Scripts

How can individuals, families, social networks, organizations, and governments support both individual and collective action in rewriting existing life-course scripts? Again, the women's movement is suggestive. In the last third of the twentieth century, women directly participated in social change as individuals and small collections of friends, club members, consciousness-raising groups,[22] and coworkers challenging the status quo. On a wide variety of personal fronts they improvised their lives by returning to school, moving into or remaining in the labor market, taking up traditionally male occupations, and climbing organizational ladders. But they also did more: protesting, rallying, litigating, and systematically pushing for policy changes in rules, regulations, and legislation around the key institutions of education, work, family, religion, government, media, and markets. In doing so, they ignited widespread social change that challenged existing gender stereotypes and restrictions, even though they did not chip away at the linear and lockstep life course.

Similarly, Boomers today are improvising by choice or by circumstance, time shifting when and how they work, serve, learn, care, connect, give back, and play. The fact is, for the moment at least, it is Boomers as individuals and couples who are reimagining and reinventing their own paths. One by one, as couples or in small groups, Boomers blessed with sufficient material resources are creating niches for themselves, forging relationships with community organizations to use their time, talent, and experience in ways that promote both their own and the next generation's well-being, inspiring others along the way. Other Boomers remain or move into public or social sector work, start their own businesses, or find positions where they can be useful while simultaneously forging new identities and more flexible ways of working.

Many are aggressively building their own paths: delaying, expediting, or postponing retirement indefinitely (neotraditional paths); remaining in jobs they love (long-game paths); customizing existing or new encore jobs, gigs, volunteer opportunities, and leisure (portfolio paths); or adapting to unexpected retirement exits (unexpected exit paths) in ways that make sense for them.

Many Boomers also occupy positions of power and influence. When will the public, private, and social sector leaders in this cohort begin to imagine and implement change? Not only personal transformation for themselves as they move through a new and uncharted life phase, but also the kinds of organizational and policy changes that will open up possibilities for everyone?

I see three possible avenues for changes aimed at fixing the life-course mismatch: the *postponing retirement* solution, the *personal responsibility* solution, and the *redesigning the life-course* solution.[23]

The Postponing Retirement Solution

What many policymakers see as the obvious solution is delaying Social Security benefits by moving the early benefit age—in the United States from 62 to 64—and delaying full benefits to age 70 or even later.[24] To my mind, postponing exits from career jobs might work for the educated segment of the Boomer workforce who still like and are able to perform their jobs. For everyone else, it would be a disaster: those with family-care responsibilities, with chronic or acute health conditions of their own, working in stressful or physically demanding job environments, with high job insecurity, or who have already been laid off. Using economic insecurity and limited social protections to keep people unwillingly working longer is, in my view, a bad idea with many unintended negative consequences, including ratcheting up stress and health problems, as well as high absenteeism and presenteeism (being at work but actually accomplishing very little).

The Personal Responsibility Solution

The personal responsibility solution is what we see at the other end of the adult life course, where those in emerging adulthood (and sometimes their parents) are expected to find their own solutions to the risks and uncertainties of their lives. As we have seen, many Boomers are developing innovative second acts on their own, even though others are unable to do so. But the premise behind personal responsibility at both edges of adulthood is that job opportunities, incomes, and other resources are there for the taking; that is simply not the case for far too many in emerging and encore adulthood or those in between. Workers of all ages confront chronic uncertainty, outdated templates, and unraveling safety nets. They feel unable to plan for the future, much less create the lives they want.

The Redesigning the Life-Course Solution

I have argued that redesigning the life course and the institutions undergirding it is the optimal solution for the mismatches we confront in the face of demographic, technological, economic, and policy forces reshaping life in the twenty-first century. Provision of nonlinear customized educational, career path, and retirement options is key to updating the life course and better fitting the reality of the portfolio careers that seem to be on the near horizon.

Including as well a portfolio of meaningful, often less than full-time paid work possibilities that attract those in the encore years is one response to the rising numbers of Boomers becoming eligible for and straining Social Security and Medicare coffers. This is why I am drawn to Marc Freedman's word "encore:"[25] it implies a voluntary activity after the main event, one that might even be more purposeful and gratifying than what came before.

3. *Recognizing the Risk-Safety Net Mismatch*

Industry leaders and elected officials—many of whom are themselves Boomers—may be slow to recognize the need for providing contemporary workers with greater life-course flexibility and possibility in the shaping of alternative career, learning, and retirement paths. But unfortunately, as we saw in chapter 3, powerful actors in organizations *are* questioning and many are eliminating the pension, seniority, and health care benefits once used to lure and retain workers, what was known as the mid-twentieth-century social contract.[26]

The workforce is changing, making older workers more attractive even as a competitive global economy has increased Boomers' uncertainty about their job security, retirement timing, and future pensions, including whether they can afford to retire or, if retired, whether they can afford not to seek paid work. This can be the impetus for employers in the public, private, and social sectors to move beyond standardized rules to facilitate time shifting, perhaps providing a portfolio of options for their employees who wish to scale back to. 8 or. 5 time, to opt for phased retirement in the form of bridge jobs, and to enable all workers—Millennials to Boomers—to customize their work and career paths. But the risks and uncertainties tied to both old and new patterns may make actually using such options unachievable.

Job and Economic Insecurity Risks

Small changes, such as employers and organizations supporting the flexibility improvisations of only a few valued employees, while helpful, are not enough. Large-scale policy shifts are necessary to shore up insurance against employment and economic insecurity. Consider how the women's movement pushed for major legislation and compliance that resulted in changing the gender compositions and wage differences of many occupations.[27] Thus, in the United States in 1963, the year Betty Friedan published *The Feminine Mystique*, Congress passed the Equal Pay Act, making it illegal for employers to pay women less than what a man would earn in the same job. In 1964, the landmark Title VII of the Civil Rights Act made discrimination in employment on the basis of race and sex illegal, though the word "sex" was inserted at the last minute. It also established the Equal Employment Opportunity Commission (EEOC) to enforce equality in employment. Title IX of the Education Amendments of 1972 revolutionized education and training as well as sports: "No person in the United States shall, on the basis of sex, be excluded from participation in, be denied the benefits of, or be subjected to discrimination under any education program or activity receiving Federal financial assistance." These structural reforms contributed to more egalitarian experiences, but also more egalitarian gender attitudes of both women and men.

There are similar prohibitions against age discrimination, but not always easy to detect or contest. The challenge is to shore up social protections for those who find themselves unwillingly out of the workforce or "retired" through forced buyouts and to fashion realistic options for those who feel too burdened by health, demanding jobs, or caregiving to continue to work full time.

Many Boomers are finding themselves on the edge of new responsibilities such as caring for their aging parents or grandchildren, and facing new risks—layoffs and unexpected retirements, age-related diseases that come with extended lifespans, and chronic uncertainty. Boomers see the need for change in the face of unraveling labor market exit and pension policies, and practices that their parents took for granted. Unfortunately, there is no single or simple vision, no single or simple solution. Needed are broad safety nets that can kick in when necessary for workers of all ages as well as new ways of working and retiring beyond full-time work and full-time retirement.

Health Risks

Health issues are another set of risks concerning Boomers who want to stave off the next life stage—of debilitating health conditions—as long as possible. The traditional solution to institutionalized long-term care was nursing homes. That is now being challenged as unsustainable in light of the coming age wave of Boomers.[28] New social inventions—like continuing care retirement communities and paid home care—and new technologies to facilitate continued living at home are offering promising alternatives. Policies promoting aging in place provide supports for older adults to continue to live independently in their own homes. However, aging in place reinforces the inequalities in quality of residence and neighborhood of different subgroups of Boomers, disparities established years ago when they moved into certain neighborhoods.[29]

Such discussions don't resonate at all with relatively healthy Boomers and those managing their health conditions who are looking for new beginnings, not endings. But most will face these dilemmas, whether with their aging parents or in their own lives. As we saw in chapter 6, Boomers themselves are concerned about maintaining their vitality and independence as long as possible. Many are changing the ways they eat, adding in exercise regimens, and thinking about scaling back at work, becoming social entrepreneurs, or else taking on new jobs or community service as ways of pressing the refresh button.

My point throughout this book is that we are witnessing in the early twenty-first century an unstable equilibrium characterizing the contemporary adult life course, with the green shoots of new life stages at both ends of adulthood. This is occurring just as Boomers move to and through their fifties, sixties, and seventies, with some postponing retirement from their career jobs even as others are retiring in their fifties or shifting to new jobs. In this incipient encore stage many are seeking but not always finding new ways to make ends meet, create new routines, remain engaged, or promote the greater good. But too many Boomers find it difficult, if not impossible, to fashion the life they *want* given the life they *have*. They are constrained by the inertia of outdated rules and expectations combined with a climate of employment and economic risks and uncertainties, skill deficits, and limited educational, income, and health resources.

The Way Forward

To promote and maintain the health and well-being of those in the encore adult years requires policies that better cushion the shock of unemployment or unexpected retirement and provide more economic security before existing social protections like Medicare and Social Security kick in. Unlike Europe and Canada, safety nets in the United States are limited. For example, Social Security provides at best modest levels of support, and yet two in 10 retirees rely on Social Security as their only source of income. Fully three in 10 rely on it for 90 percent of their income. Safety nets need to be devised for the risks and uncertainties of portfolios of work, rather than the linear careers of the past.

Third Party Intermediaries and Protections

As discussed in chapter 7, some enterprising entrepreneurs are developing innovative ways to manage the talents and skills of workers of all ages, becoming inventive third parties in the space between work opportunities and those seeking them. These new organizational arrangements can promote new ways of working that work for everyone. Sara Horowitz is one such change-maker. The founder and executive director of Freelancers Union, a third-party support system for independent workers, she has even created a social-purpose insurance company to serve Freelancers Union members. This third-party arrangement meets the needs of all kinds of entrepreneurs, including those in the encore adult years. The Freelancers Union aims to assist those who have started their own business or else engage in contract or project work, what Horowitz sees as tomorrow's workforce. Horowitz observes the outdatedness of policies, practices, and assumptions:

> The rules for the new economy haven't been written yet. Well, they have... it's just that they were written 50+ years ago when the 9-to-5, 30-years-and-a-gold-watch career path was the rule, not the exception.[30]

Mae O'Malley is another change maker, an attorney who founded a third-party arrangement for legal services, Paragon Legal. This San Francisco-based legal placement service benefits clients by enabling them to quickly "ramp up legal resources with flexible arrangements designed for your specific situation," enabling attorneys of all ages by offering an escape from the rigidity of traditional jobs through more flexible, project-based assignments with premier clients and dynamic, challenging work.[31] Paragon's policies and practices are especially unique and pathbreaking. For example, it provides attorneys with health insurance, malpractice insurance, and other benefits. Paragon also enables its attorneys to work flexibly and sanely; no job is billed at more than 40 hours a week. And it offers just two tiers of salary—one for those with less than eight years and one for those with eight or more years of legal experience. This is important, because sometimes Boomers who have previously commanded exorbitant fees because of their prior experience effectively price themselves out of the market. They may want to move away from the inflexibility and high pressures of traditional in-house or law firm positions, but there's not a big market for independent and expensive lawyers-at-large. At Paragon, attorneys with 10 or 30 years' experience operate under the same compensation structure, retaining a high degree of flexibility, freedom, and control. This two-tier remuneration policy effectively removes age discrimination by making older workers with years of experience both more attractive and affordable. Yes, it also means a trade-off between commanding higher wages and higher pressure and commanding higher flexibility, but it keeps Boomers in the workplace on their own terms—a job perk most can't yet fathom. Paragon Legal is one of the fastest-growing women- and minority-owned firms in the United States.

New types of unions or collective groups such as Paragon Legal could serve as employment agencies for their members, Richard Sennett calls these parallel institutions, offering continuity and sustainability in an occupational environment with what he calls "short and erratic" time frames.[32]

Life, Not Career or Retirement, Planning

Most Boomers don't want to talk to their bosses or human resource departments about retirement plans. Many fear that showing up at planning workshops or even asking questions online signals that they are expecting to leave soon. Older workers are not ready to tip their hands if they don't know what might come next. Moreover, most workers of all ages haven't really thought about when they will be retiring or at least exiting their current jobs, worried about keep their jobs in a climate of insecurity. Others have seen their plans unravel in this competitive and uncertain economic climate.

People have difficulty planning given the short time horizons of their employers. For example, in the IT workforce the Work, Family, and Health Network is studying, when asked in 2014 about the odds of their working, in any job, at age 67, the average answer was about 50/50 (actually 46 on a scale of 100, where 100 is certain they will be working). Fifty-fifty suggests to me that they don't know—that many Boomers simply can't or are reluctant to see around the corner. There are just too many unknowns.

In the midst of career uncertainty and ambiguity, more information about possibilities would be helpful. Changing retirement planning materials, websites, and workshops to focus on age-integrated talent development and career or life planning at all ages would shift the conversation from outdated linear career progression and retirement to what both older and younger workers want to do now and next, and how they can develop a sense of continuity in a climate of uncertainty and change. This is a way to showcase possibilities—training for new skills, trying out other positions, being detailed for a time to a nonprofit while still on the employers' payroll, and other options.

But long-term planning requires a sense of narrative and continuity, difficult in a time when most jobs are insecure and futures increasingly ambiguous.[33] This means that governments will have to provide some form of guaranteed income floor or public service job opportunities to fill in between contract and project work. Whether the United States will recognize and respond to this new reality in a timely way is doubtful.

Removing Existing Impediments

The women's movement showed that removing existing impediments can have big payoffs. Today, governments can address issues of risk and uncertainty in the encore years by removing legal barriers to re-employment. Governments and corporations could open up training programs and jobs to people of all ages; colleges and universities could welcome back Boomers to retool their skill sets, serve as mentors for younger students, or simply provide the structured space to reimagine their lives and their options; corporations could be allowed and take up options to rehire their pensioned retirees, even those recently retired.

Divisions around Boomers' age, race, nationality, nativity, education, and gender further isolate and marginalize some subgroups from the rest of society. As Boomers from all walks of life improvise their own encores, they are redefining this stage of the life course as encompassing a wide range of pathways. Educated Boomers, in particular, are discarding outdated practices and embracing new possibilities, becoming the engines of social change that will give form to and legitimate this new encore stage.[34] But, as with the women's movement, to fully engage the large numbers of Boomers who are not able to forge their own paths requires systemic changes in policies and practices in organizations, governments, schools, and communities. What is different is that unlike the women's movement, many Boomers are occupying positions of power. Those advantaged through elected office or corporate hierarchies are well positioned to reassess and remedy gaps in the safety net for this stage of the life course.

Alternative Career Paths

No one, from the youngest Millennial to the oldest Boomer, has much confidence in the career mystique today. That lockstep linear work path feels like a shaky, no longer a viable way of making a living, much less a path to material success or even fulfillment. Instead, given chronic uncertainty and risk in this, the second machine age,[35] most are focusing on employability and continuous skill development. But the edifice and assumptions of conventional careers remain very much with us, and people following alternative paths often pay a price for doing so in terms of earnings, status, and insecurity.

We need to legitimate alternative paths, together with alternative protections. Matilda White Riley described age-integrated careers.[36] And practice professor of management at the Wharton School, Stewart Friedman describes "slow" careers.[37] Cathleen Benko and Anne Weisberg review the ways Deloitte has offered customized career policies.[38] This is already happening informally, given the unraveling of the social contract rewarding seniority with security and the disappearance of established corporate ladders. But who can or will lead this change, providing the language, customs, and rules and regulations for time shifting work, education, and retirement, involving a wide range of alternative pathways through jobs, occupations, organizations, and the twenty-first-century life course? People of all ages want to feel useful, and as Sennett points out, there is much useful work, paid and unpaid, that needs doing, including the unpaid or low-paid care work that is so essential to families and society.[39] Recognizing the value of care and community service work, and paying a living wage for it, would help to recognize its importance. Such civic and family work could also serve to anchor individuals' life narratives as including different types of productive engagement across the life course and across generations.

A Social Movement?

Are there lessons to be learned from the incomplete gender revolution that might inform what could become a budding encore adult revolution? Social movements have power in both defining problems and proposing solutions. Social organization scholars Hayagreeva Rao, Calvin Morrill, and Mayer Zald describe the role of social movements in creating new organizational forms by deinstitutionalizing existing and establishing new beliefs, norms, and values.[40] The women's movement showcased and challenged widely accepted gender inequalities.[41] Critical political economy and feminist scholars have examined how institutional arrangements are developed and maintained by those in power to promote their own positions of advantage, thereby preserving existing inequalities in the distribution of resources across gender, race, class, and age.[42]

Women's organizations in the 1970s framed prevailing employment policies and legislation as creating and perpetuating gender inequality. But the women's movement stalled in that it failed to focus on changing the structure and culture—institutionalized clockworks and calendars—of paid work. I recall being in a toy store in the 1970s, asking a young stranger around seven years old if she thought my niece about her age would like a certain toy. She hesitated, then said, "I prefer boys' toys." The women's movement opened up opportunities for women to get men's things, including men's jobs. But it did not address the ways those jobs were organized, as if someone else—a wife—was still around to take care of everything else.

To be sure, the women's movement challenged the traditional division of labor. Women asked the men in their lives, at home and at work, to make the coffee and clean up. But they also accepted the full-time, inflexible lockstep of the career mystique as given, and have, for decades since, tried to mold their lives around it. If they couldn't, they would step out of career-type jobs, forgo promotions, or outsource some of the work of home life to keep all the balls in the air. Women became responsible for their own work lives *plus* their husbands' careers, their children's development, their parents' care, and their community obligations.[43] Like the young girl wanting "boy's" toys, equality meant the opportunity to obtain men's jobs and aim for, if not attain, men's wages. But that chance at better jobs and better wages came with continuous, inflexible, long-hour employment that discounted the competing logics and claims of family care and domesticity. What used to be life off the clock for women and growing numbers of men became the famous second shift.[44] And now both men and women are recognizing the death of the career mystique; the lockstep path to security and success has disappeared.

Boomers' improvisations have the markings of a social movement, and the makings of such a major undertaking can be found in organizations like AARP and encore.org. AARP's initiative, Life Reimagined, aims to assist those 50-plus explore what's next in their lives by offering "resources, tools, coaching services and ways to connect with like-minded people."[45] Marc Freedman's invention, encore.org, "invests in innovation and encourages colleges and social sector employers to work together to unleash the potential of boomers as a new workforce for social change."[46] Both organizations aim to push elected officials, service organizations, and employers to open up possibilities for the encore adult years.

We all know the names of important change-makers in the women's movement, such as Gloria Steinem, who founded *Ms.* magazine, and Bella Abzug, activist and member of the US House of Representatives. Similarly, social entrepreneurs like Marc Freedman and Marci Alboher are leading contemporary change by framing the promise of encore careers for the greater good. If this incipient revolution succeeds in changing the linear life course by opening up options, their names, too, will be remembered for generations.

Conclusions

I began this book with stories about camels to point out the ways we categorize everything and then treat the categories as concrete, unchangeable realities. It seems appropriate to end with elephants—those in the room but rarely discussed when talking about the promise of this new life stage. Too often these elephants are also assumed to be self-evident realities, but not really held up for inspection. Their very presence impedes the resets of outdated policies and practices as well as the development of new social inventions that could institutionalize viable nonlinear paths of work as well as an operative encore adult stage.

One such elephant in the room is the belief about greedy geezers. This is the presumption that as they grow older Boomers will focus on what they care about most: themselves. And yet study after study shows a great many Boomers want to give back, to do something that can help build community and the next generation. Boomers are already making a real difference in the lives of their adult children and grandchildren, as well as the children of the world. They need more identifiable paths like those offered by Experience Corps in chapter 7 as ways to assist schools, after-school programs, and other community organizations. Many of those in the encore adult years see the promise of this stage of their lives, bringing to it a happy combination of vitality and healthy life expectancy. Most want to lean out of their increasingly unstable career jobs, time shifting to fresh starts, refurbishing their identities and following purpose, whether in the form of helping bring grandchildren up right, giving aging parents the care they deserve, working with a nonprofit to address pressing social issues, mentoring younger coworkers, doing special projects, working part time, or starting a new business. But how to do so? Precisely where are all these opportunities. . . . what I call not-so-big jobs?

Another elephant is the belief that older Boomers seeking work compete directly with Millennials who are having a difficult time locating jobs. Most of us have seen seniors alongside teens at fast food cash registers, mostly because they both need the wages and have no other options. But the reality is that Boomers and Millennials typically compete for different types of jobs in different labor markets. Many Boomers are looking to make a difference, to work in not-so-big jobs in the public or social sectors or even in volunteer projects that offer small stipends. By contrast, most Millennials are looking for full-time jobs and chances to learn and grow, even if they don't see prospects for advancement and rising salaries. A growing economy may well precipitate greater demand for all employees, regardless of their ages or life stages.

Then there is the elephant depicting encore adults as wanting full-time leisure, challenging the very idea of ongoing engagement at this stage of life. Too be sure there are lots of folks wanting or needing conventional retirement, and that is fine. But when 72 percent of people in this age group say they want to work in retirement it suggests that the options for the kinds of work they want need to be out there.

Finally, there is the specter in the corner, the elephant of true old age, when Boomers will need assistance and supports for activities of daily living. Imaginative pockets of technological and social innovations are cropping up for this stage as well, but that is a topic for another book.

Despite these elephants in the room, I believe the United States and other high-income countries are poised for the recognition and encouragement of an encore stage of adult life. Outdated institutions may seem static and intractable, but they can be transformed through nonconformity, negotiation, improvisation, institutional entrepreneurs, and social movements.[47] Will employers and managers ease their older employees' passage from their current jobs to less demanding, more flexible jobs in their own and other establishments? Will they retain and recruit older workers who are seeking flexible full-time or part-time jobs, including them as an integral part of their workforces? Can governments, nonprofits, and businesses embrace the idea of purposive jobs with reduced-hour and flexible alternative work arrangements, as well as alternative career/exit paths, and implement them in their own organizations to extend the tenure of their older employees? Those who say yes to these questions may well gain a competitive advantage in the valued resources of creativity, imagination, commitment, experience, knowledge, productivity, and motivation—for all their workers, Millennials included, who want new ways to work.

The encore revolution will, like the social movements that have come before, require moving beyond taken-for-granted templates, assumptions, and discrimination. All kinds of efforts are needed to experiment with what works best, inventing new ways of living and working that better match not only encore adults' interests, but that of a twenty-first-century workforce. A multi-pronged approach will confront institutional inertia and learn from incubating pockets of innovation (chapter 7) to structure and legitimate a menu of options throughout the life course, as well as for ongoing engagement in what can be a true encore to adulthood. But the short-term time horizons of organizations mean new forms of economic security—new social protections—are required for people of all ages.

As they turn 60, 65, and 70 at the rate of 10,000 a day, Boomers' experiences and impacts as part of the workforce and the retired population are key policy issues that should be high on government, business, and community agendas. When they exit the workforce for the last time is consequential for the pool of available labor, the costs of social security and pensions, the availability of and costs of health care, and family economic viability.[48] To date, the push has been to delay retirement from full-time jobs by effectively punishing early exits. And yet the evidence shows that ongoing engagement before or after retirement can only promote health if the work, paid or unpaid, is characterized by certain conditions—voluntarily pursued, greater control, flexible or reduced time commitments—opportunities yet to be widely considered, much less adopted in either government or corporate policies and practices.

So, what does a vital encore adulthood look like? The peculiarly American focus on busyness and productivity has equated successful aging with ongoing full-time paid work, just as success has been equated with income, wealth, and status. But as we have seen, the key to realization of an encore to conventional adulthood is the fit between Boomers' needs and preferences and available, sustainable options for engagement as well as social protections. Life in encore adulthood may mean retiring from a demanding and unsatisfactory job as soon as possible in order to care for an ailing spouse, aging parents, grandchildren, or simply to get healthy before deciding what is next. It may mean delaying retirement from an ideal job as long as possible, keeping a long-held identity and sense of purpose intact. It may mean second acts and second chances, sometimes as a result of forced layoffs, when some seek fresh starts as business or social entrepreneurs solving a business or community need. It may mean connecting with like-minded networks to save the environment, help children, or build community. It may mean scaling back on current jobs or seeking contract or project work, for pay or not, that can draw on a lifetime of skills. It most definitely means recognizing the promise of a large, experienced, and capable portion of the population in danger of being sidelined. Governments and organizations can transform work, education, and retirement policies and practices to enable encore adults to have the means and opportunities to choose from a broad pool of widely available, easily accessible, affordable, and desirable options to remain engaged. Redesigning pathways with Boomers in mind will generate a new lens with which to view the institutions of work, retirement, schooling, family care, and the gendered life course, opening up possibilities for men and women of all ages and stages.

Employers and governments are just now coming to terms with the twenty-first-century labor market. Workers are more diverse than ever in terms of age, gender, race/ethnicity, immigrant status, health, and ability. This diversity—including the new reality of multiple generations working together—shows the need for creative problem-solving. To be sure, this is a time of upheaval: a new demography, a global risk economy, new digital technologies, and the individualizations of risk are contributing to the deinstitutionalization of big jobs and big careers as private pensions, job security, worry-free retirements, and predictable, orderly paths go by the wayside.

Almost three decades ago, in 1988, University of Minnesota political scientist Paul Light wrote about the future and especially the year 2016. He noted two things would be important that year: Boomers beginning to turn 70, and the political election marking half a century of Boomers' political participation, for some their 18th presidential election. Professor Light also observed that for Boomers in 1988 the year 2016 seemed a long way off: "They are still in their first jobs, their first marriages, and changing diapers on their first children."[49] Nevertheless, he felt that 2016 to the middle of the 2000s would be about Boomers' leadership, and more broadly about their contribution to society.

We are now here, with Boomers in positions of power in politics, business, and communities, in positions to reset the rules and launch new customs and clockworks around work, careers, schooling, and retirement. They know what they want in encore adulthood, and, like Gray the VP who went on to head a homeless shelter, will likely contribute in many different ways. The challenge is whether they will broaden their search for individual meaning—what C. Wright Mills called a private trouble—into recognition of the public issue, the possibilities and perils of the twenty-first-century life course, and the corollary need for updating the central institutions shaping our lives. The political is personal, even as the personal was political half a century ago.

Will Boomers, along with GenXers and Millennials in the corporate, state, and social sectors, work to actively redesign the ways work, careers, schooling, caregiving, service, and retirement are organized? Do policymakers at all levels and in all industries have the ability, insight, and motivation to make and sustain change? Will scholars theorize and investigate the changing life course, instead of making assumptions about the status quo? As with emerging adulthood, creating a true encore adult stage will require deliberate shifts in how we think about, legitimate, legislate, and regulate the life course for people of all ages. Not doing so would be a failure of imagination. Given Boomers' sheer numbers, enabling the customizing of careers, retirement, and the life course will offer enormous dividends of creativity, talent, health, and possibility for renewal—for individuals, but also for their families, workplaces, and communities.

APPENDIX A

Data Sources and Funding

This book draws on both quantitative and qualitative data from a range of sources.

Quantitative Data

Most of the quantitative data come from the March 2014 Current Population Survey. With the help of Joe Grover from the Minnesota Population Center (MPC) (NICHD R24HD041023), I analyzed the circumstances of four groups of Boomers divided by gender and birth year (leading edge born 1946–1954 versus the trailing edge born 1955–1964). The details of this analysis are provided in the tables in appendix B. With Dr. Sarah Flood I also used data from the American Time Use Survey (R01HD053654), looking at Boomers' sense of meaning, happiness, and stress based on their activities at the time. We also examined time use by this age group separately by age and gender. And with the assistance of Brit Henderson (sociology graduate student and MPC fellow), I also analyzed data across cohorts from the US Census. This research was supported by funds from the McKnight Foundation, as part of my McKnight Presidential Chair, as well as by the Minnesota Population Center.

Qualitative Data

I use qualitative evidence from in-depth interviews collected in four different research projects: the Work, Family, and Health Network Study, the Boomers at Work/In Transition Study, the Cornell Couples and Careers Study along with the Couples Managing Change Study, and some additional interviews and follow-ups. The in-depth interviews were conducted by myself, Stephen Sweet, Erin Kelly, Kimberly Fox, Erik Kojola, Kate Schaefers, and other trained interviewers as part of these four studies. They took place across the country but mostly in New York, Minnesota, and the South and Western regions of the country. Some were conducted in person, but most were by phone. The earliest were collected in 2002, the most recent in 2015, with the majority conducted in 2014. Interviews in Germany were conducted with the assistance of my colleague Joachim Savelsberg. Names and identifying information have been changed to protect respondents' privacy. William, James, and Matt are the real names of my grandsons, and Donna is the real name of my friend.

The Work, Family, and Health Network Survey

This study involved both qualitative and quantitative data collected at various points in time over a five-year period from employees and managers in two cities who were part of the Information Technology (IT) division of this major US firm. Recruitment materials emphasized the value of a study investigating the connections between employees' work, family, and health for the employees (who received some personal health information), the employing organization, and scientific knowledge more broadly. Computer-assisted personal interviews, lasting approximately 60 minutes, were conducted at the workplace on company time. At baseline, 70 percent of eligible employees participated (N=823) with 87 percent (N=717) and 85 percent (N=701) of baseline employee participants retained in the six-month and the twelve-month follow-ups, respectively. The response rate at baseline among managers was 86 percent (N=221), and 89 percent (N=196) and 85 percent (N=188) of baseline managers completed the six-month and twelve-month surveys. This study is described in detail elsewhere (Bray et al. [2013]; Kelly et al. [2014]; King et al. [2012]; Kossek et al. [2014]; Moen et al. [2016]). I draw on the in-depth interview data from this study throughout the volume. Interviews continued through the spring of 2015.

This research was conducted as part of the Work, Family, and Health Network (www.WorkFamilyHealthNetwork.org), which was funded by a cooperative agreement through the National Institutes of Health and the Centers for Disease Control and Prevention: Eunice Kennedy Shriver National Institute of Child Health and Human Development (Grant # U01HD051217, U01HD051218, U01HD051256, U01HD051276), National Institute on Aging (Grant # U01AG027669), Office of Behavioral and Social Sciences Research, and National Institute for Occupational Safety and Health (Grant # U01OH008788, U01HD059773). Grants from the National Heart, Lung, and Blood Institute (Grant #R01HL107240), William T. Grant Foundation, Alfred P. Sloan Foundation, and the Administration for Children and Families have provided additional funding. The contents of this publication are solely my responsibility and do not necessarily represent the official views of these institutes and offices. Special acknowledgement goes to Extramural Staff Science Collaborator Rosalind Berkowitz King, PhD and Lynne Casper, PhD for their design of the original Workplace, Family, Health and Well-Being Network Initiative. I also wish to express gratitude to the worksites, employers, and employees who participated in this research.

Boomers at Work/In Transition Study

To explore changes in retirement pathways and innovative policies, graduate student Erik Kojola, Dr. Kate Schaefers, and I interviewed individual Boomers and representatives of organizations that are seeking to respond to the shifting goals/needs of their older workers. Recruitment occurred from September 2013 to November 2014, although interviews continued into 2015. We interviewed decision-makers and human resource managers from 23 organizations (eleven private-sector firms, four government agencies, and eight nonprofits), all located in the Twin Cities and surrounding areas (including Rochester). We selected firms based on recognition for innovation (i.e., recipients of Sloan Award for Excellence in Workplace Effectiveness and Flexibility and Forbes list of top employers) and with a reputation as a great place to work, as well as others recommended by informants. We sought to capture theoretically meaningful variations in industry, ownership structure, size, and workforce, asking questions about work policies and informal practices and accommodations for older workers. Several interviews included visits to the actual organizations and a tour of their facilities. We also reviewed organizations' websites and documents, including employee handbooks, written policies, and other workforce reports.

In addition, we conducted 27 in-depth semistructured interviews with white-collar Boomers in Minnesota who were working, semiretired, and retired to examine their current work arrangements, and plans and expectations for work and retirement. We sought participants working for different types of employers with variation in industry and size. Four Boomers who participated in an internship program for older workers sponsored by the nonprofit organization SHIFT were also recruited into the study. Several of the individuals were also from the organizations we studied. The goal was to maximize diversity and variation amongst participants in order to make theoretical comparisons and to capture the wide range of Boomer's experiences. Participants were selected who are working full time or part time, fully or partially retired, or unemployed. In addition, we sought participants working for different types of employers to capture variation in industry and size. We anticipated that workplace policies might be different in large and small organizations and between nonprofit, public, and private employers, and that these differences could affect Boomers expectations and experiences. We also wanted the voices of several people who are self-employed, consultants, or small business owners, because these types of encore jobs are increasingly common for Boomers after exiting their full-time career jobs. The sample was mostly limited to white-collar workers because of the large differences between professional and non-professional workers in work experiences, retirement trajectories, and the salience of career identities (Price [2003]); however, some nonprofessionals were also interviewed.

The final sample was nearly equally divided between women (14) and men (12), with ages ranging from 52 to 68 with an average just above 60 years old. Most participants were working in some form—only one was retired and not working or looking for work. Most (15) were working full time, but there was a mix of people who are both retired and working (4) or define themselves as unemployed (3). Participants primarily worked at for-profit companies (13), but there were also people employed by nonprofits (5) and public institutions (3). We interviewed divorced and single Boomers, those with and without children, those are caring for older infirm parents, partners, or grandchildren, and one man who was never married and has no children.

Our interviews were primarily with human resource managers and other top leaders who were knowledgeable about employment policies. We asked questions about doing institutional work through formal policies, but also through informal practices and arrangements. When possible we spoke with multiple organizational representatives, either in a multiperson interview or in separate meetings. Interviews were primarily conducted in-person at the University of Minnesota as well as at the employing organizations' offices, along with several on the phone with one or several members of the research team. The semistructured conversations lasted between one and one and a half hours and were directed by a set of pertinent topics, with interviewers also asking follow-up and organizationally specific questions.

Several interviews included visits to the actual organizations and a tour of their facilities. We also reviewed organizations' websites and collected documents from them, including employee handbooks, written policies, and other workforce reports. These materials allowed us to capture specific written policies and workforce demographics and compare official policies with informants' perceptions and interpretations. This project was made possible through funding and support from the Center on Urban and Regional Affairs (CURA) at the Humphrey School, University of Minnesota as well as the support from the Minnesota Population Center. For more information see Moen, Kojola, and Shaefers (2016); Kojola and Moen (2016).

Ecology of Careers and Couples Managing Change Study

I also draw on data from a subsample of the Ecology of Careers Study, involving interviews of both members of dual-earner households and designed such that at least one spouse works for one of 10 participating organizations. This subsample constituting Couples' Managing Change study initiated by Stephen Sweet is well suited to the examination of the contingent and coinciding relationships between spouses' experiences and plans, as well as the organizational contexts shaping them. Approximately hour-long telephone interviews were conducted with both spouses (in separate interviews) in dual-earner, mostly middle-class households in upstate New York (following as well those who had left the area). Respondents were asked to report their family, work, and biographical experiences and expectations, including extensive life histories (N=1283 couples).

The 10 strategically selected organizations from which we obtained random samples of married workers and subsequently interviewed workers' spouses represent both manufacturing and service (utilities, health care, and higher education) industries. These data are supplemented with additional couple respondents (N=85) in a sample drawn from census block groups rather than companies. We followed individuals and couples who were laid off, retired, or took a new job, as well as those not experiencing such changes. For more information on this study see Sweet and Moen [2012]; Moen, Sweet, and Hill [2010]). This research was supported by a grant for a study called "Downsizing and Dual Earner Couples: How Corporate Restructuring Affects Couples in Upstate New York" from the Alfred P. Sloan Foundation. Stephen Sweet and Phyllis Moen were co-PIs. The larger Ecology of Careers Study was also funded by the Alfred P. Sloan Foundation, Phyllis Moen PI.

Method of Analysis

Interview transcripts from all these studies were analyzed using an inductive and iterative process of thematic coding to develop codes and theoretical insights from the data. Transcripts from each data set were first uploaded into Atlas.ti or other software to facilitate data management. Then descriptive open codes were developed from the participants' responses with theoretical sensitivity to topics around work, career paths, family care, retirement, and the life course. For example, in the Boomers at Work/In Transition study we developed eleven axial codes that comprised the dominant themes and theoretical patterns identified in the data: desire for flexible and less demanding work, staying active and engaged, wanting purposeful work or volunteer options, concerns about finances, timing based on eligibility and policies, excitement about retirement, negative perceptions of retirement, difficulty on the job market, physical nature of aging, and family and personal care work. These same themes were found to be repeated in each data set. Emblematic quotes are reported that are indicative of how respondents talked about different themes.

Acknowledgments

THIS BOOK IS the result of collaborations with many people in the Minnesota Population Center. Joe Grover provided invaluable assistance with the CPS data and ways of presenting it. Steven Ruggles and Cathy Fitch were enablers in all kinds of ways. Rachel Magennis, Yagmur Karakaya, and Erin Hoekstra all helped with the qualitative data from the Work, Family, and Health Network (WFHN). Erik Kojola conducted many interviews as part of the WFHN and in connection with the Center for Urban and Regional Affairs (CURA) project. Kris Michaelson managed our various budgets. Sarah Flood and Katie Genadek assisted with helping me understand the data. Graduates students on the shifting Flexible Work and Well-Being team (including Anne Kaduk, Brit Henderson, and Wen Fan, as well as Erik Kojola) were very helpful. And my dear friend and colleague Erin L. Kelly was enthusiastic and supportive, as always.

I also want to acknowledge the support of Margaret Levi and the Center for Advanced Study in the Behavioral Sciences (CASBS) at Stanford University. My CASBS fellowship provided the time necessary to complete the volume as well as supportive atmosphere, and my cohort of fellows provided important insights.

Thanks to Letta Page for her terrific editing assistance, and to Deborah Moen, Roberta and Miles Maguire, Bill Kelly, and Donna Dempster-McClain for their valuable suggestions. James Cook, Amy Klopfenstein, and the anonymous reviewers provided important and useful feedback. Gwen Colvin was fantastic.

The Sociology Department at the University of Minnesota was also helpful, including the budgeting by Hilda Mork. Undergraduate Sarah Simpson did an enormous amount of legwork on the latest studies. Dean Coleman and the College of Liberal Arts made it possible for me to accept the fellowship at Stanford. The McKnight Foundation supported this research through my McKnight Presidential Chair funds.

Thanks as well to all the people who agreed to be interviewed, generously sharing their stories. And to SHIFT, the fantastic Minnesota nonprofit, for permitting me to reinterview people who had participated in their Midternship program. Special thanks to Kate Schaefers, who also conducted interviews for me. And much appreciation goes to the German interviewees and to my colleague and dear friend Joachim Savelsberg who made them possible.

Beyond Dick Shore, who has endured my writing yet another book, there are two people who deserve my deepest gratitude: Marc Freedman for his ideas, inspiration, and encouragement, and Jane Peterson, who has tracked references, names, interviews, and chapters through numerous iterations, remaining unfailingly supportive all along the way.

Notes

1. AN ENCORE TO CONVENTIONAL ADULTHOOD

1. Also called schema or mindsets. For a deeper discussion see Sewell (1992).
2. Institutional logics are defined by Thornton and Ocasio (2008: 2) as "socially constructed, historical patterns of cultural symbols and material practices, including assumptions, values, and beliefs, by which individuals and organizations provide meaning."
3. The second industrialization included electrification and steel production.
4. These ideas draw in part from Sennett (2006).
5. See Arnett (1997, 2000); Benson and Furstenberg (2006); Hartmann and Swartz (2007); Lee and Mortimer (2009).
6. See the publications in the previous note, but also Arnett (2004, 2010); Arnett and Eisenberg (2007); Mortimer and Moen (2016); Settersten, Furstenberg, and Rumbaut (2005).
7. See Freedman (2007, 2011).
8. See Sennett (2006).
9. See Moen and Roehling (2005) and Tronto (2013).
10. Coser (1974); Heinz and Marshall (2003); Lawrence, Suddaby, and Leca (2009); Mills and Tancred (1992); Scott (1995); Thornton, Ocasio, and Lounsbury (2012).
11. For a discussion of the career mystique and the lockstep life course see Moen and Roehling (2005).
12. Beck (1997); Brückner and Mayer (2005); Heinz (1999).
13. Kohli (1986, 2007); Kohli and Meyer (1986); Kohli, Rein, Guillemard, and van Gunsteren (1991); Moen and Peterson (2009).
14. These are called institutional logics undergirding and reinforced by existing rules and expectations. See Lawrence, Suddaby, and Leca (2009); Thornton, Ocasio, and Lounsbury (2012).
15. See Riley, Kahn, and Foner (1994).
16. AARP (2014).

17. Moen (2007).
18. See Hurst (2014).
19. AARP (2014).
20. See the important insights in Sennett (2006).
21. See Bidewell, Griffin, and Hesketh (2006); Ekerdt (2010); Munnell and Sass (2008); OECD (2006); Williamson (2011).
22. Hedge, Borman, and Lammlein (2006).
23. Asked of workers age 45–74. See AARP (2014).
24. The "leaning in" language comes from Sheryl Sandberg's *Lean In: Women, Work, and the Will to Lead* (2013), which argues that women (and men) should lean into their jobs in order to get the salaries they deserve and to advance in their occupations.
25. Alboher (2013); Freedman (2007, 2011).
26. See Arnett (1997, 2000, 2004, 2010); Arnett and Eisenberg (2007); Benson and Furstenberg (2006); Crocker (2007); Gillon (2004); Hartmann and Swartz (2007); Lee and Mortimer (2009); Macmillian (2007); Mortimer (2003); Mortimer and Moen (2016); Mortimer et al. (2005); Settersten, Furstenberg, and Rumbaut (2004); Settersten and Ray (2010); Swartz et al. (2011).
27. See AARP (2014).
28. AARP (2014).
29. Moen (2001); Moen and Spencer (2006).
30. Toossi (2012).
31. See Riley, Kahn, and Foner (1994).
32. See Riley et al. (1994).
33. Arnett (2004); Hartmann and Swartz (2007); Macmillan (2007); Settersten and Ray (2010).
34. For a discussion about the changing transition to adulthood, see Arnett (2004); Buchmann (1989); Hogan (1981); Mortimer and Moen (2016); Settersten and Ray (2010).
35. Clarke and Wheaton (2005, 271). If Millennials are on the path to adult roles and responsibilities in a phase of early adulthood, Boomers are creating a third stage of adulthood, an encore period with new responsibilities and commitments, not the disengagement associated with old age.
36. Lawrence, Suddaby, and Leca (2009, 52).
37. Institutional logics are "socially constructed, historical patterns of cultural symbols and material practices, including assumptions, values, and beliefs, by which individuals and organizations provide meaning" (Thornton and Ocasio [2008, 2]). As Aaron Hurst (2014: 4), points out, "people gain purpose when they grow personally, when they establish meaningful relationships, and when they are in service to something greater than themselves."
38. Bronfenbrenner (2005).
39. In many ways, this book builds on the pathbreaking book by Linda George (1980) on later life transitions.

2. OUTDATED CAREER AND LIFE-COURSE TEMPLATES

1. See appendix A for a fuller description of data sources.
2. Elder (1992, 1121). See also Elder and George (2016).
3. Moen and Roehling (2005); Riley, Kahn and Foner (1994); Thornton, Ocasio, and Lounsbury (2012).
4. Mills (1951).
5. See Mills (1951); Walker and Guest (1952); Whyte (1956).
6. See Moen and Roehling (2005).
7. See Becker and Strauss (1956); Granovetter (1995); Hughes (1937, 413); Wilensky (1960, 1961). As white-collar professional jobs came into prominence in the 1950s and 1960s, sociologist Harold Wilensky defined career as "a succession of related jobs, arranged in a hierarchy of prestige, through which persons move in an ordered (more-or-less predictable) sequence." Even earlier, another famous sociologist, Everett Hughes, recognized that careers have a subjective as well as objective component: "the moving perspective in which the person sees his life as a whole and interprets the meaning of his various attributes, actions, and the things that happen to him."
8. Though starting with Betty Friedan (1963), the study of women's unpaid work became much more mainstream.
9. See Hughes (1937, 413) "Mannheim would limit the term 'career' to this type of thing. Each step in it one receives a neat package of prestige and power whose size is known in advance. Its keynote is security; the unforeseen is reduced to the vanishing-point ("Uber das Wesen und die Bedeutung des wirtschaftlichen Erfolgstrebens," Archivfiir Sozialwissenschaft und Sozialpolitik, LXIII [I1930], 458).
10. Super (1957); Brown, Brooks, and Associates (1984).
11. Holland (1973).
12. Mayer and Mueller (1986, 167). Such a framework, based on the notion of an (occupational) status sequence (Merton [1968]), is how sociologists and economists have usually characterized the typical (male) biography. Developmentalists have also viewed careers as orderly, once people are past the early matching process between persons and jobs as they move into employment.
13. Barley (1989).
14. Sennett (2006).
15. Arthur and Rousseau (1996); Arthur, Inkson, and Pringle (1999); Arthur, Khapova, and Wilderom (2005).
16. Lips-Wiersma and Hall (2007).
17. Aisenbrey, Evertsson, and Grunow (2009), Blair-Loy (1999); Fuller (2008); Gangl and Ziefle (2009); Miller (2011).
18. Staff and Mortimer (2012).

19. See Aries (1962); Costa (1998). Brückner and Mayer (2005) describe process of differentiation, standardization, and destandardization of the life course, as do Widmer and Ritschard (2013).
20. Arnett (2000; 2010); Arnett and Eisenberg (2007); Settersten and Ray (2010).
21. A term first proposed by Peter Laslett (1987), see also Gilleard and Higgs (2007); Karisto (2007); McCullough and Polak (2007); Moen and Altobelli (2007); Sadler (2006); Silva (2008).
22. Elder (1975).
23. See Gillon (2004).
24. Mortimer and Moen (2016).
25. See Arnett and Eisenberg (2007); Settersten and Ray (2010); as well as Macmillan (2007).
26. Furstenberg et al. (2004); Massoglia and Uggen (2010); Swartz (2009).
27. Swartz (2009).
28. Swartz et al. (2011).
29. Ferraro (2016).
30. See American Community Survey Report by He and Larsen (2014).
31. Settersten and Angel (2011); Settersten and Hagestad (1996 a, b). Mortimer, Oesterle, and Krüger (2005) discuss age norms and institutional structures. See also Sennett (2006).
32. See Laslett (1989).
33. Of course the "third age" depends on how you count. Is "emerging adulthood" becoming a new life stage? If so, then this would be the "fourth age." Hence my preference for the term "encore adulthood."
34. See Laslett (1987; 1989). For third age, see Gilleard and Higgs (2007); James and Wink (2007); Karisto (2007); McCullough and Polak (2007); Moen and Altobelli (2007); Moen and Spencer (2006); Sadler (2006); Silva (2008); Weiss and Bass (2002). The "third chapter" is used by Lawrence-Lightfoot (2009), and the "encore years" was coined by Freedman (2007, 2011); see also Alboher (2013); Goggin (2009).
35. James and Wink (2007); Laslett (1989); Weiss and Bass (2002).
36. Gillon (2004, 317).
37. Arnett (2004); Hartmann and Swartz (2007); Macmillan (2007); Settersten and Ray (2010).
38. See book on the purpose economy by Hurst (2014, 18).
39. The one exception in the United States is the 2014 Affordable Care Act, which means that those in their fifties or early sixties who lose jobs or else wish to exit for health or other reasons no longer face a health insurance gap until they are eligible for Medicare at age 65.
40. See Moen (2003a). For discussions about the third age, see references in note 34.
41. Biggart and Beamish (2003); Moen (2013); Scott (1995); Sewell (1992). Borrowing is also called "institutional isomorphism"; see DiMaggio and Powell (1983).
42. Sewell (1992).

43. These perks also became ways of not giving employees' raises.
44. Kohli (1986); Riley (1987); Riley and Riley (1989).
45. Moen and Roehling (2005).
46. Moen and Roehling (2005).
47. Biggart and Beamish (2003); Stryker (1994).
48. Moen and Flood (2013); see also Han and Moen (1999b) and O'Rand and Henretta (1999).
49. Moen and Altobelli (2007).
50. Lachman and James (1997).
51. See for example the spate of recent books by Alboher (2013); Freedman (2011); Leider and Webber (2013); Pauley (2014); Schenck (2014); Thomas (2014).
52. Lawrence, Suddaby, and Leca (2009); Thornton, Ocasio, and Lounsbury (2012).
53. Riley, Kahn, and Foner (1994).
54. See Posthuma, Wagstaff, and Campion (2012) for an overview of age discrimination and stereotypes.
55. See overview by Schwall (2012). He also discusses age and cognitive age as well as age norms and contextual age.
56. See Montez and Hayward (2014); Montez, Hummer, and Hayward (2012).
57. By this I mean a less than full-time or less demanding job. See Moen (2007).
58. Fifteen percent of the Canadian and 14 percent of the US populations were 65 or older in 2013, respectively, and this will escalate of the coming decades. The proportion is even higher in the Netherlands (24 percent) and Germany (21 percent). Aging is occurring in parts of Asia as well, with one fourth of the Japanese population 65 or older. See Population Reference Bureau (2013). See also Jacobsen et al. (2011); Phillips and Siu (2012).
59. Dentinger and Clarkberg (2002); Moen, Kim, and Hofmeister (2001); Pleau (2010); Venn, Davidson, and Arber (2011).
60. For a discussion of couples, see Moen, Kim, and Hofmeister (2001); Moen et al. (2006); Smith and Moen (2003). For a discussion of caregiving, see Pavalko (2011).
61. Age and gender are also key markers in research; both data and discourse divide people along age and gender lines.
62. See Bird and Rieker (2008) and Venn, Davidson, and Arber (2011).
63. Jackson and Berkowitz (2005) discuss gender and racioethnic variations in the life course. Clarke and Wheaton (2005) describe how neighborhood effects on mental health operate through life-course transitions.
64. See Montepare (2009); Schwall (2012).
65. See Posthuma, Wagstaff, and Campion (2012).
66. These data come from the Current Population Survey (March 2014 Supplement). See table 2–1 in appendix B.
67. Current Population Survey (March 2014 Supplement). See table 2–1 in appendix B.
68. Current Population Survey (March 2014 Supplement). See table 2.1 in appendix B.
69. Data from the Pew Research Center (2007). See Taylor (2014).

70. Carstensen, Isaacowitz, and Charles (1999). See also Carstensen (2011).
71. Carstensen (2011). For the links between time and aging see McFadden and Atchley (2001).
72. Moen (2003a).
73. See Aumann, Galinsky, and Matos (2011), who show that men as well as women increasingly experience the pressure of work and home; Galinsky et al. (2005). Also see books by the journalist Brigid Schulte (2014) and economist Juliet Schor (1992). Others shift time-demanding roles to different ages, such as those who delay having children until later in life, retire early or late, or else return to school to learn new things, get a long-desired degree, or embark on a new career.
74. There are important distinctions between cohort and generation. Many use "cohort" to capture distinctions across groups born at different times, and "generation" to refer to kinship relations, though Mannheim (1952) defined generations as affinity groups based on common experiences. See also Foster (2013) for a different view of generations, as well as chapters by Elder and George (2016) and Alwin and McCammon (2003).
75. See Suitor, Sechrist, Gilligan, and Pillemer (2011).
76. Alwin, McCammon, and Hofer (2006, 52). Europe, Australia, Canada, and New Zealand also had "baby booms." See discussion about the baby boom in Finland (peaking in August 1945) by Karisto (2007).
77. Easterlin (1987); Macunovich (2002).
78. This is also precipitating concerns about the aging of the Boomers. See "The 2030 Problem: Caring for Aging Baby Boomers" by Knickman and Snell (2002).
79. Stewart and Torges (2006); Alwin, McCammon, and Hofer (2006) describe conceptual and methodological issues around cohorts. Glen Elder's classic *Children of the Great Depression* (1974) demonstrates the effect of historical events in shaping a cohort's views and expectations.
80. Easterlin (1987); see also Ryder (1965).
81. See Mills's widely read book, *The Sociological Imagination* (1959).
82. Data are derived from the Current Population Survey (March 2014 Supplement). See table 2.1 in appendix B.
83. See Bradburn, Moen, and Dempster-McClain (1995); Elman and O'Rand (1998 a, b); Farkas and O'Rand (1998); Moen (1994).
84. See Moen (2003b); Han and Moen (1999 a, b).
85. Life-course trajectories and options vary for Boomer women and men with and without a college education, as well as for whites, minorities, and immigrants, and those in the leading edge or the trailing edge. Social markers such as gender, education, age, race, and ethnicity accentuate inequalities in Boomers' resources, risks, lifestyles, and options. Some call this a "cumulation of advantage or disadvantage (Dannefer [2003]; DiPrete and Eirich [2006]; Ferraro and Shippee [2009]). Women experience greater longevity but poorer health along the way. Also, women are more apt than men to see a doctor annually or to go to the doctor at all. For more on gender distinctions and disparities,

see also Bird and Rieker (2008); Eggebeen and Sturgeon (2006); Levy and Widmer (2013); Moen (1994); Moen and Roehling (2005).

86. Data are derived from the 2014 Current Population Survey March Supplement. Their family income differs as well: $72,016 for leading-edge women, compared to $84,018 for leading-edge men. See table 2.1 in appendix B.
87. See Hulbert (2003); Gillon (2004). Data are from the Current Population Survey (March 2014 Supplement). See table 2.1 in appendix B.
88. Easterlin, Schaeffer, and Macunovich (1993).
89. Eggebeen and Sturgeon (2006).
90. Eggebeen and Sturgeon (2006, 12–13).
91. See Blossfeld, Buchholz, and Kurz (2011); Kalleberg (2012).
92. See Brynjolfsson and McAfee (2014) and Sennett (2006).
93. Moen, Lam, Ammons, and Kelly (2013).
94. Hochschild (1997); Moen, Lam, Ammons, and Kelly (2013); Schulte (2014).
95. See, for example, Gamson (2015).
96. Bronfenbrenner (2005); Bronfenbrenner et al. (1996).
97. See discussions of the gendered life course in Levy and Widmer (2013); Moen (2001, 2013); Moen and Spencer (2006).
98. Elder (1974); House, Lantz, and Herd (2005); Mayer (2004); Settersten and Mayer (1997).
99. Dannefer (2003); Ferraro and Shippee (2009).
100. This book draws on an institutional and gendered life-course perspective to examine Boomer women's and men's socially patterned experiences as they move through encore adulthood—typically the fifties, sixties, and early seventies.

3. CONTEXT: INERTIA, UPHEAVALS, INEQUALITY

1. As a "solution," the owners first removed the counter stools, and eventually the lunch counters altogether.
2. See Tilly (1998).
3. Tilly (1998, 8).
4. See for example Blossfeld and Hofmeister (2006); Charles and Grusky (2004); Folbre (2012); Kalleberg (2011); Lamont (2000); Luce, Luff, McCartin, and Milkman (2014); Williams and Boushey (2010).
5. Epstein (1988).
6. For overviews, see Markides and Gerst (2011); Mutchler and Burr (2011); Venn, Davidson, and Arber (2011). Nice empirical examples are Gerstel, Clawson, and Huyser (2007) and Willson, Shuey, and Elder (2007).
7. For more on institutional logics, see Lawrence, Suddaby, and Leca (2009).
8. This discussion of the institutionalized life course draws on Buchmann (1989); Heinz and Marshall (2003); Kohli and Meyer (1986); Marshall et al. (2001); Mayer and Mueller (1986).

9. However, mandatory retirement is now against the law for most US occupations.
10. For more on institutional logics, see Lawrence, Suddaby, and Leca (2009).
11. Moen and Roehling (2005) discuss the career mystique. The term "feminine mystique" was coined in 1963 by Betty Friedan in her book by that name.
12. Friedan (1963); Moen and Roehling (2005).
13. For a discussion of the primary and secondary workforce in terms of "good" and "bad" jobs and how they are changing, refer to Kalleberg (2011).
14. See Lawrence, Suddaby, and Leca (2009).
15. See, for example, *Retirement Heist* by Schultz (2011). The ideal worker is described in Williams (2000).
16. Globalization refers to "the enormous increase in the intensity and scope of cross-border interactive relationships over the last two to three decades—be they economic transactions or processes of informational, cultural, and political exchange" (Buchholz et al. [2011, 5]). It reflects the rising importance of and vulnerability to international markets, the intensification of economic competition as a result of deregulation, and the diffusion through new information technologies of knowledge and networks. See also Higo and Williamson (2011); Mills and Blossfeld (2005); Schmid (2011); Weil (2014).
17. See Blossfeld, Buchholz, and Kurz (2011); Lam, Moen, Lee, and Buxton (2015).
18. National Research Council (2011).
19. MetLife Mature Market Institute (2013).
20. Kalleberg (2012); Rubin (1996); Stone and Arthurs (2013).
21. Kalleberg (2011) and Drobnič, Beham, and Präg (2010).
22. Betty Friedan published *The Feminine Mystique* in 1963, describing the middle-class belief that women's fulfillment was achieved through raising families and supporting their husbands.
23. Moen and Roehling (2005).
24. The links between social policies and the life course are discussed by Kohli (2007) and Korpi (2003), as well as in the volume edited by Saraceno (2008) and the edited volume by Levy and Widmer (2013). See also Allmendinger and Hinz (2009) and Schmid (2009).
25. The book *Cubed* (2014) by Nikil Saval provides a great overview of office work and the rules and expectations that developed around work life.
26. Blossfeld and Drobnič (2001); Blossfeld and Hofmeister (2006); Budig and England (2001); Budig and Hodges (2010); Stone (2007).
27. Mr. William B. ran the company together with his brother who was the CEO and his brother-in-law who was in charge of finances. The company was started by their father Otto Orkin, to deal with rats in Richman, Virgina in 1912, moving its headquarters to Atlanta in 1926. In 1964, Rollins, Inc. purchased Orkin Exterminating Company, Inc. from the Orkin family.
28. Moen and Roehling (2005).
29. It is important not to paint a monolithic picture. Some women have always worked; some have always worked part time. Some men have never been able to hold jobs for long periods.

30. See Kalleberg's (2011) and Drobnič et al.'s (2010) discussion of "good" and "bad" jobs.
31. See Hochschild (1989). Today, many who can afford it are solving the second shift problem by outsourcing much of their personal lives (Hochschild [2012]).
32. Kathleen Gerson makes this point in *The Unfinished Revolution: How a New Generation is Reshaping Family, Work, and Gender in America* (2010); see also England (2010); Esping-Andersen (2009); and Slaughter (2015).
33. Pixley (2008); Pixley and Moen (2003).
34. Budig and England (2001); Budig and Hodges (2010); Harrington Meyer and Herd (2007); Harrington Meyer and Parker (2011a and b); Stone (2007).
35. See Han and Moen (1999 a).
36. Galinsky, Bond, and Friedman (1996); Galinsky et al. (2005).
37. Chesley and Moen (2006); Neal and Hammer (2007); Pavalko (2011); Seltzer and Li (2000).
38. See Mills and Blossfeld (2005) and Buchholz et al. (2011).
39. See Weil (2014, 42).
40. Brynjolfsson and McAfee (2014).
41. Brynjolfsson and McAfee (2014, 9).
42. See Stone and Arthurs (2013) and especially chapter 4 by Katherine Stone (2013) on the standard contract.
43. The primary workforce consists of those in career mystique jobs traditionally rewarding full-time commitment and full-time employment throughout work life. The secondary workforce consists of those on the margins of the labor market, in low-paid, insecure jobs. See Farber (2008, 2010); Kalleberg (2009, 2011).
44. Kalleberg (2000, 2009).
45. Gesthuizen and Wolbers (2011).
46. Lam, Fan, and Moen (2014).
47. A significant proportion of women are combining paid work with caring for grandchildren, often as a way of helping out their time-strapped adult children by taking on childcare duties. See the book by Madonna Harrington Meyer, *Grandmothers at Work* (2014).
48. Bismarck, who was the Chancellor of Germany, initiated both disability and retirement benefits and is seen as creating the first "welfare" state with public provision for those needing assistance. See Social Security History, Otto von Bismarck, at www.ssa.gov/history/ottob.html.
49. More correctly, the Old Age and Survivors Insurance (OASI).
50. See Clark, Strauss, and Knox-Hayes (2012).
51. Costa (1998).
52. Quadagno (1988). Del Webb originated communities designed for and restricted to older adults with his Sun City in 1960; see www.delwebb.com/value-of-del-webb/History.aspx.
53. Han and Moen (1999a).
54. See Ebbinghaus (2006); Gruber and Wise (2004); Kohli et al. (1991).
55. As Mayer and Mueller (1986) note, such institutions like retirement also fostered the segmentation of the life course.

56. Rubin (1996); Sweet and Meiksins (2013).
57. Jensen (2004) describes changes in Denmark, de Vroom (2004) focuses on the Netherlands, while Teipen and Kohli (2004) note the continued early retirement in Germany; see also Rinklake and Buchholz (2011). For a European perspective, see also Maltby, de Vroom, Mirabile, and Øverbye (2004).
58. See Blau and Goodstein (2010).
59. There is evidence that the CPS understates pension income, but that expectations of future pension incomes are typically higher than their actual amounts. See Gustman, Steinmeier, and Tabatabai (2012).
60. See Schultz (2011, 5).
61. See Banerjee and Blau (2013). The authors explain the decline in young men's employment rate as due to delays in age at first marriage and increases in older Americans' labor force participation as due to change in Social Security regulations.
62. Neumark and Song (2013).
63. See Neumark (2008).
64. See Riley et al. (1994).
65. See Brynjolfsson and McAfee (2014).
66. See Christensen and Schneider (2010); Green (2006); Kelliher and Anderson (2010); Maume and Purcell (2007); Schieman, Milkie, and Glavin (2009).
67. Jacobs and Gerson (2004); Moen, Lam, Ammons, and Kelly (2013); Schulte (2014).
68. Folbre (2012); Harrington Meyer (2014); Livingston and Parker (2010); Lou et al. (2012); Tronto (2013). See also discussion on purpose in Hurst (2014).
69. Pitt-Catsouphes (2009); Pitt-Catsouphes, Sano, and Matz-Costa (2009).
70. Harrington Meyer (2014).
71. Chesley (2005).
72. Blair-Loy and Wharton (2002).
73. Daly and Beaton (2005); Hochschild (1989); Moen (2001, 2003a); Moen and Roehling (2005); Sweet (2014); Sweet and Moen (2006).
74. See DeLong (2006); Gringart, Helmes, and Speelman (2005); Heidkamp and Van Horn (2008); Hutchens and Grace-Martin (2006); Neumark (2008).
75. Kohli (2007).
76. The problems of those confronting or fearing layoffs and their spouses are investigated in Moen, Sweet, and Hill (2010); Sweet (2014); Sweet and Moen (2006, 2012); Sweet, Moen, and Meiksins (2007).
77. Europeans in particular refer to this type of employer flexibility. See Blossfeld, Buchholz, and Kurz (2011) and Esping-Andersen (2009).
78. There are other negative stereotypes as well. See Maurer, Wrenn, and Weiss (2003).
79. Rinklake and Buchholz (2011).
80. Blossfeld et al. (2011). Those in the Netherlands, for example, who retire at ages 59–61 receive the highest pension incomes, even though most are apt to retire at ages 64–65 (Gesthuizen and Wolbers [2011]).

81. Buchholz et al. (2011); Blossfeld, Buchholz, and Hofäcker (2006); Ebbinghaus (2006); Gruber and Wise (2004); Kohli et al. (1991).
82. Gesthuizen and Wolbers (2011).
83. Cappelli and Novelli (2010). A 2002 AARP Survey.
84. Sixty-seven percent. See AARP (2002, 2014); Cappelli and Novelli (2010); Nelson (2002).
85. Bendick Jr., Brown, and Wall (1999); Morgeson et al. (2008); Nelson (2002).
86. See Brynjolfsson and McAfee (2014).
87. See Blossfeld et al. (2011); Ebbinghaus (2006); Hacker (2006); Lane (2011).
88. Barbieri and Scherer (2011). Given their less lucrative safety nets, work remains key to British Boomers turning fifty. In the United Kingdom 70 percent of men who are part of the leading-edge Boomers were working full time at age 50 (at the turn of the century), and another 17 percent were self-employed. Virtually no men were working part-time, and only 8 percent were not in the labor force. About half (52 percent) of 50-year-old women in the United Kingdom were working full time, only 8 percent were self-employed, and 13 percent worked in part-time jobs. Twenty-three percent of women in this cohort were not in the labor force at age fifty. The leading edge of the Boomers in Great Britain were born somewhat later than in the United States, beginning in 1948, not 1945 (Schmelzer [2011]).
89. Schilling and Larsen (2011, 149). See also Viebrock and Clasen (2009).
90. Kalleberg (2000, 2009, 2011); Sweet, Moen, and Meiksins (2007).
91. Sennett (2006).
92. See Brynjolfsson and McAfee (2014).
93. Sennett (2006, 181).

4. IMPROVISING PLANS FOR THE FUTURE

1. Shocked after receiving our first tax bill for this land, we donated it to Cornell University with the understanding that nothing would be built there.
2. Brynjolfsson and McAfee (2014).
3. Sandberg (2013).
4. Cahill, Giandrea, and Quinn (2015, 399).
5. Moen (2007).
6. MetLife Mature Market Institute (2013). Exact age of being old is 78.5.
7. Taylor (2014).
8. See Bronfenbrenner (2005).
9. Goode (1960).
10. Pearlin (1988).
11. Worries about money often occur regardless of actual income.
12. Kim and Moen (2001); Kohli (1986); Moen (1998).
13. Frankel and Picascia (2008, 1).
14. This is the underpinning of rational choice theory. See Becker (1981) and Coleman (1990). For an empirical European example, see De Preter et al. (2013).

15. Breiger (1995); Giddens (1984).
16. Hobson (2014, 8). Hobson draws on the capabilities framework of Amartya Sen (see Sen [1992]).
17. Burtless and Quinn (2001); Hayward and Hardy (1985).
18. See Kahneman and Tversky (1984, 341).
19. Tversky and Kahneman (1981, 453).
20. See Kahneman and Tversky (1984, 341).
21. Kahneman (2003); Kahneman and Tversky (1979); Tversky and Kahneman (1974, 1991).
22. Clark, Strauss, and Knox-Hayes (2012).
23. This is also an example of field theory—people act within a bounded sphere according to understood "rules", expectations, and hierarchies. See for example, Kurt Lewin (1943).
24. Clark, Strauss, and Knox-Hayes (2012, 25).
25. Drawing on data from the HRS. See Angrisani, Hurd, and Meijer (2012).
26. He and Larsen (2014).
27. Esping-Andersen (2009); OECD (2012).
28. Burtless and Quinn (2001); Gustman and Steinmeier (2012); McNamara and Williamson (2013).
29. Hayward, Hardy, and Grady (1989).
30. This was accentuated during the "Great Recession;" see Altindag, Schmidt, and Sevak (2012).
31. Moen and Flood (2013); Quinn (1999).
32. Haider and Stephens (2007), who draw on the Retirement History Survey and HRS; "retired" is measured by whether respondents say they are retired.
33. Laughlin (2013).
34. Grandparents care for 24 percent of children of working mothers; see Laughlin (2013). See Cherlin (2010) and Agree and Glaser (2009).
35. Smith, Taylor, and Sloan (2001).
36. Haider and Stephens (2007).
37. MetLife Mature Market Institute (2013).
38. Carstensen et al. (1999).
39. Chesley and Moen (2006).
40. Baltes (1997); Baltes and Baltes (1990); Baltes and Mayer (1999).
41. Kahneman and Tversky (1984); Kahneman et al. (1982); Tversky and Kahneman (1991).
42. This is an interdisciplinary network (funded by NIH and NICHD as well as several foundations) of scholars investigating the effects of an innovation promoting employees having greater control over their time as well as family supportive supervisor behaviors. See Kelly et al. (2014); Kossek et al. (2014).
43. Knoll (2011); Li, Hurd, and Loughran (2008); McGarry (2004); Szinovacz, Martin, and Davey (2014).

44. Administration on Aging (2013).
45. AARP (2014).
46. Wooten and Hoffman (2008, 130). See also Moen (2013).
47. Becker (1981); Gruber and Wise (2004).
48. Heinz and Marshall (2003); Marshall and Clarke (2010); O'Rand (2006).
49. Butrica, Iams, and Smith (2003/2004); Purcell (2009).
50. A study comparing non-Hispanic Whites with Mexican Hispanics in California found the Mexican group (whether native born, naturalized, or noncitizen) to have higher odds of diabetes, high blood pressure, and fair or poor self-reported health.
51. AARP (2014).
52. Riley et al. (1994).
53. Ekerdt (2010); MetLife (2009).
54. Brückner and Mayer (2005); and Moen (2013); as well as Heinz, Huinink, and Weyman (2009).
55. Moen, Fields, Quick, and Hofmeister (2000).
56. *Cornell Retirement and Well-Being Study Final Report*. See Moen, Erickson, Agarwal, Fields, and Todd (2000).
57. Blau and Gilleskie (2001); Johnson, Davidoff, and Perese (2003); Quinn (1999).
58. Dentinger and Clarkberg (2002); Esping-Andersen (2009); Levy and Widmer (2013); Moen (2013); Moen et al. (2001); Pleau (2010); Venn et al. (2011).
59. Bailyn (1993); Blair-Loy (2003); Blossfeld and Drobnič (2001); Blossfeld and Hofmeister (2006); Han and Moen (2001), Kanter (1977); Scott, Crompton, and Lyonette (2010).
60. Hochschild (2012).
61. For a discussion of greedy institutions, see Coser (1974); Coser and Coser (1974). For a discussion of the gendered life course, see Levy and Widmer (2013); Moen (2001 and 2011b); Moen and Spencer (2006).
62. Moen, Huang, Plassman, and Dentinger (2006); Moen, Sweet, and Swisher (2005); Smith and Moen (1998, 2003).
63. Han and Moen (1999b); Weiss (1977).
64. Han and Moen (1999b); Stone (2007).
65. Harrington Meyer and Herd (2007), also Estes et al. (2013).
66. A MetLife Mature Market Institute (2011) study found that nearly one in four women (23 percent) experienced a change in their planned retirement age, 16 percent retiring later than expected and 7 percent earlier than expected.
67. Or sometimes "his" and "his" or "hers" and "hers." Gay and lesbian couples face similar dilemmas as do heterosexual couples about when and how to exit career jobs and what to do next.
68. Pienta (2003); Pienta and Hayward (2002); Shepard (1985); Whyte (1956). See also Hutchens and Dentinger (2003).
69. For discussions on career prioritization, see Becker and Moen (1999); Bielby and Bielby (1992); Pixley (2008); Pixley and Moen (2003).

70. Ross and Mirowsky (2002); Ross and Wright (1998); Sastry and Ross (1998).
71. See Denaeghel, Mortelmans, and Borghgraef (2011).
72. MetLife Mature Market Institute (2011).
73. Han and Moen (1999b); Kim and Moen (2001; 2002); Moen et al. (2006); Moen, Sweet, and Swisher (2005); Smith and Moen (2003, 1998).
74. MetLife Mature Market Institute (2013).
75. Moen et al. (2006).
76. Moen, Fields, Quick, and Hofmeister (2000).
77. See Moen, Sweet, and Swisher (2005); Moen et al. (2006).
78. Moen, Kim, and Hofmeister (2001).
79. Current Population Survey (March 2014 Supplement). See table 2.1 in appendix B. See also Lin and Brown (2012).
80. Current Population Survey, 2013. Consider the change in the number of divorced older women. In 1995, just 7 percent of women age 65 and older were divorced; by 2009, fully 12 percent were. (US Department of Health and Human Services, Administration on Aging 2013).
81. Pudrovska, Schieman, and Carr (2006); Rendall, Weden, Favreault, and Waldron (2011); Waite and Gallagher (2000).
82. The Supplemental Security Income (SSI) program pays benefits to disabled adults and children who have limited income and resources. SSI benefits also are payable to people 65 and older without disabilities who meet the financial limits.
83. Knoll (2011). See also Current Population Survey (March 2014 Supplement), table 4.1 in appendix B.
84. MetLife Mature Market Institute (2011).
85. See MetLife Mature Market Institute (2011).
86. Clausen (1993).
87. Prenda and Lachman (2001).
88. For a discussion of this study see Kelly et al. (2014); King et al. (2012); Kossek, Hammer, Kelly, and Moen (2014).
89. MetLife Mature Market Institute (2013).
90. Elder (1985); Hitlin and Elder (2007a).
91. Pearlin (1989, 2010).
92. MetLife Mature Market Institute (2013).

5. IMPROVISING WORK, CIVIC ENGAGEMENT, RETIREMENT

1. See Kotter (1995); Moen (2011a); Moen and Flood (2013); Moen and Peterson (2009); Sweet and Meiksins (2013); Warren et al. (2012); Williamson (2011); Wong and Hardy (2009).
2. For the case of Millennials, see Mortimer, Lam, and Lee 2015.
3. See Brynjolfsson and McAfee (2014). They see the first machine age, starting with the steam engine, as augmenting people's physical power. The second machine

age—the digital revolution—is augmenting people's mental power. There are declines in the form of postponing full eligibility for social security and the shift away from private pensions.

4. Adams and Rau (2011); Blossfeld, Buchholz, and Kurz (2011); Clark, Strauss, and Knox-Hayes (2012); McFall (2011); Moen, Sweet, and Swisher (2005).
5. I use "encore adulthood" in the way others characterize this stage as the "third age"; see James and Wink (2007); Laslett (1989); Mortimer and Moen (2016); Weiss and Bass (2002).
6. See Arnett (2000); Furstenberg et al. (2004).
7. See appendix A.
8. See MetLife Mature Market Institute (2013).
9. Supplemental Security Income, available to those with low incomes under 65 with disabilities and those over 65 without disabilities.
10. Current Population Survey (March 2014 Supplement). See tables 5.1–5.4 in appendix B.
11. I am defining retirement as not being in the labor force and calling themselves retired.
12. The official retirement age is 65 for men and 60 for women in Great Britain.
13. Hedge, Borman, and Lammlein (2006); Mermin, Johnson, and Murphy (2007).
14. The SHIFT community connects individuals making midlife transitions, people who seek greater meaning in life and work. Some members of our community want encore careers that combine income with personal meaning and social impact. Others want to volunteer their experience and skills as a way of giving back to the larger community. SHIFT serves as a compass to help midlifers navigate these transitions.
15. Edsall (2012); Grusky, Western, and Wimer (2011); Reich (2011).
16. Current Population Survey (March 2014 Supplement). See tables 5.1–5.4 in appendix B. See also Flood and Moen (2015).
17. Marc Freedman (2007, 2011) coined the term "encore" to capture second careers in the social sector to advance the public good.
18. Greenfield and Marks (2004); Li and Ferraro (2005, 2006); Morrow et al. (2001); Musick et al. (1999); Wilson (2000, 2012); Wilson and Musick (1997).
19. Current Population Survey (March 2014 Supplement). See tables 5.1–5.4 in appendix B.
20. Only 2 to 3 percent of leading-edge Boomers—those 59 to 68 in 2014—switched jobs in 2014, but again fewer were in the workforce (see table 5.4 in appendix B).
21. Drawing on data from the GSOEP (1984–2007), Rinklake and Buchholz (2011) also show that 86 percent of men in the 1946–1951 post World War II (Boomer) cohort were employed full time while only 38 percent of women in this cohort were working full time. Over one in four (26 percent) women worked part time, while only 1 percent of men in this cohort worked part time. Over one in five (22 percent) of women were inactive, compared to 5 percent of men in this cohort.

22 Appold (2004); Bidewell, Griffin, and Hesketh (2006); Gendell (2008); Hardy (2011); Hardy, Hazelrigg, and Quadagno (1996).
23. For more on institutional logics see Thornton, Ocasio, and Lounsbury (2012).
24. Vuolo, Staff, and Mortimer (2012).
25. Angel and Settersten (2013).
26. This also is intertwined with race and ethnicity, since four in five leading-edge college-educated men and women are non-Hispanic white, compared to only two in five of those without a high school education.
27. See Brynjolfsson and McAfee (2014). See appendix B tables 5.1–5.4.
28. Current Population Survey (March 2014 Supplement). See table 5.1 in appendix B.
29. Workers at Boeing, a multinational corporation headquartered in Seattle, Washington that designs, manufactures, and sells aircraft, were threatened with the loss of their jobs if they didn't accept pullbacks in pension benefits. See Bill Saporito, "Why Boeing is Going to War With Its Employees," http://business.time.com/2013/11/19/why-boeing-is-going-to-war-with-its-employees.
30. Scholars like Dannefer (1987) and Schafer, Ferraro, and Mustillo (2011) call this the "cumulation of advantage and disadvantage" or the "cumulation of inequality."
31. For more on agency or a sense of control see Hitlin and Elder (2007 a); Marshall (2005); Schafer et al. (2011); Willson, Shuey, and Elder (2007).
32. The individualization of risk is discussed by Beck and Beck-Gernsheim (2002) as well as O'Rand (2003).
33. Edsall (2012); Grusky, Western, and Wimer (2011); Reich (2011).
34. See Elder, Johnson, and Crosnoe (2003); Moen and Hernandez (2009).
35. See Milkie, Bierman, and Schieman (2008).
36. Ekerdt (2004, 2010).
37. Riley et al. (1994).

6. IMPROVISING HEALTH, WELL-BEING, PURPOSE

1. Herd, Goesling, and House (2007). For more insight into the disparities by socioeconomic status, see also Link and Phelan (1995); Marmot (2004); Marmot and Wilkinson (2006); Pampel, Krueger, and Denney (2010); Phelan, Link, and Tehranifar (2010); Siegrist and Marmot (2006).
2. Derek Bok (2010) summarizes the research evidence on happiness, concluding that 1) while those with more incomes and wealthier incomes report higher levels of happiness, happiness in the United States has neither increased nor decreased over time; 2) people adapt to situations making them happy or unhappy, thereby returning to previous levels; 3) growing inequality has not altered levels of happiness; and 4) there is no difference in happiness, health, or longevity of populations by the amount of income countries devote to social welfare.
3. Thomas and Thomas (1928, 572).
4. See Wheaton (1990, 1999).
5. See Moen (2007).

6. This means those surviving 65 and older are less likely to smoke. See National Research Council and Institute of Medicine (2013).
7. Almost three in 10 (28.3) of the leading-edge Boomer men (who were in the first half of their fifties in 2004) were obese, as were over a third (34.1 percent) of Boomer women. This contrasts with members of the 1936–41 cohort when they were in their early fifties; only one in five (21.3 percent) men and one in four (24.6 percent) women from this generation were obese.
8. See, for example, Berkman, Kawachi, and Glymour (2014); House (2002); Tausig and Fenwick (2011), as well as Aneshensel, Rutter, and Lachenbruch (1991); Link and Phelan (1995); Turner, Wheaton, and Lloyd (1995); Wheaton (2001); Wheaton and Clarke (2003); Wickrama et al. (1997).
9. See, for example, Keyes (1998); Mirowsky and Ross (2003a, b); Muhonen and Torkelson (2004); Ross and Mirowsky (1992, 2003); Ryff and Keyes (1995).
10. Pearlin (1999); Pearlin, Menaghan, Lieberman, and Mullan (1981).
11. Link and Phelan (1995).
12. Karasek (1979); Karasek and Theorell (1990).
13. Marmot (2004); Marmot and Wilkinson (2006); Marmot, Siegrist, and Theorell (2006).
14. Kaplan (1983).
15. See work by Aneshensel (1992); Lazarus and Folkman (1984); Mirowsky and Ross (2003a, b); Pearlin et al. (1981); Pearlin et al. (2005); Turner et al. (1995).
16. Goode (1960, 483).
17. Gotlib and Wheaton (1997); Muhonen and Torkleson (2004); Pearlin et al. (2005).
18. Pearlin 1989; Pearlin et al. (1981); Aneshensel, Pearlin, Mullan, Zarit, and Whitlatch (1995).
19. Elder (1998); Elder, Johnson, and Crosnoe (2003); Pearlin et al. (1981); Pearlin et al. (2005).
20. Pearlin (1989, 241).
21. Tilly (1998). See, for example, McLeod and Nonnemaker (1999); Turner (2010).
22. Berkman and Lochner (2002); Marmot and Wilkinson (2006); Siegrist and Marmot (2006); Stockdale et al. (2007); Taylor, Repetti, and Seeman (1997).
23. Mortimer, Lam, and Lee (2015, 323); Skorikov and Vondracek (2011, 706).
24. See King, Calasanti, and Sorensen (2013).
25. Data are derived from the 2014 Current Population Survey (March Supplement).
26. Weir (2007) defined the leading edge as those born 1948–1953. Men in this study reported an average of two health limitations, while the women averaged three.
27. As opposed to results of medical diagnoses. See Yang (2008).
28. The number of years people expect to live also predicts their life expectancy. See Benyamini and Idler (1999); Idler and Benyamini (1997); Kotter-Grühn, Grühn, and Smith (2010); Smith, Taylor, and Sloan (2001).
29. Mokdad et al. (2003).
30. See Weir (2007).

31. Weir (2007) defined the leading edge as those born 1948–1953. Men in this study reported an average of two health limitations, while the women averaged three.
32. Taylor (2014).
33. Kaufman and Elder (2002).
34. See Martin, Freedman, Schoeni, and Andreski (2009).
35. National Research Council and Institute of Medicine (2013).
36. In 2011, life expectancy at birth was 76.4 and 81.1 respectively for the non-Hispanic white population of men and women compared to 71.6 and 77.8 for non-Hispanic Black men and women, and 78.9 and 88.7 for Hispanic men and women; see table 6 in Hoyert and Xu (2012).
37. Flood and Moen (2015).
38. See Ross, Masters, and Hummer (2012).
39. This is based on data from the American Time Use Survey. See Flood and Moen (2015).
40. Taylor (2014).
41. See Dickens and Flynn (2001); Flynn (1999); Wicherts et al. (2004).
42. See Willis and Schaie (2006).
43. See Stone and Mackie (2013).
44. See Vega and Rumbaut (1991); Williams et al. (2010).
45. Flood and Moen (2016).
46. See Yang (2008).
47. Bok (2010, 16) says, "Why the happiness of white women should have declined is something of a mystery, since the opportunities for a career that they have long sought have become far greater than they were in earlier decades. Perhaps these possibilities have raised aspirations to a level that is hard to fulfill, or perhaps conflicts between work and family have proved difficult to reconcile."
48. Aumann et al. (2011); Galinsky et al. (2011); Kelly et al. (2014).
49. See also Burgard et al. (2009) and Gallo et al. (2000).
50. See Forbes, Spence, Wuthrich, and Rapee (2015) as well as Wang et al. (2011).
51. Westerlund et al. (2009).
52. The gap between women's expectations of working full time and reality did not predict their life satisfaction, however (Clarke, Marshall, and Weir [2012]).
53. Carstensen et al. (2011).
54. See discussion of role captivity in relation to caring for an older relative by Aneshensel, Pearlin, and Schuler (1993).
55. Almeida, Serido, and McDonald (2006: 166).
56. Mallers, Almeida, and Neupert (2005); also Lazarus and Folkman (1984) and Wheaton (1999).
57. Almeida, Serido, and McDonald (2006). See also Grzywacz, Almeida, Neupert, and Ettner 2004.
58. See Kojola, Karakaya, Moen (2015).
59. See Cahill et al. 2006; Hershey, Henkens, and Van Dalen (2007); Quick and Moen (1998); Taylor and Geldhauser (2007); Wang (2007).

60. See Burgard, Brand, and House (2009).
61. See chapter by Thoits (2010).
62. See Johnson (2001); Johnson and Mortimer (2011), Johnson, Sage, and Mortimer (2012); Mortimer, Lam, and Lee (2015).
63. This book reinforces the fact that standardized life course is a thing of the past for many young adults. See Silva (2013).
64. De Lange et al. (2003 and 2004); Ibrahim, Smith, and Muntaner (2009); Karasek and Theorell (1990).
65. Kahn (1981); Karasek and Theorell (1990).
66. Kahn (1981).
67. Ibrahim, Smith, and Muntaner (2009).
68. See Karasek (1979, 290); Karasek and Theorell (1990); Marmot, Siegrist, and Theorell (2006).
69. E.g., Argyle (1999); Bennett et al. (2003); Carayon and Zijlstra (1999); Elsass and Veiga (1997); Karasek (1979); Karasek and Theorell (1990); Keyes (1998); Kivimäki et al. (2005); Lundberg (1996); Mirowsky and Ross (1998); Muhonen and Torkelson (2004); Pearlin et al. (1981); Rau and Triemer (2004).
70. Karasek and Theorell (1990). The job strain model proposes that those with the greatest strain—in high-demanding jobs with low job control (and later low support was added) are the most at risk of poor health. Karasek (1979, 290) describes job control as an employee's "potential control over his tasks and his conduct during the working day," operationalizing job control as having two related components: "decision authority" and "intellectual [or skill] discretion." Scholars have demonstrated, in cross-sectional and longitudinal studies, that job control over how work is done has both direct effects on health and buffering effects by reducing the impacts of job demands on health and well-being. Job control has been empirically linked to exhaustion and depressive symptoms (Mausner-Dorsch and Eaton [2000]), psychophysiological stress responses (e.g., alcohol use, blood pressure, and heart disease; see Bosma, Stansfeld, and Marmot [1998]; Rau and Triemer [2004]), mental and physical health (D'Souza et al. [2003]; Stansfeld and Candy [2006]), work-family conflict and strain (Thomas and Ganster [1995]), and organizational wellness (Bennett, Pelletier, and Cook [2003]). Thus, there is ample evidence linking job control with health and subjective well-being (see also de Lange et al. 2004; Van der Doef and Maes [1999]).
71. See, for example, Moen, Kelly, Tranby, and Huang (2011).
72. Burgard, Brand, and House (2009).
73. Moen, Lam, Ammons, and Kelly (2013); Roxburgh (2009).
74. See the large body of work linking job insecurity to poor health: Burgard et al. (2009); Burgard, Kalousova, and Seefeldt (2012); Ferrie et al. (2003, 2005, 2014); Kalil et al. (2010); László et al. (2010); Rugulies et al. (2008); Scott-Marshall (2010).
75. Kelly and Moen (2007); Moen et al. (2008a and b); Thomas and Ganster (1995).

76. See Moen (2011 a and b); Moen, Kelly, and Lam (2013); Moen, Fan, and Kelly (2013); Lam, Fan, and Moen (2014). ROWE is no longer an active program at Best Buy, but is still used by some teams off the record. It has been adopted in many other organizations. See gorowe.com.
77. See studies described in Moen, Kelly, and Lam (2013) and Moen, Fan, and Kelly (2013).
78. See Kelly et al. (2014) showing declines in work-family conflict in conjunction with the organizational intervention we call STAR. Moen, Kelly, Fan et al. (2016) describes the increases in subjective well-being as a result of STAR; see also Moen, Kelly, Oakes et al. (forthcoming).
79. Artazcoz et al. (2009); Davis et al. (2008); Floderus et al. (2009); Jacobs and Gerson (2004); Kalleberg (2009); Kleiner and Pavalko (2010); Sekine et al. (2009).
80. Chandola et al. (2006); Ertel et al. (2008); Moen et al. (2008a and b).
81. Folbre (2012); Glenn (2010).
82. See Moen (2011c); Moen, Kelly, and Huang (2008a and b); McNamara et al. (2013).
83. Schulte (2014); Moen, Lam, Ammons, and Kelly (2013).
84. See Burgard, Brand, and House (2009); Gallo et al. (2000); Moen, Sweet, and Hill (2010); Sweet and Meiksins (2013).
85. See Karasek and Theorell (1990); Moen, Kelly, Tranby, and Huang et al. (2011); van Solinge and Henkens (2007); Shultz and Wang (2008).
86. See data on Boomers from the 2004 Health and Retirement Study in Weir (2007).
87. See van Solinge and Henkens (2007) and Kim and Moen (2002).
88. See Kubicek et al. (2011).
89. Clarke, Marshall, and Weir (2012) found that when US men with a history of job instability had high expectations about working past age 62 but were unable to do so, they had lower life satisfaction. Research suggests that the mental well-being in retirement is often contingent on prior work and family trajectories (the path people took before they retired), how long they've been retired and their spouses' retirement status, and the voluntariness of this exit. For instance, as we find at TOMO, a worker who puts in long hours at her job prior to retiring is likely to report experiencing relief, and a major decrease in stress.
90. Westerlund et al (2009). This is the GAZEL study of almost 15,000 employees working for the French national gas and electric company. Respondents were surveyed for up to seven years before and seven years after retirement.
91. See Kim and Moen (2002); Moen, Kim, and Hofmeister (2001); Szinovacz and Davey (2004).
92. Ho and Raymo (2009).
93. Mein et al. (2003).
94. Westerlund et al. (2009).
95. Mein et al. (2003).
96. Westerlund et al. (2009).
97. Johnson (2001, 318). See also Mortimer (2003). and Mortimer, Lam, and Lee (2015).

98. Associated with 2.2 (95 percent confidence interval = 1.7 to 2.8) and 2.2 (1.7 to 2.7) points higher mental health and with 1.0 (.6 to 1.5) and 1.1 (.8 to 1.4) points higher physical functioning.
99. Retirement due to ill health was associated with poorer mental health (-.7 points [-1.62 to .2]) and physical functioning (-4.5 points [-5.1 to -3.9]). Research indicates that an unexpected retirement plays an important (and negative) role in subsequent retirement satisfaction (Floyd et al. [1992]; Martin Matthews and Brown [1987]; Szinovacz [1987]; Szinovacz, Martin, and Davey [2014]). Involuntary retirees have the most negative retirement experience, whereas voluntary retirees (who retired to pursue their own interests, for example) report high satisfaction with retirement (Floyd et al. [1992]). Men and women who retire for family needs or health reasons are more likely to have preferred a later retirement, a preference that is negatively related to their retirement satisfaction (Szinovacz [1987]).
100. See Dingemans and Henkens (2015).
101. See also McMunn et al. (2006).
102. The majority of this oldest set of Boomers turning 65 in 2011 like the word "retirement" to describe their life stage and feel it is as they expected it to be.
103. See Kim and DeVaney (2005); Wang et al. (2008).
104. See Allen et al. (2004); Johnson et al. (2009); Price (2003); Sargent et al. (2013); Ulrich and Brott (2005); von Bonsdortff et al (2009).
105. See Ho and Raymo 2009; Li and Ferraro (2005); Morrow-Howell et al. (2003).
106. See Van Solinge and Henkens (2008); Wang (2007; 2012); Wang and Shultz (2010).
107. Glenn (2010).
108. See Mirowsky and Ross (2003a and b); Moen, Dempster-McClain, and Williams (1989).
109. Mirowsky and Ross (2003a and b).
110. See Flood and Moen (2015).
111. See Mirowsky and Ross (2008); Ross and Mirowsky (2010).
112. Klinenberg (2012, 162).
113. Taylor (2014).
114. See Klinenberg (2012, 162).
115. Bird and Rieker (2008); Luoh and Herzog (2002).
116. For general case see Ganster and Rosen (2013); Karasek and Theorell (1990); Nixon et al. (2011). For retirees see Wahrendorf, et al. (2012).
117. Moen and Fields (2002); Morrow-Howell et al. (2003); Thoits and Hewitt (2001).
118. Li and Ferraro (2005, 2006).
119. Moen, Dempster-McClain, and Williams (1989); Musick, Herzog, and House (1999).
120. Thomas (2011, 2012).
121. Greenfield and Marks (2004); Pavlova and Silbereisen (2012); Thoits (2012).
122. See Rowe and Kahn (1998).

123. Rowe and Kahn (1998, 38).
124. Rowe and Kahn (1998, 40, 46).
125. Rowe and Kahn (1998, 54).
126. Estes and Mahakian (2001).
127. Morrow-Howell, Hinterlong, and Sherraden (2001).
128. Bass and Caro (2001, 41).
129. Hurst (2014).
130. Flood and Moen (2016). Unpublished data.
131. Hitlin and Elder (2007b, 39).
132. Bandura (1997).
133. Taylor, Repetti, and Seeman (1997, 411).
134. Ross and Mirowsky (1989, 207).
135. Keyes (1998); Pearlin et al. (1981); Pearlin et al. (2007).
136. Farrell (2014).
137. Schulz and Heckhausen (1996). Skinner (1996, 559) says, "a sense of control includes a view of the self as competent and efficacious and a view of the world as structured and responsive." See also Pearlin and Schooler (1978).
138. Skaff (2006, 200).
139. Moen (2012).
140. See Sweet and Meiksins (2013); Sweet, Moen, and Meiksins (2007).
141. Estes et al. (2013). Diener (1984, 542–543) describes happiness or well-being as experiencing "life satisfaction and frequent joy, and only infrequently… unpleasant emotions such as sadness or anger."

7. INSTITUTIONAL WORK, POCKETS OF CHANGE

1. They were actually two different newspapers then.
2. Johnson (2001); Johnson and Mortimer (2011); Johnson et al. (2012); Mortimer, Lam, and Lee (2015).
3. Hartmann and Swartz (2007, 279).
4. See Hartmann and Swartz (2007).
5. Lawrence, Suddaby, and Leca (2009); Thornton, Ocasio, and Lounsbury (2012).
6. See Whyte (1987, 45).
7. See Brynjolfsson and McAfee (2014).
8. AARP (2014).
9. See Fligstein and McAdam (2012).
10. Kalev, Dobbin, and Kelly (2006).
11. DiMaggio and Powell (1983) talk about the iron cages of work. See also Kalev, Dobbin, and Kelly (2006).
12. Milkman and Appelbaum (2013).
13. Mills (1959).

14. Powell and DiMaggio (1991). Sennett (2006) describes how they are being dismantled through processes of casualization, delayering, and nonlinear sequencing.
15. See Hurst (2014).
16. See for example Lewis, Brannen, and Nilsen (2009); and Kossek and Friede (2006)
17. See Schubert, Hegelich, and Bazant (2009).
18. Gesthuizen and Wolbers (2011).
19. See van Oorschot (2009).
20. See article by Ben Riley-Smith, website is www.telegraph.co.uk/news/politics/11149224/Bar-employers-from-advertising-jobs-for-recent-graduates-says-Coaltions-older-workers-tsar.html, and The Christian Science Monitor's article by Editorial Board, www.csmonitor.com/Commentary/the-monitors-view/2014/0808/Redefining-age-in-aging-societies.
21. See article by Ben Riley-Smith.
22. AARP (2014); Moen (2007).
23. See the Bernard Osher Foundation website at www.osherfoundation.org/index.php?olli; also Road Scholar website at www.roadscholar.org.
24. American Council on Education (2007).
25. See Experience Matters Explore Your Future website at http://experiencematters-az.org/skilled-talent/learning-opportunities/explore-your-future.
26. See SHIFT website at http://shiftonline.org/.
27. See Life Planning Network website at www.lifeplanningnetwork.org/.
28. See University of Connecticut's Department of Public Policy website at http://nonprofit.leadership.uconn.edu/encore/overview.
29. See Harvard University's Advanced Leadership Initiative website at http://advancedleadership.harvard.edu/.
30. See Portland Community College's Center for Advancement at the website www.pcc.edu/climb/life/discover.html.
31. See Stanford University's Distinguished Careers Institute website at http://dci.stanford.edu/.
32. See Greenblatt (2007).
33. Matos and Galinsky (2012). Studies of a flexibility initiative are described in Kelly, Moen, and Tranby (2011); King et al. (2012); Kossek et al. (2014); Moen, Kelly, Tranby, and Huang (2011).
34. Henly and Lambert (2014) and Lambert et al. (2012).
35. King et al. (2012); Kossek et al. (2014).
36. See Kelly, Moen, Fan, et al. (2014); Moen, Kelly, Fan, Lee, Kossek and Buxton (2016); Moen, Kelly, Oakes, et al. (2016).
37. Susanka (1998).
38. I describe not-so-big jobs in Moen (2007). The term is based on books by architect Sarah Susanka on not-so-big houses.
39. See Encore.org website at https://encore.org/.

40. See AARP Foundation Experience Corps website at www.aarp.org/experience-corps.
41. See the Corporation for National & Community Service's webpage at www.nationalservice.gov/programs/senior-corps.
42. See the Volunteer Alberta website at http://volunteeralberta.ab.ca/networks/volunteer-centres www.volunteercalgary.ab.ca; Volunteers of America's website at www.voa.org/; Environmental Alliance for Senior Involvement's website at www.easi.org/; Volunteers in Medicine's website at http://volunteersinmedicine.org/.
43. See Paragon: Corporate Counsel on Demand's website at www.paragonlegal.com/; Experienced Resource's website at www.experiencedresources.net/; Jeane Thorne Staffing website at http://jeanethorne.com/.
44. See Robert Half's website at www.roberthalf.com.
45. Lawrence, Suddaby, and Leca (2009); Thornton, Ocasio, and Lounsbury (2012).

8. TRANSFORMING INSTITUTIONS AND LIVES

1. Lawrence and Suddaby (2006, 215). See also Thornton, Ocasio, and Lounsbury (2012) and Lawrence, Suddaby, and Leca (2009).
2. Battilana and D'Aunno (2009) write about this paradox.
3. Galinsky, Sakai, and Wigton (2011); Matos and Galinsky (2012).
4. For an empirical example, Moen, Lam, Ammons, and Kelly (2013). The insecurity is real. See Sennett (2006) for a discussion of the new job insecurity.
5. See England (2010); Esping-Andersen (2009); Gerson (2010); Slaughter (2015).
6. See Friedland and Alford (1991); Sewell (1992).
7. Galinsky et al. (2011).
8. See Sennett (2006).
9. Though Great Britain is planning for large cuts in the public sector, according to Larry Elliott (2014).
10. Powell and DiMaggio (1991).
11. DeLong (2004).
12. Biggart and Beamish (2003).
13. Dychtwald (1989, 1999).
14. See Carroll Estes (2004); Estes et al. (2013) and Pruchno (2015).
15. Dychtwald (1999, 57).
16. Gilleard and Higgs (2005, 157).
17. Institutions such as higher education, labor, business, the military, retirement, religion, the media, social welfare, nonprofits, family, and health care. These regimes have different logics, and not always internally consistent ones. Existing institutional arrangements cannot usefully be thought of or studied separately, since they are closely connected and interdependent (de Vroom and Bannink (2008); Ebbinghaus (2006); Kohli (2007).
18. Esping-Andersen (2009, 11).
19. Gerson (2010). See also Slaughter (2015).

20. See Tronto (2013).
21. Date of birth has always been a key marker in religious practices and has become a dominant method for tracking people as citizens, patients, consumers, customers, and, despite laws against age discrimination, employees and job applicants.
22. In 1970 Carol Hanisch wrote about consciousness-raising taking place in small groups as women shared their own experiences, and began to see similar patterns in "The Personal is Political." See also the 1970 anthology *Sisterhood is Powerful* edited by Robin Morgan.
23. There are conflicts among economists and other experts about whether either system is actually in trouble; some estimate that the Boomers will effectively kill Social Security since there aren't as many people in cohorts following to pay in, while some believe that's just ridiculous, given inflation and wages in some sectors rising faster than inflationary changes to Social Security payouts.
24. Munnell and Sass (2008).
25. Freedman (2007, 2011).
26. See Rubin (1996); Schultz (2011).
27. In "Congress, Social Movements and Public Opinion: Multiple Origins of Women's Rights Legislation," Anne N. Costain and Steven Majstorovic (1994) describe how public opinion both led and was changed by congressional legislation.
28. See Ken Dychtwald (1989, 1999).
29. See Gilleard and Higgs (2005); Gilleard, Hyde, and Higgs (2007); Mahmood and Keating (2012).
30. Freelancers Union website: see www.freelancersunion.org/blog/authors/shorowitz/.
31. Paragon: Corporate Counsel on Demand website, see www.paragonlegal.com/.
32. Sennett (2006, 183–184).
33. Sennett (2006).
34. New cohorts replacing earlier ones are a key mechanism of social change; see Alwin and McCammon (2007); Ryder (1965).
35. Brynjolfsson and McAfee (2014).
36. See Riley, Kahn, and Foner (1994).
37. Friedman (2013, 76).
38. Benko and Weisberg (2007).
39. Sennett (2006).
40. Rao, Morrill, and Zald (2000, 240).
41. For an overview of feminism and the women's movement, see Ferree and Mueller (2004); Soule et al. (1999). The women's movement occurred even as the labor market became more skilled and automated, with computers gaining ascendance. We are now in a new labor market age, what some call a second industrial revolution. See Brynjolfsson and McAfee (2014) and Gordon (2009).
42. See Acker (1992); Arber and Ginn (1991); Estes (2004); Harrington Meyer and Herd (2007); Pampel (1994); Quadagno (1988).

43. Hochschild (2012) describes how much of personal life is now being outsourced.
44. See Hochschild (1989; 2012).
45. See Life Reimagined at AARP.org.; Leider and Webber (2013).
46. Encore.org was founded by social entrepreneur Marc Freedman. It aims to promote "second acts for the common good." To learn more see Freedman (2007, 2011) and Alboher (2013).
47. DiMaggio (1988).
48. Munnell and Sass (2008).
49. Light (1988, 277).

References

AARP. 2002. *Staying Ahead of the Curve: The AARP Work and Career Study*. National survey conducted for AARP by Roper ASW. Washington, DC: AARP.

AARP. 2014. *Staying Ahead of the Curve 2013: AARP Multicultural Work and Career Study: Older Workers in an Uneasy Job Market*. Washington, DC: AARP.

Acker, Joan. 1992. "Sex Roles to Gendered Institutions." *Contemporary Sociology* 21(5): 565–569.

Adams, Gary A., and Barbara L. Rau. 2011. "Putting Off Tomorrow to Do What You Want Today: Planning for Retirement." *American Psychologist* 66(3): 180–192.

Administration on Aging. 2013. *A Profile of Older Americans: 2012*. Washington, DC: US Department of Health and Human Services.

Agree, Emily M., and Karen Glaser. 2009. "Demography of Informal Caregiving." In *International Handbook of Population Aging*, edited by Peter Uhlenberg (pp. 647–668). New York: Springer.

Aisenbrey, Silke, Marie Evertsson, and Daniela Grunow. 2009. "Is There a Career Penalty for Mothers' Time Out? A Comparison of Germany, Sweden and the United States." *Social Forces* 88(2): 573–605.

Alboher, Marci. 2013. *The Encore Career Handbook: How to Make a Living and a Difference in the Second Half of Life*. New York: Workman Publishing Company.

Allen, Steven G., Robert L. Clark, and Linda S. Ghent. 2004. "Phasing into Retirement." *Industrial and Labor Relations Review* 58(1): 112–127.

Allmendinger, Jutta, and Thomas Hinz. 2009. "Occupational Careers under Different Welfare Regimes: West Germany, Great Britain and Sweden." In *The Life Course Reader: Individuals and Societies across Time*, edited by Walter R. Heinz, Johannes Huinink, and Ansgar Weymann (pp. 234–251). Frankfurt: Campus Verlag.

Almeida, David M., Joyce Serido, and Daniel McDonald. 2006. "Daily Life Stressors of Early and Late Baby Boomers." In *The Baby Boomers Grow Up*, edited by Susan K. Whitbourne and Sherry L. Willis (pp. 165–183). Mahwah, NJ: Lawrence Erlbaum.

Altindag, Onur, Lucie Schmidt, and Purvi Sevak. 2012. "The Great Recession, Older Workers with Disabilities, and Implications for Retirement Security." University of

Michigan Retirement Research Center (Research Brief 277). Ann Arbor: University of Michigan.

Alwin, Duane F., and Ryan J. McCammon. 2003. "Generations, Cohorts, and Social Change." In *Handbook of the Life Course*, edited by J. T. Mortimer and M. J. Shanahan (pp. 23–49). New York: Kluwer Academic/Plenum Publishers.

Alwin, Duane F., and Ryan J. McCammon. 2007. "Rethinking Generations." *Research in Human Development* 4(3–4): 219–237.

Alwin, Duane F., Ryan J. McCammon, and Scott M. Hofer. 2006. "Studying Baby Boom Cohorts within a Demographic and Developmental Context: Conceptual and Methodological Issues." In *The Baby Boomers Grow Up: Contemporary Perspectives on Midlife*, edited by Susan Krauss Whitbourne and Sherry L. Willis (pp. 45–71). Mahwah, NJ: Lawrence Erlbaum.

American Council on Education. 2007. *Framing New Terrain: Older Adults & Higher Education*. Washington, DC: American Council on Education.

Aneshensel, Carol S. 1992. "Social Stress: Theory and Research." *Annual Review of Sociology* 18: 15–38.

Aneshensel, Carol S., Leonard I. Pearlin, and Roberleigh H. Schuler. 1993. "Stress, Role Captivity, and the Cessation of Caregiving." *Journal of Health and Social Behavior* 34(1): 54–70.

Aneshensel, Carol S., Carolyn M. Rutter, and Peter A. Lachenbruch. 1991. "Social Structure, Stress, and Mental Health: Competing Conceptual and Analytic Models." *American Sociological Review* 56(2): 166–178.

Aneshensel, Carol S., Leonard I. Pearlin, Joseph T. Mullan, Steven H. Zarit, and Carol J. Whitlatch. 1995. *Profiles in Caregiving: The Unexpected Career*. New York: Academic Press.

Angel, Jacqueline L., and Richard A. Settersten Jr. 2013. "The New Realities of Aging: Social and Economic Contexts." In *Perspectives on the Future of the Sociology of Aging*, edited by Linda Waite (pp. 95–119). Washington, DC: National Research Council.

Angrisani, Marco, Michael D. Hurd, and Erik Meijer. 2012. "Investment Decisions in Retirement: The Role of Subjective Expectations." University of Michigan Retirement Research Center (WP 2012-274). Ann Arbor: University of Michigan.

Appold, Stephen J. 2004. "How Much Longer Would Men Work If There Were No Employment Dislocation? Estimates from Cause-Elimination Work Life Tables." *Social Science Research* 33(4): 660–680.

Arber, Sara, and Jay Ginn. 1991. *Gender and Later Life: A Sociological Analysis of Resources and Constraints*. London: Sage Publications.

Argyle, Michael. 1999. "Causes and Correlates of Happiness." In *Well-Being: The Foundations of Hedonic Psychology*, edited by Daniel Kahneman, Ed Diener, and Norbert Schwarz (pp. 353–377). New York: Russell Sage Foundation.

Aries, Philippe. 1962. *Centuries of Childhood: A Social History of Family Life*. New York: Vintage Books.

Arnett, Jeffrey J. 1997. "Young People's Conceptions of the Transition to Adulthood." *Youth and Society* 29(1): 1–23.

Arnett, Jeffrey J. 2000. "Emerging Adulthood: A Theory of Development from the Late Teens through the Twenties." *American Psychologist* 55(5): 469–480.

Arnett, Jeffrey J. 2004. *Emerging Adulthood: The Winding Road from Late Teens through the Twenties*. New York: Oxford University Press.

Arnett, Jeffrey J. 2010. *Adolescence and Emerging Adulthood: A Cultural Approach* (4th Edition). Upper Saddle River, NJ: Prentice Hall.

Arnett, Jeffrey J., and Nancy Eisenberg. 2007. "Introduction to the Special Section: Emerging Adulthood around the World." *Child Development Perspectives* 1(2): 66–67.

Artazcoz L., I. Cortes, C. Borrell, V. Escriba-Aguir, L. Cascant, and R. Villegas. 2009. "Understanding the Relationship of Long Working Hours with Health Status and Health-Related Behaviours." *Journal of Epidemiology and Community Health* 63(7): 521–527.

Arthur, Michael B., and D. M. Rousseau. 1996. *The Boundaryless Career: A New Employment Principle for a New Organizational Era*. New York: Oxford University Press.

Arthur, Michael B., Kerr Inkson, and Judith K. Pringle. 1999. *The New Careers: Individual Action and Economic Change*. Thousand Oaks, CA: Sage Publications.

Arthur, Michael B., Svetlana N. Khapova, and Celeste P. M. Wilderom. 2005. "Career Success in a Boundaryless Career World." *Journal of Organizational Behavior* 26(2): 177–202.

Aumann, Kerstin., Ellen E. Galinsky, and Kenneth Matos. 2011. *The New Male Mystique*. New York: Families and Work Institute.

Bailyn, Lotte. 1993. *Breaking the Mold: Women, Men, and Time in the New Corporate World*. New York: The Free Press.

Baltes, Paul B. 1997. "On the Incomplete Architecture of Human Ontogeny: Selection, Optimization, and Compensation as Foundation of Developmental Theory." *American Psychologist* 52(4): 366–380.

Baltes, Paul B., and Margret M. Baltes. 1990. *Successful Aging: Perspectives from the Behavioral Sciences*. Cambridge: Cambridge University Press.

Baltes, Paul B., and Karl U. Mayer. 1999. *The Berlin Aging Study: Aging from 70 to 100*. New York: Cambridge University Press.

Bandura, Albert. 1997. *Self-Efficacy: The Exercise of Control*. New York: Freeman.

Banerjee, Sudipto, and David Blau. 2013. "Employment Trends by Age in the United States: Why are Older Workers Different?" University of Michigan Retirement Research Center (WP 2013-285). Ann Arbor: University of Michigan.

Barbieri, Paolo, and Stefani Scherer. 2011. "Retirement in Italy: Rising Social Inequalities across Generations." In *Aging Populations, Globalization and the Labor Market: Comparing Late Working Life and Retirement in Modern Societies*, edited by Hans-Peter Blossfeld, Sandra Buchholz, and Karin Kurz (pp. 91–120). Cheltenham, UK/ Northampton, MA: Edward Elgar.

Barley, Stephen R. 1989. "Careers, Identities and Institutions." In *The Handbook of Career Theory*, edited by M. B. Arthur, D. T. Hall, and B. S. Lawrence (pp. 41–60). Cambridge: Cambridge University Press.

Bass, Scott, and Francis G. Caro. 2001. "Productive Aging: A Conceptual Framework." In *Productive Aging: A Conceptual Framework*, edited by Nancy Morrow-Howell, James Hinterlong, and Michael Sherraden (pp. 37–80). Baltimore, MD: Johns Hopkins University Press.

Battilana, Julie, and Thomas D'Aunno. 2009. "Institutional Work and the Paradox of Embedded Agency." In *Institutional Work: Actors and Agency in Institutional Studies of Organizations*, edited by T. B. Lawrence, R. Suddaby, and B. Leca (pp. 31–58). New York: Cambridge University Press.

Beck, Ulrich. 1997. *The Reinvention of Politics: Rethinking Modernity in the Global Social Order*. Cambridge: Polity.

Beck, Ulrich, and Elisabeth Beck-Gernsheim. 2002. *Individualization: Institutionalized Individualism and its Social and Political Consequences*. Thousand Oaks, CA: Sage Publications.

Becker, Gary S. 1981. *A Treatise on the Family*. Cambridge, MA: Harvard University Press.

Becker, Howard S., and Anselm L. Strauss. 1956. "Careers, Personality, and Adult Socialization." *American Journal of Sociology* 62(3): 253–263.

Becker, Penny Edgell, and Phyllis Moen. 1999. "Scaling Back: Dual-Career Couples' Work-Family Strategies." *Journal of Marriage and the Family* 61(4): 995–1007.

Bendick, Marc Jr., Lauren E. Brown, and Kennington Wall. 1999. "No Foot in the Door: An Experimental Study of Employment Discrimination against Older Workers." *Journal of Aging and Social Policy* 10(4): 5–24.

Benko, Cathleen, and Anne Weisberg. 2007. *Mass Career Customization: Aligning the Workplace with Today's Nontraditional Workforce*. Boston: Harvard Business School Publishing.

Bennett, Joel B., Royer F. Cook, and Kenneth R. Pelletier. 2003. "Toward an Integrated Framework for Comprehensive Organizational Concepts, Practices, and Research in Workplace Health Promotion." In *Handbook of Occupational Health Psychology*, edited by James C. Quick and Lois E. Tetrick (pp. 69–98). Washington, DC: American Psychological Association.

Benson, Janel, and Frank F. Furstenberg Jr. 2006. "Entry into Adulthood: Are Adult Role Transitions Meaningful Markers of Adult Identity?" *Advances in Life Course Research* 11: 199–214.

Benyamini, Yael, and Ellen L. Idler. 1999. "Community Studies Reporting Association between Self-Rated Health and Mortality Additional Studies, 1995 to 1998." *Research on Aging* 21(3): 392–401.

Berkman Lisa F., and Kimberly A. Lochner. 2002. "Social Determinants of Health: Meeting at the Crossroads." *Health Affairs* 21(2): 291–293.

Berkman, Lisa, Ichiro Kawachi, and Maria Glymour. 2014. *Social Epidemiology, Second Edition*. New York: Oxford University Press.

Bidewell, John, Barbara Griffin, and Beryl Hesketh. 2006. "Timing of Retirement: Including a Delay Discounting Perspective in Retirement Models." *Journal of Vocational Behavior* 68(2): 368–387.

Bielby, William T., and Denise D. Bielby. 1992. "I Will Follow Him: Family Ties, Gender-Role Beliefs, and Reluctance to Relocate for a Better Job." *American Journal of Sociology* 97(5): 1241–1267.

Biggart, Nicole W., and Thomas D. Beamish. 2003. "The Economic Sociology of Conventions: Habit, Custom, Practice and Routine in Market Order." *Annual Review of Sociology* 29: 443–464.

Bird, Chloe E., and Patricia P. Rieker. 2008. *Gender and Health: The Effects of Constrained Choices and Social Policies*. New York: Cambridge University Press.

Blair-Loy, Mary. 1999. "Career Patterns of Executive Women in Finance: An Optimal Matching Analysis." *American Journal of Sociology* 104(5): 1346–1397.

Blair-Loy, Mary. 2003. *Competing Devotions: Career and Family among Women Executives*. Cambridge, MA: Harvard University Press.

Blair-Loy, Mary, and Amy S. Wharton. 2002. "Employees' Use of Work-Family Policies and the Workplace Social Context." *Social Forces* 80(3): 813–845.

Blau, David M., and Donna B. Gilleskie. 2001. "Retiree Health Insurance and the Labor Force Behavior of Older Men in the 1990s." *Review of Economics and Statistics* 83(1): 64–80.

Blau, David M., and Ryan Goodstein. 2010. "Can Social Security Explain Trends in Labor Force Participation of Older Men in the United States?" *Journal of Human Resources* 45(2): 328–363.

Blossfeld, Hans-Peter, and Sonja Drobnič. 2001. *Careers of Couples in Contemporary Societies: From Male Breadwinner to Dual-Earner Families*. Oxford: Oxford University Press.

Blossfeld, Hans-Peter, and Heather Hofmeister. 2006. *Globalization, Uncertainty, and Women's Careers: An International Comparison*. Cheltenham, UK/Northampton, MA: Edward Elgar.

Blossfeld, Hans-Peter, Sandra Buchholz, and Dirk Hofäcker. 2006. *Globalization, Uncertainty and Late Careers in Society*. London/New York: Routledge.

Blossfeld, Hans-Peter, Sandra Buchholz, and Karin Kurz. 2011. *Aging Populations, Globalization and the Labor Market: Comparing Late Working Life and Retirement in Modern Societies*. Northampton, MA: Edward Elgar.

Bok, Derek. 2010. *The Politics of Happiness: What Government Can Learn From the New Research on Well-Being*. Princeton, NJ: Princeton University Press.

Bosma, Hans, Stephen A. Stansfeld, and Michael G. Marmot. 1998. "Job Control, Personal Characteristics, and Heart Disease." *Journal of Occupational Health Psychology* 3(4): 402–409.

Bradburn, Ellen Marie, Phyllis Moen, and Donna Dempster-McClain. 1995. "An Event History Analysis of Women's Return to School." *Social Forces* 73(4): 1517–1551.

Bray, Jeremy W., Erin L. Kelly, Leslie B. Hammer, David M. Almeida, James W. Dearing, Rosalind B. King, and Orfeu M. Buxton. 2013. "An Integrative, Multilevel, and Transdisciplinary Research Approach to Challenges of Work, Family, and Health." RTI Press publication No. MR 0024-1303. Research Triangle Park, NC: RTI Press.

Breiger, Ronald L. 1995. "Social Structure and the Phenomenology of Attainment." *Annual Review of Sociology* 21: 115–136.

Bronfenbrenner, Urie. 2005. *Making Human Beings Human: Bioecological Perspectives on Human Development*. Thousand Oaks, CA: Sage Publications.

Bronfenbrenner, Urie, Peter McClelland, Elaine Wethington, Phyllis Moen, and Stephen J. Ceci. 1996. *The State of Americans: This Generation and the Next*. New York: The Free Press.

Brown, Duane, Linda Brooks, and Associates. 1984. *Career Choice and Development*. San Francisco: Jossey-Bass.

Brückner, Hannah, and Karl Ulrich Mayer. 2005. "De-Standardization of the Life Course: What It Might Mean? And If It Means Anything, Whether It Actually Took Place?" *Advances in Life Course Research* 9: 27–53.

Brynjolfsson, Erik, and Andrew McAfee. 2014. *The Second Machine Age: Work, Progress, and Prosperity in a Time of Brilliant Technologies*. New York: Norton.

Buchholz, Sandra, Annika Rinklake, Julia Schilling, Karin Kurz, Paul Schmelzer, and Hans-Peter Blossfeld. 2011. "Aging Populations, Globalization and the Labor Market: Comparing Late Working Life and Retirement in Modern Societies." In *Aging Populations, Globalization and the Labor Market: Comparing Late Working Life and Retirement in Modern Societies*, edited by Hans-Peter Blossfeld, Sandra Buchholz, and Karin Kurz (pp. 3–32). Cheltenham, UK/Northampton, MA: Edward Elgar.

Buchmann, Marlis. 1989. *The Script of Life in Modern Society: Entry into Adulthood in a Changing World*. Chicago: University of Chicago Press.

Budig, Michelle J., and Paula England. 2001. "The Wage Penalty for Motherhood." *American Sociological Review* 66(2): 204–225.

Budig, Michelle J., and Melissa J. Hodges. 2010. "Differences in Disadvantage: Variation in the Motherhood Wage Penalty across White Women's Earnings Distribution." *American Sociological Review* 75(5): 705–728.

Burgard, Sarah A., Jennie E. Brand, and James S. House. 2009. "Perceived Job Insecurity and Worker Health in the United States." *Social Science & Medicine* 69(5): 777–785.

Burgard, Sarah, Lucie Kalousova, and Kristin Seefeldt. 2012. "Perceived Job Insecurity and Health: The Michigan Recession and Recovery Study." *Journal of Occupational Environmental Medicine* 54(9): 1101–1106.

Burtless, Gary, and Joseph F. Quinn. 2001. "Retirement Trends and Policies to Encourage Work among Older Americans." In *Ensuring Health and Income Security for an Aging Workforce*, edited by Peter P. Budetti, Richard V. Burkhauser, Janice M. Gregory, and H. Allan Hunt (pp. 375–415). Kalamazoo, MI: W. E. Upjohn Institute for Employment Research.

Butrica, Barbara A., Howard M. Iams, and Karen E. Smith. 2003/2004. "The Changing Impact of Social Security on Retirement Income in the United States." *Social Security Bulletin* 65(3): 1–13.

Cahill, Kevin E., Michael D. Giandrea, and Joseph F. Quinn. 2006. "Retirement Patterns from Career Development." *The Gerontologist* 46(4): 514–523.

Cahill, Kevin E., Michael D. Giandrea, and Joseph F. Quinn. 2015. "Retirement Patterns and the Macroeconomy, 1992–2010: The Prevalence and Determinants of Bridge Jobs, Phased Retirement, and Reentry Among Three Recent Cohorts of Older Americans." *The Gerontologist* 55(3): 384–403.

Cappelli, Peter, and William Novelli. 2010. *Managing the Older Works: How to Prepare for the New Organizational Order*. Boston: Harvard Business School Publishing.

Carayon, Pascale, and Fred Zijlstra. 1999. "Relationship between Job Control, Work Pressure and Strain. Studies in the USA and The Netherlands." *Work & Stress* 13(1): 32–48.

Carstensen, Laura L. 2011. *A Long Bright Future: Happiness, Health and Financial Security in an Age of Increased Longevity*. New York: Public Affairs.

Carstensen, Laura L., Derek M. Isaacowitz, and Susan T. Charles. 1999. "Taking Time Seriously: A Theory of Socioemotional Selectivity." *American Psychologist* 54(3): 165–181.

Carstensen, Laura L., Bulent Turan, Susanne Scheibe, Nilam Ram, Hall Ersner-Hershfield, Gregory R. Samanez-Larkin, Kathryn P. Brooks, and John R. Nesselroade. 2011. "Emotional Experience Improves with Age: Evidence Based on Over 10 Years of Experience Sampling." *Psychology and Aging* 26(1): 21–33.

Chandola Tarani, Eric Brunner, and Michael Marmot. 2006. "Chronic Stress at Work and the Metabolic Syndrome: Prospective Study." *British Medical Journal* 332(7540): 521–525.

Charles, Maria, and David B. Grusky. 2004. *Occupational Ghettos: The Worldwide Segregation of Women and Men*. Redwood City, CA: Stanford University Press.

Cherlin, Andrew. 2010. "Demographic Trends in the United States: A Review of Research in the 2000s." *Journal of Marriage and Family* 72(3): 403–419.

Chesley, Noelle. 2005. "Blurring Boundaries? Linking Technology Use, Spillover, Individual Distress, and Family Satisfaction." *Journal of Marriage and Family* 67(5): 1237–1248.

Chesley, Noelle, and Phyllis Moen. 2006. "When Workers Care: Dual-Earner Couples' Caregiving Strategies, Benefit Use, and Psychological Well-Being." *American Behavioral Scientist* 49(9): 1248–1269.

Christensen, Kathleen, and Barbara Schneider. 2010. *Workplace Flexibility: Realigning 20th Century Jobs for a 21st Century Workforce*. Ithaca, NY: Cornell University Press.

Clark, Gordon L., Kendra Strauss, and Janelle Knox-Hayes. 2012. *Saving for Retirement*. Oxford: Oxford University Press.

Clarke, Philippa, and Blair Wheaton. 2005. "Mapping Social Context on Mental Health Trajectories through Adulthood." *Advances in Life Course Research* 9: 269–301.

Clarke, Philippa J., Victor Marshall, and David Weir. 2012. "Unexpected Retirement from Full Time Work after Age 62: Consequences for Life Satisfaction in Older Americans." *European Journal of Ageing* 9(3): 207–219.

Clausen, John A. 1993. *American Lives: Looking Back at the Children of the Great Depression*. Berkeley: University of California Press.

Coleman, James S. 1990. "Commentary: Social Institutions and Social Theory." *American Sociological Review* 55(3): 333–339.

Coser, Lewis. 1974. *Greedy Institutions: Patterns of Undivided Commitment*. New York: The Free Press.

Coser, Lewis, and Rose L. Coser. 1974. "The Housewife and Her Greedy Family." In *Greedy Institutions: Patterns of Undivided Commitment*, edited by Lewis Coser (pp. 89–100). New York: The Free Press.

Costa, Dora L. 1998. *The Evolution of Retirement: An American Economic History, 1880–1990*. Chicago: University of Chicago Press.

Costain, Anne N., and Steven Majstorovic. 1994. "Congress, Social Movements and Public Opinion: Multiple Origins of Women's Rights Legislation." *Political Research Quarterly* 47(1): 111–135.

Crocker, Richard. 2007. *The Boomer Century, 1946–2046: How America's Most Influential Generation Changed Everything*. New York: Alexandria Productions, Inc.

Daly, Kerry J., and John Beaton. 2005. "Through the Lens of Time: How Families Live in and Through Time." In *Sourcebook of Family Theory & Research*, edited by Vern L. Bengtson, Alan C. Acock, Katherine R. Allen, Peggye Dilworth-Anderson, and David M. Klein (pp. 241–263). Thousand Oaks, CA: Sage Publications.

Dannefer, Dale. 1987. "Aging as Intracohort Differentiation: Accentuation, the Matthew Effect, and the Life Course." *Sociological Forum* 2(2): 211–236.

Dannefer, Dale. 2003. "Cumulative Advantage/Disadvantage and the Life Course: Cross-Fertilizing Age and Social Science Theory." *Journal of Gerontology* 58(6): 327–337.

Davis, Kelly D., W. Benjamin Goodman, Amy E. Pirretti, and David M. Almeida. 2008. "Nonstandard Work Schedules, Perceived Family Well-being, and Daily Stressors." *Journal of Marriage and Family* 70(4): 991–1003.

De Lange, Annet H., Toon W. Taris, Michiel A.J. Kompier, Irene L. D. Houtman, and Paulien M. Bongers. 2004. "The Relationships between Work Characteristics and Mental Health: Examining Normal, Reversed and Reciprocal Relationships in a 4-Wave Study." *Work & Stress* 18(2): 149–166.

De Lange, Annet H., Toon W. Taris, Michiel A.J. Kompier, Irene L. D. Houtman, and Paulien M. Bongers. 2003. "The Very Best of the Millennium: Longitudinal Research and the Demand-Control-(Support) Model." *Journal of Occupational Health Psychology* 8(4): 282–305.

De Preter, Hanne, Dorien Van Looy, Dimitri Mortelmans, and Kim Denaeghel. 2013. "Retirement Timing in Europe: The Influence of Individual Work and Life Factors." *The Social Science Journal* 50(2): 145–151.

DeLong, David W. 2004. *Lost Knowledge: Confronting the Threat of an Aging Workforce*. New York: Oxford University Press.

DeLong, David. 2006. "The Paradox of the 'Working Retired'—Identifying Barriers to Increased Labor Force Participation by Older Workers in the U.S." Paper submitted for Academy of Management CMS Research Workshop, August 11, 2006.

Denaeghel, Kim, Dimitri Mortelmans, and Annelies Borghgraef. 2011. "Spousal Influence on the Retirement Decisions of Single-Earner and Dual-Earner Couples." *Advances in Life Course Research* 16(3): 112–123.

Dentinger, Emma, and Marin Clarkberg. 2002. "Informal Caregiving and Retirement Timing among Men and Women: Gender and Caregiving Relationships in Late Midlife." *Journal of Family Issues* 23(7): 857–879.

De Vroom, Bert. 2004. "The Shift from Early to Late Exit: Changing Institutional Conditions and Individual Preferences: The Case of the Netherlands." In *Ageing and the Transition to Retirement: A Comparative Analysis of European Welfare States*, edited by Tony Maltby, Bert de Vroom, Maria Luisa Mirabile, and Einar Øverbye (pp. 120–153). Burlington, VT: Ashgate Publishing Company.

De Vroom, Bert, and Duco Bannink. 2008. "Changing Life Courses and New Social Risks: The Case of Old Age Pensions." *Journal of Comparative Policy Analysis* 10(1): 75–92.

Dickens, William T., and James R. Flynn. 2001. "Heritability Estimates Versus Large Environmental Effects: The IQ Paradox Resolved." *Psychological Review* 108(2): 346–369.

Diener, Ed. 1984. "Subjective Well-Being." *Psychological Bulletin* 95(3): 542–575.

Dingemans, Ellen A. A., and Kène Henkens. 2015. "How Do Retirement Dynamics Influence Mental Well-Being in Later Life: A 10-Year Panel Study." *Scandinavian Journal of Work Environment & Health* 41(1): 16–23.

DiMaggio, Paul J. 1988. "Interest and Agency in Institutional Theory." In *Institutional Patterns and Organizations: Culture and Environment*, edited by Lynne G. Zucker (pp. 3–21). Cambridge, MA: Ballinger.

DiMaggio, Paul J., and Walter W. Powell. 1983. "The Iron Cage Revisited: Institutional Isomorphism and Collective Rationality in Organizational Fields." *American Sociological Review* 48(2): 147–160.

DiPrete, Thomas A., and Gregory M. Eirich. 2006. "Cumulative Advantage as a Mechanism for Inequality: A Review of Theoretical and Empirical Developments." *Annual Review of Sociology* 32: 271–297.

D'Souza, R. M., L. Strazdins, L. Y. Lim, D. H. Broom, and B. Rodgers. 2003. "Work and Health in Contemporary Society: Demands, Control and Insecurity." *Journal of Epidemiology and Community Health* 57(11): 849–854.

Drobnič, Sonja, Barbara Beham, and Patrick Präg. 2010. "Good Job, Good Life? Working Conditions and Quality of Life in Europe." *Social Indicators Research* 99(2): 205–225.

Dychtwald, Ken. 1989. *Age Wave: How the Most Important Trend of our Time Will Change Your Future*. Los Angeles: J. P. Tarcher.

Dychtwald, Ken. 1999. *Age Power: How the 21st Century Will be Ruled by the New Old*. Los Angeles: J. P. Tarcher.

Easterlin, Richard A. 1987. *Birth and Fortune: The Impact of Numbers on Personal Welfare*. Chicago: University of Chicago Press.

Easterlin, Richard A., Christine M. Schaeffer, and Diane J. Macunovich. 1993. "Will the Baby Boomers be less well off than Their Parents? Income, Wealth, and Family Circumstances over the Life Cycle in the United States." *Population and Development Review* 19(3): 497–522.

Edsall, Thomas. 2012. "The Hollowing Out." *New York Times*. July 8.

Ebbinghaus, Bernhard. 2006. *Reforming Early Retirement in Europe, Japan and the USA*. New York: Oxford University Press.

Eggebeen, David J., and Samuel Sturgeon. 2006. "Demography of the Baby Boomers." In *The Baby Boomers Grow Up: Contemporary Perspectives on Midlife*, edited by Susan Krauss Whitbourne and Sherry L. Willis (pp. 3–21). Mahwah, NJ: Lawrence Erlbaum.

Ekerdt, David J. 2004. "Born to Retire: The Foreshortened Life Course." *The Gerontologist* 44(1): 3–9.

Ekerdt, David J. 2010. "Frontiers of Research on Work and Retirement." *Journal of Gerontology* 65B(1): 69–80.

Elder, Glen H. Jr. 1974. *Children of the Great Depression: Social Change in Life Experience*. Chicago: University of Chicago Press.

Elder, Glen H. Jr. 1975. "Adolescence in the Life Cycle." In *Adolescence in the Life Cycle*, edited by Sigmund E. Dragastin and Glen H. Elder Jr. (pp. 1–22). Washington, DC: Hemisphere/Halsted Press.

Elder, Glen H. Jr. 1985. *Life Course Dynamics: Trajectories and Transitions, 1968–1980*. Ithaca, NY: Cornell University Press.

Elder, Glen H. Jr. 1992. "The Life Course." In *The Encyclopedia of Sociology*, edited by Edgar F. Borgatta and Marie L. Borgatta (pp. 1120–1130). New York: Macmillan.

Elder, Glen H. Jr. 1998. "The Life Course and Human Development." In *Handbook of Child Psychology: Theoretical Models of Human Development*, Vol 1, 5th Ed, edited by R. M. Lerner (pp. 939–991). New York: Wiley.

Elder, Glen H. Jr. and Linda K. George. 2016. "Age, Cohorts, and the Life Course." In *Handbook of the Life Course, Volume II*, edited by M. J. Shanahan, J. T. Mortimer, and M. Kirkpatrick Johnson (pp. 59–85). New York: Springer.

Elder, Glen H. Jr., Monica Kirkpatrick Johnson, and Robert Crosnoe. 2003. "The Emergence and Development of the Life Course." In *Handbook of the Life Course*, edited by Jeylan T. Mortimer and Michael J. Shanahan (pp. 3–19). New York: Plenum.

Elliott, Larry. 2014. "Public Sector Jobs Are Set to Be Cut by 40% Throughout Britain." *The Guardian*, February 13, 2014. www.theguardian.com/society/2014/feb/14/public-sector-jobs-cuts-britain.

Elman, Cheryl, and Angela M. O'Rand. 1998a. "Midlife Entry into Vocational Training: A Mobility Model." *Social Science Research* 27(2): 128–158.

Elman, Cheryl, and Angela M. O'Rand. 1998b. "Midlife Work Pathways and Educational Entry." *Research on Aging* 20(4): 475–505.

Elsass, Priscilla M., and John F. Veiga. 1997. "Job Control and Job Strain: A Test of Three Models." *Journal of Occupational Health Psychology* 2(3): 195–211.

England, Paula. 2010. "The Gender Revolution: Uneven and Stalled." *Gender & Society* 24(2): 149–166.

Epstein, Cynthia Fuchs. 1988. *Deceptive Distinctions: Sex, Gender, and the Social Order*. New Haven, CT: Yale University Press.

Esping-Andersen, Gøsta. 2009. *The Incomplete Revolution: Adapting to Women's New Roles*. Cambridge: Polity Press.

Estes, Carroll L. 2004. "Social Security Privatization and Older Women: A Feminist Political Economy Perspective." *Journal of Aging Studies* 18(1): 9–26.

Estes, Carrol L., and Jane L. Mahakian. 2001. "The Political Economy of Productive Aging." In *Productive Aging: Concepts and Challenges*, edited by Nancy Morrow-Howell, James Hinterlong, and Michael Sherraden (pp. 197–213). Baltimore, MD: Johns Hopkins University Press.

Estes, Carroll, Susan Chapman, Catherine Dodd, Brooke Hollister, and Charlene Harrington. 2013. *Health Policy: Crisis and Reform* (sixth edition). Burlington, MA: Jones & Bartlett Learning.

Ertel, K. A., K. C. Koenen, and Lisa F. Berkman. 2008. "Incorporating Home Demands into Models of Job Strain: Findings from the Work, Family and Health Network." *Journal of Occupational and Environmental Medicine* 50(11): 1244–1252.

Farber, Henry S. 2008. *Employment Insecurity: The Decline in Worker-Firm Attachment in the United States*. Princeton, NJ: Center for Economic Policy Studies, Princeton University.

Farber, Henry S. 2010. "Job Loss and the Decline in Job Security in the United States." In *Labor in the New Economy*, edited by Katharine Abraham, James Speltzer, and Michael Harper (pp. 223–262). Chicago: University of Chicago Press.

Farkas, Janice I., and Angela M. O'Rand. 1998. "The Pension Mix for Women in Middle and Late Life: The Changing Employment Relationship." *Social Forces* 76(3): 1007–1032.

Farrell, Chris. 2014. *Unretirement: How Baby Boomers are Changing the Way We Think about Work, Community, and the Good Life*. New York: Bloomsbury Press.

Ferree, Myra Marx, and Carol McClurg Mueller. 2004. "Feminism and the Women's Movement: A Global Perspective." In *The Blackwell Companion to Social Movements*, edited by David A. Snow, Sarah A. Soule, and Hanspeter Kriesi (pp. 576–607). Oxford: Blackwell Publishing, Ltd.

Ferrie, Jane E., Martin J. Shipley, Stephen A. Stansfeld, George Davey Smith, and Michael Marmot. 2003. "Future Uncertainty and Socioeconomic Inequalities in Health: The Whitehall II Study." *Social Science and Medicine* 57(4): 637–646.

Ferrie, Jane E., Martin J. Shipley, Katherine Newman, Stephen A. Stansfeld, and Michael Marmot. 2005. "Self-Reported Job Insecurity and Health in the Whitehall II Study: Potential Explanations of the Relationship." *Social Science and Medicine* 60(7): 1593–1602.

Ferrie, Jane E., Marianna Virtanen, and Mika Kivimäki. 2014. "The Healthy Population-High Disability Paradox." *Occupational and Environmental Medicine* 71(4): 232–233.

Ferraro, Kenneth F. 2016. "Life Course Lens on Aging and Health." In *Handbook of the Life Course, Volume II*, edited by M. J. Shanahan, J. T. Mortimer, and M. Kirkpatrick Johnson (pp. 389–406). New York: Springer.

Ferraro, Kenneth F., and Tetyana P. Shippee. 2009. "Aging and Cumulative Inequality: How does Inequality Get under the Skin?" *The Gerontologist* 49(3): 333–343.

Fligstein, Neil, and Doug McAdam. 2012. *A Theory of Fields*. New York: Oxford University Press.

Floderus, Birgitta, M. Hagman, G. Aronsson, S. Marklund, and A. Wikman. 2009. "Work Status, Work Hours and Health in Women with and without Children." *Occupational and Environmental Medicine* 66(1): 704–710.

Flood, Sarah, and Phyllis Moen. 2015. "Healthy Time Use in the Encore Years: Do Work, Resources, Relations, and Gender Matter?" *Journal of Health and Social Behavior* 56(1): 74–97.

Flood, Sarah, and Phyllis Moen. 2016. "Does Life Satisfaction Vary by Age, Employment, Health, and Gender?" Unpublished draft.

Floyd, Frank J., Stephen N. Haynes, Elizabeth Rogers Doll, David Winemiller, Carolyn Lemsky, Tria Murphy Burgy, Mary Werle, and Nancy Heilman. 1992. "Assessing Retirement Satisfaction and Perceptions of Retirement Experiences." *Psychology and Aging* 7(4): 609–621.

Flynn, James R. 1999. "Searching for Justice: The Discovery of IQ Gains over Time." *American Psychologist* 54(1): 5–20.

Forbes, Miriam K., Karen M. Spence, Viviana M. Wuthrich, and Ronald M. Rapee. 2015. "Mental Health and Wellbeing of Older Workers in Australia." *Work, Aging and Retirement* 1(3): 202–213.

Folbre, Nancy. 2012. *For Love and Money: Care Provision in the United States*. New York: Russell Sage Foundation.

Foster, Karen. 2013. *Generations, Discourse, and Social Change*. New York: Routledge.

Frankel, Lois P., and Susan Picascia. 2008. "Workplace Legacy: Making the Most of the Final Five." *Employment Relations Today* 35(1): 1–7.

Freedman, Marc. 2007. *Encore: Finding Work That Matters in the Second Half of Life*. New York: Public Affairs.

Freedman, Marc. 2011. *The Big Shift: Navigating the New Stage beyond Midlife*. New York: Public Affairs.

Friedan, Betty. 1963. *The Feminine Mystique*. New York: Bantam Doubleday Dell.

Friedland, Roger, and Robert R. Alford. 1991. "Bringing Society Back In: Symbols, Practices, and Institutional Contradictions." In *The New Institutionalism in Organizational Analysis*, edited by Walter W. Powell and Paul J. DiMaggio (pp. 232–266). Chicago: University of Chicago Press.

Friedman, Stewart D. 2013. *Baby Bust: New Choices for Men and Women in Work and Family*. Philadelphia: Wharton Digital Press.

Fuller, Sylvia. 2008. "Job Mobility and Wage Trajectories for Men and Women in the United States." *American Sociological Review* 73(1): 158–183.

Furstenberg, Frank Jr., Sheela Kennedy, Vonnie C. Mcloyd, Ruben G. Rumbaut, and Richard A. Settersten Jr. 2004. "Growing Up Is Harder To Do." *Contexts* 3(3): 33–41.

Galinsky, Ellen, James T. Bond, and Dana E. Friedman. 1996. "The Role of Employers in Addressing the Needs of Employed Parents." *Journal of Social Issues* 52(3): 111–136.

Galinsky, Ellen, James T. Bond, Stacey S. Kim, Lois Backon, Erin Brownfield, and Kelly Sakai. 2005. *Overwork in America: When the Way We Work Becomes too Much*. New York: Families and Work Institute.

Galinsky, Ellen, Kelly Sakai, and Tyler Wigton. 2011. "Workplace Flexibility: From Research to Action." *Work and Family* 21(2): 141–161.

Gallo, William T., Elizabeth H. Bradley, Michele Siegel, and Stanislav V. Kasl. 2000. "Health Effects of Involuntary Job Loss among Older Workers: Findings from the Health and Retirement Survey." *Journal of Gerontology* 55B(3): S131–S140.

Gamson, Joshua. 2015. *Modern Families: Stories of Extraordinary Journeys to Kinship*. New York: New York University Press.

Gangl, Markus, and Andrea Ziefle. 2009. "Motherhood, Labor Force Behavior, and Women's Careers: An Empirical Assessment of the Wage Penalty for Motherhood in Britain, Germany, and the United States." *Demography* 46(20): 341–369.

Ganster, Daniel C., and Christopher C. Rosen. 2013. "Work Stress and Employee Health: A Multidisciplinary Review." *Journal of Management* 39(5): 1085–1122.

Gendell, Murray. 2008. "Older Workers: Increasing their Labor Force Participation and Hours of Work." *Monthly Labor Review* (January): 41–54.

George, Linda K. 1980. *Role Transitions in Later Life: A Social Stress Perspective*. Monterey, CA: Brooks/Cole Publishing Co.

Gerson, Kathleen. 2010. *The Unfinished Revolution: How a New Generation is Reshaping Family, Work, and Gender in America*. New York: Oxford University Press.

Gerstel, Naomi, Dan Clawson, and Dana Huyser. 2007. "Explaining Job Hours of Physicians, Nurses, EMTs, and Nursing Assistants: Gender, Class, Jobs, and Families." *Research in the Sociology of Work* 17: 369–401.

Gesthuizen, Maurice, and Maarten H.J. Wolbers. 2011. "Late Career Instability and the Transition into Retirement of Older Workers in the Netherlands." In *Aging Populations, Globalization and the Labor Market: Comparing Late Working Life and Retirement in Modern Societies*, edited by Hans-Peter Blossfeld, Sandra Buchholz, and Karin Kurz (pp. 65–90). Cheltenham, UK/Northampton, MA: Edward Elgar.

Giddens, Anthony. 1984. *The Constitution of Society: Outline of the Theory of Structuration*. Berkeley: University of California Press.

Gilleard, Christopher, and Paul Higgs. 2005. *Contexts of Ageing: Class, Cohort and Community*. Cambridge: Polity.

Gilleard, Chris, and Paul Higgs. 2007. "Third Age and the Baby Boomers: Two Approaches to the Social Structuring of Later Life." *International Journal of Ageing and Later Life* 2(2): 13–30.

Gilleard, Chris, Martin Hyde, and Paul Higgs. 2007. "The Impact of Age, Place, Aging in Place, and Attachment to Place on the Well-Being of the over 50s in England." *Research on Aging* 29(6): 590–605.

Gillon, Steve. 2004. *Boomer Nation: The Largest and Richest Generation Ever, and How it Changed America*. New York: The Free Press.

Glenn, Evelyn Nakano. 2010. *Forced to Care: Coercion and Caregiving in America*. Cambridge, MA: Harvard University Press.

Goode, William I. 1960. "A Theory of Role Strain." *American Sociological Review* 25(4): 483–496.

Goggin, Judy. 2009. "Encore Careers for the Twenty-First Century Aging-Friendly Community." *Generations* 33(2): 95–97.

Gordon, Edward E. 2009. *Winning the Global Talent Showdown: How Businesses and Communities Can Partner to Rebuild the Jobs Pipeline*. San Francisco: Berrett-Koehler Publishers, Inc.

Gotlib, Ian H., and Blair Wheaton. 1997. *Stress and Adversity over the Life Course: Trajectories and Turning Points*. New York: Cambridge University Press.

Granovetter, Mark. 1995. *Getting a Job: A Study of Contacts and Careers*. Chicago: Chicago University Press.

Green, Francis. 2006. *Demanding Work: The Paradox of Job Quality in the Affluent Economy*. Princeton, NJ: Princeton University Press.

Greenblatt, Alan. 2007. "Aging Baby Boomers." *CQ Researcher* 71(37): 867–887.

Greenfield, Emily A., and Nadine F. Marks. 2004. "Formal Volunteering as a Protective Factor for Older Adults' Psychological Well-Being." *Journal Gerontology: Series B* 59(5): S258–S264.

Gringart, Eyal, Edward Helmes, and Carig Paul Speelman. 2005. "Exploring Attitudes towards Older Workers among Australian Employers: An Empirical Study." *Journal of Ageing and Social Policy* 17(3): 85–103.

Gruber, Jonathan, and David Wise. 2004. *Social Security Programs and Retirement around the World: Micro Estimation*. Chicago: University of Chicago Press.

Grusky, David B., Bruce Western, and Christopher Wimer. 2011. *The Great Recession*. New York: Russell Sage Foundation.

Grzywacz, Joseph G., David M. Almeida, Shevaun D. Neupert, and Susan L. Ettner. 2004. "Socioeconomic Status and Health: A Micro-Level Analysis of Exposure and Vulnerability to Daily Stressors." *Journal of Health and Social Behavior* 45(1): 1–16.

Gustman, Alan L., and Thomas L. Steinmeier. 2012. "Behavioral effects of Social Security Policies on Benefit Claiming, Retirement and Saving." University of Michigan Retirement Research Center (WP 2012-263). Ann Arbor: University of Michigan.

Gustman, Alan L., Thomas L. Steinmeier, and Nahid Tabatabai. 2012. "Mismeasurement of Pensions Before and After Retirement: The Mystery of the Disappearing

Pensions with Implications for the importance of Social Security as a Source of Retirement Support." University of Michigan Retirement Research Center (WP 2012-268). Ann Arbor: University of Michigan.

Hacker, Jacob S. 2006. *The Great Risk Shift: The Assault on American Jobs, Families, Health Care and Retirement and How You Can Fight Back*. New York: Oxford University Press.

Haider, Steven J., and Melvin Stephens Jr. 2007. "Is There a Retirement-Consumption Puzzle? Evidence Using Subjective Retirement Expectations." *The Review of Economics and Statistics* 89(2): 247–264.

Han, Shin-Kap, and Phyllis Moen. 2001. "Coupled Careers: Pathways through Work and Marriage in the United States." In *Careers of Couples in Contemporary Societies: From Male Breadwinner to Dual Earner Families*, edited by Hans-Peter Blossfeld and Sonja Drobnič (pp. 201–231). Oxford: Oxford University Press.

Han, Shin-Kap, and Phyllis Moen. 1999a. "Clocking Out: Temporal Patterning of Retirement." *American Journal of Sociology* 105(1): 191–236.

Han, Shin-Kap, and Phyllis Moen. 1999b. "Work and Family over Time: A Life Course Approach." *Annals of the American Academy of Political and Social Sciences* 562: 98–110.

Hanisch, Carol. 1970. "The Personal is Political." In *Notes from the Second Year: Women's Liberation: Major Writing of the Radical Feminists*, edited by Shulamith Firestone and Anne Koedt (pp. 59–62). New York: Radical Feminism.

Hardy, Melissa A. 2011. "Rethinking Retirement." In *Handbook of Sociology of Aging*, edited by Richard A. Settersten Jr. and Jacqueline L. Angel (pp. 213–228). New York: Springer.

Hardy, Melissa A., Lawrence E. Hazelrigg, and Jill Quadagno. 1996. *Ending a Career in the Auto Industry: Thirty and Out*. New York: Plenum Publishing.

Harrington Meyer, Madonna. 2014. *Grandmothers at Work: Juggling Families and Jobs*. New York: New York University Press.

Harrington Meyer, Madonna, and Pamela Herd. 2007. *Market Friendly or Family Friendly? The State and Gender Inequality in Old Age*. New York: Russell Sage Foundation.

Harrington Meyer, Madonna, and Wendy Parker. 2011a. "The Changing Worlds of Family and Work." In *Handbook of Sociology of Aging*, edited by Richard Settersten and Jacqueline Angel (pp. 263–277). New York: Springer Publications.

Harrington Meyer, Madonna, and Wendy Parker. 2011b. "Gender, Aging, and Social Policy." In *Handbook of Aging and the Social Sciences*, 7th edition, edited by Robert Binstock and Linda K. George (pp. 323–335). San Diego, CA: Academic Press.

Hartmann, Douglas, and Teresa Swartz. 2007. "The New Adulthood? The Transition to Adulthood from the Perspective of Transitioning Young Adults." *Advances in Life Course Research* 11: 253–286.

Hayward, Mark D., and Melissa A. Hardy. 1985. "Early Retirement Processes among Older Men." *Research on Aging* 7(4): 491–515.

Hayward, Mark D., Melissa A. Hardy, and William R. Grady. 1989. "Labor Force Withdrawal Patterns among Older Men in the United States." *Social Science Quarterly* 70(2): 425–448.

He, Wan, and Luke J. Larsen. 2014. US Census Bureau, American Community Survey Reports, ACS-29, *Older Americans with a Disability: 2008–2012*. Washington, DC: US Government Printing Office.

Hedge, Jerry W., Walter C. Borman, and Steven E. Lammlein. 2006. *The Aging Workforce: Realities, Myths, and Implications for Organizations*. Washington, DC: American Psychological Association.

Heidkamp, Maria, and Carl E. Van Horn. 2008. *Older and Out of Work: Trends in Older Displacement Trends*, Issue Brief 16. Boston: Sloan Center for Aging and Work.

Heinz, Walter R. 1999. *From Education to Work: Cross-National Perspectives*. New York: Cambridge University Press.

Heinz, Walter R., and Victor W. Marshall. 2003. *Social Dynamics of the Life Course: Transitions, Institutions, and Interrelations (The Life Course and Aging)*. Weinheim: Deutscher Studien Verlag.

Heinz, Walter R., Johannes Huinink, and Ansgar Weymann. 2009. *The Life Course Reader: Individuals and Societies across Time*. Frankfurt and New York: Campus Verlag.

Henly, Julia R., and Susan Lambert. 2014. "Unpredictable Work Timing in Retail Jobs: Implications for Employee Work-Life Outcomes." *Industrial and Labor Relations Review* 67(3): 986–1016.

Herd, Pamela, Brian Goesling, and James S. House. 2007. "Socioeconomic Position and Health: The Differential Effects of Education versus Income on the Onset versus Progression of Health Problems." *Journal of Health and Social Behavior* 48(3): 223–238.

Hershey, Douglas A., Kène Henkens, and Hendrik P. Van Dalen. 2007. "Mapping the Minds of Retirement Planners: A Cross-Cultural Perspective." *Journal of Cross-Cultural Psychology* 38(3): 361–382.

Higo, Masa, and John B. Williamson. 2011. "Global Aging." In *Handbook of Sociology of Aging*, edited by Richard A. Settersten Jr. and Jacqueline L. Angel (pp. 117–129). New York: Springer.

Hitlin, Steven, and Glen H. Elder Jr. 2007a. "Time, Self, and the Curiously Abstract Concept of Agency." *Sociological Theory* 25(2): 170–191.

Hitlin, Steven, and Glen H. Elder Jr. 2007b. "Agency: An Empirical Model of an Abstract Concept." *Advances in Life Course Research* 11: 33–67.

Ho, Jeong-Hwa, and James M. Raymo. 2009. "Expectations and Realization of Joint Retirement among Dual-Worker Couples." *Research on Aging* 31(2): 153–179.

Hobson, Barbara. 2014. *Worklife Balance: The Agency and Capabilities Gap*. New York: Oxford University Press.

Hochschild, Arlie Russell. 1989. *The Second Shift*. New York: Avon Books.

Hochschild, Arlie Russell. 1997. *The Time Bind: When Work Becomes Home and Home Becomes Work*. New York: Metropolitan Books.

Hochschild, Arlie Russell. 2012. *The Outsourced Self: Intimate Life in Market Times.* New York: Henry Holt.

Hogan, Dennis. 1981. *Transitions and Social Change: The Early Lives of American Men.* New York: Academic Press.

Holland, John. 1973. *Making Vocational Choices: A Theory of Careers.* Englewood Cliffs, NJ: Prentice-Hall.

House, James S. 2002. "Understanding Social Factors and Inequalities in Health: 20th Century Progress and 21st Century Prospects." *Journal of Health and Social Behavior* 43(2): 125–142.

House, James S., Paula M. Lantz, and Pamela Herd. 2005. "Continuity and Change in the Social Stratification of Aging and Health over the Life Course: Evidence from the Nationally Representative Longitudinal Study From 1986 to 2001/2002 (American's Changing Lives Study)." *Journals of Gerontology* 60B(2): 15–26.

Hoyert, Donna L., and Jiaquan Xu. 2012. "Deaths: Preliminary Data for 2011—Selected Causes." *National Vital Statistics Reports (NVSS)*; 61(6): 40–42. Hyattsville, MD: US Department of Health and Human Services, Centers for Disease Control Prevention, Division of Vital Statistics.

Hughes, Everett C. 1937. "Institutional Office and the Person." *American Journal of Sociology* 43(3): 404–413.

Hulbert, Ann. 2003. *Raising America: Experts, Parents, and a Century of Advice about Children.* New York: Random House.

Hurst, Aaron. 2014. *The Purpose Economy: How your Desire for Impact, Personal Growth and Community is Changing the World.* Boise, ID: Elevate.

Hutchens, Robert M., and Emma Dentinger. 2003. "Moving toward Retirement." In *It's About Time: Couples and Careers*, edited by Phyllis Moen (pp. 259–274). Ithaca, NY: Cornell University Press.

Hutchens, Robert M., and Karen Grace-Martin. 2006. "Employer Willingness to Permit Phased Retirement: Why Are Some More Willing Than Others?" *Industrial & Labor Relations Review* 59(4): 525–46.

Ibrahim, Selahadin, Peter Smith, and Carles Muntaner. 2009. "A Multi-Group Cross-Lagged Analyses of Work Stressors and Health using Canadian National Sample." *Social Science & Medicine* 68(1): 49–59.

Idler, Ellen L., and Yael Benyamini. 1997. "Self-Rated Health and Mortality: A Review of Twenty-Seven Community Studies." *Journal of Health and Social Behavior* 38(1): 21–37.

Jackson, Pamela Braboy, and Alexandra Berkowitz. 2005. "The Structure of the Life Course: Gender and Racioethnic Variation in the Occurrence and Sequencing of Role Transitions." *Advances in Life Course Research* 9: 55–90.

Jacobs, Jerry A., and Kathleen Gerson. 2004. *The Time Divide: Work, Family, and Gender Inequality.* Cambridge, MA: Harvard University Press.

Jacobsen, Linda A., Mary Kent, Marlene Lee, and Mark Mather. 2011. "America's Aging Population." *Population Bulletin* 66(1): 1–16.

James, Jacquelyn B., and Paul Wink. 2007. *The Crown of Life: Dynamics of the Early Postretirement Period.* New York: Springer.

Jensen, Per H. 2004. "Ageing and Work: From 'Early' Exit to 'Late' Exit in Denmark." In *Ageing and the Transition to Retirement: A Comparative Analysis of European Welfare States*, edited by Tony Maltby, Bert de Vroom, Maria Luisa Mirabile, and Einar Øverbye (pp. 41–66). Burlington, VT: Ashgate Publishing Company.

Johnson, Monica Kirkpatrick. 2001. "Change in Job Values During the Transition to Adulthood." *Work and Occupations* 28(3): 315–345.

Johnson, Monica Kirkpatrick, and Jeylan T. Mortimer. 2011. "Origins and Outcomes of Orientations toward Work." *Social Forces* 89(4): 1239–1260.

Johnson, Monica Kirkpatrick, Rayna Sage, and Jeylan T. Mortimer. 2012. "Work Values, Early Career Difficulties, and the U.S. Economic Recession." *Social Psychology Quarterly* 75(3): 242–267.

Johnson, Richard W, Janette Kawachi, and Eric K. Lewis. 2009. "Older Workers on the Move: Recareering in Later Life." Washington, DC: AARP Public Policy Institute.

Johnson, Richard W., Amy J. Davidoff, and Kevin Perese. 2003. "Health Insurance Costs and Early Retirement Decisions." *Industrial and Labor Relations Review* 56(4): 716–729.

Kahn, Robert L. 1981. *Work and Health*. New York: Wiley.

Kahneman, Daniel. 2003. "A Perspective on Judgment and Choice: Mapping Bounded Rationality." *American Psychologist* 58(9): 697–720.

Kahneman, Daniel, and Amos Tversky. 1979. "Prospect Theory: An Analysis of Decision under Risk." *Econometrica* 47(2): 263–292.

Kahneman, Daniel, and Amos Tversky. 1984. "Choices, Values and Frames." *American Psychologist* 39(4): 341–350.

Kahneman, Daniel, Paul Slovic, and Amos Tversky. 1982. *Judgment under Uncertainty: Heuristics and Biases*. New York: Cambridge University Press.

Kalev, Alexandra, Frank Dobbin, and Erin L. Kelly. 2006. "Best Practices or Best Guesses? Assessing the Efficacy of Corporate Affirmative Action and Diversity Policies." *American Sociological Review* 71(4): 589–617.

Kalil, Ariel, Kathleen M. Ziol-Guest, Louise C. Hawkley, and John T. Cacioppo. 2010. "Job Insecurity and Change over Time in Health among Older Men and Women." *Journal of Gerontology* 65B(1): 81–90.

Kalleberg, Arne L. 2000. "Nonstandard Employment Relations: Part-time, Temporary, and Contract Work." *Annual Review of Sociology* 26: 341–365.

Kalleberg, Arne L. 2009. "Precarious Work, Insecure Workers: Employment Relations in Transition." *American Sociological Review* 74(1): 1–22.

Kalleberg, Arne L. 2011. *Good Jobs, Bad Jobs: The Rise of Polarized and Precarious Employment Systems in the United States, 1970s—2000s*. New York: Russell Sage Foundation.

Kalleberg, Arne L. 2012. "Job Quality and Precarious Work: Clarifications, Controversies, and Challenges." *Work and Occupations* 39(4): 427–448.

Kanter, Rosabeth. 1977. *Work and Family in the United States: A Critical Review and Agenda for Research and Policy*. New York: Russell Sage Foundation.

Kaplan, Howard B. 1983. *Psychosocial Stress: Trends in Theory and Research*. New York: Academic Press.

Karisto, Antti. 2007. "Finnish Baby Boomers and the Emergence of the Third Age." *International Journal of Ageing and Later Life* 2(2): 91–108.

Karasek, Robert A. 1979. "Job Demands, Job Decision Latitude, and Mental Strain: Implications for Job Redesign." *Administrative Science Quarterly* 24(2): 285–308.

Karasek, Robert A., and Töres Theorell. 1990. *Healthy Work: Stress, Productivity and the Reconstruction of Working Life*. New York: Basic Books.

Kaufman, Gayle, and Glen H. Elder Jr. 2002. "Revisiting Age Identity: A Research Note." *Journal of Aging Studies* 16(2): 169–176.

Kelliher, Clare, and Deirdre Anderson. 2010. "Doing More with Less? Flexible Working Practices and the Intensification of Work." *Human Relations* 63(1): 83–106.

Kelly, Erin, and Phyllis Moen. 2007. "Rethinking the Clockwork of Work: Why Schedule Control May Pay Off at Home and at Work." *Advances in Developing Human Resources* 9(4): 487–506.

Kelly, Erin L., Phyllis Moen, and Eric Tranby. 2011. "Changing Workplaces to Reduce Work-Family Conflict: Schedule Control in a White-Collar Organization." *American Sociological Review* 76(2): 1–26.

Kelly, Erin L., Phyllis Moen, Wen Fan, J. Michael Oakes, Cassandra Okechukwu, Kelly D. Davis, Leslie Hammer, Ellen Kossek, Rosalind Berkowitz King, Ginger Hanson, Frank Mierzwa, and Lynne Casper. 2014. "Changing Work and Work-Family Conflict in an Information Technology Workplace: Evidence from a Group-Randomized Trial." *American Sociological Review* 79(3): 1–32.

Keyes, Corey L. M. 1998. "Social Well-Being." *Social Psychology Quarterly* 61(2): 121–140.

Kim, Haejeong, and Sharon DeVaney. 2005. "The Selection of Partial or Full Retirement by Older Workers." *Journal of Family and Economic Issues* 26(3): 371–394.

Kim, Jungmeen, and Phyllis Moen. 2001. "Moving into Retirement: Preparation and Transitions in Late Midlife." In *Handbook of Midlife Development*, edited by Margie Lachman (pp. 487–527). New York: Wiley.

Kim, Jungmeen, and Phyllis Moen. 2002. "Retirement Transitions, Gender, and Psychological Well-Being: A Life-Course, Ecological Model." *Journal of Gerontology* 57B: P212–P222.

King, Rosalind B., Georgia Karuntos, Lynne M. Casper, Phyllis Moen, Kelly D. Davis, Lisa Berkman, Mary Durham, and Ellen Ernst Kossek. 2012. "Work-Family Balance Issues and Work-Leave Policies." In *Handbook of Occupational Health and Wellness*, edited by Robert J. Gatchel and Izabela Z. Schultz (pp. 323–339). New York: Springer.

King, Neal, Toni Calasanti, and Amy Sorensen. 2013. "Occupational Aging on Men's Jobs." Presentation at Southern Sociological Society Annual Meeting (April), Atlanta, Georgia.

Kivimäki, Mika, Jussi Vahtera, Marko Elovainio, Hans Helenius, Archana, Singh-Manoux, and Jaana Pentti. 2005. "Optimism and Pessimism as Predictors of Change in Health after Death or Onset of Severe Illness in Family." *Health Psychology* 24(4): 413–421.

Kleiner, Sibyl, and Eliza K. Pavalko. 2010. "Clocking In: The Organization of Work Time and Health in the United States." *Social Forces* 88(3): 1463–1486.

Klinenberg, Eric. 2012. *Going Solo: The Extraordinary Rise and Surprising Appeal of Living Alone*. New York: Penguin.

Knickman, James R., and Emily K. Snell. 2002. "The 2030 Problem: Caring for Aging Baby Boomers." *Health Services Research* 37(4): 849–884.

Knoll, Melissa A. Z. 2011. "Behavioral and Psychological Aspects of the Retirement Decision." *Social Security Bulletin* 71(4): 15–32.

Kohli, Martin. 1986. "Social Organization and Subjective Construction of the Life Course." In *Human Development and the Life Course: Multidisciplinary Perspectives*, edited by Aage B. Sørensen, Franz E. Weinert, and Lonnie R. Sherrod (pp. 271–92). Mahwah, NJ: Lawrence Erlbaum.

Kohli, Martin. 2007. "The Institutionalization of the Life Course: Looking Back to Look Ahead." *Research in Human Development* 4(3-4): 253–271.

Kohli, Martin, and John W. Meyer. 1986. "Social Structure and Social Construction of the Life Stages." *Human Development* 29(3): 145–149.

Kohli, Martin, Martin Rein, Anne-Marie Guillemard, and Herman van Gunsteren. 1991. *Time for Retirement: Comparative Studies of Early Exit from the Labor Force*. Cambridge: Cambridge University Press.

Kojola, Erik, and Phyllis Moen. Forthcoming 2016. "No More Lock-Step Retirement: Boomers' Shifting Meanings of Work and Retirement." *Journal of Aging Studies*.

Kojola, Erik, Yagmur Karakaya, and Phyllis Moen. 2015. "Exit Strategies: Contingencies and Dynamics of IT Boomers' Retirement Plans." Presentation at Midwest Sociological Society Annual Meeting, Kansas City, MO, March.

Korpi, Walter. 2003. "Welfare-State Regress in Western Europe: Politics, Institutions, Globalization, and Europeanization." *Annual Review of Sociology* 29: 589–609.

Kossek, Ellen Ernst, and Alyssa Friede. 2006. "The Business Case: Managerial Perspectives on Work and the Family." In *The Work–Family Handbook: Multi-Disciplinary Perspectives, Methods, and Approaches*, edited by Marcie Pitt-Catsouphes, Ellen Ernst Kossek, and Stephen Sweet (pp. 611–628). Mahwah, NJ: Lawrence Erlbaum.

Kossek, Ellen Ernst, Leslie B. Hammer, Erin L. Kelly and Phyllis Moen. 2014. "Designing Work, Family & Health Organizational Change Initiatives." *Organizational Dynamics* 43(1): 53–63.

Kotter, John P. 1995. *The New Rules: How to Succeed in Today's Post-corporate World*. New York: The Free Press.

Kotter-Grühn, Dana, Daniel Grühn, and Jacqui Smith. 2010. "Predicting One's Own Death: The Relationship between Subjective and Objective Nearness to Death in Very Old Age." *European Journal of Ageing* 7(4): 293–300.

Kubicek, Bettina, Christian Korunka, James M. Raymo, and Peter Hoonakker. 2011. "Psychological Well-Being in Retirement: The Effects of Personal and Gendered Contextual Resources." *Journal of Occupational Health Psychology* 16(2): 230–246.

Lachman, Margie E., and Jacquelyn B. James. 1997. *Multiple Paths of Midlife Development*. Chicago: University of Chicago Press.

Lam, Jack, Wen Fan, and Phyllis Moen. 2014. "Is Insecurity Worse for Well-Being in Turbulent Times? Mental Health in Context." *Society and Mental Health* 4(1): 55–73.

Lam, Jack, Phyllis Moen, Shi-Rong Lee, and Orfeu M. Buxton. Forthcoming 2016. "Boomer and Gen X Managers and Employees at Risk: Evidence from the Work, Family and Health Network Study." In *Beyond the Cubicle: Insecurity Culture and the Flexible Self*, edited by Allison Pugh. New York: Oxford University Press.

Lambert, Susan J., Anna Haley-Lock, and Julia R. Henly. 2012. "Schedule Flexibility in Hourly Jobs: Unanticipated Consequences and Promising Directions." *Community, Work and Family* 15(3): 293–315.

Lamont, Michele. 2000. *The Dignity of Working Men: Morality and the Boundaries of Race, Class, and Immigration*. Cambridge, MA: Harvard University Press.

Lane, Carrie M. 2011. *A Company of One: Insecurity, Independence, and the New World of White-Collar Unemployment*. Ithaca, NY: Cornell University Press.

Laslett, Peter. 1987. "The Emergence of the Third Age." *Ageing and Society* 7(2): 133–160.

Laslett, Peter. 1989. *A Fresh Map of Life: The Emergence of the Third Age*. Cambridge, MA: Harvard University Press.

Laughlin, Lynda. 2013. *Who's Minding the Kids? Child Care Arrangements: Spring 2011*. Current Population Reports (pp. 70–136). Washington, DC: US Census Bureau. www.census.gov/prod/2013pubs/p70-135.pdf.

Lawrence, Thomas B., and Roy Suddaby. 2006. "Institutions and Institutional Work." In *Handbook of Organziation Studies*, Second Edition, edited by S. R. Clegg, C. Hardy, T. B. Lawrence, and W. R. Nord (pp. 215–254). London: Sage Publications.

Lawrence, Thomas B., Roy Suddaby, and Bernard Leca. 2009. *Institutional Work: Actors and Agency in Institutional Studies of Organizations*. New York: Cambridge University Press.

Lawrence-Lightfoot, Sara. 2009. *The Third Chapter: Passion, Risk, and Adventure in the 25 years after 50*. New York: FSG.

László, Krisztina D., Hynek Pikhar, Mária S. Kopp, Martin Bobak, Andrzej Pajak, Sofia Malyutina, Salavecz Gyöngyvér, and Michael Marmot. 2010. "Job Insecurity and Health: A Study of 16 European Countries." *Social Science & Medicine* 70(6): 867–874.

Lazarus, Richard S., and Susan Folkman. 1984. *Stress, Appraisal, and Coping*. New York: Springer.

Lee, Jennifer C., and Jeylan T. Mortimer. 2009. "Family Socialization, Economic Self-Efficacy, and the Attainment of Financial Independence in Early Adulthood." *Longitudinal and Life Course Studies* 1(1): 45–62.

Leider, Richard J., and Alan M. Webber. 2013. *Life Reimagined: Discovering Your New Life Possibilities*. San Francisco: Berrett –Koehler Publishers, Inc.

Levy, René, and Eric Widmer. 2013. *Gendered Life Courses between Individualization and Standardization. A European Approach Applied to Switzerland*. Wien: Lit Verlag.

Lewin, Kurt. 1943. "Defining the 'Field at a Given Time.'" *Psychological Review* 50(3): 292–310.

Lewis, Suzan, Julia Brannen, and Ann Nilsen. 2009. *Work, Families and Organisations in transition: European Perspectives*. Bristol: Policy Press.

Li, Yunqing, and Kenneth F. Ferraro. 2005. "Volunteering and Depression in Later Life: Social Benefit or Selection Processes?" *Journal of Health and Social Behavior* 46(1): 68–84.

Li, Yunqing, and Kenneth F. Ferraro. 2006. "Volunteering in Middle and Later Life: Is Health a Benefit, Barrier or Both?" *Social Forces* 85(1): 497–519.

Li, Xiaoyan, Michael Hurd, and David S. Loughran. 2008. *The Characteristics of Social Security Beneficiaries Who Claim Benefits at the Early Entitlement Age*. AARP Public Policy Institute Research Report No. 2008-19. Washington, DC: AARP.

Light, Paul C. 1988. *Baby Boomers*. New York: Norton.

Lin, I-Fen, and Susan L. Brown. 2012. "Unmarried Boomers Confront Old Age: A National Portrait." *Gerontologist* 52(2): 153–165.

Link, Bruce G., and Jo C. Phelan. 1995. "Social Conditions as Fundamental Causes of Disease." *Journal of Health and Social Behavior* 35(Extra Issue): 80–94.

Lips-Wiersma, Marjolein, and Douglas T. Hall. 2007. "Organizational Career Development is not Dead: A Case Study on Managing the New Career during Organizational Change." *Journal of Organizational Behavior* 28(6): 771–792.

Livingston, Gretchen, and Kim Parker. 2010. *Since the Start of the Great Recession, More Children Raised by Grandparents*. Washington, DC: Pew Research Center.

Lou, Ye, Tracey A. LaPierre, Mary Elizabeth Hughes, and Linda J. Waite. 2012. "Grandparents Providing Care to Grandchildren: A Population-Based Study of Continuity and Change." *Journal of Family Issues* 33(9): 1143–1167.

Luce, Stephanie, Jennifer Luff, Joseph A. McCartin, and Ruth Milkman. 2014. *What Works for Workers? Public Policies and Innovative Strategies for Low-Wage Workers*. New York: Russell Sage Foundation.

Lundberg, Ulf. 1996. "Influence of Paid and Unpaid Work on Psychophysiological Stress Responses of Men and Women." *Journal of Occupational Health Psychology* 1(2): 117–130.

Luoh, Ming-Ching, and A. Regula Herzog. 2002. "Individual Consequences of Volunteer and Paid Work in Old Age: Health and Mortality." *Journal of Health and Social Behavior* 43(4): 490–509.

Macmillan, Ross. 2007. *Constructing Adulthood: Agency and Subjectivity in Adolescence and Adulthood*, Vol. 11. New York: Elsevier.

Macunovich, Diane J. 2002. *Birth Quake: The Baby Boom and its Aftershocks*. Chicago: University of Chicago Press.

Mahmood, Atiya, and Norah Keating. 2012. "Inclusive Built Environment for Older Adults." In *From Exclusion to Inclusion in Old Age: A Global Challenge*, edited by Thomas Scharf and Norah Keating (pp. 145–165). Bristol: The Policy Press.

Mallers, Melanie Horn, David M. Almeida, and Shevaun D. Neupert. 2005. "Women's Daily Physical Health Symptoms and Stressful Experiences across Adulthood." *Psychology and Health* 20(3): 389–403.

Maltby, Tony, Bert de Vroom, Maria Luisa Mirabile, and Einar Øverbye. 2004. *Ageing and the Transition to Retirement: A Comparative Analysis of European Welfare States.* Burlington, VT: Ashgate Publishing Company.

Mannheim, Karl. 1952. *Essays on the Sociology of Knowledge*. London: Routledge.

Markides, Kyriakos S., and Kerstin Gerst. 2011. "Immigration, Aging, and Health in the United States." In *Handbook of Sociology of Aging*, edited by Richard A. Settersten and Jacqueline L. Angel (pp. 103–116). New York: Springer.

Marmot, Michael. 2004. *The Status Syndrome: How Social Standing Affects our Health and Longevity*. New York: Henry Holt.

Marmot, Michael, and Richard G. Wilkinson. 2006. *Social Determinants of Health*. New York: Oxford University Press.

Marmot Michael, Johannes Siegrist, and Tores Theorell. 2006. "Health and the Psychosocial Environment at Work." In *Social Determinants of Health*, edited by Michael Marmot and Richard G. Wilkinson (pp. 97–130). Oxford: Oxford University Press.

Marshall, Victor W. 2005. "Agency, Events, and Structure at the End of the Life Course." In T*owards an Interdisciplinary Perspective on the Life Course, Advances in Life Course Research*, edited by Rene Levy, Paolo Ghisletta, Jean-Marie LeGoff, Dario Spini, and Eric Widmer (pp. 57–91). New York: Elsevier Science.

Marshall, Victor W., and Philippa J. Clarke. 2010. "Agency and Social Structure in Aging and Life Course Research." In *International Handbook of Social Gerontology*, edited by Dale Dannefer and Chris Phillipson (pp. 294–305). London: Sage Publications.

Marshall, Victor W., Walter Heinz, Helga Krueger, and Anil Verma. 2001. *Restructuring Work and the Life Course*. Toronto: University of Toronto Press.

Martin, Linda G., Vicki A. Freedman, Robert F. Schoeni, and Patricia M. Andreski. 2009. "Health and Functioning among Baby Boomers Approaching 60." *Journal of Gerontology*, 64B(3): 369–377.

Martin Matthews, Anne, and Kathleen H. Brown. 1987. "Retirement as a Critical Life Event: The Differential Experiences of Women and Men." *Research on Aging* 9(4): 548–571.

Massoglia, Michael, and Christopher Uggen. 2010. "Settling Down and Aging Out: Toward an Interactionist Theory of Desistance and the Transition to Adulthood." *American Journal of Sociology* 116(2): 543–582.

Matos, Kenneth, and Ellen Galinsky. 2012. *National Study of Employers*. New York: Families and Work Institute.

Maume, David J., and David A. Purcell. 2007. "The 'Over-Paced' American: Recent Trends in the Intensification of Work." *Research in the Sociology of Work* 17: 251–283.

Maurer, Todd J., Kimberly A. Wrenn, and Elizabeth M. Weiss. 2003. "Toward Understanding and Managing Stereotypical Beliefs about Older Workers' Ability and

Desire for Learning and Development." *Research in Personnel and Human Resources Management* 22: 253–285.

Mausner-Dorsch, Hilde, and William W. Eaton. 2000. "Psychosocial Work Environment and Depression: Epidemiologic Assessment of the Demand-Control Model." *American Journal of Public Health* 90(11): 1765–1770.

Mayer, Karl Ulrich. 2004. "Whose Lives? How History, Societies, and Institutions Define and Shape Life Course." *Research in Human Development* 1(3): 161–187.

Mayer, Karl U., and Walter Mueller. 1986. "The State and the Structure of the Life Course." In *Human Development the Life Course: Multidisciplinary Perspectives F.E.W.*, edited by Aage B. Sorensen, Franz E. Weinert, and Lonnie R. Sherrod (pp. 217–245). Mahwah, NJ: Lawrence Erlbaum.

McCullough, Michael E., and Emily Polak. 2007. "Change and Stability during the Third Age: Longitudinal Investigations of Self-Rated Health and Religiousness with the Terman Sample." In *The Crown of Life: Dynamics of the Early Postretirement Period*, edited by Jacqueline James and Paul Wink (pp. 175–192.) New York: Springer.

McFadden, Susan H., and Robert C. Atchley. 2001. *Aging and the Meaning of Time: A Multidisciplinary Exploration*. New York: Springer.

McFall, Brooke Helppie. 2011. "Crash and Wait? The Impact of the Great Recession on Retirement Planning of Older Americans." *American Economic Review* 101(3): 40–44.

McGarry, Kathleen. 2004. "Health and Retirement: Do Changes in Health Affect Retirement Expectations?" *Journal of Human Resources* 39(3): 624–648.

McLeod, Jane D., and James M. Nonnemaker. 1999. "Social Stratification and Inequality." In *Handbook of the Sociology of Mental Health*, edited by C. S. Aneshensel and J. C. Phelan (pp. 321–344). New York: Klewer Academic/Plenum.

McMunn, Anne, Elizabeth Breeze, Alissa Goodman, James Nazroo, and Zoe Oldfield. 2006. "Social Determinants of Health in Older Age." In *Social Determinants of Health*, edited by Michael Marmot and Richard G. Wilkinson (pp. 267–296). New York: Oxford University Press.

McNamara, Tay, and John B. Williamson. 2013. *Unequal Prospects: Is Working Longer the Answer?* New York: Routledge.

McNamara, Tay K., Marcie Pitt-Catsouphes, Christina Matz-Costa, Melissa Brown, and Monique Valcour. 2013. "Across the Continuum of Satisfaction with Work-Family Balance: Work Hours, Flexibility-Fit, and Work-Family Culture." *Social Science Research* 42(2): 283–298.

Mein, G, Pekka Martikainen, H. Hemingway, Stephen A. Stansfeld, and Michael Marmot. 2003. "Is Retirement Good or Bad for Mental and Physical Health Functioning? Whitehall II Longitudinal Study of Civil Servants." *Journal of Epidemiology and Community Health* 57(1): 46–49.

MetLife. 2009. Study of Employee Benefits Trends: Findings from the 7th Annual National Survey of Employers and Employees. New York: Metropolitan Life Insurance Company. http://whymetlife.com/trends/downloads/MetLife_EBTS09.pdf.

MetLife Mature Market Institute. 2011. *The MetLife Study of Women, Retirement, and the Extra-Long Life: Implications for Planning*. New York: Metropolitan Life Insurance Company. www.metlife.com/assets/cao/mmi/publications/studies/2011/mmi-women-retirement-extra-long-life.pdf.

MetLife Mature Market Institute. 2013. *The MetLife Report on the Oldest Boomers: Healthy, Retiring Rapidly and Collecting Social Security*. New York: Metropolitan Life Insurance Company.

Mermin, Gordon B. T., Richard W. Johnson, and Dan P. Murphy. 2007. "Why Do Boomers Plan to Work Longer?" *Journal of Gerontology* 62B(5): S286-S294.

Merton, Robert K. 1968. "The Matthew Effect in Science." *Science* 159(3810): 56–63.

Milkie, Melissa A., Alex Bierman, and Scott Schieman. 2008. "How Adult Children Influence Older Parents' Mental Health: Integrating Stress-Process and Life-Course Perspectives." *Social Psychology Quarterly* 71(1): 86–105.

Milkman, Ruth, and Eileen Appelbaum. 2013. *Unfinished Business: Paid Family Leave in California and the Future of U.S Work-Family Policy*. Ithaca, NY: ILR/Cornell University Press.

Miller, Amalia R. 2011. "The Effects of Motherhood Timing on Career Paths." *Journal of Population Economics* 24(3): 1071–1100.

Mills, C. Wright. 1951. *White Collar: The American Middle Classes*. New York: Oxford University Press.

Mills, C. Wright. 1959. *The Sociological Imagination*. New York: Oxford University Press.

Mills, Albert J., and Peta Tancred. 1992. *Gendering Organizational Analysis*. Thousand Oaks, CA: Sage Publications.

Mills, Melinda, and Hans-Peter Blossfeld. 2005. "Globalization, Uncertainty and the Early Life Course: A Theoretical Framework." In *Globalization, Uncertainty and Youth in Society*, edited by Hans-Peter Blossfeld, Erik Klijzing, Melinda Mills, and Karin Kurz (pp. 1–24). New York: Routledge.

Mirowsky, John, and Catherine E. Ross. 1998. "Education, Personal Control, Lifestyle and Health: A Human Capital Hypothesis." *Research on Aging* 20(4): 415–449.

Mirowsky, John, and Catherine E. Ross. 2003a. *Education, Social Status and Health*. New Brunswick, NJ: Aldine Transaction.

Mirowsky, John, and Catherine E. Ross. 2003b. *Social Causes of Psychological Distress, Second Edition*. New Brunswick, NJ: Aldine Transaction.

Mirowsky, John, and Catherine E. Ross. 2008. "Education and Self-Rated Health: Cumulative Advantage and its Rising Importance." *Research on Aging* 30(1): 93–122.

Moen, Phyllis. 1994. "Women, Work and Family: A Sociological Perspective on Changing Roles." In *Age and Structural Lag: The Mismatch between People's Lives and Opportunities in Work, Family and Leisure*, edited by Matilda White Riley, Robert L. Kahn, and Anne Foner (pp. 151–70). New York: Wiley.

Moen, Phyllis. 1998. "Reconstructing Retirement: Careers, Couples, and Social Capital." *Contemporary Gerontology* 4(4): 123–125.

Moen, Phyllis. 2001. "The Gendered Life Course." In *Handbook of Aging and the Social Sciences*, edited by Linda George and Robert. H. Binstock (pp. 179–196). San Diego: Academic Press.

Moen, Phyllis. 2003a. "Midcourse: Navigating Retirement and a New Life Stage." In *Handbook of the Life Course*, edited by Jeylan Mortimer and Michael J. Shananhan (pp. 269–291). New York: Kluwer Academic/Plenum.

Moen, Phyllis. 2003b. *It's About Time: Couples and Careers*. Ithaca, NY: Cornell University Press.

Moen, Phyllis. 2007. "Not So Big Jobs and Retirements: What Workers (and Retirees) Really Want." *Generations* 31(1): 31–36.

Moen, Phyllis. 2011a. "Living the Gendered Life Course in Time and Space." In *Handbook of the Sociology of Aging and the Life Course*, edited by Richard Settersten and Jacqui Angel (pp. 655–657). New York: Springer.

Moen, Phyllis. 2011b. "A Life Course Approach to the Third Age." In *Gerontology in the Era of the Third Age: Implications and Next Steps*, edited by Dawn C. Carr and Kathrin Komp (pp. 13–32). New York: Springer.

Moen, Phyllis. 2011c. "From 'Work-Family' to 'Life Course Fit': Five Challenges to the Field." *Community, Work and Family* 14(1): 1–16.

Moen, Phyllis. 2012. "Retirement Dilemmas and Decisions." In *The Oxford Handbook of Work and Aging*, edited by Jerry Hedge and Walter Borman (pp. 549–569). New York: Oxford University Press.

Moen, Phyllis. 2013. "Constrained Choices: The Shifting Institutional Contexts of Aging and the Life Course." In *Perspectives on the Future of the Sociology of Aging*, edited by Linda Waite (pp. 175–216). Washington, DC: National Research Council.

Moen, Phyllis, Erin L. Kelly, Wen Fan, Shi-Rong Lee, Ellen E. Kossek, and Orfeu Buxton. 2016. "Does a Flexibility/Support Organizational Initiative Improve High Tech Employee's Well-being: Evidence from the Work, Family and Health Network." *American Sociological Review* 81(1): 1–31.

Moen, Phyllis, and Joyce Altobelli. 2007. "Strategic Selection as a Retirement Project: Will Americans Develop Hybrid Arrangements." In *The Crown of Life: Dynamics of the Early Postretirement Period*, edited by Jacqueline James and Paul Wink (pp. 61–81). New York: Springer.

Moen, Phyllis, Donna Dempster-McClain, and Robin Williams Jr. 1989. "Social Integration and Longevity: An Event History Analysis of Women's Roles and Resilience." *American Sociological Review* 54(4): 635–647.

Moen, Phyllis, Vivian Fields, Heather Quick, and Heather Hofmeister. 2000. "A Life Course Approach to Retirement and Social Integration." In *Social Integration in the Second Half of Life*, edited by Karl Pillemer, Phyllis Moen, Elaine Wethington, and Nina Glasgow (pp. 75–107). Baltimore, MD: Johns Hopkins University Press.

Moen, Phyllis, William A. Erickson, Madhurima Agarwal, Vivian Fields, and Laurie Todd. 2000. *The Cornell Retirement and Well-Being Study: Final Report*. Ithaca, NY: Bronfenbrenner Life Course Center, Cornell University.

Moen, Phyllis, and Vivian Fields. 2002. "Midcourse in the United States: Does Unpaid Community Participation Replace Paid Work?" *Aging International* 27(3): 21–48.

Moen, Phyllis, and Sarah Flood. 2013. "Limited Engagements? Women's and Men's Work/Volunteer Time in the Encore Life Course Stage." *Social Problems* 60(2): 206–233.

Moen, Phyllis, and Elaine Hernandez. 2009. "Social Convoys: Studying Linked Lives in Time, Context, and Motion." In *The Craft of Life Course Research*, edited by Glen Elder Jr. and Janet Giele (pp. 258–279). New York: Guilford Press.

Moen, Phyllis, and Jane Peterson. 2009. "A Third Path? Multiplex Time, Gender, and Retirement Encores in the United States." *Nova Acta Leopoldina* 106(370): 41–58.

Moen, Phyllis, and Patricia Roehling. 2005. *The Career Mystique: Cracks in the American Dream*. Boulder, CO: Rowman & Littlefield.

Moen, Phyllis, and Donna Spencer. 2006. "Converging Divergences in Age, Gender, Health, and Well-Being: Strategic Selection in the Third Age." In *Handbook of Aging and the Social Sciences*, edited by Robert Binstock and Linda George (pp. 127–144). Burlington, VT: Elsevier Academic Press.

Moen, Phyllis, Wen Fan, and Erin L. Kelly. 2013. "Team-Level Flexibility, Work-Home Spillover, and Health Behavior." *Social Science & Medicine* 84: 69–79.

Moen, Phyllis, Jungmeen E. Kim, and Heather Hofmeister. 2001. "Couples' Work/Retirement Transitions, Gender, and Marital Quality." *Social Psychology Quarterly* 64(1): 55–71.

Moen, Phyllis, Stephen Sweet, and Rachelle Hill. 2010. "Risk, Resilience, and Life-Course Fit: Older Couples' Encores following Job Loss." In *New Frontiers in Resilient Aging*, edited by Prem S. Fry and Corey L. M. Keyes (pp. 283–309). New York: Cambridge University Press.

Moen, Phyllis, Erin L. Kelly, and Qinlei Huang. 2008a. "Work, Family, and Life-Course Fit: Does Control over Work Time Matter?" *Journal of Vocational Behavior* 73(3): 414–425.

Moen, Phyllis, Erin L. Kelly, and Reiping Huang. 2008b. "'Fit' Inside the Work-Family Black Box: An Ecology of the Life Course, Cycles of Control Reframing." *Journal of Occupational and Organizational Psychology* 81(3): 411–433.

Moen, Phyllis, Erin L. Kelly, and Jack Lam. 2013. "Healthy Work Revisited: Do Changes in Time Strain Predict Well-Being?" *Journal of Occupational Health Psychology* 18(2): 157–172.

Moen, Phyllis, Erin L. Kelly, Eric Tranby, and Qinlei Huang. 2011. "Changing Work, Changing Health: Can Real Work-Time Flexibility Promote Health Behaviors and Well-Being?" *Journal of Health and Social Behavior* 52(4): 404–429.

Moen, Phyllis, Erin L. Kelly, Michael J. Oakes, Shi-Rong Lee, Jeremy Bray, David Almeida, Leslie Hammer, David Hurtado, and Orfeu Buxton. Forthcoming. "Can a Flexibility/Support Initiative Reduce Turnover? Results from the Work, Family, Health Network." *Social Problems*.

Moen, Phyllis, Erik Kojola, and Kate Schaefers. Forthcoming 2016. "Institutional Work around an Older Workforce." *The Gerontologist*.

Moen, Phyllis, Jack Lam, Samantha Ammons, and Erin L. Kelly. 2013. "Time Work by Overworked Professionals: Strategies in Response to the Stress of Higher Status." *Work & Occupations* 40(2): 79–114.

Moen, Phyllis, Stephen Sweet, and Raymond Swisher. 2005. "Embedded Career Clocks: The Case of Retirement Planning." *Advances in Life Course Research* 9: 237–265.

Moen, Phyllis, Vivian Fields, Heather Quick, and Heather Hofmeister. 2000. "A Life Course Approach to Retirement and Social Integration." In *Social Integration in the Second Half of Life*, edited by Karl Pillemer, Phyllis Moen, Elaine Wethington, and Nina Glasgow (pp. 75–107). Baltimore: Johns Hopkins University Press.

Moen, Phyllis, Qinlei Huang, Vandana Plassman, and Emma Dentinger. 2006."Deciding the Future: Do Dual-Earner Couples Plan Together for Retirement?" *American Behavioral Scientist* 49(10): 1422–1443.

Mokdad Ali H., Earl S. Ford, Barbara A. Bowman, William H. Dietz, Frank Vinicor, Virginia S. Bales, and James S. Marks. 2003. "Prevalence of Obesity, Diabetes, and Obesity-Related Health Risk Factors, 2001." *JAMA* 289(1): 76–79.

Montepare, Joann M. 2009. "Subjective Age: Toward a Guiding Lifespan Framework." *International Journal of Behavioral Development* 33(1): 42–46.

Montez, Jennifer Karas, and Mark D. Hayward. 2014. "Cumulative Childhood Adversity, Educational Attainment, and Active Life Expectancy among U.S. Adults." *Demography* 51(2): 413–435.

Montez, Jennifer Karas, Robert A. Hummer, and Mark D. Hayward. 2012. "Educational Attainment and Adult Mortality in the United States: A Systematic Analysis of Functional Form." *Demography* 49(1): 315–336.

Morgan, Robin. 1970. *Sisterhood is Powerful: An Anthology of Writings from the Women's Liberation Movement*. New York: Random House.

Morgeson, Frederick P., Matthew H. Reider, Michael A. Campion, and Rebecca A. Bull. 2008. "Review of Research on Age Discrimination in the Employment Interview." *Journal of Business and Psychology* 22(3): 223–232.

Morrow-Howell, Nancy, James Hinterlong, and Michael Sherraden. 2001. *Productive Aging: Concepts and Challenges*. Baltimore, MD: Johns Hopkins University Press.

Morrow-Howell, Nancy, Jim Hinterlong, Philip A. Rozario, and Fengyan Tang. 2003. "Effects of Volunteering on Well-Being in Later Life." *Journal of Gerontology* 58(3): S137–S145.

Mortimer, Jeylan T. 2003. *Working and Growing Up in America*. Cambridge, MA: Harvard University Press.

Mortimer, Jeylan, and Phyllis Moen. 2016. "The Changing Social Construction of Age and the life Course: Precarious Identity and Enactment of 'Early' and 'Encore' Stages of Adulthood." In *Handbook of the Life Course, Volume II*, edited by M. J. Shanahan, J. T. Mortimer, and M. Kirkpatrick Johnson (pp. 111–129). New York: Springer International Publishing.

Mortimer, Jeylan, Jack Lam, and Shi-Rong Lee. 2015. "Transformation, Erosion, or Disparity in Work Identity? Challenges During the Contemporary Transition to

Adulthood." In *The Oxford Handbook of Identity Development*, edited by K. McLead and M. Syed (pp. 319–336). New York: Oxford University Press.

Mortimer, Jeylan T., Sabrina Oesterle, and Helga Krüger. 2005. "Age Norms, Institutional Structures, and the Timing of Markers of Transition to Adulthood." *Advances in Life Course Research* 9: 175–203.

Muhonen, Tuija, and Eva Torkelson. 2004. "Work Locus of Control and its Relationship to Health and Job Satisfaction from a Gender Perspective." *Stress and Health* 20(1): 21–28.

Munnell, Alicia Haydock, and Steven A. Sass. 2008. *Working Longer: The Solution to the Retirement Income Challenge*. Washington, DC: Brookings Institution Press.

Musick, Marc A., A. Regula Herzog, and James S. House. 1999. "Volunteering and Mortality among Older Adults: Findings from A National Sample." *Journal of Gerontology: Social Sciences* 54B(3): S173–80.

Mutchler, Jan E., and Jeffrey A. Burr. 2011. "Social Dimensions of Aging: Race and Ethnicity." In *Handbook of the Sociology of Aging*, edited by Richard Settersten and Jacqueline Angel (pp. 83–101). New York: Springer.

National Research Council. 2011. *Assessing the Impact of Severe Economic Recession on the Elderly: Summary of a Workshop*. Washington, DC: The National Academies Press.

National Research Council and Institute of Medicine. 2013. *U.S. Health in International Perspective: Shorter Lives, Poorer Health*. Washington, DC: The National Academies Press.

Neal, Margaret B., and Leslie B. Hammer. 2007. *Working Couples Caring for Children and Aging Parents: Effects on Work and Well-Being*. Mahwah, NJ: Lawrence Erlbaum.

Nelson, Todd D. 2002. *Ageism: Stereotyping and Prejudice Against Older Persons*. Cambridge, MA: MIT Press.

Neumark, David. 2008. "The Age Discrimination in Employment Act and the Challenge of Population Aging." *Research on Aging* 31(1): 41–68.

Neumark, David, and Joanne Song. 2013. "Do Stronger Age Discrimination Laws make Social Security Reforms More Effective?" *Journal of Public Economics* 108: 1–16.

Nixon, Ashley E., Joseph J. Mazzola, Jeremy Bauer, Jeremy R. Krueger, and Paul E. Spector. 2011. "Can Work Make you Sick? A Metaanalysis of the Relationships between Job Stressors and Physical Symptoms." *Work & Stress* 25(1): 1–22.

Organisation for Economic Co-operation and Development (OECD). 2006. *Live Longer, Work Longer*. Paris: OECD.

Organisation for Economic Co-operation and Development (OECD). 2012. *OECD Pensions Outlook 2012*. OECD Publishing. doi: 10.1787/9789264169401-en.

O'Rand, Angela. 2003. "The Future of the Life Course: Late Modernity and Life Course Risks." In *Handbook of the Life Course*, edited by Jeylan T. Mortimer and Michael J. Shanahan (pp. 693–701). New York: Springer.

O'Rand. Angela. 2006. "Stratification and the Life Course: Social Origins, Life Course Capital and Cohort Inequality." In *Handbook of Aging and the Social Sciences*, Sixth

Edition, edited by Richard H. Binstock and Linda K. George (pp. 145–162). New York: Academic Press.

O'Rand, Angela M., and John C. Henretta. 1999. *Age and Inequality: Diverse Pathways through Later Life*. Boulder, CO: Westview Press.

Pampel, Fred C. 1994. "Population Aging, Class Context, and Age Inequality in Public Spending." *American Journal of Sociology* 100(1): 153–195.

Pampel, Fred C., Patrick M. Krueger, and Justin T. Denny. 2010. "Socioeconomic Disparities in Health Behaviors." *Annual Review of Sociology* 36: 349–370.

Pauley, Jane. 2014. *Your Life Calling: Reimaging the Rest of your Life*. New York: Simon & Schuster.

Pavlova, Maria K., and Rainer K. Silbereisen. 2012. "Participation in Voluntary Organizations and Volunteer Work as a Compensation for the Absence of Work and Partnership? Evidence from Two German Samples of Younger and Older Adults." *Journals of Gerontology, Series B: Psychological Sciences and Social Sciences* 67(4): 514–524.

Pavalko, Eliza K. 2011. "Caregiving and the Life Course: Connecting the Personal and the Public." In *Handbook of Sociology of Aging*, edited by Richard A. Settersten Jr. and Jacqueline L. Angel (pp. 603–617). New York: Springer.

Pearlin, Leonard I. 1988. "Social Structure and Social Values; The Regulation of Structural Effects." In *Surveying Social Life*, edited by Hubert O'Gorman (pp. 252–264). Middletown, CT: Wesleyan University Press.

Pearlin, Leonard I. 1989. "The Sociological Study of Stress." *Journal of Health and Social Behavior* 30(3): 241–256.

Pearlin, Leonard I. 1999. "The Stress Process Revisited: Reflections on Concepts and their Interrelationships." In *The Handbook of the Sociology of Mental Health*, edited by C. S. Aneshensel and J. C. Phelan (pp. 395–415). New York: Kluwer.

Pearlin, Leonard I. 2010. "The Life Course and the Stress Process: Some Conceptual Comparisons." *Journals of Gerontology* 65B(20): 207–215.

Pearlin, Leonard I., and Carmi Schooler. 1978. "The Structure of Coping." *Journal of Health and Social Behavior* 19(1): 2–21.

Pearlin, Leodard. I., Elizabeth G. Menaghan, Morton A. Lieberman, and Joseph T. Mullan. 1981. "The Stress Process." *Journal of Health and Social Behavior* 22(4): 337–356.

Pearlin, Leonard I., Scott Schieman, Elena M. Fazio, and Stephen C. Meersman. 2005. "Stress, Health, and the Life Course: Some Conceptual Perspectives." *Journal of Health and Social Behavior* 46(2): 205–219.

Pearlin, Leonard I., Kim B. Nguyen, Scott Schieman, and Melissa A. Milkie. 2007. "The Life-Course Origins of Mastery among Older People." *Journal of Health and Social Behavior* 48(2): 164–179.

Pew Research Center. 2007. "Working After Retirement: The Gap Between Expectations and Reality." A Social Trends Report. www.pewsocialtrends.org/2006/09/21/working-after-retirement-the-gap-between-expectations-and-reality.

Pew Research Center. 2009. "Growing Old in America: Expectations vs. Reality." A Social & Demographic Trends Report. www.pewsocialtrends.org/2009/06/29/growing-old-in-america-expectations-vs-reality.

Phelan, Jo C., Bruce G. Link, and Parisa Tehranifar. 2010. "Social Conditions as Fundamental Causes of Health Inequalities: Theory, Evidence, and Policy Implications." *Journal of Health and Social Behavior* 51(S): S28–S40.

Phillips, David R., and Oi-ling Siu. 2012. "Global Aging and Aging Workers." In *The Oxford Handbook of Work and Aging*, edited by Walter C. Borman and Jerry W. Hedge (pp. 11–32). New York: Oxford University Press.

Pienta, Amy M. 2003. "Partners in Marriage: An Analysis of Husbands' and Wives' Retirement Behavior." *Journal of Applied Gerontology* 22(3): 340–358.

Pienta, Amy M., and Mark D. Hayward. 2002. "Who Expects to Continue Working After Age 62: The Retirement Plans of Couples." *Journal of Gerontoology* 57B(4): S199–S208.

Pitt-Catsouphes, Marcie. 2009. "Between a Twentieth- and a Twenty-First-Century Workforce: Employers at the Tipping Point." *Generations* 31(1): 50–56.

Pitt-Catsouphes, Marcie, Joelle Sano, and Christina Matz-Costa. 2009. "Unions' Responsiveness to the Aging of the Workforce." *Journal of Workplace Behavioral Health* 24(1–2): 125–146.

Pixley, Joy E. 2008. "Life Course Patterns of Career-Prioritizing Decisions and Occupational Attainment in Dual-Earner Couples." *Work and Occupations* 35(2): 127–163.

Pixley, Joy E., and Phyllis Moen. 2003. "Prioritizing Careers." In *It's About Time: Couples and Careers*, edited by Phyllis Moen (pp. 183–200). Ithaca, NY: Cornell University Press.

Pleau, Robin. 2010. "Gender Differences in Postretirement Employment." *Research on Aging* 32(3): 267–303.

Population Reference Bureau. 2013. "World Population Data Sheet 2013." www.prb.org/Publications/Datasheets/2013/2013-world-population-data-sheet.aspx.

Posthuma, Richard A., Maria Fernanda Wagstaff, and Michael A. Campion. 2012. "Age Stereotypes and Workplace Age Discrimination: A Framework for Future Research." In *The Oxford Handbook of Work and Aging*, edited by Walter C. Borman and Jerry W. Hedge (pp. 298–312). New York: Oxford University Press.

Powell, Walter W., and Paul J. DiMaggio. 1991. *The New Institutionalism in Organizational Analysis*. Chicago: University of Chicago Press.

Prenda, Kimberly M., and Margie E. Lachman. 2001. "Planning for the Future: A Life Management Strategy for Increasing Control and Life Satisfaction in Adulthood." *Psychology and Aging* 16(2): 206–216.

Price, Christine A. 2003. "Professional Women's Retirement Adjustment: The Experience of Reestablishing Order." *Journal of Aging Studies* 17(3): 341–355.

Pruchno, Rachel. 2015. "Successful Aging: Contentious Past, Productive Future." *The Gerontologist* 55(1): 1–4.

Pudrovska, Tetyana, Scott Schieman, and Deborah Carr. 2006. "Strains of Singlehood in Later Life: Do Race and Gender Matter?" *Journal of Gerontology: Psychological Sciences and Social Sciences* 61(6): 315–322.

Purcell, Patrick. 2009. *Income and Poverty among Older Americans in 2008*. Washington, DC: Congressional Research Service.

Quadagno, Jill. 1988. *The Transformation of Old Age Security: Class and Politics in the American Welfare State*. Chicago: University of Chicago Press.

Quick, Heather, and Phyllis Moen. 1998. "Gender, Employment, and Retirement Quality: A Life Course Approach to the Differential Experiences of Men and Women." *Journal of Occupational Health Psychology* 3(1): 44–64.

Quinn, Joseph F. 1999. *Retirement Patterns and Bridge Jobs in the 1990s*. EBRI Issue Brief no. 206. Washington, DC: Employee Benefit Research Institute.

Rao, Hayagreeva, Calvin Morrill, and Mayer N. Zald. 2000. "Power Plays: How Social Movements and Collective Action Create New Organizational Forms." *Research in Organizational Behavior* 22: 239–282.

Rau, Renate and Antje Triemer. 2004. "Overtime in Relation to Blood Pressure and Mood during Work, Leisure, and Night Time." *Social Indicators Research* 67(1): 51–73.

Reich, Robert. 2011. "Why Inequality is the Real Cause of our Ongoing Terrible Economy." *New York Times*. September 4.

Rendall, Michael S., Margaret M. Weden, Melissa M. Favreault, and Hilary Waldron. 2011. "The Protective Effect of Marriage for Survival: A Review and Update." *Demography* 48(2): 481–506.

Riley, Matilda White. 1987. "On the Significance of Age in Sociology." *American Sociological Review* 52(1): 1–14.

Riley, Matilda W., and John W. Riley. 1989. "The Lives of Older People and Changing Social Roles." *Annals of the American Academy of Political and Social Science* 503: 14–28.

Riley, Matilda W., Robert L. Kahn, and Anne Foner. 1994. *Age and Structural Lag: Society's Failure to Provide Meaningful Opportunities in Work, Family, and Leisure*. New York: Wiley.

Rinklake, Annika, and Sandra Buchholz. 2011. "Increasing Inequalities in Germany: Older People's Employment Lives and Income Conditions Since the Mid-1980s." In *Aging Populations, Globalization and the Labor Market: Comparing Late Working Life and Retirement in Modern Societies*, edited by Hans-Peter Blossfeld, Sandra Buchholz, and Karin Kurz (pp. 35–64). Cheltenham, UK/Northampton, MA: Edward Elgar.

Ross, Catherine E., and John Mirowsky. 1989. "Explaining the Social Patterns of Depression: Control and Problem-Solving or Support and Talking." *Journal of Health and Social Behavior* 30(2): 206–219.

Ross, Catherine E., and John Mirowsky. 1992. "Households, Employment, and the Sense of Control." *Social Psychology Quarterly* 55(3): 217–235.

Ross, Catherine E., and John Mirowsky. 2002. "Family Relationships, Social Support, and Subjective Life Expectancy." *Journal of Health and Social Behavior* 43(4): 469–489.

Ross, Catherine E., and John Mirowsky. 2003. "Social Structure and Psychological Functioning: The Sense of Personal Control, Distress, and Trust." In *The Handbook of the Social Psychology*, edited by J. DeLamater (pp. 411–447). New York: Kluwer-Plenum.

Ross, Catherine E., and John Mirowsky. 2010. "Why Education is Key to Socioeconomic Differentials in Health." *In Handbook of Medical Sociology*, sixth edition, edited by Chloe E. Bird, Peter Conrad, Allen M. Fremont, and Stefan Timmermans (pp. 33–51). Nashville, TN: Vanderbilt University Press.

Ross, Catherine E., and Marylyn P. Wright. 1998. "Women's Work, Men's Work and the Sense of Control." *Work and Occupations* 25(3): 333–355.

Ross, Catherine E., Ryan K. Masters, and Robert A. Hummer. 2012. "Education and the Gender Gaps in Health and Mortality." *Demography* 49(4): 1157–1183.

Rowe, John W., and Robert L. Kahn. 1998. *Successful Aging*. New York: Pantheon.

Roxburgh, Susan. 2009. "Untangling Inequalities: Gender, Race, and Socioeconomic Differences in Depression." *Sociological Forum* 24(2): 357–381.

Rubin, Beth A. 1996. *Shifts in the Social Contract: Understanding Change in American Society*. Thousand Oaks, CA: Pine Forge Press.

Rugulies Reiner, B. Aust, H. Burr, and U. Bültmann. 2008. "Job Insecurity, Chances on the Labour Market and Decline in Self-Rated Health in a Representative Sample of the Danish Workforce." *Journal of Epidemiology and Community Health* 62(3): 245–250.

Ryder, Norman B. 1965. "The Cohort as a Concept in the Study of Social Change." *American Sociological Review* 30(6): 843–861.

Ryff, Carol D., and Corey L. M. Keyes. 1995. "The Structure of Psychological Well-Being Revisited." *Journal of Personality and Social Psychology* 69(4): 719–727.

Sadler, William A. 2006. "Changing Life Options: Uncovering the Riches of the Third Age." *Lifelong Learning Institute Review* 1(1): 11–20.

Sandberg, Sheryl. 2013. *Lean In: Women, Work, and the Will to Lead*. New York: Knopf.

Saraceno, Chiara. 2008. *Families, Aging and Social Policy: Intergenerational Solidarity in European Welfare States*. Cheltenham, UK/Northampton, MA: Edward Elgar Publishing.

Sargent, Leisa D., Mary D. Lee, Bill Martin, and Jelena Zikic. 2013. "Reinventing Retirement: New Pathways, New Arrangements, New Meanings." *Human Relations* 66(1): 3–21.

Sastry, Jaya, and Catherine E. Ross. 1998. "Asian Ethnicity and the Sense of Personal Control." *Social Psychology Quarterly* 61(2): 101–120.

Saval, Nikil. 2014. *Cubed: A Secret History of the Workplace*. New York: Random House.

Schafer, Markus H., Kenneth F. Ferraro, and Sarah A. Mustillo. 2011. "Children of Misfortune: Early Adversity and Cumulative Inequality in Perceived Life Trajectories." *American Journal of Sociology* 116(4): 1053–1091.

Schenck, Dwain. 2014. *Reset: How to Beat the Job-Loss Blues and Get Ready for your Next Act*. Boston: Da Capo Press.

Schieman, Scott, Melissa Milkie, and Paul Glavin. 2009. "When Work Interferes with Life: The Social Distribution of Work-Nonwork Interference and the Influence of Work-related Demands and Resources." *American Sociological Review* 74(6): 966–987.

Schilling, Julia, and Mona Larsen. 2011. "How 'Flexicure" are Older Danes? The Development of Social Inequality in Later Life since the 1980s." In *Aging Populations, Globalization and the Labor Market: Comparing Late Working Life and Retirement in Modern Societies*, edited by Hans-Peter Blossfeld, Sandra Buchholz, and Karin Kurz (pp. 149–178). Cheltenham, UK/Northampton, MA: Edward Elgar.

Schmelzer, Paul. 2011. "Income Development of Older People: Consequences of Pension Reforms and Unstable Careers in the UK." In *Aging Populations, Globalization and the Labor Market: Comparing Late Working Life and Retirement in Modern Societies*, edited by Hans-Peter Blossfeld, Sandra Buchholz, and Karin Kurz (pp. 259–282). Cheltenham, UK/Northampton, MA: Edward Elgar.

Schmid, Günther. 2011. "Non-Standard Employment in Europe." *Germany Policy Studies* 7(1): 171–210.

Schmid, Günther. 2009. "Transitional Labour Markets, from Theory to Policy Application. Transitional Labour Markets and Flexicurity: Managing Social Risks over the Lifecourse." Documents de Travail du Centre d'Economie de la Sorbonne 75: 1–26.

Schor, Juliet. 1992. *The Overworked American: The Unexpected Decline of Leisure*. New York: Basic Books.

Schubert, Klaus, Simon Hegelich, and Ursula Bazant. 2009. *The Handbook of European Welfare Systems*. London: Routledge.

Schulte, Brigid. 2014. *Overwhelmed: Work, Love, and Play When No One has the Time*. New York: FSG.

Schulz, Richard, and Jutta Heckhausen. 1996. "A Life Span Model of Successful Aging." *American Psychologist* 51(7): 702–714.

Schultz, Ellen E. 2011. *Retirement Heist: How Companies Plunder and Profit from the Nest Eggs of American Workers*. New York: Penguin.

Schwall, Alexander R. 2012. "Defining Age, and Using Age-Relevant Constructs." In *The Oxford Handbook of Work and Aging*, edited by Walter C. Borman and Jerry W. Hedge (pp. 169–186). New York: Oxford University Press.

Scott, W. Richard 1995. *Institutions and Organizations*. Thousand Oaks, CA: Sage Publications.

Scott, Jacqueline, Rosemary Crompton, and Clare Lyonette. 2010. *Gender Inequalities in the 21st Century: New Barriers and Continuing Constraints*. Cheltenham, UK: Elgar Edgar Publishing.

Scott-Marshall, Heather. 2010. "The Social Patterning of Work-Related Insecurity and its Health Consequences." *Social Indicators Research* 96(2): 313–337.

Seltzer, Marsha Mailick, and Lydia Wailing Li. 2000. "The Dynamics of Caregiving: Transitions during a Three-Year Prospective Study." *The Gerontologist* 40(2): 165–178.

Sekine, Michikazu, Tarani Chandola, Pekka Martikainen, Michael Marmot, and Sadanobu Kagamimori. 2009. "Socioeconomic Inequalities in Physical and Mental Functioning of British, Finnish, and Japanese Civil Servants: Role of Job Demand, Control, and Work Hours." *Social Science & Medicine* 69(10): 1417–1425.

Sen, Amartya. 1992. *Inequality Reexamined*. New York: Russell Sage Foundation.

Sennett, Richard. 2006. *The Culture of the New Capitalism*. New York: Yale University Press.

Settersten, Richard A. Jr., and Jacqueline L. Angel. 2011. *Handbook of Sociology of Aging*. New York: Springer.

Settersten, Richard A. Jr., and Gunhild O. Hagestad. 1996a "What's the Latest? Cultural Age Deadlines for Family Transitions." *The Gerontologist* 36(2): 178–188.

Settersten, Richard A. Jr., and Gunhild O. Hagestad. 1996b. "What's the Latest? II. Cultural Age Deadlines for Educational and Work Transitions." *The Gerontologist* 36(5): 602–613.

Settersten Richard A. Jr., and Karl Ulrich Mayer. 1997. "The Measurement of Age, Age Structuring and the Life Course." *Annual Review of Sociology* 23: 233–261.

Settersten, Richard A. Jr., and Barbara Ray. 2010. *Not Quite Adults: Why 20-Somethings are Choosing a Slower Path to Adulthood and Why It's Good for Everyone*. New York: Bantam/Random House.

Settersten, Richard A. Jr., Frank F. Furstenberg, and Rubén G. Rumbaut. 2005. *On the Frontier of Adulthood: Theory, Research, and Public Policy*. Chicago: University of Chicago Press.

Sewell, William H. Jr. 1992. "A Theory of Structure: Duality, Agency, and Transformation." *American Journal of Sociology* 98(1): 1–29.

Shepard, Herbert. 1985. "Men and Organizational Cultures." In *Beyond Sex Roles*, edited by Alice G. Sargent (pp. 374–381). St. Paul, MN: West Publishing Company.

Shultz, Kenneth S., and Mo Wang. 2008. "The Changing Nature of Mid- and Late Careers." *In 21st Century Management: A Reference Handbook*, edited by Charles Wankel (pp. 130–138). Thousand Oaks, CA: Sage Publications.

Slaughter, Anne-Marie. 2015. *Unfinished Business: Women, Men, Work, Family* New York: Random House.

Siegrist, Johannes, and Michael Marmot. 2006. *Social Inequalities in Health: New Evidence and Policy Implications*. New York: Oxford University Press.

Silva, Jennifer M. 2013. *Coming Up Short: Working-Class Adulthood in an Age of Uncertainty*. New York: Oxford University Press.

Silva, Luna Rodrigues Freitas. 2008. "From Old Age to Third Age: The Historical Course of the Identities Linked to the Process of Ageing." *História, Ciências, Saúde—Manguinhos* 15(1): 155–68.

Skaff, Marilyn McKean. 2006. "The View from the Driver's Seat: Sense of Control in the Baby Boomers at Midlife." In *The Baby Boomers Brow Up: Contemporary Perspectives on Midlife*, edited by Susan Krauss Whitbourne and Sherry L. Willis (pp. 185–204). Mahwah, HJ: Lawrence Erlbaum.

Skinner, Ellen A. 1996. "A Guide to Constructs of Control." *Journal of Personality and Social Psychology* 71(3): 549–570.

Skorikov, Vladimir B., and Fred W. Vondracek. 2011. "Occupational Identity." In *Handbook of Identity Theory and Research*, edited by S. J. Schwartz, K. Luyckx, and V. L. Vignoles (pp. 693–714). New York: Springer.

Smith, Deborah B., and Phyllis Moen. 1998. "Spousal Influence on Retirement: His, Her, and Their Perceptions." *Journal of Marriage and the Family* 60(3): 734–744.

Smith, Deborah B., and Phyllis Moen. 2003. "Retirement Satisfaction for Retirees and Their Spouses: Do Gender and the Retirement Decision-Making Process Matter?" *Journal of Family Issues* 25(2): 262–285.

Smith, V. Kerry, Donald H. Taylor Jr., and Frank A. Sloan. 2001. "Longevity Expectations and Death: Can People Predict Their Own Demise?" *American Economic Review* 91(4): 1126–1134.

Soule, Sarah A., Doug McAdam, John McCarthy, and Yang Su. 1999. "Protest Events: Cause or Consequences of State Action? The U.S. Women's Movement and Federal Congressional Activities, 1956-1979." *Mobilization: An International Journal* 42(2): 239–256.

Stansfeld, Stephen, and Bridget Candy. 2006. "Psychosocial Work Environment and Mental Health—A Meta-analytic Review." *Scandinavian Journal of Work, Environment and Health* 32(6): 443–462.

Staff, Jeremy, and Jeylan T. Mortimer. 2012. "Explaining the Motherhood Wage Penalty during the Early Occupational Career." *Demography* 49(1): 1–21.

Stewart, A. J., and Cynthia M. Torges. 2006. "Social, Historical and Developmental Influences on the Psychology of the Baby Boom at Midlife." In *The Baby Boomers Grow Up: Contemporary Perspectives on Midlife*, edited by Susan Krauss Whitbourne and Sherry L. Willis (pp. 23–43). Mahwah, NJ: Lawrence Erlbaum.

Stockdale, Susan E., Kenneth B. Wells, Lingqui Tang, Thomas R. Belin, Lily Zhang, and Cathy D. Sherbourne. 2007. "The Importance of Social Context: Neighborhood Stressors, Stress-Buffering Mechanisms, and Alcohol, Drug, and Mental Health Disorders." *Social Science & Medicine* 65(9): 1867–1881.

Stone, Katherine. 2013. "The Decline of the Standard Contract of Employment in the United States: A Socio-Regulatory Perspective." In *Rethinking Workplace Regulation: Beyond the Standard Contract of Employment*, edited by Katherine Stone and Harry Arthurs (pp. 58–72). New York: Russell Sage Foundation.

Stone, Pamela. 2007. *Opting Out? Why Women Really Quit Careers and Head Home.* Berkeley: University of California Press.

Stone, Arthur, and Christopher Mackie. 2013. *Subjective Well-Being: Measuring Happiness, Suffering, and Other Dimensions of Experience*. Washington, DC: The National Academies Press.

Stone, Katherine, and Harry Arthurs. 2013. *Rethinking Workplace Regulation: Beyond the Standard Contract of Employment*. New York: Russell Sage Foundation.

Stryker, Robin. 1994. "Rules, Resources, and Legitimacy Processes: Some Implications for Social Conflict, Order, and Change." *American Journal of Sociology* 99(4): 847–910.

Suitor, J. Jill, Jori Sechrist, Megan Gilligan, and Karl Pillemer. 2011. "Intergenerational Relations in later-Life Families." In *Handbook of Sociology of Aging*, edited by Richard A. Settersten Jr. and Jacqueline L. Angel (pp. 161–178). New York: Springer.

Super, Donald Edwin. 1957. *The Psychology of Careers: An Introduction to Vocational Development*. New York: Harper & Brothers.

Susanka, Sarah. 1998. *The Not So Big House: A Blueprint for the Way We Really Live*. Newtown, CT: The Tauton Press, Inc.

Swartz, Teresa Toguchi. 2009. "Intergenerational Family Relations in Adulthood: Patterns, Variations, and Implications in the Contemporary United States." *Annual Review of Sociology* 35: 191–212.

Swartz, Teresa Toguchi, Minzee Kim, Mayumi Uno, Jeylan Mortimer, and Kirsten Bengtson O'Brien. 2011. "Safety Nets and Scaffolds: Parental Support in the Transition to Adulthood." *Journal of Marriage and Family* 73(2): 414–429.

Sweet, Stephen. 2014. *The Work-Family Interface: An Introduction*. Thousand Oaks, CA: Sage Publications.

Sweet, Stephen, and Peter Meiksins. 2013. *Changing Contours of Work: Jobs and Opportunities in the New Economy* (2nd Edition). Thousand Oaks, CA: Pine Forge Press.

Sweet, Stephen, and Phyllis Moen. 2006. "Advancing a Career Focus on Work and Family: Insights from the Life Course Perspective." In *The Work and Family Handbook: Multi-Disciplinary Perspectives and Methods*, edited by Marcie Pitt-Catsouphes, Ellen Ernst Kossek, and Stephen Sweet (pp. 189–208). Mahwah, NJ: Lawrence Erlbaum.

Sweet, Stephen, and Phyllis Moen. 2012. "Dual Earners Preparing for Job Loss: Agency, Linked Lives, and Resilience." *Work and Occupations* 39(1): 35–70.

Sweet, Stephen, Phyllis Moen, and Peter Meiksins. 2007. "Dual Earners in Double Jeopardy: Preparing for Job Loss in the New Risk Economy." *Research in the Sociology of Work* 17: 439–463.

Szinovacz, Maximiliane. 1987. "Preferred Retirement Timing and Retirement in Women." *International Journal of Aging and Human Development* 24(4): 301–317.

Szinovacz, Maximiliane E., and Adam Davey. 2004. "Honeymoons and Joint Lunches: Effects of Retirement and Spouses' Employment on Depressive Symptoms." *Journals of Gerontology* 59B(5): 233–245.

Szinovacz, Maximiliane E., Lauren Martin, and Adam Davey. 2014. "Recession and Expected Retirement Age: Another Look at the Evidence." *The Gerontologist* 54(2): 245–257.

Tausig, Mark, and Rudy Fenwick. 2011. *Work and Mental Health in Social Context*. New York: Springer.

Taylor, Paul. 2014. *The Next America: Boomers, Millennials, and the Looming Generational Showdown*. New York: Public Affairs.

Taylor, M. A., and Holly A. Geldhauser. 2007. "Low-Income Older Workers." In *Aging and Work in the 21st Century*, edited by K. S. Shultz and G. A. Adams (pp. 25–50). Mahwah, NJ: Lawrence Erlbaum.

Taylor, Shelley E., Rena L. Repetti, and Teresa Seeman. 1997. "Health Psychology: What is an Unhealthy Environment and How Does it Get Under the Skin?" *Annual Review of Psychology* 48: 411–447.

Teipen, Christina, and Martin Kohli. 2004. "Early Retirement in Germany." In *Ageing and the Transition to Retirement: A Comparative Analysis of European Welfare States*, edited by Tony Maltby, Bert de Vroom, Maria Luisa Mirabile, and Einar Øverbye (pp. 93–119). Burlington, VT: Ashgate Publishing Company.

Thoits, Peggy A. 2010. "Compensatory Coping with Stressors." In *Advances in the Conceptualization of the Stress Process: Essays in Honor of Leonard I. Pearlin*, edited by W. R. Avison, C. Aneshensel, S. Schieman, and B. Wheaton (pp. 23–34). New York: Springer.

Thoits, Peggy A. 2012. "Role-Identity Salience, Purpose and Meaning in Life, and Well-being among Volunteers." *Social Psychology Quarterly* 75(4): 360–384.

Thoits, Peggy A., and Lyndi N. Hewitt. 2001. "Volunteer Work and Well Being." *Journal of Health and Social Behavior* 42(2): 115–131.

Thomas. Bill. 2014. *Second Wind: Navigating the Passage to a Slower, Deeper, and More Connected Life*. New York: Simon & Schuster.

Thomas, Patricia A. 2011. "Trajectories of Social Engagement and Limitations in Late Life." *Journal of Health and Social Behavior* 52(4): 430–443.

Thomas, Patricia A. 2012. "Trajectories of Social Engagement and Mortality in Late Life. *Journal of Aging and Health* 24(4): 547–568.

Thomas, Linda Thiede, and Daniel C. Ganster. 1995. "Impact of Family-Supportive Work Variables on Work-Family Conflict and Strain: A Control Perspective." *Journal of Applied Psychology* 80(1): 6–15.

Thomas, W. I., and Dorothy Swaine Thomas. 1928. *The Child in America: Behavior Problems and Programs*. New York: Knopf.

Thornton, Patricia H., and William Ocasio. 2008. "Institutional Logics." In *The Sage Handbook of Organizational Institutionalism*, edited by R. Greenwood, C. Oliver, R. Suddaby, and K. Sahlin (pp. 1- 46). Thousand Oaks, CA: Sage Publications.

Thornton, Patricia H., William Ocasio, and Michael Lounsbury. 2012. *The Institutional Logics Perspective: A New Approach to Culture, Structure, and Process*. New York: Oxford University Press.

Tilly, Charles. 1998. *Durable Inequality*. Berkeley: University of California Press.

Toossi, Mitra. 2012. "Labor Force Projections to 2020: A More Slowly Growing Workforce." *Monthly Labor Review* (January): 43–62.

Tronto, Joan C. 2013. *Caring Democracy: Markets, Equality, and Justice*. New York: New York University Press.

Turner, R. Jay. 2010. "Understanding Health Disparities: The Promise of the Stress Process Model." In *Advances in the Conceptualization of the Stress Process: Essays in Honor of Leonard I. Pearlin*, edited by W. R. Avison, C. Aneshensel, S. Schieman, and B. Wheaton (pp. 3–21). New York: Springer.

Turner, R. Jay, Blair Wheaton, and Donald A. Lloyd. 1995. "The Epidemiology of Social Stress." *American Sociological Review* 60(1): 104–125.

Tversky, Amos, and Daniel Kahneman. 1974. "Judgment under Uncertainty: Heuristics and Biases." *Science* 185(4157): 1128–1131.

Tversky, Amos, and Daniel Kahneman. 1981. "The Framing of Decision and the Psychology of Choice." *Science* 211(4481): 453–458.

Tversky, Amos, and Daniel Kahneman. 1991. "Loss Aversion in Riskless Choice: A Reference-Dependent Model." *Quarterly Journal of Economics* 106(4): 1039–1061.

Ulrich, Lorene B., and Pamelia E. Brott. 2005. "Older Workers and Bridge Employment: Redefining Retirement." *Journal of Employment Counseling* 42(4): 159–170.

US Census Bureau. 2013. *Annual Social and Economic (ASEC) Supplement [machine-readable data file]/conducted by the Bureau of the Census for the Bureau of Labor Statistics.* Current Population Reports, March. Washington, DC: Government Printing Office. www.census.gov/prod/techdoc/cps/cpsmar13.pdf.

US Census Bureau. 2010. *Current Population Survey, September 2010: Volunteer Supplement.* Ann Arbor, MI: Inter-university Consortium for Political and Social Research. http://doi.org/10.3886/ICPSR31861.v1.

Vega, William A., and Ruben G. Rumbaut. 1991. "Ethnic Minorities and Mental Health." *Annual Review of Sociology* 17: 351–383.

Venn, Susan, Kate Davidson, and Sara Arber. 2011. "Gender and Ageing." In *Handbook of Sociology of Aging*, edited by Richard A. Settersten Jr., and Jacqueline L. Angel (pp. 71–82). New York: Springer.

Viebrock, Elke, and Jochen Clasen. 2009. "Flexicurity and Welfare Reform: A Review." *Socio-Economic Review* 7(2): 305–331.

Van der Doef, Margot, and Stan Maes 1999. "The Job Demand-Control(-Support) Model and Psychological Well-Being: A Review of 20 Years of Empirical Research." *Work and Stress* 13(2): 87–114.

van Oorschot, Wim. 2009. "The Dutch Welfare System: From Collective Solidarity Towards Individual Responsibility." In *The Handbook of European Welfare Systems*, edited by Klaus Schubert, Simon Hegelich, and Ursula Bazant (pp. 263–377). London: Routledge.

Van Solinge, Hanna, and Kène Henkens. 2007. "Involuntary Retirement: The Role of Restrictive Circumstances, Timing, and Social Embeddedness." *Journals of Gerontology* 62B(5): S295–S303.

Van Solinge, Hanna, and Kène Henkens. 2008. "Adjustment to and Satisfaction with Retirement: Two of a Kind?" *Psychology and Aging* 23(2): 422–434.

von Bonsdorff, Monika, Kenneth Shultz, Esko Leskinen, and Judith Tansky. 2009. "The Choice between Retirement and Bridge Employment: A Continuity Theory and Life Course Perspective." *International Journal of Aging and Human Development* 69(2): 79–100.

Vuolo, Mike, Jeremy Staff, and Jeylan T. Mortimer. 2012. "Weathering the Great Recession: Psychological and Behavioral Trajectories in the Transition from School to Work." *Developmental Psychology* 48(6): 1759–1773.

Wahrendorf, Morten, Grace Sembajwe, Marie Zins, Lisa Berkman, Marcel Goldberg, and Johannes Siegrist. 2012. "Long-Term Effects of Psychosocial Work Stress in Midlife on Health Functioning after Labor Market Exit—Results from the GAZEL Study." *The Journals of Gerontology* 67(4): 471–480.

Waite, Linda J., and Maggie Gallagher. 2000. *The Case of Marriage: Why Married People are Happier, Healthier, and Better off Financially*. New York: Broadway Books.

Walker, Charles R., and Robert H. Guest. 1952. *The Man on the Assembly Line*. Cambridge, MA: Harvard University Press.

Wang, Mo. 2007. "Profiling Retirees in the Retirement Transition and Adjustment Process: Examining the Longitudinal Change Patterns of Retirees' Psychological Well-Being." *Journal of Applied Psychology* 92(2): 455–474.

Wang, Mo. 2012. "Health and Fiscal and Psychological Well-Being in Retirement." In *The Oxford Handbook of Work and Aging*, edited by Jerry Hedge and Walter Borman (pp. 570–584). New York: Oxford University Press.

Wang, Mo, and Kenneth Shultz. 2010. "Employee Retirement: A Review and Recommendations for Future Investigation." *Journal of Management* 36(1): 172–206.

Wang Mo, Kène Henkens, and Hanna van Solinge. 2011. "Retirement Adjustment: A Review of Theoretical and Empirical Advancements." *American Psychologist* 66(3): 204–213.

Wang, Mo, Yujie Zhan, Songqi Liu, and Kenneth Schultz. 2008. "Antecedents of Bridge Employment: A Longitudinal Investigation." *Journal of Applied Psychology* 93(4): 818–830.

Warren, John Robert, Laurie Knies, Steven Haas, and Elaine M. Hernandez. 2012. "The Impact of Childhood Sickness on Adult Socioeconomic Outcomes: Evidence from later 19th Century America." *Social Science & Medicine* 75(8): 1531–1538.

Weil, David. 2014. *The Fissured Workplace: Why Work Became so Bad for so many and What can be Done to Improve It*. Cambridge, MA: Harvard University Press.

Weir, David R. 2007. "Are Baby Boomers Living Well Longer?" In *Redefining Retirement: How Will Boomers Fare?*, edited by Brigitte Madrian, Olivia S. Mitchell and Beth J. Soldo (pp. 95–111). New York: Oxford University Press.

Weiss, Robert S. 1977. *Marital Separation: Coping with the End of a Marriage and the Transition to being Single Again*. New York: Basic Books.

Weiss, Robert S., and Scott A. Bass. 2002. *Challenges of the Third Age*. New York: Oxford University Press.

Westerlund, Hugo, Mika Kivimäki, Archana Singh-Manoux, Maria Melchior, Jane E. Ferrie, Jaana Pentti, Markus Jokela, Constanze Leineweber, Marcel Goldberg, Maria Zins, and Jussi Vahtera. 2009. "Self-Rated Health Before and After Retirement in France (GAZEL): A Cohort Study." *Lancet* 374(9705): 1889–1896.

Wheaton, Blair. 1990. "Life Transitions, Role Histories, and Mental Health." *American Sociological Review* 55(2): 209–223.

Wheaton, Blair. 1999. "Social Stress." In *Handbook of Sociology of Mental Health*, edited by Carol S. Aneshensel and Jo C. Phelan (pp. 277–300). New York: Kluwer Academic.

Wheaton, Blair. 2001. "The Role of Sociology in the Study of Mental Health…and the Role of Mental Health in the Study of Sociology." *Journal of Health and Social Behavior* 42(3): 221–234.

Wheaton, Blair, and Philippa J. Clarke. 2003. "Space Meets Time: Integrating Temporal and Contextual Influences on Mental Health in Early Adulthood." *American Sociological Review* 68(5): 680–706.

Whyte, William H. 1956. *The Organization Man*. New York: Simon & Schuster.

Whyte, William Foote. 1987. "Social Inventions for Solving Human Problems" *Clinical Sociology Review*: 5(1): 45–63.

Wicherts, Jelte M., Conor V. Dolan, David J. Hessen, Paul Oosterveld, G. Caroline M. van Baal, Dorret I. Boomsma, and Mark M. Span. 2004. "Are Intelligence Tests Measurement Invariant Over time: Investigating the Nature of the Flynn Effect." *Intelligence* 32(5): 509–537.

Wickrama, Kandauda A. S., Frederick O. Lorenz, Rand Conger, Lisa Matthews, and Glen H. Elder Jr. 1997. "Linking Occupational Conditions to Physical Health through Marital, Social, and Intrapersonal Processes." *Journal of Health and Social Behavior* 38(4): 363–375.

Widmer, Eric D., and Gilbert Ritschard. 2013. "Life Course Changes in Late Modernity: Towards Destandardization and Degendering?" In *Gendered Life Courses between Individualization and Standardization. A European Approach Applied to Switzerland*, edited by René Levy and Eric D. Widmer (pp. 161–182.) Wien: Lit Verlag.

Wilensky, Harold L. 1960. "Work, Careers and Social Integration." *International Social Science Journal* 12(4): 543–560.

Wilensky, Harold L. 1961. "Orderly Careers and Social Participation: The Impact of Social Integration in the Middle Class." *American Sociological Review* 26(4): 521–539.

Wilson, John. 2000. "Volunteering." *Annual Review of Sociology* 26: 215–240.

Wilson, John. 2012. "Volunteerism Research: A Review Essay." *Nonprofit and Voluntary Section Quarterly* 41(2): 176–212.

Wilson, John and Marc Musick. 1997. "Who Cares? Toward an Integrated Theory of Volunteer Work." *American Sociological Review* 62(5): 694–713.

Williams, David R., Selina A. Mohammed, Jacinta Leavell, and Chiquita Collins. 2010. "Race, Socioeconomic Status and Health: Complexities, Ongoing Challenges and Research Opportunities." *Annals of the New York Academy of Science* 1186: 69–101.

Williams, Joan C. 2000. *Unbending Gender: Why Family and Work Conflict and What To Do About It*. New York: Oxford University Press.

Williams, Joan C., and Heather Boushey. 2010. *The Three Faces of Work-Family Conflict: The Poor, the Professionals, and the Missing Middle*. Washington, DC: Center of American Progress and Center for WorkLife Law.

Williamson, John B. 2011. "The Future of Retirement Security." In *Handbook of Aging and the Social Sciences*, edited by Robert H. Binstock and Linda K. George (pp. 281–94). San Diego: Academic Press.

Willis, Sherry L., and K. Warner Schaie. 2006. "Cognitive Functioning in the Baby Boomers: Longitudinal and Cohort Effects." In *The Baby Boomers Grow Up*, edited by Susan K. Whitbourne and Sherry L. Willis (pp. 205–234). Mahwah, NJ: Lawrence Erlbaum.

Willson, Andrea, Kim M. Shuey, and Glen H. Elder Jr. 2007. "Cumulative Advantage Processes as Mechanisms of Inequality in Life Course Health." *American Journal of Sociology* 112(6): 1886–1924.

Wooten, Melissa E., and Andrew J. Hoffman. 2008. "Organizational Fields: Past, Present and Future." In *Sage Handbook of Organizational Institutionalism*, edited by Royston Greenwood, Christine Oliver, Roy Suddaby, and Kerstin Sahlin (pp. 130–148). London: Sage Publications.

Wong, Jen D., and Melissa A. Hardy. 2009. "Women's Retirement Expectations: How Stable Are They?" *Journal of Gerontology: Social Sciences* 64B(1): S77–S86.

Yang, Yang. 2008. "Social Inequalities in Happiness in the United States, 1972 to 2004: An Age-Period-Cohort Analysis." *American Sociological Review* 73(2): 204–226.

Index

Figures and tables are indicated by "f" and "t" following page numbers.

CPSIA information can be obtained
at www.ICGtesting.com
Printed in the USA
BVHW032123140819
555920BV00002B/20/P

9 780199 357284